DRACULA

The First Hundred Years

DRACULA

The First Hundred Years

Edited by Bob Madison

MIDNIGHT MARQUEE PRESS, INC.

Baltimore, Maryland

ISBN 1-887664-14-9
Library of Congress Catalog Card Number 97-73132
Manufactured in the United States of America
Printed by Kirby Lithographic Company, Arlington, VA
First Printing by Midnight Marquee Press, Inc., October 1997

Acknowledgments: John Antosiewicz Photo Archives, Ronald V. Borst/Hollywood
Movie Posters, Frank Dello Stritto, Lou Gaul, Cortlandt Hull, Greg Mank, John Parnum,
Gary J. Svehla, Linda J. Walter

"I think they're after Dracula!"
—Boris Karloff, *House of Frankenstein* (1944)

Special Contributions Prepared for This Volume by
James Bernard
Nicolas Cage
Veronica Carlson
Bill Campbell
James V. Hart
John Landis
Francis Lederer
Chelsea Quinn Yarbro

Table of Contents

9   **Foreword—Dracula: The First Hundred Years** by Bob Madison

20   **Bram Stoker's Dracula: The Coffin Opens** by David J. Hogan

42   **Books of Blood: The Continued Adventures of Dracula** by Bob Madison

52   **The Changing Face of Dracula: A Portrait Gallery** by Bob Madison

88   **Abraham Van Helsing, MDD, Ph.D. Lit, Etc., Etc.** by Tom Johnson

108   **Dracula's Last Bride** by Gregory William Mank

126   **Clash of the Draculas: Bela Lugosi vs. John Carradine** by Gregory William Mank

142   **The Vampire Strikes Back!** by Frank Dello Stritto

168   **Fangs for the Funny Books: Or, Dracula in the Comics** by Rickey L. Shanklin

186   **Hammer Films and the Resurrection of Dracula** by Gary J. Svehla

200   **Sex and Eroticism From Dracula and His Brood—A Tooth-In-Cheek Overview (Or: Are Those Fangs You're Baring or Are You Just Happy to See Me?)** by Randy Vest

216   **Dracula in the 1970s: Prints of Darkness** by Steve Vertlieb

240   **The Vampire's Return: John Badham on the Making of Dracula, An Interview** by Tom Weaver

256   **Night Stalking: An Interview With John Llewellyn Moxey** by Tom Weaver

266   **The Vampire's Kiss: Echoes of Bram Stoker in the Vampire Film of the 1980s** by Gary Don Rhodes

282   **Dracula: Dead and Loving It: Dracula in the 1990s** by Bob Madison

292   **Afterword—Him and Me: A Personal Slice of the Dracula Century** by David J. Skal

302   **A Dracula Filmography** by Bob Madison

Foreword
Dracula: The First Hundred Years
by Bob Madison

> I am Dracula; and I bid you welcome.
> —*Dracula,* by Bram Stoker

He has haunted our dreams and our waking hours, a fiend with a single purpose... to disarm us, to seduce us, to take the life from us.

And Count Dracula, Bram Stoker's Vampire King, has been doing it for 100 years.

But why? Why has Stoker's vampire lasted so long, when other vampire heroes have literally and figuratively crumbled to dust? What is the hold this long undead Transylvanian nobleman has over us, and why do we willingly submit to the cold caress and chilly attentions of the Prince of Darkness?

Because Dracula is us, and we are Dracula.

As you will see in *Dracula: The First Hundred Years*, the image of Dracula is forever shifting and changing, reflecting not himself, but our own fears and secret longings. Dracula casts no reflection in the mirror, but he does not have to—it's our own faces we see when we gaze upon the visage of Count Dracula.

For Stoker, Dracula was Darwinism run amuck, a foul, smelly mixture of man and beast, complete with fangs and hairy palms. He was man's prehistoric nature, crawling from regions beyond England's empire, to challenge a rational and modern scientific world.

To Germany of the 1920s, still reeling from the devastation of the First World War, the Dracula seen in F. W. Murnau's *Nosferatu* was pestilence incarnate: a hideous force of nature that implacably plodded forward, like war, disease, and grim death.

And so on. Dracula in the 1920s and 1930s was an undead lounge lizard, a soulless alien who wore an aristocrat's face. To Americans in the 1940s, as the world slipped into the most catastrophic war in human history, Dracula and his vampiric horde represented the blood-thirsty foreigner. As the 1950s and 1960s brought greater freedom of expression to the media, the sex and violence implicit in Stoker's narrative became explicit, with liberal amounts of both in a new series of color films.

Dracula's redemption started in the warm and fuzzy 1970s, and he returned to the fold of brooding, doomed, sympathetic vampires that were in vogue before Stoker's masterwork. It is this complex Dracula, both predator and victim, that is still with us today in the current atmosphere of New Ageism, recovery programs, and cloudy morality.

But of this I am certain:

He will change, and he is not going anywhere.

The Count

Sesame Street's Count Von Count has been a favorite with children for more than 20 years. Master puppeteer and voice artist Jerry Nelson has been the man behind the cape since the character first appeared, with children and parents alike responding instantly.

The Count is just what his name implies: he loves to count. Through his myriad songs and games, children count cookies, toys, and just about anything else, while learning that math can be fun.

His appeal to children and adults is twofold: children love his mathematical antics, while his cape, evening clothes, and Lugosi-like accent remind adults of treasured movie memories.

He is one of the most successful characters ever to emerge from *Sesame Street*, with hundreds of toys, games, and hand puppets in his likeness.

The Count is just one of countless re-interpretations of Dracula for children. One hundred years later, Bram Stoker would no longer recognize his bloodthirsty Tartar. Pop culture has rendered Dracula something Stoker never imagined: Dracula has gone cuddly.

—Bob Madison

The Dracula of our children, and our children's children, will be a very different monster from the one we know today. The only certainty is that Dracula will reflect our future selves, as he has our past lives, and he will continue his symbiotic relationship with living human beings as both sucker and sucked. For though this monster takes the blood of the living, he also brings us closer to the eternal mysteries of sex, death, and immortality.

We give ourselves willingly to Dracula, for in doing so he gives much more than he takes. At the simplest level, Dracula illustrates our capacity for wonder: a "cool" monster that lives forever, caught in adventures and situations beyond our wildest imaginings. At the other end of the spectrum is a figure of almost religious significance: a being of resurrection, power, transcendence, and eternal life.

I cannot remember a time when I did not know who Dracula was.

My earliest memories of him are watching John Carradine in *House of Dracula* on the Saturday night *Creature Features*, and even then he was old news to me. A child of the 1960s, I remember the trouble my Bela Lugosi impression created with the nuns in my kindergarten class, my first intimation that not everyone was as susceptible as I to the vampire's kiss.

Dracula was a constant during my boyhood. Count Chocula—a barely disguised Dracula clone—was my breakfast cereal of choice, the Count peered at me through his monocle on *Sesame Street*, and Dracula himself showed up in comic books and children's adaptations, records, toys, games, puzzles, television, films, monster movie magazines, everywhere.

I sought no escape. Rather, I reveled under his undead tutelage. Dark blanket secured around my shoulders with a safety pin, I paraded around the house in my makeshift cape, intoning "I am Dracula" to my parents, brothers, and any other sundry friends and relatives who happened to be handy. I played *Dracula's Return* from the novelty record *Famous Monsters Speak* so often I thought I would wear the vinyl away.

Dracula did not give me a persona to hide behind, no. Instead, he gave me a vision of power, wonder, and mysticism when life was very prosaic. Dracula was something you grew *toward*, not away from.

For a young boy in the suburbs of Queens, Dracula was swanky, Dracula was Old World (with all the weight of "culture" that phrase carried), and Dracula commanded the mysterious power of adulthood, with all of its rights and privileges. He had the accumulated wisdom of the ages, the mystical insight of life after death, and all the allure of dangerous sex. What child could help but be captivated?

Dracula was something I never managed to put away, like many people pack away their baseball cards or catcher's mitts when childhood ends. Instead, my appreciation for Stoker's creation, and the various transformations he has made over ensuing decades, only increased. The enthusiasm I feel for the character, and the excitement he can generate within me, is one of the many contributing factors to my becoming a writer.

Nor am I alone in my continuing interest. There are many people who simply cannot put away the cherished "friends" of their youth. There are many clubs and societies—all filled with intelligent, accomplished people—that devote themselves to the study and appreciation of such characters as Sherlock Holmes, Tarzan, and even pulp heroes like Doc Savage and The Shadow. While my appreciation for these fictional creations is profound, none of them, I believe, have the same *bite* as Dracula.

In compiling *Dracula: The First Hundred Years*, I was flooded with a deeply nostalgic feeling. Thinking about it, I realized it was not only a longing for my youth and the Dracula films and toys that filled it, but the warm feeling of an old friend rediscovered. In a macabre way, Dracula is much like the uncle that you always took for granted; it's only after investigating his past that you realize what a remarkable man he was.

That Dracula's spell continues undiminished, I'm sure. My niece Lillian, this year 90 years younger than the bloodthirsty Count, has all but memorized Bela Lugosi's *Abbott and Costello Meet Frankenstein*. A new generation of "monster magazines" have come into their own, making Dracula that most fascinating of ogres, available to youngsters again. And with recent films like *Bram Stoker's Dracula* and Roger Corman's *Dracula Rising*, and Fred Saberhagen's acclaimed series of Dracula novels, it is apparent that Dracula is as much with us as ever.

A book like *Dracula: The First Hundred Years* is not only natural, it's inevitable.

Bram Stoker's *Dracula* has never been out of print, and has been translated into more than 100 languages the world over. In this centennial year, Norton has published the first legitimate, critical edition of the novel (edited by Dracula scholars David J. Skal and Nina Auerbach), which finally confirms the importance of a novel that readers have already savored as a classic for 100 years.

With *Dracula*, Bram Stoker created the modern horror novel. Though firmly rooted in the Gothic tradition, *Dracula* was extremely modern for its time. Stoker broke away from Gothic convention by placing his supernatural menace in a contemporary present, rather than in some distant past. Stoker is really not the last of the great Gothic writers, but the first of the modern masters of horror. Stephen King, Dean Koontz, Peter Straub, and Anne Rice all owe a debt to Stoker, as does the concept of the modern horror novel, a tradition Stoker invented. It is only fitting that the award bestowed by the Horror Writers Association is named The Stoker in his honor.

The role of Dracula has been tackled by some of the century's greatest actors, including Orson Welles, Frank Langella, and Daniel Day Lewis, and has given immortality to a host of "horror stars," Bela Lugosi and John Carradine among them. Dracula has given voice to hit records, singing ditties on the popular *Monster Mash* album, and has been a staple of both PBS and sitcoms like *F-Troop*. Adaptations for children of Stoker's novel fill bookstore shelves, and the toys inspired by the Vampire

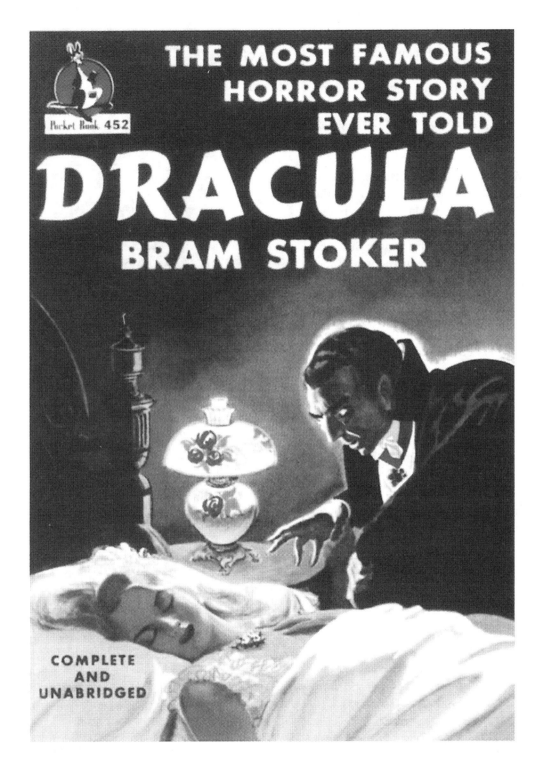

THE MOST FAMOUS
HORROR STORY
EVER TOLD

Pocket Book 452

DRACULA

BRAM STOKER

COMPLETE
AND
UNABRIDGED

King would stock a warehouse. There are several Dracula and vampire Web site pages, and not a month goes by that he is not mentioned somewhere in the world's newspapers.

The Hamilton Deane–John L. Balderston stage adaptation is in production constantly, in venues as disparate as Broadway and high school auditoriums. And new adaptations are penned regularly, adhering closely to the novel, or deconstructing it, sending it up or taking little more than the Vampire King's name and reputation in vein. Dracula has been the subject of ballets and operas, scholarly papers, and more than one doctoral thesis.

In print and on screen Dracula has battled Sherlock Holmes, Jack the Ripper, Billy the Kid, Frankenstein's Monster, and The Red Baron. As this book was in preparation, Dracula appeared in a new Marvel comic book, crossing swords with both the Amazing Spider-Man and Dr. Strange. (His earlier bout with Batman in the graphic novel *Red Rain* left the vampire down for the Count.) Even when Dracula loses he wins, for we know he will be back for round two.

This centennial year, Dracula is featured on postage stamps in the United States and Britain, and he is the focus of major conferences in New York and Los Angeles.

Dracula's fangs have penetrated every aspect of culture both high and low—with Dracula, Bram Stoker created the first multi-media star. In fact, the past 100 years have been more than The War Years, or The Space Age, or The Computer Revolution... it has been *The Dracula Century.*

Of course, it would be impossible to chronicle the myth-making 100 years of Dracula in a single volume. Instead, *Dracula: The First Hundred Years* provides a freewheeling overview of the vampire's unlife and untimes in literature, films, television, and comic books. That some things are bound to be overlooked is unavoidable, but every Dracula buff will find something to relish.

Also, very little attention is paid in the following pages to the historical Dracula, Vlad Tepes. This medieval tyrant and sadist may have lent his name to the demon we know today,

U.K. Tales of Terror Stamps

Dracula

Not to be outdone by their American cousins, the U.K. also issued a Dracula stamp as part of the 100th Anniversary of Stoker's *Dracula.* However, rather than go back to the character's cinematic roots, the stamp harks back to Stoker's original conception.

Dracula is one of four stamps celebrating the great Gothic novels, the others being *Frankenstein, Dr. Jekyll and Mr. Hyde,* and *The Hound of the Baskervilles.* Dracula's likeness graces the 26p stamp, the Monster the 31p, Dr. Jekyll/Mr. Hyde the 37p, and Dartmoor's Hound of Hell howls from the 43p. First released on May 13, 1997, the stamps are specially treated to have a glow-in-the-dark quality.

The stamps were handsomely packaged with an illustrated narrative by Gothic scholar Christopher Frayling, Professor of Cultural History and Rector of the Royal College of Art, who wrote and narrated BBC's *Nightmare* documentary.

The British philatelic press humorously took Americans to task for turning to film adaptations of the classic monsters for their set of stamps. However, the April 1997 issue of the *British Philatelic Bulletin* features cover art of Hollywood's Frankenstein Monster, played by movie Dracula Bela Lugosi!

A superb limited edition first day cover was personally signed by movie Dracula Christopher Lee. This is the second time a cinema Dracula signed first day covers: on Oct. 31, 1944, Bela Lugosi signed a three-cent stamp first day cover celebrating the 50th anniversary of motion pictures. The envelope featured stunning art of Lugosi from his stage turn as Dracula (the art can be seen next to the treatise on vampirism in Lugosi's 1944 *The Return of the Vampire*).

—Bob Madison

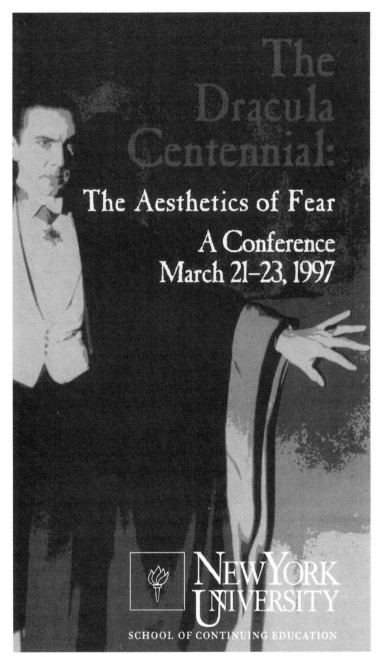

The Dracula Centennial:

The Aesthetics of Fear

A Conference
March 21–23, 1997

NEW YORK UNIVERSITY

SCHOOL OF CONTINUING EDUCATION

but little else. The Dracula that has meant so much to so many in the past 100 years—dispensing equal measures of fright and delight—owes little to his history. For those whose interests go back 500 rather than 100 years, I recommend *In Search of Dracula* by Raymond McNally and Radu Florescu, now happily back in print thanks to the fictional Dracula's anniversary, with a dazzling new cover by artist Edward Gorey.

And now, don't be afraid, turn the page. Dracula is waiting for you, just as you knew he would be. Or, as the man himself would say: "Come freely. Go safely; and leave something of the happiness you bring!"

Bob Madison
September 1997

A book like this would not have been possible without the support and contributions of many talented people. To the authors of the following chapters I tender my sincerest thanks and admiration: You have provided me with a greater knowledge of and appreciation for what Bram Stoker has wrought than I ever dreamed possible. Special thanks must go to Tom Johnson, Tom Weaver, and David J. Skal, who provided more help and inspiration than they could ever realize. Thanks also to Gary and Sue Svehla, the masterminds behind Midnight Marquee Press, who know the old man still has a lot of blood in him.

And finally, special thanks to Russell Frost, who knows why.

Dracula takes center stage at the Houston Ballet.

Houston Ballet Dracula

Always shape-shifting, Dracula has appeared in an ever-multiplying array of media. From the legitimate stage, films, and television to comic books, toys, and children's adaptations, Dracula is unending.

He's also a great little dancer.

There have been several ballet versions of *Dracula*. John L. Balderston, one of the key creators of the Dracula image as we know it, suggested a *Dracula* Broadway musical as early as 1944. His vision came complete with a vampire ballet to be choreographed by Agnes DeMille.

Unhappily, this idea never came off. But Dracula and vampires have tripped the light fantastic for more than 100 years. The first vampire ballet even predated Stoker: *Morgano,* by Paul Taglioni and J. Herzel, premiered in Berlin in 1857!

Ballet interpretations of *Dracula* have included *Love, Dracula*, presented by Les Royal Ballets Canadiens, and the Dayton Ballet and American Repertory Ballet version of *Dracula,* choreographed by Stuart Sebastian.

The Northern Ballet Theater of Halifax performed *Dracula* in October 1996. The pasty-faced make-up for dancer Denis Malinkine's Dracula was as repulsive, in its own way, as was Max Schreck's for *Nosferatu*. This production was amazingly faithful to Stoker's novel, and received critical acclaim.

As part of the 100th anniversary of Stoker's novel, the Houston Ballet held its world premiere of Ben Stevenson's *Dracula*. (The ballet was also performed in Pittsburgh and Los Angeles.)

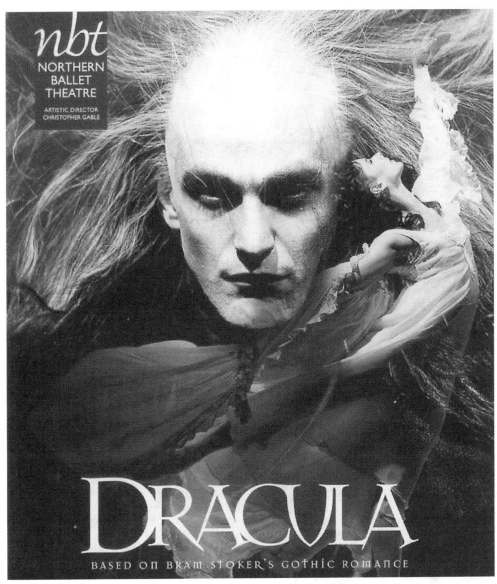

nbt
NORTHERN
BALLET
THEATRE
ARTISTIC DIRECTOR
CHRISTOPHER GABLE

DRACULA

BASED ON BRAM STOKER'S GOTHIC ROMANCE

Stevenson's *Dracula* was a terrific success, with opening night in Houston garnering headlines in newspapers in New York, Los Angeles, Boston and Chicago. ("Dracula Looks Like a Million," cried Clive Barnes.)

"I've been thinking of doing a version of *Dracula* for some time now," observed Mr. Stevenson. "*Dracula* is an amazing story. It's very gruesome, but it continues to fascinate people 100 years later."

The score for *Dracula* featured music by Hungarian composer Franz Liszt (1811-1886), in an arrangement created especially for this production by the celebrated British ballet composer John Lanchbery.

While Stevenson's version may well become a fixture with dance companies the world over, it's not particularly faithful to Stoker's novel. Here, the action takes place entirely in Transylvania, with the first and third acts transpiring in Dracula's castle and the second act in the village. There is a young lover named Frederic, a priest who confronts the Count, and two young maidens, Flora and Svetlana. (And moviemakers have trouble with the names Lucy Westenra and Mina Murray!)

All told, it seems that Dracula has no trouble walking on his points: not bad for a man pushing a hundred.

—Bob Madison

Dracula in the Witch's Dungeon

Dracula has been held in captivity for more than 30 years in the world's foremost horror movie museum!

And, if you dare, you can visit with the undead Count each and every Halloween.

When Cortlandt Hull started making his faithful recreations of the classic movie monsters of yesteryear, he had no idea that he was starting a tradition that would continue for decades. Hull's Witch's Dungeon, the only museum to display full-sized recreations of the movies' all-time favorite fiends, opens annually to the public for the three weekends nearest Halloween.

What began as a hobby for the talented Mr. Hull has become an East Coast Halloween tradition, with fans flocking from around the country annually to see the great movie monsters brought back to "life." Located in the quiet suburban town of Bristol, Connecticut, the Dungeon holds the remains not only of Dracula, but the other classic movie monsters as well.

Hull, a professional painter, sculptor, and make-up artist, first became obsessed with Dracula and monsters when he was a little boy. "Lots of my friends were afraid of Dracula," he recalls. "But I always thought there was something sad about him. He never frightened me."

Hull created the Dungeon when he was only 13 years old, starting with just a few figures. The Dracula figure was sculpted from an actual lifemask of actor Bela Lugosi's face. He also built Dracula's coffin, and recreated the famous Dracula crest designed by Universal studios for its lid. Other figures, such as the Creature from the Black Lagoon and the Mole Man, were cast from original studio molds of the movie masks, then recast and painted by Hull.

The late Vincent Price donated the costume he wore in his first horror film hit *House of Wax* (1953), and it can now be seen on the museum's Price figure. Price, a long-time friend of Hull, also recorded the voice-over narration for visitors to the Dungeon. Other celebrity voices include Mark Hamill, John Agar, and June Foray.

To celebrate the 100th anniversary of Dracula, Hull is adding a new figure for the 1997 Halloween season. After years of meticulous preparation, Hull has created a life-size recreation of actor Max Schreck, as seen in the 1922 vampire classic *Nosferatu*.

"He was really interesting to do," said Hull. "There are no supplementary materials to work with, and not much is known about Schreck. But I knew I couldn't let Dracula's birthday go by without commemorating it in some way."

The Witch's Dungeon is located at 90 Battle Street in Bristol, Connecticut. The exhibit opens at sundown (naturally) and is not recommended for children under six. For those brave enough to trace Dracula, Nosferatu, and a score of other movie monsters to their lair, send a self-addressed, stamped envelope for directions to: The Witch's Dungeon, 90 Battle Street, Bristol, CT 06010.

—Bob Madison

Dracula for Children

It's safe to say that Dracula is one of the century's most popular icons with children.

For more than four decades, the Vampire King has been de-fanged and rendered harmless for generations of baby-boomers, a trick of making the undead cuddly that continues into this Generation X age.

Children's versions of Stoker's novel abound in the nation's bookstores. The brothers Hilderbrandt, the famed illustrators of children's stories, are responsible for a particularly lavish, full-color version that has been a consistent seller for the past several years, and there are even "pop-up" versions of the story available to kids.

More interesting are the series of books featuring *Bunnicula*, the vampire rabbit. The total sales for this series of books—featuring a rabbit hare to Dracula's throne—numbers well into the millions, with children

taking delight in the antics of the carrot-victimizing, buck-toothed juice sucker.

Dracula merchandising for children has included dolls, toys, fast-food chain soda cups, candy, rubber stamps, fake fangs, watches, party-effects records, Halloween costumes, and a host of products featuring *Sesame Street*'s The Count. Another television star inspired by Dracula who spoke directly to children was Drac from the *Groovy Ghoulies* animated series of the early 1970s, who was featured in comics, coloring books, and a series of plastic dolls.

But perhaps one of the most influential of these figures is Count Chocula. For more than 20 years the Count has been, along with Frankenberry and Booberry, spokescharacter for one of the nation's most popular children's cereals. With his Lugosi-inspired voice (which has become universal for "Dracula"), cape, and medallion, Count Chocula allowed children to become familiar with Dracula iconography while laughing away any fears the character may inspire.

General Mills, the creators of the Count and his coterie of monster companions, may have bitten off more than they could chew with their initial design for the Count's cereal box. Original boxes featuring Bela Lugosi on the front are now prized collector's items after they were pulled from supermarket shelves when Jewish groups complained that the vampire's medallion looked too much like the Star of David. (The medallion worn by Chocula is little more than a tiny skull.)

There have been several Chocula tie-ins, available to kids with the purchase of a box of his cereal, many of them now collected by both Americana and vampire buffs.

And, of course, by children everywhere.

—Bob Madison

Dracula *by* BRAM STOKER

Frankenstein *by* MARY SHELLEY

Dracula *is the first modern horror novel. Without it, there would be no Stephen King, no Anne Rice, no cult of "Gothic" music and, most definitely, no heritage of horror films as we know it.*

In this essay, critic and historian David J. Hogan looks at both creation and creator as he examines Bram Stoker's Dracula, *and the tumultuous times in which Stoker lived.*
—Bob Madison

Bram Stoker's Dracula: The Coffin Opens

by David J. Hogan

Dracula was not the first vampire story, or even the first vampire novel. Its antecedents are numerous, and range from epic poetry to penny dreadfuls. The novel was published in 1897, and although the late Victorian era produced some great writers, the author of *Dracula*, an Irishman named Bram Stoker, was not one of them. Like many second-tier novelists of the time, he was prey to windy verbosity, sentimentality, and a reliance on uncomfortable contrivance. His idealized notions of women and masculine friendship made sophisticated readers squirm even in 1897. His language can be maddeningly coy, and his tendency to digress is often tedious. The novel begins strongly but then sags and does not recover until its mid-point. By accepted literary standards, then, *Dracula* is a deeply flawed work. It might legitimately be called mediocre.

And yet...

Dracula is now 100 years old, and has never been out of print. Nor is it likely to ever be. It is a work of unusual, often shocking power, and succeeds brilliantly at challenging many of our most cherished notions about death and dying; love, commitment, and sexuality; and our relationships to God and nature. To read *Dracula* is akin to submitting to a genteel physician who unexpectedly restrains us, then produces a small but wicked instrument that he indelicately inserts behind our eyeball. Completely in control, he probes. We are shocked, held fast by something terrible and compelling.

Although Count Dracula dominates the novel's every page and paragraph, he is mostly offstage. Unlike Sherlock Holmes, Tarzan, Robin Hood, and other indelible fictional characters known across the globe, Dracula does not personally dominate every scene. Yet his dominance of the book's action and themes is absolute. He motivates both the text and subtext of the novel, and awes, terrifies, and motivates most of the book's many characters. He remains imprinted on the reader's brain even when absent for long stretches of the narrative.

Because Dracula the character so forcefully seizes us, because he is a figure who, once encountered, is never forgotten, *Dracula* is, indisputably, a great work. It is a masterpiece that rises above its obvious shortcomings. It is not great literature but it is a titanic imaginative achievement. The novel is desire and panic, naked power and the whisper of seduction. We imagine ourselves not merely Dracula's victims but his accomplices. He is murderous and alluring in equal measure. Dracula exists at the summit of our desires and at the lowest depths of our potential for depravity. If he represents shocking extremes of human behavior, it's no accident, for Stoker intended the character to be a metaphor for each of us.

With regret, one suspects that *Dracula* is not widely read today. Although the novel can be found in every chain bookstore across the globe, these are places frequented mainly by people who purchase non-fiction. The relatively few who buy fiction are most likely to leave with undemanding legal thrillers, Hollywood romances, techno adventures—and horror fiction, most of which has only the barest fraction of the force and resonance of *Dracula*.

Admittedly, the surprise and subtexts of *Dracula* have been diluted by a century of imitation and adaptation. People who have absorbed the story through a sort of cultural osmosis have no desire—and perhaps not even a need—to read it. More significantly, the book's potential audience has been coarsened by an assaultive popular culture, by the undisciplined, colloquial prose of shoddy books and magazines, and by aural and visual entertainments that hack and chop at the senses and encourage the brain to sink into stupor. In this milieu of grade-school verbiage, the careful, frequently arch Victorian prose of *Dracula* cannot be finding many takers.

The novel's most recent popularity came in the wake of Francis Ford Coppola's *Bram Stoker's Dracula,* when the novel placed on *The New York Times* bestseller list for several weeks. Hollywood has provided Stoker and his creation with many much-needed transfusions, and will undoubtedly provide many more in the future.

Briefly, *Dracula* concerns the efforts of the title character, an undead Transylvanian Count, to establish himself in England while, simultaneously, a disparate group of men and women come together in common purpose to stop and destroy him.

The novel is told mainly via excerpts from the journals, diaries, letters, and telegrams of Dracula's antagonists. This device gives the novel a sense of immediacy and urgency. We first meet Jonathan Harker, a young solicitor who travels to Transylvania and Castle Dracula in order to help the Count negotiate a property deal in London. Just days after his arrival, Harker realizes that—for reasons unknown to him—he is Dracula's prisoner. Harker is horrified when he witnesses Dracula's nighttime, face-down crawl down a sheer wall of his castle. Later, after entering a forbidden room, Harker is enthralled by three beautiful women—Dracula's vampire brides—and very nearly becomes their prey. A furious Dracula storms in, feeding a wailing infant to his castle harpies.

Later, Dracula forces Harker to write misleading, post-dated letters to Mina Murray, his fiancée, and others. With mounting dread, Harker realizes that Dracula means to kill him.

Meanwhile, in London, Mina's friend, Lucy Westenra, receives proposals of marriage from three men: Arthur Holmwood, an affable young lord; Dr. John Seward, a young doctor who runs a sanitarium; and Quincey Morris, a Texas cowboy. She accepts Holmwood, and the others pledge continued love of her.

At his sanitarium nearby, Dr. Seward puzzles over one of his patients, Renfield, a deeply disturbed man who raves about "the master," and who compulsively gobbles spiders and flies.

At Castle Dracula, Harker fails in his attempt to use local gypsies to smuggle letters home. Later, Slovak workmen deliver large wooden boxes to the castle. The desperate Harker climbs along a parapet and descends to the bowels of the castle, where he discovers Dracula comatose in an earth-filled box.

Although Harker gashes Dracula's forehead with a spade, the Count and his boxes soon leave Romania on the schooner *Demeter*. As the ship slowly makes its way toward England, crewmen begin to disappear. In London, the madman Renfield becomes more agitated: he eats a flock of sparrows he has gathered and demands to have a kitten.

Mina receives the first of Harker's false letters, and her friend, Lucy, is suddenly troubled by sleepwalking. The *Demeter* is beached at Whitby during a terrific storm, and witnesses claim that a wolf or dog fled the wreck. The ship is empty except for the captain's body, bound to the wheel.

One of the most important parts of Bram Stoker's novel that is most often overlooked by film adaptations are the key scenes set in Whitby.

Whitby, a North Yorkshire seaside port, plays a major part in the novel, and first appears in Chapter Three. It is at Whitby that Stoker's Vampire King first enters London, hoping to feast upon the "rush of humanity" far from his barren homeland.

When visiting Whitby, remember that not much has changed there since Dracula's planned conquest of the British Isles. This tiny seaport continues to be a busy fishing town despite European fishing quotas. In Stoker's day, Whitby was bustling and prosperous with trading vessels from ports all over the world.

One of the major commodities of contemporary Whitby is Dracula himself. The town is proud of its *Dracula* connections, and numerous shops sell memorabilia and cards to visitors. There is also *The Dracula Experience*, a sort of seaside haunted house, featuring eerie lighting and sound effects coupled with tableaux of wax dummies. Be warned, though, for as you move through the dark corridors a blood-thirsty female vampire will pounce upon you! A friend and I discovered this to our cost, and while it gave us a delicious chill, we were relieved that it was an actress in pancake make-up and not a real vampire.

At least, I hope it was just an actress.

The Parish Church of St. Mary's and its surrounding graveyard are also interesting. Still and silent at most times, on moonlit nights it is rich in *Dracula* atmosphere. Following the same trail as Lucy and Mina, you will climb the 199 steps to the church where you will be greeted by the breathtaking view of the town, the raging sea, and the distant horizon.

Journey a little further and see the ruins of Whitby Abbey, whose spires are amazingly photogenic against the Yorkshire skies. Whatever the weather, the sea and sky-scapes are always stunning. Much of the town is unchanged since Stoker spent his family holidays there; indeed the library still has the local history books and tourist guides which Stoker used for research. Walking through the cobbled streets and quaint shops, you can feel the past reach out for you with vampiric hands...

The local Tourist Information Centre will furnish you with a *Dracula Trail* booklet if you left your own well-thumbed paperback of the novel at home. It includes a map so you can stand right where the action happened.

The Bram Stoker Memorial Seat, dedicated to the author on the 68th anniversary of his death, is an important monument to visit. The seat itself has been carefully situated so that visitors can share the principal views seen by Stoker as he conceived his famous masterpiece. Its panoramic setting allows you to enjoy all the novel's locations at once, and is a unique experience.

So if you are a true *Dracula* fan, perhaps it's time to visit Whitby. Just remember the quaint old English custom of seaside resorts: these towns and attractions flourish in the summer, but in the winter they close down to hibernate in true undead fashion. But once there, you will understand how Bram Stoker conceived many of his ideas.

You can take home all kinds of souvenirs from your visit... but perhaps the postcard best sums it up in just three words.

WHITBY—DRACULA COUNTRY.

—Mark Walker

Lucy's somnambulism takes her to a lonely cliffside, where Dracula drinks her blood. He feeds off her many times more, coming to her in the guise of man, mist, and bat.

As Lucy grows progressively weaker, Renfield's agitation increases. He escapes the sanitarium and runs toward the neighboring house Carfax, where fifty boxes of Transylvanian earth—cargo from the *Demeter*—have been delivered.

Harker is discovered alive in Buda-Pesth (Budapest); Mina flies to his side and they are married abroad. While Mina is away, Dr. Seward is asked by Holmwood to examine Lucy, who has grown wan and debilitated. Seward is puzzled and sends for one of his former professors, a Dutchman, Dr. Abraham Van Helsing. Lucy receives a blood transfusion and rallies, but later weakens; Van Helsing has no choice but to give her blood transfusions, using the blood of Holmwood, Seward, Quincey, and himself.

A possessed wolf escapes from the zoo, crashes into Lucy's room, and frightens Lucy's mother to death. Lucy weakens further and dies from shock and loss of blood. Not long after her entombment, local children are attacked and bitten by the pale "Bloofer Lady" (beautiful lady). On what was to have been her wedding day, Lucy rises from her grave and lures away a child. Her resurrection is witnessed by Holmwood, Seward, Van Helsing, and Morris. In a truly grisly passage, the group enters Lucy's tomb, where Holmwood drives a stake through the heart of his undead lover.

Dracula's opponents band together. Mina reads Harker's journal and passes it on to Van Helsing; later, she and Seward exchange diaries. The pattern and purpose of Dracula's movements begins to come clear, but even this knowledge cannot prevent the Count from preying upon Mina and drinking her blood.

Renfield becomes violent, wounding Seward and lapping at the spilled blood. Then, in a moment of startling lucidity, Renfield runs to Carfax and attacks workmen as they remove some of the mysterious boxes. Renfield is soon killed by Dracula, his face and skull shattered, his back cruelly broken.

Aware that his London haven has been uncovered, Dracula makes ready to flee. In a horrific passage he preys upon Mina again, opening a vein in his chest and forcing her to drink. Van Helsing and his band of protectors break in upon the bloody scene, but Dracula escapes, first destroying their notebooks, records, and memoranda.

Seward, Harker, Van Helsing, Holmwood, and Morris track Dracula to a rented house, but the Count escapes again, this time to the *Czarina Catherine*, a ship bound for Varna, Bulgaria.

Van Helsing, the other men, and the weakened but desperate Mina take the Orient Express to Varna, arriving there before Dracula. Days later, Van Helsing and Mina—by now separated from the rest of the group, which has split up in order not to miss Dracula—discover that the *Czarina Catherine* has been diverted to Galatz. In a spectacularly unsettling scene, the pair hurry to the vicinity of Castle Dracula, where Dracula's brides attack them in the forest. Van Helsing wards them off with consecrated host, then follows them back to their lair where he kills them.

The Gypsies deliver Dracula, in his coffin, to his castle by wagon. The now re-united group of crusaders battle the Gypsies and the setting sun and they scramble toward the resting king vampire. Quincey Morris, although mortally injured, drives his Bowie knife into Dracula's heart in the same instant that Harker beheads the Count with his great *kukri* knife. As Dracula crumbles to dust, the evil is destroyed and Mina's soul is saved.

Bram (Abraham) Stoker was born in Dublin, Ireland, in 1847. He was physically disabled as a child by an unidentified (and possibly hysterical) ailment, and could neither stand nor walk until he was seven years old. Largely by force of will, he grew strong and became a star athlete at the University of Dublin.

Bram Stoker's London home, complete with historical plaque for *Dracula* pilgrims.

For much of his adult life, Stoker seemed destined to be a respectable but anonymous member of Britain's growing middle class. He worked for 10 years as a civil servant at Dublin Castle, and as an unpaid literary critic for the Dublin *Mail*. Another non-paying job, editor of the *Irish Echo* newspaper, followed.

In 1878 Stoker went to work for Sir Henry Irving, the celebrated Shakespearean actor and tragedian whom Stoker had observed and enjoyed in the past, and who now was manager of London's Lyceum Theatre. Irving had seen Stoker's drama reviews, and invited him to become the theater's hands-on manager. From 1878 until Irving's death in 1905, Stoker did not simply oversee the day-to-day operations of the Lyceum, but was Henry Irving's de facto secretary, organizing the details of the actor's career, maintaining a voluminous correspondence, and performing other nettlesome but necessary duties. Stoker became indispensable to Irving, and accompanied the actor on tours to America and elsewhere. Ironically, Irving frequently made life difficult for Stoker, mocking his ambitions and taking care to maintain the distinction between *artiste* and vassal.

A literate man of taste and ambition, Stoker could not be satisfied merely with proximity to Irving and the theatrical world. He began to write. His first novel, the historical adventure *The Snake's Pass*, was serialized in 1889 and published in book form a year later. *Dracula* (entitled *The Un-Dead* and *Count Wampyr* on Stoker's early handwritten drafts) appeared seven years later, published by Constable and Sons.

Dracula was a sensation in Stoker's lifetime, stirring passions and controversy. Many critics condemned its morbidity; others lauded its power and imagination. The book brought Stoker notoriety and a reasonable income, but would never become a runaway bestseller in his lifetime. The first American edition was published by Doubleday in 1899.

In 1897, just six days before the novel was first published, Stoker led the Lyceum Theatre company in a public reading of *Dracula*, most likely to protect the book's

DRACULA

BY BRAM STOKER

copyright from unauthorized theatrical adaptations. (Regardless, Stoker's widow, Florence, spent decades protecting her husband's literary rights, most famously against German film director F. W. Murnau, whose 1922 masterpiece, *Nosferatu: Eine Symphonie des Gravens*, adapted *Dracula* without permission. She fought to have the film destroyed, but the film, like Dracula, had traveled abroad, and copies survived in the United States. It remains one of the finest adaptations of Stoker's novel ever produced.)

Perhaps Stoker always had a play in mind while creating *Dracula*. Conceived as a vehicle for his idol, Irving, Dracula would have made a grand part for the actor, who had also scored a hit as Mephistopheles. At any rate, Stoker's stage reading ran in five acts, including 47 scenes and a prologue. A copy of his treatment exists in the British Museum, and includes Stoker's deviations from his own text, including action concerning Harker outside of Castle Dracula. Legend goes that Irving saw a few moments of the production, entitled *Dracula, or The Undead*, and pronounced it "Dreadful!"

The Lyceum was destroyed by fire in 1898, and a syndicate took over control of the venue. The theater was closed in 1902. Henry Irving became ill not long after the fire, and died in 1905.

None of Stoker's other books duplicated the visceral impact or popular success of *Dracula*. Stoker's subsequent novels are *Miss Betty* (1898); *The Mystery of the Sea* (1902); *The Jewel of Seven Stars* (1903; adapted by filmmakers in 1971 and 1980); *The Man* (1905); *The Lady of the Shroud* (1909; a commercially successful book that had seen some 20 printings by 1934); and *The Lair of the White Worm* (1911; reprinted and adapted for film in 1988).

Stoker also produced books of non-fiction: *Famous Impostors* (1910) and the two-volume *The Personal Reminiscences of Henry Irving* (1911).

Stoker suffered a stroke in 1905, and struggled to write thereafter. He subsequently was struck with Bright's disease, a debilitating kidney ailment marked by albumin (protein) in the urine. Stoker died at his home in London on April 20, 1912. His estate was valued at about £5,000.

Florence Stoker oversaw the posthumous publication, in 1914, of a story collection, *Dracula's Guest, and Other Weird Stories*; the title story is a chapter that had been deleted from the *Dracula* manuscript before publication. She followed her husband to the grave in 1937.

Dracula fits comfortably in the larger context of late-Victorian life and literature.

Queen Victoria occupied the British throne from 1837 to 1901. Her 63-year reign encompassed remarkable change in Britain: a deeper entrenchment of the ruling class; rapid population growth; tentative social and political reform; and dramatic, extremely profitable industrialization and a concomitant rise of a reasonably well-educated middle class.

However, much of the population growth of this early period of Victoria's reign occurred among the working class, who would come into increasingly frequent conflict with the nascent middle class. The latter, in turn, often locked horns with Britain's aristocracy.

Despite the simmering class warfare, the first half of Victoria's reign brought England unprecedented prosperity and political stability. England viewed itself—and was viewed by much of the world—as a paragon of progress. The period was an optimistic one, and was in many ways the second Age of Enlightenment. Van Helsing, man of science, was its logical hero just as Dracula, creature of myth, its obvious villain.

A portent of philosophical change was embodied in the Chartists, a group of politically "radical" activists who, during the period 1838-49, demanded the vote for working-class men; vote by ballot; and equal representation in electoral districts, regardless of social and economic make-up. Although Chartism failed to realize its goals during its heyday, all but one—annual parliamentary elections—were realized later.

Chartism's greatest significance was symbolic. Its dissonant voice startled Britons who had fallen prey to intellectual inertia, and suggested that even a monarch as respected as Victoria could not expect all of her subjects to be perfectly docile and obedient. Further, the movement's very existence was an explicit threat to British social and political structures that had been regarded for centuries as the natural order of things.

The second 30-year period of Victoria's rule saw a subtle but very real decline of British fortune and moral authority. A falling birth rate and mass unemployment dogged industrial expansion and damaged the morale and material lives of the lower and middle classes. Simultaneous widespread exploitation of child workers further disheartened the working class and fueled the outrage of reformers. Britain's self-confidence was shaken also by economic crises spurred by successive bad harvests that began about 1836.

Abroad, late 19th-century Britain practiced a brand of colonialism that was informed by xenophobia and *noblesse oblige* arrogance, a sort of moral and intellectual laziness that assumed that Britain's material and political dominance gave the nation the right to do whatever it chose. Britain's colonies, notably India, suffered under British rule, and the nation's exploitation of her holdings became uglier and more blatant than before. Closer to home, British malfeasance in Ireland led to violent expressions of Irish nationalism.

Like the rest of the Western world, Britain was rocked in 1859 by Charles Darwin's *On the Origin of Species by Means of Natural Selection*, a groundbreaking work that posited the theory of evolution. Writers, thinkers, and society at large suddenly were forced to question the nature of man, his origins, and his relationship to God.

Darwinian thought encouraged a liberal new school of philosophy, relativism, which appeared around 1865. By holding that knowledge and ethics are shaped *and limited* by the mind of man—and not simply pronounced by some supernatural higher power—relativism flew in the face of centuries of religious doctrine, and suggested that the cultural elite had no more ability, and thus no more right, than the lower classes to comprehend and interpret the world.

The same year as *Origin of Species,* British essayist John Stuart Mill published "On Liberty," a cry for reformation dedicated to fair treatment of the working class, and a more equitable distribution of wealth. This was followed by a pair of books by Thomas Huxley: *Man's Place in Nature* (1863) and *The Physical Basis of Life* (1868). These works had considerably less scientific foundation than Darwin's, and considerably more antipathy toward the teachings of the Church.

The social, political, and philosophical changes described above led to intellectual turmoil precipitated by the unavoidable clash of relativism with traditional values. Bram Stoker, a young adult by the time of the first flush of relativist thought, could not have avoided its implications and challenges.

It's no surprise that literature produced in England and across Europe in the late 19th century drifted toward realism and naturalism. Writers such as Gustave Flaubert, Emile Zola, Ivan Sergeyevich Turgenev, George Eliot (Mary Ann Evans), Anthony Trollope, Thomas Hardy, and Europe's two great naturalists, Charles Dickens and Honoré de Balzac, expressed concern for the working class, and focused on the physical and moral impediments of everyday life. Secondary characters and even protagonists were sharply-drawn laborers, prostitutes, criminals, adulterers, and eccentrics. Genteel observers found the works of many of these writers, notably Zola and Balzac, scandalous, not least because of the books' interest in willful female characters who were shaped, fairly or unfairly, by their environments—another cultural signpost of which Stoker must have been aware. Although Lucy in *Dracula* sometimes seems like little more than a Victorian cameo, after the vampire's kiss she boils with raw, animal passions.

DRACULA

1/6 Net.   BRAM STOKER   1/6 Net.

Late-Victorian drama, too, underwent significant change, shifting from sensational, mass-audience fare of the early-Victorian period toward a new realism and frankness, often layered with satire of the ruling class. Henrik Ibsen, Arthur Wing Pinero, Oscar Wilde, T. W. Robertson, and other playwrights were at the forefront of the new drama.

Every new movement encourages a cultural backlash. The late-Victorian realists encouraged revivals of Romantic and Gothic novels. Late-Victorian writers who looked to literature's past for inspiration include Robert Louis Stevenson, Arthur Conan Doyle, Rudyard Kipling, Sheridan Le Fanu, Wilkie Collins, and Bram Stoker. These "new romantics," whether expressing themselves with satire, mystery, adventure, or out-and-out fantasy, championed familiar values (Kipling's preoccupation with colonialism is a sterling example), with the added fillip of satire or sexual frankness. Many new-romantic works were built around emotional, non-rational points of view.

The new romantics were encouraged by a sensual, backward-looking school of British verse that emerged around 1870. This movement, dubbed the Pre-Raphaelite Brotherhood, was led by Dante Gabriel Rossetti, whose work epitomized what was called "The Fleshly School of Poetry." Rossetti and others, such as William Morris and Algernon Swinburne, combined medieval settings with paganism, mythic heroes and heroines, utopianism, and expressions of physical love—all described in colorful detail that was at once beautiful and, to straitlaced readers, unsettling.

Another quasi-backlash movement, religious poetry, also flourished in this period; Christina Rossetti (Dante Rossetti's sister) and Gerard Manley Hopkins were at the forefront of a growing fascination with things mystical. Like the new romantics, the religious poets of the period rejected academicism, turning their gift for pictorial detail to emotional, sometimes mystical interpretations of traditional religion. In this, the poetry was fresh, but many readers questioned its relevance to an increasingly materialistic society.

The imaginative Bram Stoker was a man of his era, and *Dracula* is an amalgam of much of what has been described above. It is rational and irrational. It is sexually discreet and promiscuous. It longs for an ordered society but describes one beset by a phantasmagorical agent of disorder. The book exhibits a fascination with modern science and technology: the telegraph, phonograph, and typewriter (upon which Stoker, incidentally, set down *Dracula*) are prominently mentioned; and Van Helsing, though mindful of the timeless aspect of the evil he faces, prepares to confront it with all the care of a clever detective or scientist. And yet the scientific method is effective only to a point, for in the courtyard of Castle Dracula Van Helsing protects Mina by drawing a mystic ring around her, instructing her to remain within it. And Dracula's destruction is achieved via brute force and physical sacrifice, ending in the death of Quincey Morris.

The book is stuffed with exhilarating adventure, yet has distinctly modern philosophical implications that remain thought-provoking and disturbing. Stoker implicitly supports the British Empire, condescendingly describing the people of Eastern Europe as "quaint" and "rough." However, two of the story's heroes, the Dutch Van Helsing and the American Morris, are decidedly un-British. It is a story of men and women hurtled into a new era, even as they struggle to protect the principles and values of the past.

As noted, *Dracula*, was not the first vampire story. Stoker had read Dubliner Sheridan Le Fanu's "Carmilla," a short story that originally appeared in an 1872 Le Fanu collection entitled *In a Glass Darkly*. Carmilla is a beautiful vampiress who victimizes, over a period of many years, the story's young narrator, Laura. In time, the reader discovers that Laura is a descendant of the Karnstein family, and that Carmilla is actually Mircalla Karnstein, who was born in the 17th century. Mircalla was cursed with vampirism because she had committed suicide. She is destroyed when she is staked, beheaded, and burned by two men: a physician, and a general intent on avenging the death of his daughter.

"Carmilla" profoundly affected Stoker; he suffered nightmares after reading the story, and adopted many of Le Fanu's vampiric "conventions." In both works, protagonists act partly out of a desire for revenge. Also, Le Fanu's sympathetic physician seems to have inspired two of *Dracula's* major characters, Dr. Seward and Dr. Van Helsing.

Stoker was inspired by other literary vampires as well. Early interpretations of the undead were offered in poems and stories by Euripides, Homer, Aristophanes, and Philostratus (who was intrigued by demonic shape-shifting). Much later, Goethe's 1791 poem, "The Bride of Corinth," described a repressed girl who is free to marry her lover only after she has died and was reborn a vampire. Another poem, Coleridge's "Christabel," concerns a young woman who is visited by an undead lamia (female vampire) named Geraldine.

The same 1816 literary gathering in Switzerland that produced Mary Shelley's *Frankenstein* also produced "The Vampyre," an outline written by Lord Byron. In 1819, Byron's companion, John Polidori, utilized the outline to fashion a story of the same title. The blood-drinking protagonist is Lord Ruthven, a figure who, like Dracula, possesses a primal, animalistic allure.

Ruthven is a vampire in the Byronic mode. Aristocratic, attractive to women, and possessing a dangerous sensuality, Ruthven is a mirror-image of Byron, described by his contemporaries as "mad, bad and dangerous to know."

Stoker's Dracula, a hairy, Darwinian superman, is the complete antithesis of the Byronic ideal. However, the Byronic literary tradition of vampirism is strong, and continues to this day. Most stage and screen adaptations jettison Stoker's Tartar for the more romantic, Byronic model. Every film adaptation of the novel, featuring actors and talents as disparate as Bela Lugosi, Christopher Lee, Louis Jourdan, and Frank Langella, draws to some degree upon the Byronic conceit. Anne Rice's debt to Byron is so great, she should split her royalties with his estate.

An 1836 story by Theophile Gautier, "The Dreamland Bride," revolves around Clarimonde, an elegant vampiress whom Gautier used to mount a deliberate attack on the conservative sexual mores of his time. In the story a young monk is inflamed by the richly perverse fantasy life provided by Clarimonde, and willingly offers her his blood in return.

The potent sexual aspect of these works, particularly as it reshaped traditional notions of female sexuality, clearly helped inspire the characterizations and predicaments of two of the most intriguing characters in *Dracula*, Lucy Westenra and Mina Murray Harker. Each is not simply victimized by Dracula's sickly erotic yearnings: they are painted (Lucy, in particular) as creatures with barely repressed, potentially menacing sexualities.

Finally, Stoker must surely have been aware of *Varney, the Vampyre; or, The Feast of Blood, A Romance*, an unabashedly pulpy British novel written by a onetime civil engineer named James Malcolm Rymer. *Varney's* 220 chapters (!) were originally serialized in 109 weekly, one-cent installments in the mid-1840s. In 1847, these "penny dreadful" pieces were collected and published in book form. Authorship of *Varney* is sometimes erroneously credited to Thomas Presket Prest, author of the *Sweeney Todd* penny-dreadful thrillers. However, because it was not uncommon for such works to be cobbled together by more than one writer, James Rymer may not be the sole author, and may in fact have been assisted by Prest.

Vampire poetry and fiction inspired Stoker in the specifics of his tale, but on a broader level *Dracula* was inspired by the Gothic-romantic conventions established by Robert Walpole's *The Castle of Otranto*, a novel published in 1764. The story is magical, offering a castle that is described in minute detail: the place is fitted with trapdoors and ominous suits of armor and ancient weaponry and a portrait that comes to life. The plot turns on sudden death, the imperative of carrying on a family name, and symbolic incest (the villainous protagonist schemes to marry his son's widow after confining his own wife to a convent).

The Gothic novel was refined by Ann Radcliffe in *The Mysteries of Udolpho* (1794) and *The Italian* (1797). Like Walpole, Radcliffe was preoccupied with (and tiptoed around) incest, a subject that was blatantly exploited by Matthew G. Lewis' *The Monk* (1796). Lewis' title character, launched into the sensual world following 30 years of celibacy, becomes so corrupted and debauched that he murders his mother in order to seduce a woman who turns out to be his sister. The incestuous consummation takes place in a charnel house. As in *Dracula*, traditional morality is challenged when unwholesome sex collides headlong with death.

The curse of an unnaturally long lifespan is explored in Charles Maturin's *Melmoth the Wanderer* (1820), a darkly picaresque novel describing the horrific travels of the title character, who sells his soul in order to live 150 years. Not unexpectedly (and in the sort of irony relished by the Devil), Melmoth falls into lust, violence, cannibalism, and disillusionment. The fall from grace of the later Count Dracula is no less dramatic.

The miracle of *Dracula*'s success as a unified whole is that it is a mixing bowl of so much, including one ingredient that its predecessors lacked: a true-life historical antecedent. This is Vlad III (also known as Vlad Tepes and Vlad Dracul), who was Prince of the Romanian principality of Wallachia from 1456 to 1462 and for a brief period in 1476.

Wallachia was located on the left bank of the lower Danube, unfortuitously situated between the disdainful Kingdom of Hungary and the expanding empire of the Ottoman Turks (to whom Prince Vlad was forced to pay tribute). The principality was ripe for political upheaval and violence.

Vlad was right at home.

He was born in 1431 at Sighisoara, in central Romania north of the Transylvanian Alps. While still a youth, Vlad was part of a group of hostages sent to the court of Murad II, the Ottoman Sultan. During his imprisonment the boy was brutalized and sexually assaulted regularly, a horror that undoubtedly helped to precipitate the cruelty and bloodlust he exhibited as an adult.

Historically, Vlad is just another petty nobleman who was squeezed between two enormous, unsympathetic powers. When his reign began in 1456, only three years had passed since the Ottoman Turks had overrun Constantinople. Swept up in the fervor of the final Crusade against the Muslim "infidels," the ostensibly Christian Vlad showed no mercy to Turks who fell into his hands. It is this lack of mercy—and a genius for torture—that elevated him into legend.

Vlad favored the *pala* (pointed stake), on which victims would be impaled in a variety of ways: through the chest, back, neck, and other prosaic sites; or, with exceedingly thin *palas* that had been specially greased and sharpened, through the rectum and out through the mouth. A victim so impaled, the *pala* driven into the ground, might live for days in indescribable agony. One account claims that a single expedition across the Danube netted Vlad nearly 24,000 Turkish prisoners, all of whom were impaled (countless others who had been beheaded, boiled, or burned were spared the *pala*).

Incredibly, Vlad turned his bloodlust against his own people as well, impaling some 20,000 Wallachian men, women, and children of noble birth in a single orgy of cruelty undertaken at the beginning his reign. Given his hideous obsession, it's no surprise that the Prince came to be known as Vlad the Impaler.

He enjoyed observing the death throes of his captives while he dined, and was known to drink the fresh blood of his victims; not as unreasonable as it seems, for what better way to humiliate and dominate one's enemies than by consuming them? (What better way, for that matter, to offer a cautionary example to one's own subjects and rivals?) Many victims were blinded, and the sex organs of female captives were frequently taken as trophies.

Not a nice man.

In 1462 Vlad was arrested and imprisoned by Matthias Corvinus, the King of Hungary, who was either fearful for the safety of his own subjects or simply fed up. Vlad remained in captivity in Hungary until 1474. He subsequently returned home but was assassinated in 1476, two months after regaining control of Wallachia.

Vlad's cruelty was first documented in *Geschichte Dracole Wayde*, a German book published in Vienna in 1463, thirteen years before Vlad's death. This book, the closest we will come to an accurate account of Vlad's misdeeds, is the basis for the centuries of variations and embellishments that followed. To complete the picture, we have Vlad's image—broad forehead, narrow jaw, thick mustache, piercing eyes—which was preserved in woodcuts and sculpture. His castles, located north of Bucharest at Poenari and Bran, remain extant and accessible.

Stoker was aware of Vlad Dracul, and may also have known of another real-life blood fiend, Elisabeth Bathory, a Hungarian noblewoman born in 1560. She grew up in the Carpathian Mountains and married a nobleman named Ferencz Nadasdy, who allowed her to move freely from castle to castle, where she indulged her unnatural appetites. From 1600 to 1610 Bathory ordered the abductions and murders of hundreds of peasant maidens, believing that by bathing in their blood, she could maintain her youth. After Bathory's activities were finally exposed in 1614, she was walled up alive in one of her castles.

The cruelty and apparent barbarism of Eastern Europe, and the often-distressing ramifications of a rapidly changing Britain and Western Europe, roiled in Stoker's mind. In addition, he was sharply aware that the European literary tradition was changing dramatically, and that although the story he wished to relate was, in many ways, a traditional one, he would be free (and perhaps even obligated) to utilize modern literary devices in the telling.

To present-day readers accustomed to stories told through dialogue and in "real time," Stoker's use of his characters' journals, diaries, and other writings to propel the narrative (a device borrowed from Wilkie Collins' *The Moonstone*) is likely to seem not merely artificial, but distancing. The device is additionally problematic now because few people write long letters and perhaps fewer keep a journal.

The novel opens with the journal entries of the young solicitor, Harker. They are vividly expressed and quickly impart a powerful sense of unease. Even better, because these initial impressions by Harker are long, accounting for about one-sixth of the novel's total length, the reader is caught up in a grotesque milieu that is expressed in marvelous detail.

The early stages of Harker's journey, during which he describes "green swelling hills," "mighty slopes of forest," and "an endless perspective of jagged rocks and pointed crags," takes the urban reader of Stoker's time to an exotic, wild place.

Dracula's presence hangs over the untamed landscape like a moldering shroud. Harker's unease is fueled by Dracula's mysterious driver (who is of course Dracula himself), the "jagged battlements" of the enormous castle, locked doors, and the seeming impossibility of the Count's failure to cast a reflection in a mirror. Discomfiture turns to all-out terror the night Harker is visited by Dracula's silent brides: "I thought at the time that I must be dreaming when I saw them, for, though the moonlight was behind them, they threw no shadow on the floor."

When the women's blatantly sexual assault on Harker is thwarted by Dracula's angry arrival, one of his brides asks, "Are we to have nothing to-night?" At this, Dracula

$1.25

Stoker's book of blood adapted for children.

points to what Harker describes as a "dreadful bag," which "moved as though there were some living thing within it... If my ears did not deceive me there was a gasp and a low wail, as of a half-smothered child. The women closed round, whilst I was aghast with horror..."

Other early scenes—as when Harker sees the Count's lizard-like scuttle down an exterior castle wall, and later discovery of Dracula lying in his coffin, bloated like a filthy leech—are similarly dismaying, and are small masterpieces of the odd and terrible.

Regrettably, the novel slows for a long section following Harker's misadventures. The visceral language of the solicitor's journal is swept aside by the cloying prose of journals and letters kept by the book's important female characters, Mina and Lucy. Each young woman is atremble with love and respect for the other, and almost completely preoccupied with an exalted sort of romantic love for the respective men in their lives, Harker and Holmwood.

Other important characters are introduced via the women's correspondence, including Seward ("Just fancy! He is only nine-and-twenty, and he has an immense lunatic asylum all under his own care") and Morris ("Won't you just hitch up alongside of me," Lucy recalls him asking her, "and let us go down the long road together, driving in double harness?")

Stoker's attempt at American slang and dialect is dire, but Mina's dialect-filled recollection of her conversation with an old salt at the seacoast town of Whitby is just as awful, and even more aggravating, as it goes on for pages. The artificiality of the letter-journal device becomes quite apparent here, as we are expected to believe that Mina would want to, and is capable of, reproducing paragraphs of dialect dialogue.

Stoker also had trouble expressing Van Helsing's Dutch dialect, although he does not fail as badly as he does with Morris. Much of the professor's dialogue (related, of course, in the writings of other characters) is merely clunky rather than contrived: "Now, little miss [Lucy], here is your medicine... See, I lift you so that to swallow is easy. Yes." And later: "But I shall precaution take. I shall give hypodermic injection of morphia." Although the tortured syntax suggests Van Helsing's alien aspect (an echo of Dracula), it does not really suggest an English-speaking Dutchman.

Relief from the diaries and early correspondence of Lucy and Mina arrives in the form of Seward's journal entries concerning his demented patient, Renfield. These passages are lively and amusing, not simply for the outré subject matter ("He has turned his mind now to spiders, and has got several very big fellows in a box"), but for a laudable simplicity of language. It's doubtful that Stoker intended for Seward and Renfield to function as antidotes to Mina and Lucy, but that's precisely what they are.

The hideous breaking up of the *Demeter* upon the rocks at Whitby is high adventure, related in muscular prose (a supposed newspaper story) that brims with wrenching detail. The skipper's log ("There seems some doom over this ship") is similarly eerie.

Lucy does not become an interesting figure until nearly a third of the way into the novel, when Mina and others notice her daytime listlessness and agitated sleep. Lucy's world (and, by extension, the world of all proper Victorians) has been invaded by something untoward and menacingly sexual, so in this respect the arch writings of Lucy and Mina at least function as counterpoint to the horror of Lucy's situation.

Dracula rallies back from its flowery language and over-length because of Stoker's flair for surprise and morbid detail. Lucy's tomb, where flowers hang "lank and dead," hides the vampiress, a "dim white figure" who feeds on a small child as her friends watch. Seward relates,

> My own heart grew cold as ice, and I could hear the gasp of Arthur, as we recognized the features of Lucy Westenra. Lucy Westenra, but yet how changed. The sweetness was turned to adamantine, heartless cruelty, and the purity to voluptuous wantonness... the lips were crimson with fresh blood, and... the stream had trickled over her chin and stained the purity of her lawn death-robe.
>
> We shuddered with horror... When Lucy—I call the thing that was before us Lucy because it bore her shape—saw us she drew back with an angry snarl, such as a cat gives when taken unawares; then her eyes

ranged over us. Lucy's eyes in form and colour; but Lucy's eyes unclean and full of hell-fire, instead of the pure, gentle orbs we knew.

The passage is shocking, poignant, horrifying. Scores of writers and legions of filmmakers have tried, usually unsuccessfully, to duplicate its dread.

Lucy's victimization of children is just one instance of the novel's preoccupation with the abuse and corruption of the very young. The writhing bag tossed to Dracula's brides, and the London boys and girls victimized by Lucy, the "Bloofer Lady," provoke pity and outrage. Stoker's utilization of children in this way was especially compelling in his own time because Britain's growing, industrialized middle class, free of the endless drudgery of farming, enjoyed a luxury that had previously been allowed only to the upper classes: the opportunity to regard their children as beloved family members, and not simply as additional farm hands. (Working-class children, of course, continued to labor long hours in dirty, dangerous factories.)

Writers good and bad reflected the exalted new status of middle-class children in novels, stories, and verse that ranged from warm to overly sentimental. Children were cherished and (unrealistically) idealized. By adopting this point of view, the new middle class was able to feel good about itself, perhaps even noble. Dracula's callous slaughter of children, his regard of them as livestock, was a harsh blow aimed at middle-class self-image.

Central to the novel's sexual aspect is Stoker's suggestion that the dissipated Lucy is not frightened or saddened by her condition; rather, she throbs with physical longing. She is a modern woman who *wants* the brush of the fiend's fangs against her throat, she *wants* to give her blood to him. She has become a wanton, and the reader must ponder: does a sensualist lurk inside every woman? Is Dracula merely the key that unlocks predilections that have been there all along?

While Lucy writhes in bloody abandon, Mina is enduring a sexless, anesthetized sort of marriage to Harker (whose escape from Castle Dracula, by the way, is never explained; he simply turns up at a Hungarian "sanitarium"). Harker's experience seems to have drained him of potency. Dracula's machinations, then, can turn sexuality on its head, denying it to the married and imposing it upon the innocent and unmarried.

The carnal nature of Lucy's predicament spreads to those around her, particularly the men, who are unconsciously aroused, even as they attempt to save Lucy's life. Seward, relating the transfusion of his blood into Lucy's "horribly white" body, writes: "No man knows till he experiences it, what it is to feel his own life-blood drawn away into the veins of the woman he loves." This metaphor for masochistic sexual intercourse is positively eye-opening. Also, the fact that in successive transfusions Lucy receives blood from Seward, Holmwood, Van Helsing, and Morris (that is, from multiple "lovers") puts her in a moral predicament that Victorian readers must have found unbearable.

Symbolists have no difficulty locating the novel's allusions to homosexual love, either. Once the reader accepts Stoker's symbolic substitution of blood for semen, Dracula's relationship with the pathetic Renfield is nothing if not homoerotic. The point of view comes close to explicitness when Seward is attacked and cut by Renfield at the asylum. Seward relates, "My wrist bled freely, and quite a little pool trickled on to the carpet... When the attendants rushed in, and we turned our attention to him [Renfield], his employment positively sickened me. He was lying on his belly on the floor licking up, like a dog, the blood which had fallen from my wounded wrist. He was easily secured and, to my surprise, went with the attendants quite placidly, simply repeating over and over again: 'The blood is the life! the blood is the life!'" The blood/

0 552 10698 4

Count Dracula

CORGI

A GOTHIC ROMANCE by GERALD SAVORY
BASED ON BRAM STOKER'S
DRACULA

NOW A STUNNING BBC-TV DRAMATISATION
STARRING LOUIS JOURDAN AS
COUNT DRACULA

semen symbolism inherent in Renfield's expression of appetite is obvious, but the passage's most telling word is "placidly," having enjoyed "sex" with Seward, Renfield is suddenly relaxed, at ease. The thoughtful reader, whatever his or her sexual orientation, can appreciate Renfield's satisfaction.

Stoker was interested not only in sexuality, but in opposing schools of late 19th-century thought, specifically, cool intellectualism grounded in the scientific method, and a livelier type of reasoning spurred by ancient instinct. Van Helsing and Seward are notable characters in this regard because of their interest in modern science and medicine—subjects which, as we have seen, assumed tremendous social and religious significance during Stoker's lifetime.

Seward, a young man, is thoroughly modern. It is the stolid, older Van Helsing who is the more engaging character, for he quite consciously straddles (and sometimes struggles to reconcile) the new age with which Seward is so comfortable, and the older, less knowable world of magic and legend. In this respect, Van Helsing is very much like Dracula, and as the novel progresses, the characters' similarities become increasingly clear. The Count, undead and centuries-old, is a creature of ancient origin, but also has a keen grasp of lawyers, train and ship timetables, and how to negotiate a complicated real estate deal. Van Helsing, expert in blood transfusions and nearly as interested in the new sciences of psychiatry and criminology as Seward (he describes Dracula as being afflicted with a selfish and thus predictable "child-brain"), nevertheless comprehends the timeless evil that motivates Dracula. Although Van Helsing reminds Seward that "knowledge is stronger than memory," it is the older man's understanding of things past that makes him a profound threat to Dracula. He and the Count are natural, and inevitable, antagonists.

Regarded as part of a larger canvas, Van Helsing is Stoker's highest expression of the strength and nobility of heterosexual-male commitment. The men who oppose Dracula do not do so as individuals, but as part of a loyal, deeply bonded, archetypally "male" group. They are comrades, fellow hunters, adventurers, men linked by blood and common purpose.

Amusingly, though (and quite unconsciously on Stoker's part), the descriptions of the men's expressions of friendship bring us back to the issue of homoeroticism. During a supper that follows Lucy's death, the men gather to discuss what next must be done. In the dialogue and events that follow, Van Helsing and Seward hold hands as they regard the beautiful corpse; Holmwood and Van Helsing take each other's hand, note each other's "goodness," and pledge eternal fealty; Van Helsing addresses the grieving Holmwood "sweetly" and tells the younger man, "I have grown to love you"; Holmwood repays the compliment by commending Van Helsing for his "noble heart"; Seward reflects on Holmwood's "stalwart manhood"; Holmwood throws his arms around Seward's shoulders and cries. During much of this, comically, the men suck after-dinner cigars.

Later, Seward describes Quincey Morris as "a moral Viking," and is shocked when the exhausted Van Helsing gives way to "a regular fit of hysterics," alternately laughing and crying "just as a woman does." But Van Helsing quickly gathers himself (that is, he represses his feminine side) and leads the others to Lucy's tomb, where they stake (a particularly male action and implement) and behead her, in order to free her of Dracula's curse. Meaningful violence, the novel implies, is thoroughly masculine, and therefore noble. It's also invigorating, as Harker regains his vigor, and his essential maleness, only after joining the others in physical action, and after defending his wife against the darker male presence that would steal her away. (But action and camaraderie have their limitations, as is seen late in the story, when Harker again grows weak as Dracula gathers his own strength for the final battle. Harker's potency returns for good only after he arms himself with a *kukri* knife, an immense Nepalese blade that, in another instance of unintended comedy, compensates for Harker's diminished manhood.)

If Van Helsing and his male companions are effusive in their regard for each other, they are positively rhapsodic in their love of Mina, who, though under Dracula's thrall, insists on participating in the fiend's undoing. (A transparent plot contrivance, this, for Mina, because she is partially under Dracula's thrall, is conveniently able to "read" the vampire's thoughts and alert her friends to the Count's next move.)

Although inherently condescending to women (Van Helsing notes that "young ladies" do not have "good memory for facts, for details"), the group idolizes Mina, showering her with compliments for her bravery and goodness. Van Helsing sums it up, with incredible treacle, when he informs "Madam Mina" that "it will be pleasure and delight if I may serve you as a friend... There are darknesses in life and there are lights; you are one of the lights."

Later, Van Helsing tells Harker, "She [Mina] is one of God's women, fashioned by His own hand to show us men and other women that there is a heaven where we can enter, and that its light can be here on earth. So true, so sweet, so noble, so little an egoist." The remark presages a later observation made by Mina, who notes that the caregiver's role is natural to women, who "have something of the mother in us that makes us rise above smaller matters when the mother-spirit is invoked...." In effect, Mina becomes the mother to her husband, and to Van Helsing and the rest of the men, leading a family that is infinitely stronger than the rootless, disconnected Dracula.

Even worse from Dracula's point of view is that Mina's maternal leadership imbues the group with a moral superiority against which the Count has no defense. That superiority's ultimate expression is Mina's pity for Dracula, whom she describes as a "poor soul" who is "the saddest case of all... You must be pitiful to him too," she reminds the others, "though it may not hold your hands from his destruction."

Pity aside, Stoker never lets us forget that Dracula is a malignant, formidable enemy. The book's profoundly disturbing description of the undead Lucy illustrates the horror inherent in vampirism, as explained by Van Helsing: "When they become such [undead], there comes with the change the curse of immortality; they cannot die, but must go on age after age adding new victims and multiplying the evils of the world...." The vampire is the personification of all the world's cruel ills and unhappiness. Further, like the tormented shades of Dante's *Inferno,* the vampire's plight is grotesque and unbearable.

Like the *Inferno, Dracula* is as uniquely Christian work. Van Helsing and the others are destroying a godless evil; at one point, Van Helsing likens the group to Crusaders who "go out as the old knights of the Cross." Later, the group's members make mental and spiritual preparations for their own deaths, like Christian martyrs. Their arsenal includes crucifixes and sacred wafers. In a creepily atmospheric moment near the climax, two of the crusaders, Harker and Holmwood, drift along a cold, foreboding river that is clearly intended to evoke that watery boundary of Hell, the river Styx.

Unlike Dante, however, Stoker holds out hope of redemption for the damned. Even Dracula, dispatched at the novel's climax, is spared eternal agony. In this, Van Helsing and the others become, in one (literal) stroke, avenger and savior.

Harker severs Dracula's head, and the knife thrust by Morris tears into the vampire's heart. Mina recounts,

> It was like a miracle; but before our very eyes, and almost in the drawing of a breath, the whole body crumbled into dust and passed from our sight.
> I shall be glad as long as I live that even in that moment of final dissolution, there was in the face a look of peace, such as I never could have imagined might have rested there.

That Dracula's antagonists give him back his soul is the unexpected kindness that lies at the core of this violent, overwrought, and completely fascinating novel. Although the book's creation was influenced by real-life events and numerous literary antecedents, and was pushed and pulled by shifting cultural tides, its central assertion is many centuries old, and is one that even our complacently secular age is loath to deny: the soul is eternal, and may be redeemed.

That is the strength of Bram Stoker's *Dracula.*

The Bram Stoker Award

Bram Stoker created the modern horror novel with *Dracula,* and it is only fitting that the award for outstanding achievement in this field was named after him.

The Horror Writers Association (HWA) was formed over a period of several years during the 1980s with the help of many of the horror genre's greats, including Joe Lansdale, Robert McCammon, and Dean Koontz. The organization was incorporated in 1987 with Dean Koontz as its president. The HWA is now a worldwide organization of over 700 writers and publishing professionals.

Each year, the HWA presents the Bram Stoker Awards for Superior Achievement in the horror genre. The Stoker Awards were instituted immediately after the organization's 1987 incorporation. While many members, including President Koontz, had reservations about awards—since the point of HWA was for writers to cooperate for their mutual benefit, not to compete against one another—the majority heavily favored presenting awards, both to recognize outstanding work in the horror field and to publicize HWA's activities.

To ameliorate the competitive nature of awards, the Stokers are given "for superior achievement," not for "best of the year," and the rules are deliberately designed to make ties fairly common. The first awards were presented in 1988, and they have been presented every year since.

Dracula received no such accolades during Stoker's lifetime, but the author continues to live on as part of a vital literary tradition.

—Bob Madison

The Bram Stoker Award

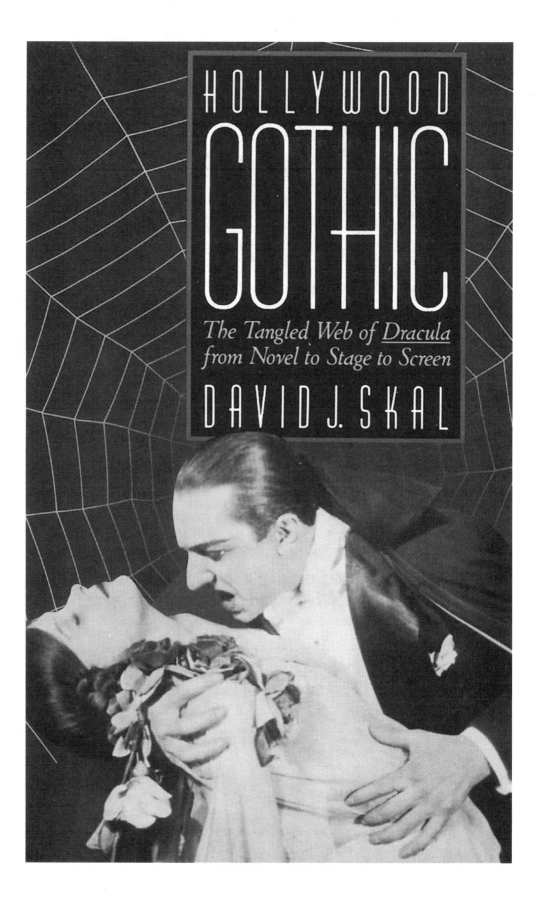

Books of Blood:
The Continued Adventures
of Dracula
by Bob Madison

"I saw the Count lying within the box upon the earth, some of which the rude falling from the cart had scattered over him. He was deathly pale, just like a waxen image, and the red eyes glared with the horrible vindictive look which I knew too well.

As I looked, the eyes saw the sinking sun, and the look of hate in them turned to triumph.

But, on the instant, came the sweep and flash of Jonathan's great knife. I shrieked as I saw it shear through the throat; whilst at the same moment Mr. Morris' bowie knife plunged into the heart.

It was like a miracle; but before our very eyes, and almost in the drawing of a breath, the whole body crumbled into dust and passed from our sight..."
—Bram Stoker, *Dracula*

Dracula did *not* die when Jonathan Harker severed the vampire's head and Quincey Morris skewered him with his great bowie knife.

But you knew that already.

Author Bram Stoker lavished so much affection and attention on his vampire creation, that it's amazing that he never wrote a sequel to *Dracula*. With such a formidable villain—and such a diverse and dedicated "family" of vampire killers—he certainly could have taken his hoary-headed demon into the 20th century.

Instead, Stoker contented himself with lesser works, such as the forgettable *Lair of the White Worm*. The cause of death on the author's death certificate read "exhaustion," but Stoker never dappled his brow creating a new Dracula story, or writing another novel to equal it.

Perhaps Stoker wisely thought any continuation of his saga would dilute the power and potency of his original. If Dracula were to return in a series of continuing adventures—novel after novel—he would become a mere stock figure of menace, a cartoon villain. Stoker maintained the integrity of his creation with a literal unwritten promise to respect his vampire in the morning: When Dracula died at the end of the novel, for Stoker at least, he stayed dead.

Happily for the legions of Dracula and vampire buffs out there (yes, I'm talking about you!), other, more enterprising authors have taken Stoker's premise and run with it. And while none of the Count's subsequent adventures will loom as large in the literary canon as Stoker's masterwork, many of them make for some terrific reading. Nor are any destined to remain a cultural force capable of controversy: in this, *Dracula*'s centennial year, the book was removed from the required reading lists for juniors and seniors in the advanced English classes at the Colony High School in Lewisville, Texas! *Dracula*'s reputation as a classic both dark and dangerous continues to grow.

Any comprehensive survey of Dracula and vampire-related books would be far outside the scope of this article. Indeed, it would take another book. Instead, I offer a smattering of some of the best Dracula books to have surfaced in recent years. Some of them, such as Robert Lory's Dracula adventure novels of the 1970s, have been long out of print. But the energetic Draculaphile can amass a respectable library of volumes about his favorite subject with a little effort and a paid-up credit card.

For convenience, I have divided Dracula's literary adventures into three categories: fiction, non-fiction, and film books.

Non-fiction:

A Clutch of Vampires by Raymond McNally (New York Graphic Society, 1974)

A complete "vampire handbook," and an essential tome for the beginning Dracula student. Penned by one of the three most profound Dracula scholars of the age (the other two being David J. Skal and McNally's frequent co-author, Radu Florescu), *A Clutch of Vampires* is an entertaining mix of fact and fiction. McNally includes extracts from Romanian periodicals, old Chinese texts, and the ramblings of Victorian vampire buff and occultist Montague Summers. An added bonus is McNally's description of a staking he personally witnessed in Transylvania in 1969!

The fiction selections include Richard Matheson's *Drink My Blood*, Robert Bloch's *The Living Dead*, and Stoker's own *Dracula's Guest*.

A Dream of Dracula by Leonard Wolf (Little, Brown & Co., 1972)

Professor Leonard Wolf was an important part of the great Dracula revival of the 1970s, and garnered considerable attention with this, his book-long meditation on Dracula and vampires.

Like most academes, Wolf strays so far from the source material that, after a while, the reader wonders just *what* it is he is talking about. One admires Wolf's energy and tenacity, but the good professor never seems to know when to stop. In his quest for Dracula, Wolf details his observations on, and visits with, motorcycle gangs, homosexual blood drinkers, a hospital ward for the terminally ill, and on and on and on. Rather than stand revealed by all of Wolf's compulsive searching, the legendary caped phantasm is only obscured further.

Wolf shines in his chapters on Stoker's novel, where he manages to deconstruct the text without descending into the sometimes interminable navel-contemplating that plagues the rest of his book.

Not to all tastes by any means, *A Dream of Dracula* is a treat for the hardiest of Dracula buffs.

The Annotated Dracula by Leonard Wolf (Clarkson Potter, 1975)

Wolf's best book on Dracula: Stoker's complete text with a line-by-line explication by Wolf. Bringing the same energy to the task that powered his *A Dream of Dracula*, Wolf provides everything the Dracula completist could want: Transylvanian recipes, railway charts, cycles of the moon, a calendar of events for the plotline of the novel; in short, any cultural, culinary, or then-contemporary reference in *Dracula* is rendered understandable in lucid, accessible prose. If you must own only one copy of Stoker's original, this is the one to get. Later reissued as *The Essential Dracula*, with much new material.

Dracula: A Biography of Vlad the Impaler by Radu Florescu and Raymond McNally (Hawthorn, 1973)

Part academic text, part popular account, *Dracula: A Biography of Vlad the Impaler* is the first complete, English-language biography of Vlad Tepes, the historical Dracula. Both authors can be credited for rescuing this little-known nobleman and sadist from obscurity with their earlier bestseller, *In Search of Dracula*. Here, they delve deeper into the man's personal history and category of misdeeds. By turns compelling history and nauseating inventory of atrocities and acts of violence, the book is both an invaluable look at medieval middle Europe and a graphic story of a state-sanctioned serial killer and petty dictator.

The Dracula Book by Donald Glut (Scarecrow Press, 1975)

Glut has managed to find every Dracula film, comic book, newspaper cartoon, toy, theatrical performance and artifact; in fact, everywhere Dracula has been, Glut has not been far behind. To determine just how far Dracula has penetrated into popular culture and mass media, one has only to page through this handsome little book. Glut makes no attempt to make sense of all the material, but lists it all compulsively and lovingly. Profusely illustrated with many rare photographs, *The Dracula Book* is a veritable encyclopedia on the subject. Now more than 20 years old, one hopes that the author would consider a revised, updated version.

The Dracula Scrapbook edited by Peter Haining (Bramhall House, 1976)

The late Peter Haining was one of Gothic fiction's greatest apologists. An indefatigable anthologist and editor, Haining also found time to compile this interesting antipasto of Draculana. Profusely illustrated, this is a fine coffee table book for the beginning vampire buff.

Dracula: The Ultimate, Illustrated Edition of the World-Famous Vampire Play, edited and annotated by David J. Skal (St. Martin's Press, 1993)

Finally, Hamilton Deane's original text published alongside John L. Balderston's later Broadway version. These two men together created the caped, evening-clothed demon of popular imagination. With annotations and notes by peerless Dracula scholar David J. Skal, this book is a handsome companion piece to his indispensable *Hollywood Gothic*.

Dracula Was a Woman: In Search of The Blood Countess of Transylvania by Raymond T. McNally (McGraw Hill, 1983)

McNally presents the true history of Elizabeth Bathory, the Transylvania vampire Countess. Though not as compelling or well-written as his earlier books, a diverting way to spend an evening.

Hollywood Gothic: The Tangled Web of Dracula from Novel to Stage to Screen by David J. Skal (W. W. Norton & Company, 1990)

If I had to recommend only one book of Dracula history and criticism, it would be this, film historian David J. Skal's terrific chronicle of the creation of Stoker's novel and its eventual migration to Hollywood, where the character became forever identified with actor Bela Lugosi. Dracula historians have been drawing on Skal's research for several years now, but no book has come close to duplicating his achievement. A must have.

In Search of Dracula by Raymond McNally and Radu Florescu (New York Graphic Society, 1972)

Arguably responsible for the entire Dracula revival of the 1970s, *In Search of Dracula* returned Stoker's creation to the popular consciousness and saved the historical Dracula from obscurity. A model for all scholars, McNally and Florescu mold their considerable erudition into an endlessly readable and enjoyable narrative. This cornerstone book chronicles the historical Dracula and Stoker's life and times, as well as the creation of his novel; it then traces their various influences on popular culture and myth. Crammed with never-seen-before illustrations and witty commentary, this book is a must for every Dracula hobbyist.

Without McNally and Florescu, Dracula may have sunk into an undeserved oblivion. Recently republished with a new cover by Edward Gorey.

A Night in Transylvania: The Dracula Scrapbook by Kurt Brokaw (Grosset & Dunlap, 1976)

One of the more amusing volumes to emerge during the Dracula-obsessed 1970s. Author Brokaw provides the reader with a tour of modern-day Transylvania, as well as a concise history of the historical and literary Draculas. Written with a wry sense of humor and beautifully designed, *A Night in Transylvania* seems forgotten except by die-hard Dracula buffs. That's a shame, for this is a terrific, crackerjack little book. Highly recommended, Brokaw's book is a delight.

V Is for Vampire: The A-Z Guide to Everything Undead by David J. Skal (Plume, 1996)

A funny, informative encyclopedia covering the vampire in fact, fiction, and film. Like spending an evening with one of the wittiest, most interesting Dracula experts.

Vampire: The Complete Guide to the World of the Undead by Manuela Dunn Mascetti (Viking Studio Books, 1992)

An entertaining, fast-moving guide to the vampire underworld. The stunning visuals include original paintings and breath-taking photographs which successfully draw attention away from the deficiencies of the text.

The Vampire Encyclopedia by Matthew Bunson (Crown Trade Paperbacks, 1993)

Just what the title says, a vampire encyclopedia, with tons of information provided by an enthused author. Though Bunson sometimes strays far afield from Dracula—and sometimes even from vampires—he is never less than informative and entertaining. A useful reference.

Vampires: Lord Byron to Count Dracula edited by Christopher Frayling (Faber & Faber, 1993)

A solid, informative look into the vampire tradition in English letters. Frayling is one of England's finest scholars of the Gothic tradition and merits wider fame in the United States. Highly recommended.

Fiction:

Anno Dracula by Kim Newman (Carrol & Graf, 1992)

Wild and woolly tale set in an alternate Victorian universe where Dracula has married Queen Victoria. The plot concerns Jack the Ripper, the rising "vampire class," and various Victorian luminaries. (The sequel, *The Bloody Red Baron*, set a score of years later, concerns the Red Baron and vampire battalions in World War I!) With cameos or mentions of all the great vampires of history, half the fun of *Anno Dracula* for vampire buffs is spotting the references and in-jokes.

Bram Stoker's Bedside Companion by Bram Stoker (Taplinger, 1974)

Stoker's deleted chapter from *Dracula*, *Dracula's Guest*, is included in this anthology of 10 stories. Though not in the same league as Poe or M. R. James, Stoker can still, after all these years, cause a sleepless night or two.

Dracula by Bram Stoker (available in dozens of editions)

If you have gotten this far, we will assume that you have already read Stoker's masterpiece. The first modern horror novel and the last great Gothic, the reverberations of Stoker's book of blood are felt to this day. One hundred years old, and still going strong. (See David J. Hogan's *Bram Stoker's Dracula: The Coffin Opens* in this volume.) Norton has just published its critical edition, featuring invaluable notes by editors David J. Skal and Nina Auerbach.

The Dracula Archives by Raymond Rudoff (Pocket Books, 1973)

Fast-moving paperback original that brings together the stories of Dracula and Elizabeth Bathory. Unlike most pastiche, Rudoff manages to get a real Victorian flavor, and tells his tale with vigor and brio. If you can find a flea market copy, don't hesitate to pick up this little winner.

Dracula: Prince of Darkness edited by Martin H. Greenberg (DAW Books, 1992)

Paperback anthology of Dracula short stories of variable quality: works by Rex Miller and P. N. Elrod are the standouts.

Dracula Returns! by Robert Lory (Pinnacle Books, 1973)

Dracula is reactivated to become a crime-fighter in this, the first of a series of pulp paperbacks. The back-cover blurb called the series "unwholesomely horrible... tales of legendary wickedness and modern-day suspense." Ahem. Dr. Damien Harmon, wheelchair-bound criminologist and scientist, controls Dracula with an electronic implant that could pierce the vampire's heart with a tiny sliver of wood. (Sort of a pacemaker in reverse, come to think of it.) In this manner, Dracula becomes a hero against his own will. If this is your cup of tea, go for it. Other books in the series include *The Hand of Dracula, Dracula's Brothers, Dracula's Gold, Drums of Dracula, The Witching of Dracula,* and *Dracula's Lost World.*

The Dracula Tape by Fred Saberhagen (Warner Paperback Library, 1975)

The first of Saberhagen's Dracula series, and a doozy. More "fang-in-cheek" than the later novels, *The Dracula Tape* was at the forefront of the Dracula revisionism of the 1970s, when the character was changed from Stoker's hoary-headed Tartar with bad breath, to a more romantic, Byronic anti-hero. That such a take was miles away from Stoker's original intention is unimportant; like Deane and Balderston before him, Saberhagen managed to successfully remold the vampire in a way to make him palatable to modern audiences. Ensuing volumes in the series include *The Holmes-Dracula File*, *Thorn*, *An Old Friend of the Family*, *A Matter of Taste*, and *A Question of Time*.

With the release of Francis Ford Coppola's *Bram Stoker's Dracula*, Saberhagen wrote the official movie tie-in paperback, based on the screenplay by James V. Hart. Saberhagen's Dracula books have many devoted followers, and the series may continue the Vampire King's adventures well into the next century.

The Ultimate Dracula edited by Byron Preiss (Dell Books, 1993)

Anthology of well-chosen vampire stories, only some of which deal with Dracula. Philip Jose Farmer and Dan Simmons provide the best works.

Film Books:

Bram Stoker's Dracula: The Film and the Legend by James V. Hart (Newmarket Press, 1992)

James V. Hart's screenplay lushly illustrated with color photographs from the movie. Also includes notes on the production and an afterword by Leonard Wolf. A quick look at the photographs from the smaller details of the production design amply illustrates that Coppola's realization of Hart's screenplay is one of the most complete, ornate, and pictorially beautiful renderings of Stoker's tale.

Dracula: The Original Shooting Script, edited by Philip J. Riley (MagicImage Filmbooks, 1990)

The original shooting script for the Tod Browning–Bela Lugosi classic, complete with a production history by Riley and George Turner. Lavishly illustrated, this book contains the original pressbook and other little-

Chelsea Quinn Yarbro On Her Brides of Dracula Trilogy

Had Stoker said more about the three women in Dracula's castle, I would probably never have tackled a trilogy about them. Stoker's vision is so all-encompassing, I would not have had any room to work with had he given us more information about them.

As it is, knowing from Stoker only that the blonde is the oldest—or the longest vampiric—of them, and that they appear young and attractive, provides me with just enough material to give me a starting point for these three very different women. Had Stoker given them names or ages, my work would have been more difficult, but since he left those two vital elements out of his classic narrative, I had free rein with Kelene, Fenice, and Zhameni, extrapolating as much as possible from the little bit we know about them in *Dracula*.

Now they will have what they never had in Stoker: fully realized characters, each worthy of her own story. It's my contribution to Stoker's venerable literary reputation.

—Chelsea Quinn Yarbro

seen material. The only flaw in this otherwise handy book is the reproduction of the Louis Bromfield treatment for his version of *Dracula*—the type is so small as to be nearly invisible. The book's other treats help to make up for this oversight.

A Heritage of Horror by David Pirie (Avon, 1974)

Pirie argues that the English horror film is the only body of film work Britain can claim as its own. Written for the serious film scholar, Pirie clearly has an agenda in his long defense of the Hammer Films productions. A fine examination of that studio's small contribution to Gothic cinema.

An Illustrated History of the Horror Film by Carlos Clarens (Putnam, 1967)

The first champion history of the horror film, one that still holds up handsomely 30 years later. Clarens may be the first real scholar of the fantastic film—predating the yeoman work of such authors as Gregory William Mank, Tom Weaver, and David J. Skal—who saved it from the cheesy, cloying type of material found in such juvenilia as *Famous Monsters of Filmland*.

The Monster Show by David J. Skal (W. W. Norton & Company, 1993)

The first book to put the horror film in a cultural perspective, *The Monster Show* is a terrific amalgam of trenchant cultural observation, dazzling scholarship, and deft prose. Easily the best book on the horror film genre ever written, and destined to become a classic. Skal continues to be one of the wittiest, most intelligent commentators on the horrific resonances of popular culture.

The Vampire Film by Alain Silver and James Ursini (Limelight Editions, 1993)

A sober analysis of the vampire film, from *Nosferatu* to the present. For serious vampire-film buffs only.

The Changing Face of Dracula: A Portrait Gallery

by Bob Madison

Author Bram Stoker played with various ideas for *Dracula* that never made it to the finished novel.

The author's notes, now at the Rosenbach Museum and Library in Philadelphia, contain a wealth of characters that Stoker had considered bringing to life, only to discard them in favor of his final band of vampire killers.

One such character was Cotford, a detective hot on the Vampire King's trail. (*Dracula* was written during the height of the Sherlock Holmes craze.) It also involved a "psychic research agent" named Alfred Singleton, an "American inventor from Texas," and various mute and mysterious servants to the Count.

One of the most intriguing elements that never made it into *Dracula* was a subplot about the artist, Francis Aytown, and his efforts to paint Count Dracula's portrait. According to Stoker's notes, Aytown tries throughout the novel to paint the vampire's portrait, meeting failure as every picture turns out looking like somebody else.

And so it is with Dracula's movie career.

Just as every generation has its Hamlet, it also finds its own Dracula. Inspired by the greatest Shakespearean actor of his day, Sir Henry Irving, to whom Stoker acted as manager and factotum, Dracula is the kind of part that leaves an indelible stamp on an actor's career. Too long the province of that talented group of thespians that became solely identified by their roles in horror films, Dracula has finally reached pantheon status. Some of the finest players of this century—including Orson Welles, Daniel Day Lewis, and Frank Langella—have tackled the role, each bringing to it his own individual talents. It has attracted—and created—some of Hollywood's leading cinema personalities, such as John Carradine and Bela Lugosi; and a surprising number of established actors of various types have taken their turn under the cape, including Francis Lederer, Martin Landau, and Terence Stamp. Television star Judd Hirsch made a memorable Dracula for children and teeny-bopper idol Christopher Atkins was one of cinema's few *blond* Draculas. Others, like Zandor Vorkov, tried the role once, only to slink back to a well-deserved obscurity.

Like Aytown's pictures, all of these Draculas are portraits that resemble someone else. Each actor was able, for the most part, to deliver different and distinct interpretations, but all were recognizably Count Dracula.

That movie-goers might show some confusion as to the *real* Count Dracula is understandable. The Dracula of popular myth is less an invention of author Bram Stoker than of actor-playwright Hamilton Deane and Deane's later collaborator, John L. Balderston. (Proving that, from the very beginning, Dracula was the dark patron saint of needy actors.)

Stoker's Dracula is not the elegant figure that haunts the popular imagination. More old goat than lounge lizard, Stoker's Dracula is a hairy-palmed, hoary-headed old Tartar, whose rank breath and pointy ears hardly brand him a lady-killer. The Dracula that Stoker introduces to his protagonist, Jonathan Harker, is described as:

> ...a tall old man, clean shaven save for a long white mustache, and clad in black from head to foot, without a single speck of colour about him anywhere. He held in his hand an antique silver lamp, in which the flame burned without chimney or globe of any kind, throwing long shadows as it flickered in the draught of the open door. The old man motioned me in with his right hand with a courtly gesture...

Dracula's handshake is strong enough to make Harker "wince," and his fingers ended in nails "long and fine, and cut to a sharp point." Once inside Castle Dracula, drawing near the fire after a meal prepared for him by the Count, Harker better observes his host's "very marked physiognomy."

> His face was a strong—a very strong—aquiline, with high bridge of the thin nose and peculiarly arched nostrils; with lofty domed forehead, and hair growing scantily round the temples, but profusely elsewhere. His eyebrows were massive, almost meeting over the nose, and with brushy hair that seemed to curl in its own profusion. The mouth, so far as I could see under the heavy mustache, was fixed and rather cruel looking, with peculiarly sharp white teeth; these protruded over the lips, whose remarkable ruddiness showed astonishing vitality in a man of his years. For the rest, his ears were pale and at the tops extremely pointed; the chin was broad and strong, and the cheeks firm though thin. The general effect was one of extraordinary pallor.

Stoker's Dracula is revolting. When Dracula lies supine in his coffin after feeding, Harker likens him to a loathsome, bloated leech. While Dracula grows younger, he never grows attractive. Once in London, the Count shows a marked affinity for the wolves kept in the London Zoo, which is only natural: the Dracula of the novel is more animal than man.

The hallmarks that we come to expect with Dracula—the full-dress evening clothes, the red-lined cape, the signet ring, the Continental accent—these were all the inventions of Stoker's successors. The aristocratic manner and debonair demeanor of many of his impersonators rings false when compared to Stoker's original: it is less likely for the novel's Dracula to entertain guests in Dr. Seward's drawing room than for him to be outside on the lawn, baying at the moon.

The changes in Dracula were necessary if he was to become a viable theatrical property. And it was just such a property that actor-manager Hamilton Deane happened to be looking for. If it wasn't for Deane, it is unlikely that Stoker's *Dracula* would have remained deeply entrenched in the public consciousness, or that his centennial would be celebrated today.

If Stoker was Dracula's creator, then three other men must hold honored positions as the vampire's godfathers. First among these three godfathers was actor-manager-playwright Hamilton Deane (who died in 1958), who was also responsible for bringing together the other two.

Deane was one of Dracula's earliest fans, admiring the novel since its publication. His mother was a Dublin friend of Stoker's, and the Irish actor secured the rights to the book from the author's widow, Florence Stoker, in 1924.

Mrs. Stoker, desperate for money at this stage, authorized the adaptation while still smarting over the first movie version of her husband's masterpiece, F. W. Murnau's *Nosferatu*. (Ironically, it is only *Nosferatu*, of all of the many adaptations of *Dracula*, that is considered something of a genuine cinematic classic.) Bridling at her lack of recompense for this, to her mind, Germanic travesty, and horrified by the vampire's rat-like countenance as well, Mrs. Stoker embraced Deane's efforts to legitimize her husband's rancid revenant.

It is Deane's play that is really responsible for the Dracula of popular myth. All of the accouterments we expect from Dracula are found within it: the Count's hypnotic powers, the cape and evening clothes, the courtly manner, and Dracula's emergence as a romantic figure. In doing so, Deane was simply showing good sense: mystery plays were enjoying a tremendous vogue at the time, and by making Dracula a villain accessible to drawing rooms, he was copying commercially acceptable conventions.

Deane originally wanted to play the Transylvanian Count himself, but took on the role of Van Helsing instead once the play was finished and he realized that Dracula's scenes were limited. He and his troupe of players toured with *Dracula* successfully in the provinces for three years before taking the show to London, where it became a hit. Critics crucified the vampire play as outlandish and silly, but *Dracula* became an unqualified hit on London's West End, too late for Irving to sneer and Stoker to gloat.

Deane also starred in a touring company of Peggy Webling's dramatization of *Frankenstein*. Sometimes he cut both plays for time and played them on a double-bill, continuing the long and natural connection between these two great Gothic villains. Deane eventually played Dracula in a 1939 revival of the play. This production was directed by Bernard Jukes, who essayed Renfield in both the British and American stage versions, playing the role more than 4,000 times. Deane played Dracula until 1941, when he turned his back on the vehicle forever. He dissolved his company of players sometime later, but continued to remain active. He can be seen as one of the courtiers in Laurence Olivier's *Hamlet* (1948).

It was in 1927 that Jazz Age producer-publisher-entrepreneur Horace Liveright purchased Deane's play for the American stage. And it was Liveright who introduced the undying vampire to his second most important godfather: John L. Balderston.

Balderston (who died in 1954) was a journalist, playwright, and screenwriter. As a reporter, he covered the discovery of King Tut's tomb, an experience that he would later put to good use when writing *The Mummy* (1932) for Boris Karloff at Universal Pictures.

Liveright had Balderston completely re-write Deane's play, making it smarter and slicker for Broadway's more sophisticated audiences. Balderston excised Quincey Morris from Deane's play (no great loss to the novel's fidelity as Deane usually had a woman play the role!), and sharpened the conflict between Van Helsing and the Count. Sifting the crude dramatics of Deane for the gold buried in the vampire's coffin, Balderston was able to refine the version of Dracula that would migrate to California and Universal studios, becoming the world's most recognizable monster.

Thanks to *Dracula*, Balderston found himself a lucrative line as scribe for the classic monsters. He rewrote Peggy Webling's *Frankenstein* for Broadway and, when funding for the project fell through, sold the property to Universal. The studio used none of his material, but on the strength of *Dracula* and *The Mummy*, Balderston was hired for an (unused) draft of *Bride of Frankenstein* (1935).

He also penned a truly outlandish treatment of *Dracula's Daughter*, including whips, blood slaves, and enthralled, helpless men. This fevered vision (difficult to imagine today and impossible to realize in 1936) is one of the significant unproduced projects of Hollywood's golden age of horror films.

In the 1950s, Balderston sued Universal, claiming that the conception they popularized of Frankenstein's Monster was his creation, and that he was unfairly exploited. Universal coughed up some $100,000 to Balderston and the Peggy Webling estate for all rights to the character.

Dracula's migration to America also gave the character his final, and most legendary, godfather.

Actor Bela Lugosi *is* Dracula in the popular imagination. Never before—or since—has an actor become so defined by a solitary part. The identification was so great that for the rest of his life, the actor was billed as Bela "Dracula" Lugosi. No other actor's face, voice, inflections, or body language holds greater supremacy over the part than those of the Hungarian expatriate. Nor has any other actor so obsessively identified with the role; Lugosi was buried in his Dracula costume after playing the Count in two films and for decades on the stage.

When *Dracula* premiered in Broadway's Fulton Theater, neither the critics nor the audience realized that they were witnessing the creation of one of modern theater history's great signature roles. Though Lugosi was generally praised for his work, the thought of a supernatural protagonist on the Broadway stage was a concept that took a while to settle in. The passion that Lugosi brought to the part—he so mesmerized actress Clara Bow at a performance of *Dracula* that it was the start of a stormy romance between the "It" girl and the undead Valentino—along with his intensity, strange intonation, and charisma, made Dracula acceptable to critics and audiences alike.

Many actors to later essay the role found themselves hobbled by the long shadow of Lugosi. When Martin Landau played Dracula in a revival of the Edward Gorey production of the Deane-Balderston play, he found that audiences would accept nothing but the Lugosi conception. (And this, 10 years *before* Landau won the Academy Award for playing Lugosi in Tim Burton's *Ed Wood*.) Gary Oldman, a terrific actor who made his mark in challenging roles, frankly admitted that the voice he used in *Bram Stoker's Dracula* was "pure Lugosi."

Dracula distilled for children—everything from *Sesame Street*'s Count to General Mills' breakfast cereal Count Chocula—is simply Lugosi and water. When George

Hamilton played Dracula in *Love at First Bite*, he portrayed him as a lovelorn Bela Lugosi, caught in a world that had forgotten romance. Leslie Nielsen, the latest actor to bring Dracula to life in *Dracula: Dead and Loving It*, also closely studied Lugosi's delivery and mannerisms.

As Dracula, Bela Lugosi has appeared on toys, games, model kits, and magazine covers. Any television or radio commercial employing Dracula also employs Lugosi, for it is the actor and not the part that other players use. Posters, greeting cards, record albums, Halloween costumes, iron-on patches, candy boxes, and bubble gum cards have all borne Lugosi's likeness.

Bela Lugosi's face adorned the cover of Bram Stoker's novel as early as 1947, when the Pocket Books edition featured a painting of Lugosi hovering over a sleeping victim. His association with the novel continues to this day, and Lugosi's visage continues to appear on the covers of many editions of *Dracula*, including the inexpensive Barnes and Noble reprint sold nationally.

No actor to play the part after Bela Lugosi has achieved the same long-lasting impression or has penetrated as far into popular myth. Lugosi's Dracula is *the* yardstick by which all other interpretations are measured, a standard which has not diminished despite the many fine performances that followed in Lugosi's wake. (In this volume, authors Greg Mank and Gary J. Svehla measure later Draculas John Carradine and Christopher Lee against him.)

In the gallery of pop icons, Lugosi's hold over his role is unshakable. Mention Sherlock Holmes to the casual fan, and images as diverse as Basil Rathbone, Peter Cushing, or Jeremy Brett may come to mind. Tarzan is little more than a generic muscleman, and Johnny Weissmuller, Buster Crabbe, and Gordon Scott all blur in the memory. It is the costumes of both Batman and Superman that resonate with audiences, and not particular performances. But show a photograph of Bela Lugosi to anybody on the street and the identification comes immediately: *that's* Dracula.

Any celebration of Dracula is also, by necessity, also a celebration of Lugosi. The part consumed Lugosi more completely than the novel did Stoker, leaving the actor a broken and dissipated man. (Sir Henry Irving was Stoker's master, while Lugosi only had Dracula.) While Stoker's *Dracula* is 100 years old in 1997, Lugosi's vampire reaches 70 this year as well; a long-lasting codependence that shows no sign of ending.

Though Stoker was Dracula's creator, it was Deane, Balderston, and Lugosi who raised the vampire, who straightened his tie, smoothed his cape, buffed his patent leather pumps, and sent him out into an unsuspecting world.

Perhaps it's for the best that Stoker excised the portraitist subplot from his novel. The story of the artist Aytown is the story of all artists who have given their lives to the undying vampire—sacrificing their talents, their faces, and their personas to a being that ultimately drains their best efforts, only to abandon them in search of fresh artistic blood.

Despite Lugosi's unending stranglehold on the role, there has never been a *definitive* interpretation of Dracula. It's impossible, for the vampire's true likeness cannot be captured, only approximated. Just as Stoker's monster meant a host of things to his Victorian audience, Dracula has continued to evolve, reflecting the fears and desires of each generation that turns to him.

As will be seen here, the qualities that actors have brought to Dracula are many and diverse. Future performers will all build on this foundation, continuing a tradition that is rich in mythology and nearly as old as cinema itself.

THE DRACULA PORTRAIT GALLERY

"What a lovely throat!"
—Max Schreck, title card from *Nosferatu: Eine Symphonie des Grauens* (1922)

Perhaps the most acclaimed movie interpretation of *Dracula* was also the earliest: in *Nosferatu*, actor Max Schreck (1879-1936) portrayed Dracula as pestilence incarnate. With his sharp talons, pointy ears, rat-like teeth, and bald pate, Schreck's Count Orlock was hardly a creature welcome in the drawing room mystery plays of the time.

Produced by Prana Films, an artistic collective which folded after this single production, *Nosferatu* was the focus of widow Florence Stoker's wrath for nearly a decade. Though freely adapting the novel *Dracula* (names are changed and the narrative is streamlined), the film is unmistakably a retelling of Stoker's book. Designed as an "art film," *Nosferatu* was Murnau's response to the horrors of post–World War I Germany. It was an enormous success upon its release, and sustained a Continental vogue.

This enraged Mrs. Stoker, who received no royalties from the film. Not only was she outraged by the frankly horrific nature of the film (so much so that contemporary historians wonder if she ever actually *read* her husband's novel), but money was tight for the widow at this time, and *Dracula* was virtually her husband's sole legacy to her.

Her legal pursuit of Prana led to naught: the company dissolved before she could receive any money from it. She had to content herself with the promise that the negative and all existing prints of the film would be destroyed.

Fortunately for cinema buffs, this Dracula escaped to America. In its original state, the film featured color-tinted scenes and a modernist musical score, composed by Hans Erdmann. It has recently been restored, both in Europe and the United States, and can now be seen in something approximating its original glory.

Nosferatu is responsible for one of the great misconceptions of Dracula lore: that the Vampire King can be destroyed by sunlight. In Stoker's novel, Dracula's powers are minimal during the day, but sunlight will not destroy him. It was only after *Nosferatu*, when the rat-faced vampire vanished in a puff of smoke at the film's finale, that the lethal effects of sunlight were grafted onto the legend.

Schreck—whose name, coincidentally, means "terror" in German—is simply marvelous as the repugnant Orlock. Like Dorian Gray's attic portrait, Orlock seems to grow uglier as his sins escalate. His talons grow longer, the rat-like configuration of his face grows more pronounced, and his movements become yet more stylized. Though he does not physically resemble Stoker's description, Schreck probably comes closer to the author's idea conceptually than any other actor to play the role.

The film makes considerable use of location shooting—Dracula's castle is indeed a *real* castle—and the brooding Germanic countryside is more effective than any other Transylvania committed to celluloid. Here is Dracula captured on film in his homeland, only 25 years after his literary debut.

Schreck left the promise of a secure place in the business world to become an actor. He worked with Max Reinhardt before entering films, and continued to act until the

Frame blow-up of actor Max Schreck. Note his bat-like talons.

year of his death. Schreck's crowning achievement, *Nosferatu*, is now considered one
of the masterpieces of German silent cinema. The make-up used continues to linger in
the consciousness of movie-goers, and has been adapted for everything from Tobe
Hooper's *Salem's Lot* (1979), to the space vampire episode of *Superboy*. The film's
high regard has only come in recent years, long after Murnau or Schreck were alive to
enjoy its rediscovery. Like Bram Stoker before him and Bela Lugosi after him, Schreck
enjoyed his greatest success with the Count only once he was dead.

> "So after centuries of waiting, I have at last found my way back to England."
> —Raymond Huntley, from Hamilton Deane's *Dracula, The Vampire Play*

The actor with the greatest number of performances of Dracula to his credit is neither
Bela Lugosi nor Christopher Lee, but British character actor Raymond Huntley (1903-
1990).

Huntley first played the role when he was only 22 years old, and later suspected that he won the part because he owned a full kit of evening clothes. He played Dracula nearly nonstop for four years in England and America. While the play and his performance scored a great hit with the public, a patronizing press often ridiculed his work. One writer went so far as to disparage Huntley's "ill fitting mask," when, in reality, the actor wore no mask at all! It was his refusal to take the role in the Broadway debut of the rewritten Balderston version of Deane's play that cleared the way for Bela Lugosi. He later came to America in 1928, and performed in a touring company of the play.

Huntley later came to consider Dracula an indiscretion of his youth. The young actor played the part with whitened hair sweeping backward, suggesting devilish horns. There is a look of distaste on his face in the surviving photos of his performance, taken at a time when Huntley greatly resembled a young John Gielgud.

Huntley continued to work until his death, and television viewers know him best from his role in *Upstairs, Downstairs*. He also appeared in the Hammer Films version of *The Mummy* (1959), where he was murdered by later film-Dracula, Christopher Lee.

"I am Dracula."
—Bela Lugosi, *Dracula* (1931)

After years of political activism in his native Hungary, actor Bela Lugosi (1882-1956) fled to the United States to continue his career as an actor. (Always grateful for the freedom of his adopted homeland, Lugosi remained a Roosevelt-inspired liberal Democrat for the rest of his life.) He jumped ship in New Orleans, later making his way to New York and its Hungarian theater community.

There, Lugosi won several parts in well-reviewed shows, starting with *The Red Poppy*, which opened at the Greenwich Village Theater in December 1922. His impassioned performance as the Spanish Fernando—a role that the Hungarian-speaking actor had to learn phonetically—took New York by storm. According to legend, Lugosi's onstage lovemaking was so passionate he broke one of co-star Estelle Winwood's ribs. Winwood, in later interviews, both verified and denied the tale.

Whatever the truth, it was certain that Lugosi's studied intensity marked him for stardom. The actor worked in several shows, including *The Werewolf* and *Arabesque*, before landing the title role in the Deane–Balderston *Dracula*.

And the rest is history. *Dracula* both secured and destroyed the actor's future career. Lugosi went to Hollywood to repeat his stage triumph in the Universal Pictures version, directed by Tod Browning. (One of Hollywood's most notorious directors—he would later stretch the boundaries of taste with his masterwork, *Freaks*—Browning fumbled the ball badly with *Dracula*. Historians are uncertain why the final film is so lackluster, but the general belief is that without Lon Chaney, the star with whom the director made some of his finest silent films, *Dracula* meant little to Browning.)

While Lugosi worked in the American film version of *Dracula* during the day, actor Carlos Villarias starred in the Spanish-language version shot on the same sets at night. Director George Melford managed to create a much more fluid, erotic, and exciting film than Browning, missing only Lugosi's charisma. While Villarias is an adequate stand-in, he is never more than a pallid imitation of Lugosi. (Melford even included out-take footage of Lugosi in his film.)

Bela Lugosi created the popular conception of the Count in Tod Browning's *Dracula* (1931).

While Lugosi's hypnotic hand gestures often make him look like a human spider, Villarias' efforts to copy him only make the Spanish actor look like a malefic chipmunk. Though many critics find this alternate version technically better than Browning's, it is the Lugosi version that was the more influential film.

With *Dracula*, Browning and Lugosi created the contemporary horror film. Like an earlier tradition of Gothic literature, most "monsters" in Hollywood films of the era were explained away as involved contrivances on the part of the villain. It was only with *Dracula* that a supernatural anti-hero was allowed to take center stage, starting a tradition of monstrous movies that continues to this day. *Dracula* is the first modern horror film, and Lugosi, the genre's first star.

Receiving only a pittance for his work in the film, Lugosi waited for better offers to come in. They never did. Lugosi learned, as many later actors did, that Dracula is a tough act to follow. He made a tragic miscalculation in turning down the part of the Monster in *Frankenstein*, allowing future rival Boris Karloff to step into the role and eclipse Lugosi's star entirely. Together, Lugosi and Karloff starred in some of the horror genre's best-remembered films, including *The Black Cat* (1934), *The Raven* (1935), and *The Invisible Ray* (1936).

After the early 1930s, Lugosi could only secure supporting parts at the major studios. But he continued to be treated as a star by independent operations like Monogram Studios and PRC, where he made such forgettable potboilers as *The Devil Bat* (1940), *Invisible Ghost* (1941), and *The Ape Man* (1943).

Lugosi continued to play Dracula in stock and vaudeville shows throughout the 1940s and early 1950s. He repeated the role on film only once, in 1948's affectionate romp, *Abbott and Costello Meet Frankenstein*.

In the early 1950s, Lugosi committed himself for treatment for medically induced drug addiction. Lurid photos from the era show the actor an emaciated shell of his former self—the Vampire King now a victim. Amazingly, he survived the rigors of his cure, left the hospital, and married for a fifth and final time. (See Gregory William Mank's *Dracula's Last Bride* in this volume.)

Unfortunately, the desperate-for-work Lugosi was also befriended during this period by young Edward D. Wood, Jr., who would later win infamy as movieland's worst director. Lugosi appeared in several forgettable features for Wood, including *Glen or Glenda* (1953) and *Bride of the Monster* (1955), and he later shot footage that was slipped into *Plan 9 from Outer Space* (1959), Wood's tribute to his own incompetence.

Always eager for a comeback, Lugosi returned with a vengeance after death. With the advent of the Monster Craze in the late 1950s, Lugosi's image once more became valuable currency. His legend has continued to grow with time, perhaps reaching its apex when Martin Landau won an Academy Award for his portrayal of the elderly Lugosi in Tim Burton's *Ed Wood* (1994).

Other actors will play Dracula (both John Carradine and Lon Chaney, Jr. did during Lugosi's lifetime), but they will have large boots to fill. The Hungarian actor jealously holds the part from beyond the grave, staking a claim on the vampire that no other actor has managed to jump.

"You will be flesh of my flesh ..."
—Orson Welles, the Mercury Theater's radio adaptation of *Dracula* (1938)

Remembered as one of America's greatest directors, the enormous genius of Orson Welles (1915-1985) would also take a stab at Stoker's literary classic.

On radio's *Mercury Theater on the Air*, young Welles played both Dracula and Dr. Seward in an hour-long adaptation of the novel, just the kind of doubling act the radio made possible. Welles played Dracula through a filter, giving his line readings an unearthly quality. Agnes Moorehead, a staple of Welles' repertory company, played Mina, and actor Martin Gabel voiced Dr. Van Helsing.

This adaptation, widely available on tape, draws its inspiration from Stoker's novel and not the Deane-Balderston play. And despite the popularity of Lugosi's conception, Welles brings the part his own brand of chilly malice.

Always larger-than-life, Welles told Bram Stoker's great nephew and biographer Daniel Farson that Stoker said to him he originally wrote *Dracula* as a play, intending it as a vehicle for Irving. When Irving declined the honor, Stoker had his revenge by turning the play into a novel and villainizing the actor. This story sounds terrific, but one wonders how Stoker told Welles anything when the author died three years before Welles was born!

Interestingly, Welles would later play The Shadow on the air, a mysterious superhero that author Walter B. Gibson based, in part, on Lugosi's stage Dracula.

"Announce me!"
—Lon Chaney, Jr., *Son of Dracula* (1943)

Lon Chaney plies his pudgy charms in 1943's *Son of Dracula*. **His father's death allowed Bela Lugosi to step into the role for the 1931 version.**

Tod Browning had originally envisioned his *Dracula* as a big-budget mega-production for his favorite star, Lon Chaney. Together, Chaney and Browning made some of the most obsessively grotesque melodramas of the 1920s, including, *The Unholy Three* (1925), *The Road to Mandalay* (1926), and *The Unknown* (1927).

What Chaney would have done with Dracula remains a mystery. Surely this master of pantomime and make-up—known by the Hollywood press machine as "The Man of a Thousand Faces"—would have returned to Stoker for inspiration, creating a hairy, razor-toothed fiend.

Unfortunately, his son, born Creighton Chaney (1906-1973) but later known as "Lon Chaney, Jr.," got the chance instead of him.

This burly, potato-faced actor was often effectively cast: Chaney, Jr. made a credible Lennie in *Of Mice and Men* (1939) and appeared in supporting roles in some fine motion pictures, including the Western classic *High Noon* (1952). But Universal Pictures insisted (inexplicably) on replicating Chaney, Sr.'s career, a feat that his earnest but often inept son could not equal.

A crippling malaise smothers all of Chaney, Jr.'s horror film performances, where he often laments (with tedious frequency) the hard luck life of movie monsters. Most horror film buffs remember him for his turn as the Wolf Man, but Chaney, Jr. also essayed the roles of the Mummy, Frankenstein's Monster, and, in 1943, Count Dracula.

As Dracula, Chaney sported a suave mustache and widow's peak, but these touches do nothing to suggest aristocracy or sophistication to the fumbling, tragically alcoholic actor. He lumbers around in evening clothes like an under-experienced headwaiter, and he looks like he lives on five-pound bacon cheeseburgers instead of human blood.

Chaney's lack of presence and awkward performance sinks *Son of Dracula*. This is too bad because the film, directed by Robert Siodmak, has many nice touches. (For more on *Son of Dracula*, see Frank Dello Stritto's *The Vampire Strikes Back*, in this volume.) With Bela Lugosi in the role, *Son of Dracula* could have achieved classic status; with Chaney, Jr., it's just another of Universal's lesser 1940s programmers.

Chaney would continue to work until the end of his life. His last film appearance was as a mute stooge (in an eerie echo of Bela Lugosi's career) in 1971's awful *Dracula vs. Frankenstein*, with Zandor Vorkov as Dracula. A troubled man (Chaney tried to commit suicide in 1948), much research points to childhood abuse at the hands of Chaney, Sr. and later sexual despondency. Much of the pathos in Chaney, Jr.'s persona may have been endemic to the man himself—making him a truly tragic figure.

> "If I'm alive, what am I doing here? One the other hand,
> if I'm dead, why do I have to wee-wee?"
> —John Carradine, his curtain call speech during the
> Detroit run of the Deane-Balderston *Dracula*, and *Nocturna* (1978)

Though the career of John Carradine continued until his death in 1988, this superb actor seems to be more a relic of an earlier, more theatrical age.

It is easier to see Carradine (born in 1906) as a barnstorming Shakespearean actor in the early American West, delivering *Richard III* loud enough to carry to the last row (of another theater!). And though this gifted and talented actor injected a welcome bit of ham to his many horror film portrayals, John Carradine also starred in many mainstream cinema classics.

In *Jesse James* (1939), an evil and self-assured Carradine shot the famous outlaw (Tyrone Power) in the back, and came back for more in *The Return of Frank James* (1940). He was magnificent as the brutal and sadistic jailer of poor Dr. Mudd in *The Prisoner of Shark Island* (1940), and in *The Grapes of Wrath* (1940), his performance as the ebullient preacher Casy galvanized the screen. He was wonderfully subtle and mysterious in *Stagecoach* (1939); he achieved near sainthood as Bartolomeo Romagna in *Winterset* (1936), and stepped into the Bible for a turn as Aaron, brother of Moses (Charlton Heston), in *The Ten Commandments* (1956).

John Carradine shows off his mobile home to Onslow Stevens in *House of Dracula* (1945).

Indeed, it is safe to say that his horror films, though noteworthy, were only a negligible part of John Carradine's career. In his genre film performances he was capable of superior work if he respected the part or the film (see 1944's *Bluebeard*). If he respected neither, as was often the case of his later horror films, the results were often hammy overplaying or a total lack of effort.

John Carradine's Dracula seems to fall somewhere between both camps. While many critics have claimed that his appearance was closer to Stoker's conception than that of any other actor, that is simply not *quite* true. Carradine does sport white hair and a mustache, but his performance is still firmly grounded in the Deane-Balderston tradition as he elegantly amuses his hosts in both of his Universal films, impeccably attired in top hat and tails. Also, Carradine's performance lacks the frankly brutal edge necessary to bring Stoker's Dracula to life, an edge that might have been present in worthier vehicles.

Actually, this fine actor underplays the Vampire King to the point where Dracula nearly fades into the background. While it is true that his participation in his first two Dracula films—*House of Frankenstein* (1944) and *House of Dracula* (1945)—amount to little more than prolonged cameos, Carradine does very little with the part indeed. His line readings are tired and colorless, and he brings to the part none of the bravado that can be seen in his more serious, mainstream work. One of the most colorful Shakespearean actors of his generation—friend and confidante John Barrymore was said to be especially impressed by his *Lear*—none of Carradine's "classical" qualities creep into his Dracula performances. While it is easy to admire Carradine's impressive body of work, his vampire is not quite as good as his other performances.

Carradine repeated the role in the 1950s in a notorious Detroit production of the Deane-Balderston play. He starred in a straight adaptation of the tale for television in a 1958 episode of *Matinee Theater*, which is now a lost film. He would play the role again in *Billy the Kid Versus Dracula* (1966), the kind of bad film that truly needs to be seen to be believed. Here is a prime example of Carradine's hamming at its worst: bulging his eyes, gesturing wildly, and reciting his lines like a cartoon tragedian.

Carradine plays the vampire's butler in *Blood of Dracula's Castle* (1967). He did not play the title role in *Doctor Dracula* (1977) either, rather getting top billing as an occult expert named Dr. Radcliff. Even after repeat viewings the plot is still inexplicable, so help yourself. He returned as the Count himself in 1978's *Nocturna*, the first Dracula-disco comedy. Here, the aged Count turns his castle into a disco in order to pay his taxes. He is also pursued by ex-flame Yvonne De Carlo, once more a vampire 10 years after her role as Lily Munster.

Carradine played the role one last time on a 1977 episode of television's *McCloud*, *McCloud Meets Dracula*. He appears here as a horror film actor who may be the actual Count, and is primarily of interest to nostalgia buffs.

In the many still photos of his Universal performances and the Detroit production, John Carradine looks like an impressive Dracula. Unfortunately, his performance was only skin deep.

"I am your cousin from Europe."
—Francis Lederer, *The Return of Dracula* (1958)

European actor Francis Lederer (born 1906) portrayed the Count in *The Return of Dracula*, a terrific little film that is all but forgotten. This is a shame, because *The Return of Dracula* remains one of the most competent and amusing vampiric visitations between the 1931 Universal classic and the 1979 Frank Langella remake.

Set in the then-contemporary 1950s California, Dracula preys upon an American family, who believes their enigmatic visitor is really cousin Bellac from the old country. There is much black humor as the constraints of vampirism are just written off as cultural differences by members of the *Happy Days* generation. This black-and-white film also contains a color sequence—the staking of one of Dracula's female victims—that has not lost its power to shock.

Tapping into the Cold War *zeitgeist*, Lederer plays Dracula much like a James Bond villain. With a long topcoat draped over his shoulders like a cape, Lederer evokes images of evil European secret agents as well as vampires. (And to the minds of American audiences, Soviet spies fed, vampire-like, on the life-preserving American military machine.) Lederer brought an oily, sullen anger to the role, turning his back on the Deane-Balderston tradition by resolutely staying *out* of his hosts' drawing room. And, like many Red Menace infiltrators of the time, Lederer's Dracula seems to be enjoying his stay in the United States immensely, sucking up the good life and the Californian moonshine.

Francis Lederer turned Dracula into a Cold War spy for 1958 audiences.

Dracula was just one of many steps in Francis Lederer's career. Born Frantisek Lederer in Prague, Czechoslovakia, the actor was the youngest of three sons of a leather merchant. Wanting to act at an early age, Lederer won a scholarship to the Prague Academy of Dramatic Art before he was 18. He won a reputation in Europe for his stage work, and went on to make films in France and Germany.

His appearance in the 1932 Broadway musical *Autumn Crocus* earned him a Hollywood contract, and soon he was romancing the likes of Claudette Colbert in *Midnight* (1939). Before the war, Lederer was a sleek and hand-

---

Francis Lederer Remembers *The Return of Dracula*

When I was first offered the role of Dracula in *The Return of Dracula*, it was presented to me as a spoof. However, when we started making the film, we played it in a more traditional manner.

All parts are interesting for an actor to interpret. Dracula has now become a role in the classic category, and, of course, is challenging and fascinating to play.

Although the film is now more than 40 years old, I still receive a lot of mail related to *Return of Dracula*. It's like a bit of immortality...

—Francis Lederer

Christopher Lee proves to be a messy eater in 1958's *Horror of Dracula*.

some leading man; afterward he concentrated mainly on character parts. Like Bela Lugosi, this screen Dracula was active politically, and was a founder of the World Peace Foundation.

Lederer was so good as Dracula that it is a shame he never returned for a sequel. A series of contemporary, American Dracula films would have given England's Hammer Films a run for their money, and Lederer may have found another career for himself haunting tract houses. Though that was not to be, *The Return of Dracula* is available on video tape, allowing Dracula fans the opportunity to indulge in both post-war Americana and Transylvanian thrills.

Francis Lederer, now retired, lives in California.

"Hiissssttttgggguuuhhh!"
—Christopher Lee in *Horror of Dracula* (1958), *Dracula—Prince of Darkness* (1966), *Dracula Has Risen From the Grave* (1968), *Taste the Blood of Dracula* (1970), *Scars of Dracula* (1970), *Dracula A.D. 1972* (1972), and *The Satanic Rites of Dracula* (1973)

Christopher Lee (born 1922) has played Dracula on film more times than any other actor. Aside from his seven Hammer Film appearances, he also played the Count (or a Dracula-like figure) in *Uncle Was a Vampire* (1959), *The Magic Christian* (1969), *Count Dracula* (1970), *In Search of Dracula* (1972), and *Dracula and Son* (1976).

Because of his numerous appearances, Lee is fondly remembered by the baby boom generation as the first post-Lugosi Dracula of merit. Unfortunately, a close examination of this physically imposing actor's Dracula performances proves that he actually *did* very little with the role.

A stiff and wooden actor at best, it was easy for Lee to trade upon his considerable height and comparative youth in his Dracula performances, jumping and snarling his way through the role. He brought energy, but no style, to his interpretation, and milked the part for all of its aggression, but none of its subtlety. Though Hammer considered Lee to be one of their major drawing-cards, they gave him little dialogue to speak. (He does, however, hiss a great deal.) The total line-count for his seven Dracula films equals less dialogue and screen time than Bela Lugosi had in his initial, 1931 performance. Perhaps this was for the best because Lee's (few) line readings in the latter films are dull and windy, as if he knew he had to do little but mumble to receive his check. Wisely, Hammer's scenarists and directors elected to keep him mute.

The total collapse of Hammer's Dracula series is a shame, because Hammer's first two Dracula films, *Horror of Dracula* and *The Brides of Dracula* (1960), are minor classics of Dracula and horror cinema. Not surprisingly, Lee appears for less than seven minutes in the first and is totally absent from the other! Actor Peter Cushing's stalwart Van Helsing carries both films, and his absence is felt in their immediate sequels. Sadly, the bulk of Hammer's Dracula films are tawdry, exploitive affairs, liberally sprinkled with cheap sexual innuendo and unnecessary violence.

Understandably, Lee grew to hate his Dracula films, and publicly whined for a chance to play the part as written by Stoker. He received his chance in Jess Franco's ill-fated *Count Dracula*, a major embarrassment to all concerned. Lee actually mouthed some of Stoker's dialogue in this film, and showed that the character as originally conceived was completely and totally out of his limited range. Wisely, he soon returned to the nearly mute interpretation offered by Hammer, where few demands were made upon him. Lee's turn as *Count Dracula* is bland and lifeless, lacking terror or resonance, and remains the worst performance by any actor as Dracula in a serious horror film.

There has been among horror film buffs, of late, a bit of historical revisionism in regards to Lee's impact on the role. In fact, Lee's influence has been marginal. Despite his many performances as Dracula, neither his face nor his (little heard) voice are immediately identified with the role in the popular imagination.

Perhaps the unkind comments spread about Lugosi's performance among horror film aficionados (seemingly the *only* people who disparage his work in the role) originated with Lee himself. In a comment appearing in the newsletter for the Christopher Lee Fan Club in the 1970s, Lee said that Lugosi was not "The right person to play Dracula from the point of view of nationality. Because Transylvania is in Rumania and he was a Hungarian from the town of Lugos, hence his name." (Perhaps Lee thought that he, of Italian extraction and born in London, was closer to Rumanian ancestry.) And in *A Dream of Dracula*, Lee is quoted as saying: "About the Lugosi *Dracula*. I was so disappointed... Dracula is played too nice at the beginning. Practically no menace in the character... There is no shock or fright in it... Lugosi's hands too... He held them out stiffly... making him look like a puppet. His smile was not always sinister either." Here Lee fails to notice that, unlike himself, Lugosi had charisma and a way with dialogue.

Lee's interpretation was soon eclipsed once the Dracula craze of the 1970s got into full swing, and Frank Langella reinvented the role for Broadway and movie audiences.

Curiously, Peter Cushing dons the Bela Lugosi outfit for _Tendre Dracula_ (1973), skipping the iconography of co-star Christopher Lee.

(For more on Christopher Lee, see Gary J. Svehla's _Hammer Films and The Resurrection of Dracula_, in this volume.)

Christopher Lee is the last surviving horror film "personality," and continues to work in supporting roles in international films released mostly in Europe.

> "It is romance that separates man from beast."
> —Peter Cushing, _Tendre Dracula_ (1973)

Peter Cushing (1913-1994) may well be the finest actor to emerge from the horror genre. His sensitivity, quietly commanding demeanor, and unconventionally handsome good looks have been an asset to many films that would be much the worse without his heroic presence.

A classically trained character actor of the old school, Cushing's first fame came courtesy of British television, where he starred in adaptations of George Orwell's _1984_ and Terrance Rattigan's _The Browning Version_.

Cushing's career might have continued on that course, and today he would be remembered as a fine character actor in the Trevor Howard or John Mills class. Fortunately, Cushing won the role of Dr. Frankenstein in the Hammer Films production of _The Curse of Frankenstein_ (1957), a part he would continue to play (brilliantly) in five additional films.

Soon realizing that the actor was their greatest asset, Hammer also pegged Cushing to play Van Helsing in _Horror of Dracula_, thus allowing him to make an invaluable contribution to Gothic cinema. (For more on Peter Cushing's characterization, see Tom Johnson's _Abraham Van Helsing, MDD, Ph.D. Lit, Etc., Etc._ in this volume.) He would go on to play Conan Doyle's Sherlock Holmes in *The Hound of the Baskervilles* (1959), H. Rider Haggard's Major Holly in *She* (1965), and Grand Moff Tarkin in *Star Wars* (1977).

Cushing had both a warm, accessible persona and a still, chilly self-composure. It was his mastery of this fire-and-ice technique that energized his performances.

Though he doesn't play Dracula in *Tendre Dracula*, he gets into full vampire regalia as MacGregor, a horror film actor who wants to retire and play more romantic parts. Interestingly, it is not the Christopher Lee but the Deane-Balderston-Lugosi conception of the character that Cushing impersonates, complete with evening clothes, white gloves, and medallion. Cushing looks so good in the Dracula costume that one regrets that he never essayed the role in a serious production.

A fine actor and gracious gentleman, Peter Cushing is missed by legions of fans in Britain and the United States.

"That Shakespeare. What a cornball!"
—Al Lewis, *The Munsters* (1964-1966)

Perhaps the cutest personification of Bram Stoker's Vampire King can be found in the American television series *The Munsters*.

As portrayed by veteran funnyman Al Lewis, Grandpa Munster is a curious hybrid of Dracula, mad scientist, and Borscht Belt comedian. Millions of children (and adults) have delighted in his performance as patriarch of the Munster clan, which continues to enjoy a vampiric half-life in reruns.

Born in upstate New York in 1910, Lewis left home at the age of 12 to join a traveling circus. He eventually made his way to New York, working in vaudeville, Broadway, radio, and television.

A bonanza for merchandisers, *The Munsters* spawned masks, toys, games, and model kits. The Munster Koach used on the show was constructed for $20,000 out of Fiberglas and the joined bodies of a 1927 Model T and a touring roadster. The model kit version of this automobile was very popular, as was Grandpa's Dragula, a 350-horsepower, coffin-shaped hot-rod built at a cost of $10,800. (Today, the unopened model kit versions of both can be bought for only slightly less money!)

His association with Grandpa Munster continues to this day. Visitors to New York's Greenwich Village often see the avuncular vampire (a successful restaurateur) sitting in front of his Italian bistro, *Grandpa's*. He has recently hosted several home-video releases of bad horror films, as well as compilations of movie trailers. A frequent guest at film and genre conventions, this spry octogenarian seems to have a Dracula-like longevity and vitality.

"Lucy, I have come for you."
—Jack Palance, *Dracula* (1973)

Jack Palance (born 1918) changed the role of Dracula for modern audiences. He moved the character away from the atavistic monstrosity of Stoker and the leering gentleman of Deane-Balderston, taking the monster back to an earlier, more Byronic conception of vampirism. This was the start of Dracula's reclamation, a white-washing that continues to this day. After Palance's Dracula, the Vampire King would often be portrayed as a

Jack Palance started the Count's spiritual reclamation, a sentiment which continues to this day.

tragic, victimized, misunderstood outcast. No longer a villain, monster, fiend, or charnel house ghoul, Dracula will mutate into a hybrid of Romantic poet and Fabio.

It is the greatest turnaround in a character since Ebenezer Scrooge.

Palance's Dracula is a man tormented, angered, embittered by his isolation and desperately lonely. He is also commanding, powerful, and passionate. Author Richard Matheson and director Dan Curtis hint at the historical Dracula by prominently placing a portrait in the castle of the living man as military conqueror. After victimizing Harker, Dracula heads for London, there to seek out Mina, the reincarnation of his lost love.

If all this sounds familiar, it should. Everything—from the flashbacks of the historical Dracula, the castle portrait, and the vampire's reincarnated love—was recycled for Francis Ford Coppola's *Bram Stoker's Dracula*.

Unfortunately, the movie that started the Dracula conversion is competent, but not much more, and while Palance shines at what he does, he isn't given much.

Born Vladimir Palanuik in Lattimer, Pennsylvania, Palance was the son of a Ukrainian coal miner, a superb athlete, and a pilot in World War II. Burns sustained while in active service necessitated reconstructive surgery, leaving his face with spooky hollows and jutting cheek bones.

He worked on Broadway after the war, where he was Anthony Quinn's understudy in Elia Kazan's production of *A Streetcar Named Desire*. It was in 1953 that Palance won movie fame as the gunslinger in *Shane*. He has worked steadily in films ever since, some terrific and some terrible. His career started a major revival in 1989 when he played the criminal boss in Tim Burton's *Batman*, and he later won an Academy Award for his role in *City Slickers* (1991). (Palance is one of three Academy Award winners to play Dracula, the others being Orson Welles and Martin Landau.)

Critics and movie fans lauded his turn as Dracula but, unfortunately, he never repeated the role.

"Do you know the significance of a kiss? You are nourishment to me."
—Louis Jourdan, *Count Dracula* (1977)

Actor Louis Jourdan (born 1921) brought a decadent sensuality to *Count Dracula*, delivering a performance of subtle power and oily menace.

This three-part adaptation, made originally for the BBC and broadcast in the United States on PBS, is one of film's closest approximations of Bram Stoker's novel. While there is some minor rearranging—heroes Arthur Holmwood and Quincey Morris are melded into one character, for instance—*Count Dracula* still manages to serve up generous portions of Stoker's bloody and passionate narrative.

In fact, *Count Dracula* (adapted by Gerald Savory) is one of the most unnerving retellings of the original novel. Dracula's vampire brides feast upon an infant in the dark and drafty confines of Dracula's Transylvania castle, and the scenes in Carfax are moldy and fetid enough for the viewer to imagine the vampire's rancid stench. It also manages to suggest some of the novel's sweep—though the film lacks any of the book's desperate momentum—as the action moves from Transylvania to Whitby to London and back again to Transylvania. Production values are uniformly excellent, and one wishes that the entire series was committed to film rather than video tape.

The one ringer in the adaptation is Dracula himself. That is not to fault Jourdan's performance, which is excellent, but the smarmy European charm he brings to the role is at odds with Stoker's hoary-headed Genghis Khan.

Jourdan's creepy sexuality is indeed memorable, as is the air of quiet mastery he brought to his dialogue and movements. He also does well in conveying the Vampire King's intelligence, making him a more than worthy opponent for Van Helsing and his band of vampire killers. His seduction of Mina is a masterpiece of creepy, insinuating sexuality, leaving the viewer simultaneously intrigued and queasy. The actor eschews the formal dress iconography of the Deane-Balderston conception, and is dressed entirely in black clothes with a severe military cut. Jourdan brings so much to the role

Jourdan's oily sensuality made Dracula a creepy, nocturnal seducer.

that, after decades of by-the-number performances by lesser actors, his Dracula is an inspiration.

The son of a hotelier, Jourdan studied acting at the Ecole Dramatique in Paris. His first movie role was in *Le Corsaire*, in 1939. Instantly popular, he starred in nine more films before World War II interrupted his career, when he joined the Resistance.

Once the war was over, he traveled to America, where David O. Selznick cast him in Alfred Hitchcock's *The Paradine Case*. Though not a singer by any means, he is perhaps best remembered for two musicals, *Gigi* (1958) and *Can Can* (1960). A talented player, Jourdan soon found movie roles were hard to come by for Continental types, and concentrated on theater and television work (where he delivered an outstanding performance opposite Peter Falk in *Columbo*).

Jourdan's Dracula, totally evil and without apology, remains one of the most interesting and effective interpretations of the role.

> "I am king of my kind!"
> —Frank Langella, *Dracula* (1979)

Frank Langella (born 1940) is simply the finest, most gifted actor ever to play this classic vampire role.

Easily one of the two or three greatest North American classical actors of his generation, Frank Langella was the first performer to create a Dracula that was a three-dimensional, complex human being.

By turns charismatic, seductive, commanding, dangerous, romantic, melancholy, frightening, and aggressive, Langella redefined the part, rescuing the character from B-movie oblivion and bringing Dracula, for the first time, into realm of "classical" roles.

Langella tackled Dracula in much the same spirit that John Barrymore might have: a great actor delivering a fine performance grounded in a romantic, matinee idol tradition. Langella was the first actor to make Dracula sexy, and the fact that he could play Dracula as both a character part and romantic idol is a testament to his ability. He played the part hundreds of times on stage, and modified his performance for the 1979 movie version.

The actor first played the role in a Stockbridge, Massachusetts, production in 1967. The 1977 version, with a witty and amusing set design by artist Edward Gorey (who won a Tony award for his costumes), was an unqualified success. The mark that Langella made in the part was so pronounced that the production, which had been commonly referred to as "Edward Gorey's Dracula," soon became known as "Frank Langella's Dracula."

(The original Edward Gorey cover for *Playbill* was soon discarded in favor of one featuring a photo of Langella's Dracula.) Due to the character's few scenes, additional dialogue was lifted from the 1931 film to pad Langella's stage time.

The play opened at the Martin Beck Theater to mixed reviews and packed houses. Critics generally found the production design inspired and Langella a revelation (he was nominated for a Tony award for his work), but though the Deane-Balderston script anemic. Played largely for its camp quality, Langella and company managed to infuse the play with genuine melodrama, romance, and scares along with a sense of style and fun. Langella's stage performance was grandiloquent and theatrical, complete with rich flourishes and evocative gestures.

Langella realized that playing to the vanity inherent in the role made his performance more effective. At New York City's Dracula Centennial Conference in March 1997, Broadway actress Anne Sachs (Lucy) remembered that Langella enacted their seduction scene as if he were playing to a reflection of himself. Isolating Dracula by rendering him a prisoner of his charm and good looks made him all the more attractive.

Frank Langella's performance powers the elegant John Badham version. *Dracula* **(1979).**

Universal, spurred by the play's New York triumph, quickly planned a remake of their Bela Lugosi classic. Director John Badham decided to discard the evocative production design of Gorey (see *The Vampire's Return: John Badham on The Making of Dracula*, an interview by Tom Weaver, in this volume), and to increase the story's romantic possibilities. Langella left the show, allowing such accomplished actors as Raul Julia and David Dukes to take the Broadway spotlight.

Badham needed a star to match Langella's talents and recruited Shakespearean actor Laurence Olivier to play Dr. Van Helsing. Kate Nelligan, then at the beginning of a distinguished career, played Lucy. Character actor Donald Pleasence was Dr. Seward. Although a modest hit, Universal's *Dracula* was not the box office champion they had anticipated. Perhaps hoping to trade on the vogue that fantasy films were enjoying at the time (such as the phenomenally successful *Star Wars*), they did not realize that their *Dracula* was too old-fashioned and atmospheric to be appreciated by the youth market.

Langella's performance is often dismissed by a core-group of horror film aficionados and that is somewhat understandable: Langella's interpretation is bigger and more challenging than the monster movie genre. In remaking the 1931 Universal film, director John Badham and scenarist W. D. Richter set out to make less a horror film and more a tragic Gothic romance. The filmmakers turned to the Deane-Balderston play that Langella had repopularized on Broadway for their inspiration, and that is unfortunate. Had they adapted the novel instead, their film would have had more opportunities to strut its lush production design and employ a greater epic sweep in the narrative.

As a romantic reimagining of the play, Badham's film is unbeatable. Aided by a memorable score by composer John Williams, Frank Langella's *Dracula* was the movie that the character often deserved, but so seldom received.

Perhaps because *Dracula* never took flight at the box office, actor Langella has only been an occasional film actor. Fortunately, he is one of the nation's most prolific stage actors, who, along with Dracula, has played such larger-than-life figures as Lear, Cyrano, and Sherlock Holmes.

Langella's Broadway career includes *Seascape*, *Amadeus*, and *Design for Living* (where he starred with his *Dracula* replacement, Raul Julia). He is the recipient of over a dozen major acting awards: along with his Tony he has earned three Obies, three Drama Desks, National Society of Film Critics, Los Angeles Drama Critics Circle Award, and the Cable Ace Award for Best Actor in Kurt Vonnegut's *Monkey House*. Like screen Draculas George Hamilton and Duncan Regehr, he also rattled his saber as Zorro. He has often directed (at one time, he considered directing a revival of *Dracula* with Patrick Swayze in the title role), and during Dracula's 100th anniversary he once more took Broadway by storm in Noël Coward's *Present Laughter*.

Currently involved with actress-comedian Whoopi Goldberg, Langella stars in the upcoming film version of Nabokov's *Lolita*.

Langella's Dracula moved the character further down the path of reclamation started by actor Jack Palance. Reconceived as a tragic lover and not a blood-thirsty fiend, Dracula was ready to stalk the popular imagination once more.

The Show Must Go On ...

The late Raul Julia (1940-1994) took over when Frank Langella left Broadway for Hollywood. His performance was even more frankly sexual than Langella's, and was extremely popular as well. He later went on to star as an energetic Gomez Addams in *The Addams Family* (1991) and *Addams Family Values* (1993).

Actor David Dukes also appeared in the Broadway version. During the 1970s he also starred as Dr. Frankenstein in Broadway's *Frankenstein*, at that time the biggest flop in Broadway history. The show closed after one performance and also starred John Carradine as the hermit who befriends the monster.

Broadway's final Dracula was popular soap opera star Jon LeClerc. Though he did not make any notable dent in the role, he looked wonderful in costume.

Terence Stamp (born 1940) is perhaps today best remembered for his portrayal as the villainous General Zod in *Superman* (1978) and *Superman II* (1980). His best performances, however, are found in *Billy Budd* (1962) and *The Collector* (1965). He starred in the London revival of the show in 1978, which was a critical disaster. The British media liked neither his performance nor the Edward Gorey design, and the show quickly closed.

Ten years before Martin Landau won an Academy Award for playing Bela Lugosi in *Ed Wood*, he played Dracula (imitating Lugosi) in the 1984 revival of the show. He complained, at the time, that the Lugosi characterization was the only one audiences would accept from him.

The logical successor to Basil Rathbone's Sherlock Holmes was Jeremy Brett (1936-1995). Before taking up pipe and deerstalker, this flamboyant actor hid behind the cape, taking the Gorey show on tour. He brought the same outlandish quality to the Vampire King that he did to the Master Detective, investing the part with a manic, dangerous energy.

"Look at me."
—Michael Nouri, *The Curse of Dracula*, television's *Cliffhangers* (1977)

Michael Nouri played Dracula in the continuing *The Curse of Dracula* story line on television's *Cliffhangers*. Conceived as an homage to chapterplays from Hollywood's Golden Age, each episode of *Cliffhangers* juggled three continuing story lines, including one involving the infamous Transylvanian Count.

Here, Dracula is a professor at a California University where he teaches (what else?) history. He jeopardizes his immortality when he falls in love, pursuing romance throughout the limited run of the series. *The Curse of Dracula* was the only story line the writers resolved when the show was canceled after one season, finishing with the vampire consumed by flames.

Cliffhangers was just another move in further romanticizing Dracula. As the Count, Nouri isn't bad, but he isn't called upon to do much other than pout like a fashion model. With his mane of blow-dried hair and open-necked shirts, Nouri was a disco Dracula for the polyester age.

Nouri went on to star in such films as *Flashdance* (1983), *The Hidden* (1987), and *American Yakuza* (1994), among others, and on Broadway opposite Julie Andrews in *Victor/Victoria*. All were better than *Cliffhangers*.

"There goes my big bucks!"
—Judd Hirsch, *The Halloween That Almost Wasn't* (1979)

Judd Hirsch of television's *Taxi* did an outrageous impersonation of Bela Lugosi's Dracula in the delightful *The Halloween That Almost Wasn't*. This award-winning 30-minute television special, created as a Halloween treat for children, also featured the Wolf Man, Frankenstein's Monster, Ygor, and other classic monsters.

In the film, Mariette Hartley plays a witch who refuses to fly over the moon—the ceremony that officially starts Halloween—until Dracula gives in to her demands, including putting her picture on Halloween merchandising. It all ends happily, of course, with the children of America convincing her that Halloween is too important a holiday to lose over squabbling.

Hirsch enjoys himself immensely, and maintains a hectoring banter with Henry Gibson's Ygor throughout. For fans of the classic monsters, *The Halloween That Almost Wasn't* is an affectionate Halloween tribute.

Klaus Kinski as Count Dracula from *Nosferatu the Vampyre* (1979).

"You have developed a taste for the night, I see."
—Klaus Kinski, *Nosferatu the Vampyre* (1979)

Klaus Kinski (1925-1991) replaced Max Schreck in Werner Herzog's disappointing remake of the silent classic. *Nosferatu the Vampyre* was actually two films, as Herzog's cast and crew shot an English and German-language version simultaneously. He didn't get it quite right either time, as the German version is little more than an interesting failure and the English film unwatchable.

Kinski looks great in the Max Schreck make-up, and the scenes of him wooing Isabelle Adjani have a definite repulsive fascination. Unfortunately the film does not live up to its sometimes stunning visuals.

Kinski, a Polish actor raised in Berlin, often lived in extreme poverty. He toured in cabaret as a young man and did poetry recitals in Germany. He made several films with director Herzog, including *Aguirre* (1973) and *Woyzeck* (1979), but showed poor judgment in his selection of American films. He turned down *Raiders of the Lost Ark* (1981) in order to do *Venom* (1981), and had a featured role in Billy Wilder's flop *Buddy, Buddy* (1981). For Jess Franco's *Count Dracula* (1970), Kinski delivered a truly disturbing portrait of Renfield, the only capable performance in an otherwise terrible film.

Unhappily, he (and everyone else) delivers a poor performance in *Nosferatu*. Maybe Herzog didn't really care about the film. Maybe the tensions that would eventually

George Hamilton toasts his success in *Love at First Bite* (1979).

destroy the friendship between the director and the star had already started. Whatever the reason, the film is impossible to sit through.

For those Dracula completists who feel they must see this film, I recommend that they rent the German version and watch it with the sound turned off to better enjoy the movie's many visual delights.

> "In a world without romance, I'd rather be dead."
> —George Hamilton, *Love at First Bite* (1979)

The idea of Dracula as a romantic idol reached its apotheosis with George Hamilton's *Love at First Bite*.

Hamilton (born 1939) took the character back to its Broadway, matinee idol roots, reinventing the vampire as a displaced person in time. His Dracula is romantic, dashing, theatrical, and passionate in a world that is increasingly mundane, colorless, tawdry, and self-involved. Glamorous in the debonair way of 1920s and 1930s leading men, this Dracula is on a quest to find love and his place in a changing world.

Largely conceived around the pool by actor Hamilton and writer Robert Kaufman, *Love at First Bite* is surprisingly subtle, and even poignant, despite its more slapstick moments. Dracula and his servant Renfield (Arte Johnson) are banished from their Transylvanian castle by the Communists, who convert their home into efficiency apartments. That note of displacement is sustained throughout, proving that the real villain of contemporary times is not Dracula, but the modern world itself. To his dismay, Hamilton's Dracula discovers himself in a New York that has no time for myths, romance, or the grand, romantic gesture.

Hamilton suits this interpretation so well because this Dracula reflects, in a way, his own film career. With his lounge lizard good looks and smooth manner, Hamilton never found complete favor in a 1960s and 1970s culture of anti-heroes and renegades. Hamilton, to a degree, cultivated his playboy persona, spending considerable time in Monte Carlo and in the company of a succession of beautiful women, and many in the Hollywood establishment dismissed him as a lightweight.

For a while, it seemed as if Hamilton would rejuvenate his moribund career with a string of comedies spoofing the romantic heroes of a bygone age. *Love at First Bite* proved to be an enormous hit, and Hamilton followed it with *Zorro, the Gay Blade* (1981), which, unfortunately, bombed at the box office.

A sequel to *Love at First Bite* was in development for years, but never got off the ground. At one time Peter O'Toole was considered as a replacement for Hamilton, and the writers even had an ingenious way of playing with the casting change. The film, tentatively titled *Love at Second Bite*, would open in a hospital. A figure, face concealed with bandages, would lie in bed, a photo of Hamilton's Dracula on the night table. When the bandages are removed, O'Toole's Dracula was to have exclaimed: "Doctor! You made me look much older!"

"Yes," the doctor says, "But now you're a damned better actor."

Love at First Bite is a very funny film and one of the more amusing artifacts of the Dracula craze of the 1970s.

"Wake up old friend. It's our time!"
—Duncan Regehr as Dracula to the Frankenstein Monster (Tom Noonan),
The Monster Squad (1987)

Duncan Regehr has made a career of playing dangerous characters. Not only has Regehr played Dracula, but he was *Zorro* for four years on the Family Channel, impersonated Errol Flynn in the biographical film *My Wicked, Wicked Ways* (1985), and even twirled guns as Pat Garrett in *Gore Vidal's Billy the Kid* (1989).

The Monster Squad details the efforts of Dracula, Frankenstein's Monster, the Wolf Man, the Mummy, and the Creature from the Black Lagoon to gain possession of an

The classic monsters rally to defeat *The Monster Squad* (1987).

amulet that would open the gates of hell upon an unsuspecting world. They are defeated by a group of kids who belong to a monster fan club, the policeman father of the gang's leader, and an aging Holocaust survivor.

Though definitely a children's film, this effective homage to the classic Universal movie monsters is surprisingly good. The special effects are first rate, the humor funny without being cute, the monsters all strangely believable, and the relationships between the children and their parents touching. Director Fred Dekker obviously has great nostalgia for the classic monster characters, for he lovingly reinvents them for modern audiences. At times the film has the look and feel of one of the Universal "monster rallies" of the 1940s, but manages to create a slam-bang climax that the older films could never have duplicated. To anyone who grew up on Saturday night *Creature Features* or the monster magazines of decades ago, *The Monster Squad* is irresistible fun.

Regehr makes an effective Dracula. His intention was to get away from the "lady-killer" tradition of the character, but he managed to be suave and smoothly sexual nevertheless. With his precise movements, commanding manner, and determined performance, Regehr presents a Dracula who is psychotic, homicidal, and openly sadistic. As is always the case in these multiple-monster-movies, Dracula is not only the catalyst of the plot, but the leader of the monsters, as well.

Regehr was born in Lethbridge, Alberta, Canada, in 1952. An author and artist as well as an actor, Regehr's latest book is *Dragon's Eye: An Artist's View*. He also plays the continuing role of Shakaar on television's *Star Trek: Deep Space Nine*.

An unbeatable family film, *The Monster Squad* improves with repeated viewings and should become a Halloween tradition in any home with children.

"Look what your God has done to me!"
—Gary Oldman, *Bram Stoker's Dracula* (1992)

Nearly 15 years after Frank Langella's magnificent revitalization of Dracula, Gary Oldman (born 1958) took the character even further in this, the most ambitious retelling of Bram Stoker's classic yet.

Though promoted as a strictly faithful adaptation of the novel *Dracula*, *Bram Stoker's Dracula* actually incorporates elements from previous vampire films that are not present in Stoker's text. The screenplay, by James V. Hart, expands upon the historical Dracula, Vlad Tepes, whom Stoker only hinted at, and gives Dracula the motivation of pursuing his reincarnated love, Mina.

That *Bram Stoker's Dracula* is not scrupulously faithful to the text is immaterial: no previous adaptation got all the particulars right, and it is probably a mistake to believe that a film could capture the totality of Stoker's sprawling tale. However, Hart's screenplay is the first to include all of Stoker's major characters—especially the three suitors, Seward, Holmwood and Quincey—and was ambitious enough to return some of Stoker's narrative scope to the tale.

The film was fortunate in having Francis Ford Coppola as its director. Arguably one of the finest directors in recent times (his *Godfather* trilogy and *Apocalypse Now* are established film classics), Coppola moved away from the tradition of realism in which his career is grounded and created out of *Dracula* an ornate, mannered film in the Expressionist tradition. Whether *Bram Stoker's Dracula* is to everyone's taste does not matter; it is an audacious piece of filmmaking that reintroduced Dracula to a new generation.

In keeping with the innovative spirit of the production, Gary Oldman strives to bring something very different to Dracula. He bravely elects to do a Rumanian/Lugosian accent—a daring choice in itself that could have elicited chuckles instead of fear. (He is the only actor to employ an accent for the part in a serious interpretation of the role.) Instead, Oldman's speech patterns work wonders in underscoring the Count's malignant evil.

It is in the opening scenes in Dracula's Transylvania castle (the exterior of which is designed like an Epstein sphinx) that Oldman is especially effective. With his twin mounds of white hair, stylized movements, and creepy delivery, Oldman is a walking nightmare. He is perhaps less convincing after the Vampire King comes to London and woos Mina. Though a magnificent actor, Oldman is not the sort to incite white-hot passion. But still, Oldman's love scenes with Winona Ryder's Mina function at a high level of emotion, and Oldman is the first Dracula to cry on screen. He manages to convey a mix of conflicting emotions and motives, delivering a multi-leveled, powerful performance.

On the downside, Oldman's physicality is not equal to his performance. Small, reedy, and nondescript, he lacks the imposing physical presence that is so often necessary for an effective Dracula. He works extremely well in the man-sized bat and wolf make-ups, but little can be done for him in his most human guises where he loses much of his menace.

Gary Oldman's Dracula is addicted to necking while at the movies.

Gary Oldman began his career on the stage, where he was a member of the Glasgow Citizen's Theater before his fist significant movie role as punk rocker Sid Vicious in *Sid and Nancy* (1986). He followed that with a brilliant performance as playwright Joe Orton in *Prick Up Your Ears* (1987) and soon became a featured player in major films, including *True Romance* (1993) and *The Fifth Element* (1997).

Like Dracula, Oldman has grappled with a drinking problem, his sole inheritance from an abusive, alcoholic father. His drinking problem destroyed his marriage to actress Uma Thurman and his romance with Isabella Rossellini before he was able to cure himself of the addiction. He married photographer Donya Fiorentino in early 1997.

It was Bela Lugosi who created the Dracula that people have come to expect, but only actors Gary Oldman and Frank Langella dared to reinterpret the role, infusing the vampire with new life and vitality.

"Yeeouch!"
—Leslie Nielsen, *Dracula: Dead and Loving It* (1995)

With the box office bonanza of the Coppola film, it was only natural that a film parody followed. That it was made by Mel Brooks, the comedic genius behind *Blazing Saddles* (1974) and *Young Frankenstein* (1974), was the icing on the cake.

Leslie Nielsen portrayed Dracula as a bubble-headed klutz. An inept villain with two left fangs who trips on bat poop, slips while crawling down walls, and trades crude Moldavian insults, Nielsen is a delight. The film, however, is nearly stolen by Brooks' own take on the vampire's nemesis, Dr. Van Helsing, and Peter MacNichol's flawless impression of Dwight Frye as Renfield.

A leading man and television star during the 1950s and 1960s, Nielsen was cast less frequently in significant roles during the 1970s, finding refuge on *The Love Boat* and *Fantasy Island*. It was only with the outrageous comedy *Airplane!* (1980), which poked fun not only at the conventions of disaster films but at a whole generation of he-man actors like Nielsen, Robert Stack, and Lloyd Bridges, that the actor was once more a box office star. He parlayed his performance into a profitable career as a deadpan comedian in the *Naked Gun* films, receiving greater success than he ever had during his leading-man period.

Dracula: Dead and Loving It mainly pokes fun at Bela Lugosi's 1931 classic, but also parodies the Oldman and Langella films. While not in the same league as Brooks' *Young Frankenstein*, *Dracula: Dead and Loving It* guarantees chuckles for any Dracula fan.

Dracula has been in his celluloid coffin for the past couple of years. Not dead in the true sense, he is only marshaling his strength, waiting for the opportunity to strike again. It is only a matter of time before he walks among us, hungry for blood and box office returns.

I promise.

Vincent Price—The Dracula that never was!

Vincent Price Never Played Count Dracula

Without question the most beloved star of horror films of his generation, actor Vincent Price never played Count Dracula. Though he was a gifted actor in costume pictures—his series of films for AIP based on Edgar Allan Poe's stories are simply the best post World War II horror films—no enterprising producer ever saw fit to cast Vincent Price in an adaptation of Bram Stoker's novel.

But it was inevitable that these icons of horror—Count Dracula and Vincent Price—would collide in some way. Price spoofed the Dracula image in an episode of television's *F-Troop*, complete with outrageous Bela Lugosi accent. During the 1970s he regularly sported a cape for television's kiddie show, *The Horrible House of Frightenstone*, and became a vampire at the end of a Halloween special for children, where he recommended Stoker's *Dracula* to young viewers. (A dainty dish indeed to set before a young audience!)

A vampiric Vincent Price preyed upon former screen Dracula John Carradine in *The Monster Club* (1980), and he also played host and narrator to *Vincent Price's Dracula* (1982), a documentary about the historical Dracula and vampires made palatable only by his elegant presence.

Some of this must have penetrated into the public consciousness. When Price passed away in October 1993 just five days before Halloween, more than one obituary pointed out that his fans often asked about his Dracula portrayals.

Price, consummate wit and gentleman, said he never disappointed people who asked about Dracula—he bit them.

—Bob Madison

U.S. Dracula Stamp

Bela Lugosi's image is so indelibly merged with that of Bram Stoker's Dracula that it has been recognized by the United States Post Office.

The Bela Lugosi as Dracula thirty-two cent postage stamp was first distributed in October 1997. The stamp is part of a series commemorating classic portrayals of movie monsters and also features stamps of Lon Chaney as the Phantom of the Opera, Boris Karloff as Frankenstein's Monster and the Mummy, and Lon Chaney, Jr. as the Wolf Man.

The Postal Service premiered the designs for the stamps at a ceremony at Universal Studios, Florida. In attendance were Bela

Bela Lugosi is recognized as *the* Count Dracula, and his visage now can be seen on an U. S. postage stamp.

Lugosi, Jr., Sara Karloff (daughter of the late actor) and Ron Chaney, grandson of Lon, Jr.

The stamps are really the brainchild of Ms. Karloff, who campaigned for years to bring the project to fruition. "We tried to include Vincent Price as well," she said, "but the Post Office demands that 10 years pass between a celebrity's death and the issuance of a stamp."

"These actors and their monsters created a whole new genre in American film and have been sending a shiver down the spines of audiences for more than 60 years," said Postmaster General Marvin Runyon. "It is fitting that these classic characters, and the actors who portrayed them, will be honored on U.S. postage stamps."

The Postal Service handles 40 percent of the world's mail volume, processing about 580 million pieces a day, and makes deliveries to more than 128 million addresses each day.

Ironically, Bram Stoker handled all the correspondence for the great Victorian tragedian Sir Henry Irving.

—Bob Madison

The measure of any villain is his opponent.

It was the genius of Bram Stoker to give his Vampire King a nemesis as capable, as implacable, as dangerous as Dracula himself. Dr. Abraham Van Helsing may be the most popular Victorian avenger after Sherlock Holmes: it is he who provides the dramatic tension in Stoker's Dracula *and in all of its subsequent retellings.*

It is Van Helsing with whom Stoker most identified, sharing with his fictive hero his own Christian name and interest in folklore and demonism. It is not beyond possibility that he even envisioned himself in the role, and would have played Van Helsing himself had he been able to mount a production with his employer, Shakespearean actor Sir Henry Irving, as the Count... stranger things have happened in the theater.

To Stoker, Van Helsing and Dracula were equals, evenly matched opponents. To Irving, Stoker was a mere vassal who, after a lifetime of service, did not even merit remembrance in his will.

At any rate, as Irving was the model for Dracula, it's interesting that Stoker had his own surrogate mount a campaign against him, run him to earth, and destroy him.

Author and educator Tom Johnson is the co-author of Peter Cushing: The Gentle Man of Horror *and* Hammer Films: An Exhaustive Filmography. *An expert on the chillers produced by Hammer Films, he is a frequent lecturer and panelist at film conventions.*
—Bob Madison

Abraham Van Helsing, MDD, Ph.D. Lit, Etc., Etc.
by Tom Johnson

"I rose and bowed," wrote Mina Harker in her journal, "and he came towards me; a man of medium weight; strongly built, with his shoulders set back over a broad, deep chest and a neck well balanced on the trunk as the head is on the neck. The pose of the head strikes one at once as indicative of thought and power; the head is noble, well sized, broad, and large behind the ears. The face, clean shaven, shows a hard, square chin, a large, resolute, mobile mouth, a good sized nose, rather straight but with quick, sensitive nostrils, that seem to broaden as the big, bushy brows come down and the mouth tightens. The forehead is broad and fine, rising at first almost straight and then sloping back above two bumps or ridges wide apart; such a forehead that the reddish hair cannot possibly tumble over it, but falls naturally back at the sides. Big, dark blue eyes are set widely apart, and are quick and tender or stern with the man's moods."

Bram Stoker seems to have had a definite model for his vampire hunter; no other character in *Dracula*—not even the Count—is so specifically described. This description does not tally with any of the actors who gave cinematic life to Van Helsing, yet, oddly, each actor has *something* of the doctor in his manner or appearance.

Called in by Dr. Seward as a "second opinion" for the stricken Lucy, Van Helsing's character traits were laid down precisely in the doctor's journal and have been faithfully preserved by the myriad screenwriters that followed:

> I have written to my old friend and master, Professor Van Helsing of Amsterdam, who knows as much about obscure diseases as anyone in the world. Van Helsing would, I know, do anything for me for a personal reason so, no matter on what ground he comes, we must accept his wishes. He is a seemingly arbitrary man, but this is because he knows what he is talking about better than anyone else. He is a philosopher and metaphysician and one of the most advanced scientists of his day, and he has, I believe, an absolutely open mind. This, with an iron nerve, a temper of the ice-brook, an indomitable resolution, self command, and toleration. These form his equipment for the noble work he is doing for mankind; I tell you these facts that you may know why I have such confidence in him.

Considering the strain and responsibility Van Helsing labored under, it's not surprising that events occasionally got away from him. For example, the Professor can barely contain his laughter when poor Arthur Holmwood, after transfusing his blood with Lucy, feels that they have "been married in the sight of God." (The transfusions performed by Van Helsing on both page and screen do not inspire confidence; blood typing was not discovered until a quarter century after *Dracula* was written. Van Helsing's actions could have been as fatal to Lucy as Dracula's attack!)

Later, Van Helsing is overcome by the "humor" inherent in Lucy's appearance after her death. "Oh, it was the grim irony of it all," he chortled. "This so lovely lady garlanded with flowers that looked so fair as life till one by one we wondered if she were truly dead."

Seward sternly replies, "Well, for the life of me Professor, I can't see anything to laugh at in all that."

Van Helsing's boorish behavior actually makes him, fleetingly, a suspect in the mystery. "Surely there must be some rational explanation of all these mysterious things," writes Dr. Seward. "Is it possible that the Professor can have done it himself? I am loathe to think it, and indeed it would be almost as great a marvel as the other to find that Van Helsing was mad; but anyhow I shall watch him carefully."

The Professor reaches his nadir of tastelessness in a remark made soon after Mina has been attacked by Dracula.

> HARKER: The Count may come to Piccadilly earlier than we think.
> VAN HELSING: Not so!
> HARKER: But why?

VAN HELSING: Do you forget that last night he banqueted heavily and will sleep late?

Van Helsing's lack of good taste in these—especially the latter—examples is almost beyond belief... and certainly not the way in which he is thought of by movie audiences.

The Professor is also not immune to the lovely young ladies that populate the book. "She charms me," he says of Lucy. "And for her, if not for you or disease, I come." Cinematic Van Helsings showed little or no interest in that direction... with one exception: Peter Cushing in *The Brides of Dracula* (1960) got fairly chummy with the beautiful Marianne (Yvonne Monlaur). In fact, they clinch at the picture's climax. Since Van Helsing *does* have descendants (as chronicled in the miserable Hammer Dracula films of the 1970s), perhaps this is where it all began.

Equally open to speculation is Van Helsing's medical bag: a thing of wonder, not unlike Batman's utility belt. Whatever the Professor needed at any given moment was easily found within its seemingly limitless confines. Peter Cushing addressed the problem in Hammer's original *Dracula* (1958), titled *Horror of Dracula* in the U. S. "The script demanded Van Helsing to carry so many crucifixes," Cushing wrote in his *Autobiography* (Weidenfeld and Nicolson, 1986). "It read as if he were a traveling salesman in these relics." He wisely suggested to director Terence Fisher that crossed candlesticks might be more acceptable for the picture's rousing climax.

Van Helsing's most annoying characteristic in the novel—even more so than his occasionally boorish behavior—was the unbearable and unreadable Dutch (or whatever) accent foisted upon him. Why did Stoker feel this was necessary? One guess is that the accent distinguished the doctor from the (too) many vampire hunters, literally giving Van Helsing a voice in the proceedings.

The Professor *may* have been partially based—at least subconsciously—on that other paragon of Victorian rationality, Sherlock Holmes. Bram Stoker and Sir Arthur Conan Doyle, Holmes' creator, knew each other well; it's possible that Stoker borrowed some of Holmes' general characteristics. For example, both Van Helsing and Holmes are bachelors, possess knowledge denied to most, have anti-social attitudes, can be blunt with those who lack their mental prowess, confound their lesser-informed associates, seek no recognition for their expertise, are completely single-minded, and are viewed by their fellows as odd.

Van Helsing's main functions in the novel were to unify the forces attempting to destroy Dracula and to lay down the rules of vampirism. These roles have pretty much been carried on in the many film adaptations that began, officially, with Universal's 1931 *Dracula*.

Edward Van Sloan, the screen's first Van Helsing, was born in Minnesota (as Van Sloun) on November 1, 1881... 16 years before *Dracula*'s publication. Like Van Helsing, he was of Dutch origin; his father, Martin, was born in Holland. Van Sloan entered college with the expectation of following his father as an architect, but he became interested in theatrics and that was that.

After his theatrical debut in 1908, Van Sloan found steady work in plays like *Charlie's Aunt*, *The Liars*, *Morals*, and *Juarez and Maximilian*, in which he co-starred with Edward G. Robinson. This Broadway production may have caught the eye of Horace

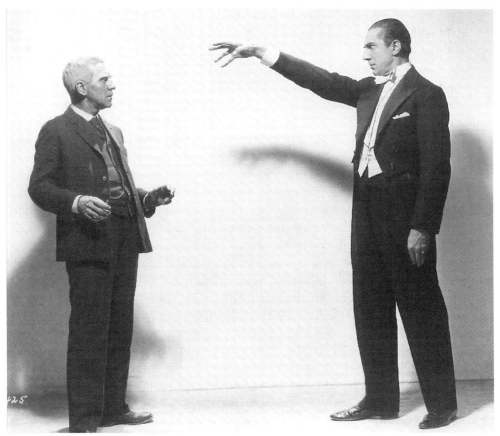

Edward Van Sloan combats the charisma of Bela Lugosi in this publicity still from *Dracula* **(1931).**

Liveright, who was interested in bringing *Dracula* to New York. Adapted by Hamilton Deane (who played Van Helsing in the London production), *Dracula* opened at the Fulton Theatre on December 5, 1927, with Bela Lugosi in the lead, and ran for 261 performances.

When director Tod Browning and producer Carl Laemmle, Jr. assembled the film version three years later, they had far less trouble casting the actor to play Van Helsing than they did for Dracula. Van Sloan was 48 when he made his movie debut in *Dracula*, but seemed at least a decade older. His success as an authority figure for monsters led to his appearance in *Frankenstein* (1931) and *The Mummy* (1932) before reprising Van Helsing (oddly renamed *Von* Helsing) in *Dracula's Daughter* (1936).

Van Sloan was, by the mid-thirties, a Hollywood fixture, appearing in such pictures as *The Last Mile* (1932), *Death Takes a Holiday* (1934), *The Last Days of Pompeii* (1935), and *The Road Back* (1937), again working with *Frankenstein* director James Whale. He returned to horror in *The Phantom Creeps*, a 1939 serial with Bela Lugosi, *Before I Hang* (1940), and *The Monster and the Girl* (1941). Van Sloan's film career ended in 1948 with *A Foreign Affair*, but he appeared on stage (under the name Van Sloun) in *The Vigil* the following year. He died on March 8, 1964, in San Francisco.

Van Sloan was not only the first film actor to play Van Helsing; he was also the first to play him in a sequel. In *Dracula* (1931), Van Sloan brought a stately authority that perfectly matched the pace of both Lugosi and the picture. Van Sloan, Lugosi, and

Dwight Frye's Renfield was anchored by the stolid under-playing of Van Sloan's Van Helsing.

Dracula have received unfavorable criticism recently due to the staginess of it all, criticism which is, by modern standards, justified. But—it must be remembered that this was not the reaction of *Dracula*'s contemporary audience. Van Sloan gave the character a quiet authority, and it's hard to imagine any other actor of the period being better cast.

Dracula, after arriving in England, quickly makes a deadly move on Lucy (Frances Dade), house guest of Dr. Seward (Herbert Bunston), and his daughter Mina (Helen Chandler). Van Helsing, an eminent authority, is called in to investigate both Lucy's death and the mysterious Renfield (Dwight Frye), a fly-eater, confined at Seward's asylum.

When we get our first look at him, Van Helsing comes across as something of a geek... white lab jacket, Coke-bottle eyeglasses, flat-top haircut... but he instantly proves that he's in charge. "Gentlemen... we are dealing with the undead. The vampire attacks the throat and leaves two little wounds... white, with red centers."

Dr. Seward blows off this grave announcement in what became a time-honored tradition. "Modern medical science does not admit to such a creature... the vampire is a pure myth... superstition."

"I may be able to bring you proof," Van Helsing insists, setting the stage for all Van Helsings to come, "that the superstition of yesterday can become the scientific reality of today."

Van Sloan returned as *Von* Helsing in *Dracula's Daughter* (1936), and played a similar role in *The Mummy* (1932).

Mina is the next to fall under the Count's spell, and her milquetoast fiancé Jonathan Harker (David Manners) isn't up to this or, presumably, *any* challenge. Thank God Van Helsing's there when Dracula smoothly insinuates himself into Seward's drawing room gathering.

The vampire and his nemesis acknowledge each other with a bow. "Van Helsing... a most distinguished scientist whose name we know, even in the wilds of Transylvania."

But the Professor isn't paying attention to the Count's chit-chat... he's noticed that Dracula casts no reflection in a cigarette box with a mirrored top.

"A moment ago," Van Helsing says, "I stumbled upon a most amazing phenomenon..." Dracula is not amused; he slaps the box away and hisses, "For one who has not lived a single lifetime, you're a wise man, Van Helsing."

Yes, he was—wise enough to find Dracula's hidden coffin and destroy the vampire, saving Mina, London, and the world... and set a standard of man over monster that endures over 70 years later.

In *Dracula's Daughter* (1936), Van Helsing was subjected to an amusing reality check; he was arrested for the murder of Count Dracula! As a suspect for much of the movie, Von Helsing ceded his vampire hunting authority into the capable hands of Dr. Garth (Otto Kruger), and became pretty much a secondary character.

A Van Helsing clone (J. Edward Bromberg as Prof. Lazlo) appeared in Universal's *Son of Dracula* (1943), but the character would remain in studio vaults, Dracula-like, until 1958.

Peter Cushing, the screen's most prolific (five films) Van Helsing, was born in Surrey, England on May 26, 1913. After the usual false starts common to most actors' careers, Cushing took the bold step of going to Hollywood to break into movies with little experience other than community theater productions. After lucking (and, he admitted, lying) his way into the cast of director James Whale's *The Man in the Iron Mask* (1939), Cushing made six more movies before returning to the U.K. due to World War II.

Cushing became associated with future Van Helsing, Sir Laurence Olivier, and appeared with him as Osric in the Academy Award–winning *Hamlet* (1947). By the mid-1950s, Cushing had become England's most honored television actor and had scored in several movies (notably *The End of the Affair,* 1954). Sought and caught by Hammer Films to play the Baron in *The Curse of Frankenstein* (1957), Cushing became typed in horror roles and never looked back, appearing in over 75 more pictures. Effectively cast as heroes (Sherlock Holmes in *The Hound of the Baskervilles,* 1959) and villains (Grand Moff Tarkin in *Star Wars,* 1977) and everyday people (Mr. Fordyce in *Cash on Demand,* 1961), Cushing was the most versatile actor to be associated with horror movies. He brought all of his considerable skills to the Van Helsing role in Hammer's *Dracula* (1958).

On the trail of his friend Jonathan Harker (John Van Eyssen), who has failed in his attempt to destroy Dracula (Christopher Lee), Van Helsing enters an inn and confronts its frightened, surly owner (George Woodbridge). "What are you afraid of?" Van Helsing asks. "Why all these garlic flowers over the window? They're not for decoration, are they?"

"I don't know what you're talking about."

"I think you do... and I think you know something about my friend. He came here with a purpose... to help you."

"We haven't asked for any help."

"You need it all the same."

"You're a stranger here in Clausenberg," the innkeeper sniffs. "Some things are better left alone... such as interfering in things which are beyond our powers."

But Van Helsing will have none of this. "Please don't misunderstand me. This is more than a superstition... I know! The danger is very real."

Christopher Lee as Dracula confronts Peter Cushing as Van Helsing, both worthy adversaries, in *Dracula A. D. 1972*

And so is Van Helsing, played by Cushing not as a cliché but as a fully developed character, a recognizable human being.

"Can Dracula really be as old as it says here?" asks a skeptical Arthur Holmwood (Michael Gough), whose wife Mina (Melissa Stribling) is the Count's next target.

"We believe it's possible," Van Helsing asserts. "Vampires have been known to have gone on from century to century."

"Another thing... I've always understood that *if* there were such things," Holmwood continues, "I thought they could change themselves into bats or wolves."

"That's a common fallacy," says Van Helsing, grounding the picture in reality and saving Hammer hundreds of pounds in special effects.

Cushing's Van Helsing dominates the movie, a combination of sensitivity and sternness, one step ahead of Dracula's fleeting, shadowy appearances. Despite Dracula's awesome powers, we are not at all surprised when Van Helsing puts him away. In the picture's famous climax, Van Helsing uses both his mental and physical prowess; trapped in a beam of sunlight by Van Helsing's make-shift cross, Dracula whips and thrashes in a well-deserved destruction.

Van Helsing was back two years later in *The Brides of Dracula*, and not a second too soon. A Transylvanian village is being ravaged by Baron Meinster (David Peel), a

Peter Cushing played Van Helsing's grandson as an occult investigator, predating *The X-Files* by more than a decade.

vicious Dracula wannabe. An ineffectual priest (Fred Johnson) fails to comfort the father of a recently vampirized girl. "Poor man," he mutters. "And I am powerless, powerless..."

"Perhaps I can help," says a confident Van Helsing.

"Who are you?"

"You sent for me... Dr. Van Helsing."

"Oh!" gushes the priest. "Thank God you've come! Thank God!"

With God's help, plus some holy water, the cross-like vanes of a windmill, and plenty of guts, Van Helsing makes short work of the upstart Baron.

Peter Cushing got it a *bit* wrong in an interview with *Little Shoppe of Horrors,* a magazine devoted to analyzing Hammer's horror films: "Stoker had described [Van Helsing] as a *little* old Dutchman with a *bald head* and sporting a small beard. Therefore, all the production team got together and decided that it would be better to inject more vigor into the character. So I played the part more or less as myself."

This meant a civilized charm that could turn a bit chilly when called for, or a wild athleticism: a perfect—and necessary—match for Christopher Lee's energetic Dracula. Cushing's greatest strength in horror pictures (other than his impeccably 19th-century look and mannerisms) was his ability to make the most absurd line or situation believable.

Unlike past and future Van Helsings, Cushing's character was a lone wolf. Combining both intellectualization and physical prowess, his Van Helsing needed no one at all to help subdue the Count or his disciple Baron Meinster. This gave Cushing's interpretation an additional boost, even though it's at odds with Stoker's gang leader. Due to Hammer's focus on action, Cushing was as perfectly cast against Lee as Van Sloan was against Lugosi.

Van Helsing did not appear in Hammer's next four "period" Draculas, but made a comeback (of sorts) in *Dracula A.D. 1972* and *Satanic Rites of Dracula* (1973). As Lorrimer Van Helsing, a descendent of the original, Peter Cushing was unable to lift both films out of the ordinary (which is testimony to their mediocrity). In these latter day versions, Van Helsing has, due to Cushing's advancing years, joined forces with the police (Michael Coles) to considerably less result.

Cushing gave his final performance as Van Helsing in *Legend of the Seven Golden Vampires* (1974). This Dracula/Kung fu combo filmed in Hong Kong isn't as bad as it sounds (how could it be?), but is almost as far from Stoker's original as it's possible to get.

After leaving the Van Helsing role, Peter Cushing appeared in 20 movies, ranging from the excellent (*Star Wars*) to the execrable (*Tendre Dracula*, 1974). He died of cancer in August 1994, leaving a legacy of fine film performances and devoted fans, both outside and inside the film industry.

Although Edward Van Sloan and Peter Cushing are poles apart in acting styles, and the films in which they played Van Helsing couldn't be more different, they pretty much define the role. Each was perfectly matched with his Dracula—strong enough to stand up to the Count without usurping the vampires' power. Each in his own way set a standard that bigger "name" actors in mega-budget productions would fail to surpass.

Following in the considerable wake of Van Sloan and Cushing came Herbert Lom, Nigel Davenport, Sir Laurence Olivier, Frank Finlay, and Sir Anthony Hopkins. All five are fine actors; the least of them is probably Nigel Davenport, who is never less than well above average, and Olivier and Hopkins are both Academy Award winners. Despite their talents, none are associated with the role (which is probably just fine with them) in the same manner as Van Sloan or Cushing.

Herbert Lom, described in 1950 by *Film World* as "Villain Number One in British Pictures," is the only member of the quintet generally associated with horror movies. Oddly, due to his performance as the luckless Dreyfuss in Peter Sellers' *Pink Panther* series, he is equally associated with comedy.

Lom was born Herbert Charles Angelo Kuchacevichze Schluderpacheru in Prague, Czechoslovakia, in 1917. After appearing in several movies, he left for England due to the Nazi threat and joined the Westminster School of Acting. His distinctive voice soon landed him a job with the BBC, broadcasting anti-Nazi propaganda to occupied Europe. His British film debut was in 1940's *Mein Kampf*, based on Adolf Hitler's autobiography.

He worked steadily through the 1940s in both films and plays, and hit the big time as a villainous "promoter" in the film noir classic *Night and the City* (1950). Lom first caught the attention of fans of fantastic films by playing Captain Nemo (*Mysterious Island*, 1961) and *The Phantom of the Opera* (1962).

Lom brought his usual assets to the Van Helsing role in *Count Dracula* (1970) and delivered a fine performance, but he might have been wiser (as would Christopher Lee)

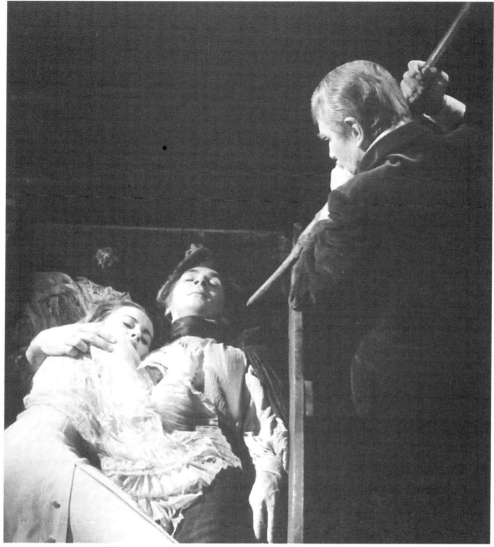

Sir Laurence Olivier's Van Helsing about to put the kibosh on the sexual revolution of the 1970s. *Dracula* **(1979)**

to have just skipped the whole thing. Praised while in production as being the most faithful version of the Stoker novel, the finished product was a crashing bore. Lee *does* get the chance to play Dracula as an old man in the opening scenes, complete with flowing white hair and mustache, but these details do not compensate for the muddled script, inappropriate music, and director Jess Franco's inability to shoot a scene without resorting to a zoom lens.

Lom and Klaus Kinski, as the most disturbing Renfield of all, more than pulled their weight, but most of the picture is just dead wood. Despite an attractive period look, it would take forever to catalogue the picture's faults; but one of its major assets is a small but interesting confrontation between Van Helsing and Dracula.

As the Professor sits, deep in thought, Dracula enters the quiet study. "You... ," says Van Helsing. "All my life I've studied the Black Arts... It's strange to finally confront the Prince of Darkness himself."

"You have learned much," the Count intones, "but you can do nothing." Van Helsing drives him from the room with a flaming cross burned into the floor.

Unfortunately, Van Helsing can do little more; he is soon confined to a wheelchair, the victim of a "slight stroke." As a result, he is unable to participate in Dracula's destruction. This in no way detracts from Herbert Lom's commanding presence—he is nearly the best Van Helsing, sadly trapped in the *worst* Dracula adaptation.

"I guess I'm cut out for strong man roles," said Nigel Davenport (*Courier Journal Times*, December 6, 1970). "I can't exactly see myself in an effeminate part. My appearance is against me, for a start."

This odd bit of self-assessment aside, Davenport made a competent, but hardly awe-inspiring, Van Helsing in Dan Curtis' 1973 *Dracula* for CBS-TV.

Born in Cambridge, England, in 1928, Davenport followed the usual step taken by British actors: a college education (Oxford!), local rep companies (1951), the London stage, then films. He made his movie debut in *Look Back in Anger* (1959), and had several brushes with the horror and fantasy genres in *Peeping Tom* (1960), *The Mind of Mr. Soames* (1970), *No Blade of Grass* (1970), *Phase IV* (1974), and *The Island of Dr. Moreau* (1977).

Author Richard Matheson, no stranger to the fantastic himself (he wrote such respected novels as *The Shrinking Man* and *I Am Legend*, as well as many of the Roger Corman–Edgar Allan Poe films in the 1960s), strayed a bit in his depiction of the Count (Jack Palance), creating a Byronic revenant seeking the reincarnation of his lost love... but perhaps Matheson was onto something. This device was later lifted for *Bram Stoker's Dracula* (1992).

Matheson introduces Van Helsing as a friend of Arthur Holmwood (Simon Ward), brought in to save his fiancée Lucy (Fiona Lewis) from Dracula.

Nigel Davenport is one of those countless British supporting players who's never bad but is equally less than memorable. He plays Van Helsing as friendly and reassuring toward Lucy but a bit dismissive toward Arthur. Oddly, Van Helsing is given no real credit for being an expert on vampires; he just seems to know more than the rest of the cast. "Your fiancée may be the unwilling victim of a vampire," he tells Arthur, as if there are many willing victims of vampires. "How can you, a man of science, believe such things?" Holmwood typically asks.

He and Holmwood, once Lucy is under Dracula's spell, are practically inseparable, which greatly reduces Van Helsing's effectiveness. Even worse, Van Helsing is curiously detached during his perfunctory staking of the vampire Lucy, spouting vampire lore as if he recently completed a course on the subject.

When the search for Dracula's hideout begins, the ineffectual Arthur has somehow taken charge as the pair become Victorian PI's, following a "paper trail" that leads to Carfax Abbey. While Arthur holds Dracula at bay with a crucifix, Van Helsing pulls the curtains, hitting the Count with deadly sunlight, then runs him through with a curtain rod.

While there's nothing specifically wrong with either Davenport's performance or "look," he is easily forgotten. Lacking the evangelistic spirit of Peter Cushing, Edward Van Sloan's grim determination, and Herbert Lom's intensity, there's little to distinguish Davenport from the rest of the cast. The movie itself is not unlike Davenport's performance and, despite many positives (including Jack Palance), Dan Curtis' *Dracula* is probably no one's favorite version.

Oddly, President Nixon pulled a "Van Helsing" himself, bumping *Dracula* into a temporary oblivion. CBS canceled the picture's planned early 1972 airing due to a Presidential address. Showing more class than one is used to in the world of television, network head Fred Silverman did not broadcast *Dracula* until 1973, so as not to upstage NBC's November 1972 *Frankenstein: The True Story*.

Frank Finlay was the third Van Helsing to be nominated for an Oscar; unfortunately, unlike Sir Laurence Olivier and Sir Anthony Hopkins, his performance as Iago in *Othello* (1965) came up short.

Finlay was born in 1927 in Lancashire, England. After the usual desultory jobs (butcher, factory worker), he caught the proverbial acting bug and joined the Halifax Rep in 1951. His talent was eventually recognized, and he was given a two-year scholarship to the Royal Academy of the Dramatic Arts. Finlay's career began in earnest when he joined the Guilford Rep, and his first big success was in *Chips With Everything* at the Vaudeville in London (1962). Before long, he was appearing with Maggie Smith, Lynn Redgrave, Ian McKellan, and Robert Stephens at the National Theatre under Sir Laurence Olivier's direction.

"I've been in about 30 films," Finlay said (*The New York Daily News*, February 14, 1986), "but I'm basically a theater and television actor." He played small parts in *The Loneliness of the Long Distance Runner* and *Life for Ruth* (both 1962), then landed a major supporting role as Inspector Lestrade in 1965's horrific *A Study in Terror* in which Sherlock Holmes (John Neville) battled Jack the Ripper. Oddly, he played the same part in 1979's *Murder by Decree* starring Christopher Plummer's Sherlock Holmes, which told a similar but more "realistic" story. Perhaps Finlay's best film performances were as a vindictive policeman out to get Sean Connery in *The Molly Maguires* (1970) and as Porthos in *The Three Musketeers* (1974).

In 1968, the BBC televised its first version of *Dracula*, starring Denholm Elliot and Bernard Archard. It has either been destroyed or rots away in its vaults. A second version, *Count Dracula*, was aired in 1978, with Louis Jourdan, creepy and oily as Dracula.

As Van Helsing to Jourdan's Dracula, Frank Finlay was physically impressive with his shock of white hair and a commanding, no nonsense attitude: "I do not joke... there is purpose in all that I do." He deftly pulls off the Professor's accented speech patterns, making a nice compromise between accuracy to the novel and alienating the viewer.

Van Helsing is not opposed to getting down to the necessary dirty work: "Am I, friend Quincey [Richard Barnes], to proceed?" as he demonstrates his staking technique... then stuffs the vampire Lucy's mouth with garlic before calmly beheading her. He also demonstrates his knowledge of the occult by drawing the sacred circle around himself and Mina (Judi Bowker), proves his courage while presiding over a shoot-out between the Brits and Slavs at Castle Dracula, and delivers as professional a staking of the Count as one could wish.

Count Dracula is a mixed bag. Jourdan turns in an impeccably low key performance; unmoved by Van Helsing's cross, he sneers that he cannot be *truly* harmed by "an instrument of torture and humiliation." The rest of the cast is uniformly fine (Jack Shepherd is especially impressive as Renfield), the Whitby scenes were shot on location, and the sets and costumes beautifully suggest the period.

The teleplay takes the unexpected liberties (Mina and Lucy are "sisters"; Lucy is presented as a semi-libertine, that sort of thing), but the picture easily survives them. It self-destructs, however, with unnecessary and poorly conceived video "tricks" like close-ups of Jourdan's eyes in negative, which seem like out-takes from kitsch like *Count Yorga, Vampire*.

Surely, the most prestigious "name" actor to play Van Helsing was Sir Laurence Olivier. One of the few actors to be generally considered the greatest of all time, much of his well-deserved reputation was based on his stage performances, notably in Shakespearean roles.

He wasn't too bad in movies, either.

Olivier was born on May 22, 1907, in Dorking, England, the son of a minister. His stage debut came at age 15, playing a girl in *The Taming of the Shrew* at Stratford-on-Avon. After attending Oxford, Olivier joined the Birmingham Repertory (1926) and, three years later, made his Broadway debut.

His classically good looks and outstanding voice made him a natural for the movies, and he returned to England in 1930 to appear in *The Temporary Widow*. Greta Garbo turned Olivier down as her co-star in *Queen Christina* (1933); most of his 1930s films are either undistinguished or forgotten.

Olivier's career caught fire with *Wuthering Heights* (1939), and he never looked back. He married Vivien Leigh in 1940, joined the Air Fleet in 1941, and was released from World War II service to run, with Ralph Richardson, the Old Vic Theatre. He directed himself in *Henry V* (1944), and again in *Hamlet* (1947), for which he won the Academy Award for Best Actor in the Best Picture of 1948. *Hamlet* featured future movie Van Helsing, Peter Cushing, in a supporting role, and he and Olivier soon left with the Old Vic for a tour of Australia.

Olivier's success in *Hamlet* placed him at the top of his profession and, during the 1950s and 1960s, he chose his film roles carefully, appearing in *Richard III* (1955) and *Spartacus* (1960), making fewer than 20 pictures.

By the 1970s, Olivier's film career had changed. Instead of *Hamlet* and *Othello*, Lord Larry was now associated with big budget thrillers: *Sleuth* (1972), *Marathon Man* (1974), *The Seven Percent Solution* (1976), and *The Boys from Brazil* (1978). He would be Oscar nominated for all of these appearances, except for his turn as Prof. Moriarty in *Solution*.

By 1979, he was ready to go slumming in *Dracula*.

Following the path Bela Lugosi blazed nearly 50 years earlier, Frank Langella followed his stage success as Dracula with this movie version, an entertaining amalgam of the novel, the Hamilton Deane–John Balderston play, Hammer Horror, and every junior high school girl's sex fantasy.

The picture opens in Edwardian England, with Dracula's ship sinking at Whitby. The vampire quickly insinuates himself into the lives of asylum director Dr. Seward (Donald Pleasence), his daughter Lucy (Kate Nelligan), her fiancé Jonathan Harker (Trevor Eve), and Lucy's friend Mina Van Helsing (Jan Francis), daughter of you-know-who.

Mina is the first to fall under the Count's low-key, dreamy-eyed power. After her death from you-know-what, her father (Olivier, dapper, distracted by grief, and accented) arrives, with little previous knowledge or interest in the undead. He chats with Lucy at Mina's grave: "You know the legends of Central Europe of the werewolf and vampire... creatures who suck the blood of the living..."

Olivier's screen presence lent power and conviction to his portrayal of Van Helsing.

Just then, the Count rides up and exchanges a knowing glance with the Professor over the crucifix he's just given to Lucy. Van Helsing learns fast and, after tracking the reanimated Mina to her underground lair, accidentally—but effectively—puts her away with a stake, allowing Olivier to cut loose as Van Helsing is consumed by grief.

He's now in charge ("There is a grim purpose in all I do"), and it's just as well; Trevor Eve as Harker makes David Manners, the *original* ineffectual Harker, look like James Bond. Van Helsing proves again he's a fast learner when he confronts Dracula with a handful of garlic and barely survives a battle of wills.

With Lucy now under the Count's sensual spell, Harker springs into action, donning a driving cap (this *is* the Edwardian period) for the climactic car chase.

Dracula abducts Lucy to Scarborough port, to take her back to Transylvania, with Van Helsing, Harker, and Seward in pursuit. Leaving Seward on the dock, the pair board the ship and, after the *Professor* is staked by Dracula, Harker is forced to show some backbone. With his dying effort, Van Helsing sinks a hook into the Count, sending him up to the sails and the sunlight.

Perhaps any disappointment viewers may find with Olivier stems from the role as conceived by W. D. Richter's script. This Van Helsing is not the scientific avenger of Stoker or Cushing's able soldier of Christ, but an elderly man in deep mourning, thrust into action by outrage and a desire for revenge. Easily the most gifted and brilliant actor to essay the role, Olivier aptly makes the most of what he's handed... but one wishes he were handed more.

"I was so very lonely as a child," he told *Newsday* (March 10, 1976), "I used to play by myself at one end of the street while all the other kids were up at the other end. I had no confidence and felt I was doomed to be a miserable failure."

Olivier died in 1989, his legacy intact.

Sir Anthony Hopkins, one of the world's most successful actors, was born in Port Talbot, Wales, in 1937. Diagnosed as dyslexic, he was sent to a boarding school where, during a term break in 1955, he chanced upon a YMCA acting troupe and landed a small role in an Easter play.

Hopkins' career choice became more certain when he went to the sister's home of fellow Welshman Richard Burton to get the star's autograph. As Hopkins stood nervously on the doorstep, Burton magically appeared at the curb in his Jaguar.

The young man's path was clear.

By the mid 1960s, courtesy of the Cardiff College of Music and Drama, the Royal Academy of Dramatic Arts, and Sir Laurence Olivier's influence at the National Theatre, Hopkins was being called "the next Richard Burton."

After playing a Burton-like Richard the Lionheart in 1968's *The Lion in Winter*, Claudius in Nicol Williamson's *Hamlet* (1969), and Lloyd George in *Young Winston* (1971), Hopkins' film career was set. He played his first horror film role as a batty ventriloquist in the equally batty *Magic* (1978) as a warm-up for the screen's most dangerous psycho, Hannibal "the Cannibal" Lechter in *The Silence of the Lambs* (1991), for which he received a well-deserved Oscar.

Hopkins was the trendy choice to play Van Helsing in Francis Ford Coppola's movie of *Bram Stoker's Dracula* (1994). But Hopkins, like the picture itself, was a bit *too* impressive.

"I've taken the liberty," says Dr. Seward (Richard E. Grant) to Lucy's army of suitors, "of cabling Abraham Van Helsing, the metaphysician-philosopher. Van Helsing knows more about obscure diseases than any man in the world."

We meet the metaphysician-philosopher as he lectures a class on diseases of the blood... specifically, venereal disease. "The very name venereal disease," he smirks,

Hopkins made Van Helsing dark and dangerous... and more menacing than the lovelorn Count! *Bram Stoker's Dracula* **(1992)**

"the diseases of Venus, imputes to them divine origin. They are involved in that sex problem about which the ethics and ideals of Christian civilization are concerned."

Dr. Seward's telegram hurtles Van Helsing to England a bit too late (as usual) to help poor Lucy. "Where did the blood go?" he asks.

"Something just went up there," sneers Seward, "sucked it out of her, and flew away, I suppose?"

"Ya... why not?" Van Helsing counters. "Do you not think that there are things in this universe which you cannot understand and which are true? Those marks on your dear Lucy's neck were made by something unspeakable... dead but not dead... it stalks us for some dread purpose I do not yet comprehend."

Naturally, Van Helsing soon comprehends it all and ably marshals his troops against Dracula, who appears in several guises, including one in which, in blue-tinted glasses, he vaguely resembles John Lennon.

Van Helsing is a volatile sort, spontaneously dancing with Mina seconds after they meet, manhandling a demonic Lucy, laughing wildly in a driving wind. "Guard her well," he tells Quincey Morris (Bill Campbell). "Do not fail here tonight. We are dealing with forces beyond all human experience. Otherwise your precious Lucy will become a bitch of the devil!"

Sir Anthony Hopkins, although he gives an acceptable performance, is the least attractive of all Van Helsings, since he plays the part pretty much as Stoker wrote it: more than a bit rough around the edges. At Lucy's wake, Van Helsing quietly says to the grieving Seward, "I know how deeply you loved her... that's why you must trust me and believe. I want you to bring me before night fall a set of postmortem knives."

Lucy (Sadie Frost) recoils from Anthony Hopkins' performance in *Bram Stoker's Dracula* (1992).

"An autopsy... for Lucy?" stammers Seward.

"No, no, no... not exactly. I want to cut off her head and take out her heart."

"You're a sick old buzzard," opines Quincey.

An understatement, that.

Hopkins has been criticized for being a bit over the top... and he certainly is. But so is the whole movie, and Gary Oldman's portrayal of Dracula is one of the screen's most remarkable. Hopkins' sweaty performance may be extreme, but, as we've seen, Stoker's original Van Helsing was a piece of work himself.

The inevitable question remains: Who's the best Van Helsing? It's a tough call and, of course, a matter of opinion. That understood, let me say that, if my family and friends were being savaged by Dracula, I'd call Peter Cushing... a Van Helsing with unmatched mental and physical skills, charm, sophistication, and a snappy wardrobe.

If Cushing isn't an exact copy of Stoker's model, so be it; do you *really* want Sir Anthony Hopkins cutting out your sister's heart?

Dracula's Ring

One of the most famous pieces of Dracula folklore—the hypnotic power of his signet ring—came not from Bram Stoker's novel, but from the pen of Universal Studios script writers.

Though Bela Lugosi wore a distinctive ring in the 1931 movie *Dracula* (if you look closely you can see it in his other films of the early 1930s, including *Murders in the Rue Morgue* and *Broad Minded*), the famous Dracula crest was not created until 1943's *Son of Dracula*. Later John Carradine took the ring from Lon Chaney's chubby finger for his stay in the *House of Frankenstein* (1944), where he used it to hypnotize actress Anne Gwynne. Screen hero Peter Coe instantly recognizes the "Dracula crest" on her finger, creating another "authentic" bit of Dracula lore. When Gwynne is free from the Vampire

One of Bela Lugosi's original Dracula rings, now part of the Cortlandt Hull collection.

King's spell, the ring falls to the ground, somehow eluding the searches of the best souvenir hunters.

Carradine sported the Dracula crest on his finger (and coffin lid) for 1945's *House of Dracula*. It was only in 1948 that Bela Lugosi assumed the vampire's ring during his final screen appearance as Dracula, *Abbott and Costello Meet Frankenstein*. According to legend, Lugosi was supposed to return the ring to Universal's prop department but didn't—and they were too afraid to ask for it back!

Lugosi commissioned eight reproductions of the ring, passing them along to close friends. Now highly prized collectibles, these rings are among the rarest of Lugosi relics.

The legend of the Dracula ring continued. In the record album *Famous Monsters Speak*, Gabriel Dell's Count Dracula (speaking in Lugosian tones) first hypnotizes his victims with his ring. Starting with 1968's *Dracula Has Risen From the Grave*, actor Christopher Lee sported one of Lugosi's own copies of the ring in a welcome note of continuity. And in 1971's abysmal *Dracula vs. Frankenstein*, Dracula's ring also functions as some kind of ray gun, an utterly ridiculous embellishment.

Today a spate of reproductions are available on the market, from the cheesy to the top drawer. The fan magazine *Famous Monsters of Filmland* now offers what must be the worst reproduction on the market, while there are some truly beautiful replicas available at "monster conventions" nationwide starting at about $250.

—Bob Madison

It was Dracula that adolescent Hope Lininger fell in love with, and not actor Bela Lugosi. Sitting there, in the darkness of a Depression-era movie house, the black-and-white image of the undead Vampire King stepped out of the shadows and stole something more vital, more elemental than her blood.

He took her heart.

Hope spent more than 20 years obsessively hunting her vampiric ideal, a classic case of Hollywood Gothic brought vividly to life. And when she had finally lured the undead Count to her lair, it was no longer the powerful, commanding figure she had seen on screen, but the older, despairing actor who portrayed him, Bela Lugosi.

Hope's story is a perfect example of the vampire's hold on the individual imagination. To her, Dracula epitomized seducer, lover, friend, and father. A veritable "Dracula's curse" has dogged such diverse figures as Florence Stoker, Bela Lugosi, Helen Chandler, and Christopher Lee; a list that must also include Hope Lininger Lugosi's name.

Unfortunately, Hope Lugosi died during the preparation of this volume. But here film historian Gregory William Mank shares her memories with Dracula buffs. Mank is simply one of the most profound scholars of fantastic film alive today. His book on the classic series of Frankenstein films made by Universal Pictures in the 1930s and 1940s, It's Alive, *remains the final word on the subject. He is also the author of* Karloff and Lugosi, *which chronicles the careers and lives of America's two most famous bogeymen. Here is an intimate look at the woman whose life was shaped by Dracula, the Vampire King's final bride...*

—Bob Madison

Dracula's Last Bride
by Gregory William Mank

Dracula's hypnotic spell is legendary.

I did not know the full extent of his influence until July 1993, when my friend Charles Heard called me with a surprise. Just the evening before, he'd talked on the telephone with Hope Lugosi—Bela Lugosi's fifth, final, and most notorious wife.

"Would you like to call her?" asked Charles.

I wasn't sure. After all, I'd accepted (and, in my book *Karloff and Lugosi*, reported) the Hope Lugosi legend that had become part of Bela's ever-growing folklore: Hope, the crazy, blonde fan-vamp, who adored Lugosi since seeing *Dracula* when she was 12 years old... the self-proclaimed witch, who dreamed and schemed obsessively for 25 years to become Mrs. Bela Lugosi... the last Bride of Dracula.

She was the young, macabre *femme fatale* who sank her fangs into a lonely, forlorn, 72-year-old Bela as he left Metropolitan State Hospital after purging his drug addiction, marrying him only two weeks later; the bride-harpy who sadistically added to the woes and torments of Bela's final year; the widow who had vowed to "forget all about having been Mrs. Bela Lugosi," supposedly giving away "all" her memorabilia, avoiding all interviews, and keeping a bitter exile.

Years after Bela's death, she was still Mrs. Bela Lugosi, having fled the West Coast many years before to go to Hawaii—and work at the leper hospital on Molokai.

Frankly, her reputation scared me. I remembered my 1988 interview with Chuck Moses, former associate of Howard W. Koch, producer of Lugosi's final professional film, *The Black Sleep*. In June of 1956, Chuck had gone to San Francisco to supervise *The Black Sleep*'s personal appearance tour with cast-members Lon Chaney, John Carradine, Tor Johnson, and Lugosi. (Vampira, not in the picture, joined the tour later on.) As we began talking, Chuck asked me if Mrs. Lugosi was still alive. When I replied she was, he forbade me to print the punchline of his anecdote, fearing the redoubtable widow might sue me *and* him.

Chuck Moses had arrived at San Francisco's St. Francis Hotel, where the actors had stayed the previous night. There he found not only a drunken Carradine, but an "extremely nervous" Tor Johnson, who met Chuck in the lobby. The giant actor-wrestler was terrified by the severity of the drinking by his hotel roommate Bela, who, as Johnson told Chuck, "was running around the walls" of the hotel room. The aged actor was cured of his drug addiction, but tragically still addicted to alcohol.

Tor Johnson confided to Chuck that he had put in an emergency call to Hope in Hollywood, Tor asking what he should do if an intoxicated Bela once again began careening around the room, literally running into the walls high in the St. Francis Hotel. Hope's response shocked Tor—and still gave Chuck Moses chills over 30 years later:

"Open the window."

Two months later, Bela Lugosi was dead—not in a fall from a window, but from a heart attack. He had died peacefully in bed at his Hollywood apartment, and was buried at Holy Cross Cemetery—in his Dracula cape.

His legend would grow. And so would the legend of Hope Lugosi—as the virtual lady vampire who had lured, agonized, and buried Hollywood's Dracula.

Did I really want to talk to this woman?

Well... yes.

I made the call.

I was never in the first-floor, front apartment at 5620 Harold Way in Hollywood, where Mr. and Mrs. Bela Lugosi spent their single year of marriage. And I can't fairly say what happened behind the closed doors, or who victimized whom.

But I can say this: Hope Lugosi was great to me.

By the time I'd completed two long, candid, sometimes hilarious and sometimes horrifying telephone interviews with her, we were friends. We stayed friends. Over the last three years, every holiday saw cards from Hope—the envelopes elaborately decorated with stickers, the cards invariably containing delightful letters with maverick opinions on everything and everybody.

She had a salty, incredibly caustic sense of humor. But also, beneath the cynicism and the bombast, behind the Don Rickles–style timing and delivery, she had a kindness and sensitivity. She was deeply appreciative to have friends late in her life.

Bela Lugosi's Dracula stole young Hope Lininger's heart. The man proved to be different than the myth.

And, despite all the melodrama of her final marriage, she was proud to have been Mrs. Bela Lugosi, the final bride of Dracula.

Hope Lininger was born in Johnstown, Pennsylvania, March 23, 1919. When she married the 72-year-old Lugosi in 1955, she was 36; she told the papers she was 39, feeling it was less embarrassing to her bridegroom to marry a woman not exactly half his age.

Her passion for Dracula was a natural extension of her upbringing. She grew up with a fascination for the fantastic and the macabre, amidst the "Hex" signs of the

Helen Chandler stands-in for Hope Lininger, forever enthralled by the vampire's spell.

Pennsylvania countryside. Hope adored bats and black cats, and would enjoy (for many years) telling people she was a witch. Naturally, she loved Halloween, her favorite holiday. Her All Hallow's Eve cards were always a treat, and she told me:

> I do recall wonderful Halloween parties at home. My mother's birthday was October 29 and she always cooked up a party. We'd all sit in the dark and shiver as she told marvelous scary tales and passed around peeled grapes as the victim's eyeballs... Once, in my black cat suit, I had water poured on me by a farmer and, worse, caught my tail in the fence and thereby lost the most essential part of my costume. Good fun!

At age 12, she saw the movie *Dracula*. True to her legend, she was a passionate Lugosi fan from then on, dreaming of one day marrying him. She first saw Bela "in the flesh" in New York—probably in Ed Sullivan's *Stardust Cavalcade* stage show, which played Broadway's Loew's State Theatre in April 1940. Lugosi, resplendent in his formal Dracula attire, continued to fascinate her.

"Oh, I was thrilled!" Hope told me. "I went three times. I went without dinner so I could afford to go."

Hope came to Hollywood to be nearer the demon lover of her fantasies. In 1942, she began working for RKO Studios as a continuity writer (i.e., preparing a complete script of each film, with music cued, lengths of scenes measured, etc., to be filed with each film's negative). In Hollywood, she met the still-dashing, cigar-smoking Bela two more times: at the Music Box Theatre on Hollywood Boulevard, after a performance of *Arsenic and Old Lace* in late summer, 1943; and at RKO, during the shooting of *The Body Snatcher*, in the fall of 1944.

"He and Karloff were there," said Hope, "and I could go on the set."

While Hope followed Bela's life and career, she didn't "save herself" for her idol. In fact, contrary to the legend, she actually married twice before her union with Lugosi. She never discussed husband number one with me, but listening to Hope remembering husband number two was an experience:

> That second one, Jose, was the best man in the world. Just won-derful. He had that old world charm—South American, Colombian. How did I know he had a wife curled away somewhere in Cuba? I knew it was illegal for us to marry, but I didn't care. But he made a bad mistake—he gave me up for Lent. Nobody gives me up for Lent! *Nobody!* I handed him his guitar, and said good-bye.

> So he went out and drowned himself! I know he didn't do it on purpose, because he was a devout Catholic, and the horror of his life was to die without a priest. Well, no priest went down with him to the bottom of Clear Lake, I'm quite sure of it!

Living and working in Hollywood, Hope had observed many famous stars and personalities. Of course, she had her opinions of them:

> *Marilyn Monroe*: She lived for a while in the orphanage right below where I lived. She was put there because nobody could stand her! Her mother went to the loony bin, and her aunt had worked with us at RKO as a negative cutter. The aunt had it with her! Everybody called Mon-roe Norma Jean, and she was so damned jealous! She just couldn't stand anyone who might be better-looking than she was! Ech! She had something that titillated audiences—that "come hither" look. It certainly wasn't brains!

> *Cary Grant:* One day I was wearing a pale blue skirt and a pink angora sweater, and I thought I looked pretty hot! Grant came by and said, "You look just like an ice cream cone." I don't care what they say

about him... he was as straight as an arrow. The boys in the cutting room would have told me if he weren't. They knew who was who in the zoo!

Vincent Price: I went to Vincent Price's home—not with Lugosi, but with my second husband, Jose... I was staring at one of the paintings—he painted, Price—and I stared at it, and I thought, "What the hell is that?" And Price said, "Well, turn it upside down, maybe it will look better." So I turned it around and I didn't see any difference—it looked horrible one way or the other!

Also, at RKO, Hope came to know producer Val Lewton, whose horror unit created such melodramas as *Cat People*, *I Walked With a Zombie*, *The Seventh Victim*, *The Curse of the Cat People*, and the Karloff and Lugosi *The Body Snatcher*:

The funniest part was Lewton and Robert Wise and the men who did the horror films—they were funny. By God, they had everybody laughing—everything was hysterically funny! The men who did the comedies—they walked around like mortuary attendants. Couldn't get a smile out of them. It was really weird!

I scared the hell out of the horror crowd one night. They were up in the projection room, and I was horsing around down in editorial, and we'd been invited to a party. Well, we had privileges of borrowing whatever dress we wanted from the wardrobe department. Midriffs were all the rage, and I had one all lined up. That was fine, except that I'd broken a rib, and I'd had it taped ...

So I went to head of shipping for film, and I said, "Charlie, I've got to get rid of this thing, it's not going to look very nice with my two-piece dress." "Oh sure," said Charlie, "just hang onto the desk and I'll give a good pull." Well, he pulled all right—not only the tape came off, but half of my hide! All around the middle! That was the end of the party, the dress, and everything else, and I let out a *scream* that lifted Lewton and those men up above in the projection room right out of their seats!

Of course, Hope's most fascinating stories concerned her one-year marriage to Bela Lugosi.

"My body grew hot, then cold. I tried to eat the bed sheets, my pajamas," said Bela—describing the horrors of recovery from drug addiction. In April of 1955, Bela, divorced from his fourth wife, Lillian, out of money, suffering the terrors of his addiction, committed himself to Metropolitan State Hospital in Norwalk, California. Documentation of this event is heartbreaking. The pictures of a 125 pound Bela, so sadly desperate for attention that he posed for the press in hospital sackcloth, showing the needle marks on his skeletal legs, is Hollywood Gothic at its most chilling.

Dracula fetishist Hope claims the ultimate trophy as her own as she marries aged actor Bela Lugosi.

Hope now made her move. She wrote to him constantly, offering encouragement ("There was a method to my madness!" she admitted). Bela was released August 5, 1955; at Bela's invitation, she went to visit him.

"I had to get him, now or never!" she told me.

Bela and Hope were married the night of Wednesday, August 24, 1955. The nuptials took place at the home of Dr. Manly P. Hall, like Stoker's Van Helsing, a metaphysician, writer, and lecturer, who had supposedly hypnotized Bela as a publicity stunt on Universal's 1940 Karloff/Lugosi opus, *Black Friday*. Bela Lugosi, Jr., then 17 years old, was best man.

In 1993, Hope had no romantic illusions about the wedding—nor about Bela's last-minute reluctance to marry her.

> I had a friend, Pat Delaney, my matron of honor, a big, tough Irish woman. She was ugly as a mud fence—but boy, she could keep Lugosi in line! Yes, indeed. She came to pick him up for the wedding. By this time he'd been drinking, and was having a few misgivings. Pat said, "No you're not—*get dressed!*"
>
> She got him dressed (to her husband's horror); she then hustled Lugosi up to Manly Hall's house, and said, "He's not going to stand up a friend of mine, with all this publicity and all! No, no!" So we got married. We had a glass of champagne, he probably had a bottleful, I don't remember...

So began Bela Lugosi's fifth marriage, and Hope Lininger's third. The chauffeur for their honeymoon to Big Bear Lake was Ed Wood himself—who already had directed Bela in the infamous *Glen or Glenda?* (1953) and *Bride of the Monster* (1955). (*Plan 9 from Outer Space* was looming in both men's futures.) The newlyweds were the first tenants of the brand new apartment house at 5620 Harold Way, in the heart of Hollywood. Hope kept working at RKO; Bela entertained thoughts of a comeback and the demons that haunted him during his last year.

Some people have claimed that one of the chief demons was Hope. She, in turn, had to cope with Bela's severe jealousy:

> He was jealous like hell because I was at the studio all day... I never dared take a ride home with any of the men who were going my way, because if he ever found out, he'd raise holy hell...Very jealous man. I don't know why—I wasn't *that* gorgeous!

Bela's heavy drinking, too, was a terrible problem. Yet Hope kept many happy memories. For example, she warmly remembered the night that Bela, she, and Richard Sheffield (Bela's loyal young fan, and ringleader of a group of teen-aged boys Hope affectionately called "the fan club"), visited Bela's former houses: the red-brick castle at 2835 Westshire Drive, high on a cliff below the HOLLYWOODLAND sign; the colonial mansion at 2227 Outpost Drive, in the Hollywood Hills; and Bela's "Dracula House" at 10841 Whipple Street in North Hollywood—complete with steeple, pond, and banana trees. Bela had shared all these homes with his former wife Lillian, but Hope went along on the pilgrimage with no rancor:

> That was a most enjoyable evening! The house in North Hollywood was very interesting—it had all his original furniture in it. Big heavy piano, big heavy staircase. And one of the houses in the Hollywood Hills had a fireplace—you could burn up six bodies in there at once—that fascinated me! They had his dining room set there; evidently he sold it with the furniture, because the furniture had been custom-made.

Here Lugosi dispels the rumor that he "never drinks wine." Lugosi marries Hope Lininger on August 24, 1955.

Oh, the people were delighted to see us! Even in the pitch dark. "Sure! Come on in!" Lugosi didn't have to say much—everybody looked at him and they *knew* who he was! Sure! Then he announced he'd lived there. He was very, very affable that evening. We had a good time!

Then there were nights at the Little Gypsy Restaurant, out on the Sunset Strip. ("Now they're Girlie houses," lamented Hope of the "lovely" restaurants and clubs that used to be on the Strip. "You wouldn't believe how nice it was.")

We had a good time going to the Little Gypsy Restaurant, because they had real Hungarian Gypsies playing. And that was fun! I liked that—up to a point. You know how Hungarian music is. It starts out, "Oh, Whoop-dee-Doo," and then it gets sadder and sadder and *sadder*—and everybody's finally crying.

Would Bela cry? Oh, my God! Does a cat have whiskers? *Certainly*! Especially while everyone was drinking all the time... Once, Bela decided he was going to buy wine for the whole orchestra. And since *I* bought, I thought, "God—I'm buying for everyone, I'll buy one for me!" I took my bottle home with me, a Hungarian wine called "The Blood of the Bull," and polished it off there, where I could fall over, you know. The next morning, I felt just marvelous—trouble was, I couldn't move! Lugosi said, "Wouldn't you like to fix breakfast?" I said, "Fix it yourself!" And I think he understood!

Of course, Hope came to know Bela's friends and co-workers—such as Ed Wood:

I remember Eddie and his wife having a big fight one time, and she threw hot coffee in his face! As for Eddie being a transvestite... well, he stole one of my nightgowns once! Maybe Bela gave it to him, or maybe I had it drying it in the bathroom or something (Ed would never go through the drawers)—but it vanished! I never got it back. After Eddie had it, I didn't *want* it back! But I guarantee you—Ed was always a perfect gentleman around me.

And there was bald, giant Tor Johnson:

Tor Johnson would bring his wife over... I trembled when he sat on my velvet chairs, because he was so damn big! So I made him sit on something else, rather than have him break the legs on the chair!

Then there were the trips to the movies—Bela, Hope, Sheffield, and "the fan club"—including an eventful return visit to see Universal's 1934 "KARLOFF and Bela LUGOSI" classic, *The Black Cat*:

Oh, Lugosi liked to go to the movies—especially his own pictures. Once we went to a downtown theatre (L.A. was safe in those days) to see *The Black Cat*. Oh yeah, he loved *The Black Cat*! I think that was his favorite film—he was very good-looking in it. Very. Well, right in the middle, while we're looking at *The Black Cat* all over again, Lugosi screams out, so everybody can turn around and see who he is—"OH, WHAT A HANDSOME BASTARD I WAS!"

Yeah, he just loved it! I'd rarely go to the movies with him anymore—I made the boys take him. It was embarrassing!

In February 1956, Bela made a new movie: *The Black Sleep*. It starred Basil Rathbone as a mad doctor, Lon Chaney as a bestial goon, John Carradine as a madman in a long

"A _terrible_ thing!" Hope Lugosi remembers _The Black Sleep_ (1956).

gray beard ("Kill the infidels!")—and Bela as a mute servant. (The late Reginald LeBorg, director of _The Black Sleep_, remembered that Bela pleaded for dialogue, even though his role was written as mute.) Hope visited the set—and was hardly impressed:

> _The Black Sleep_—yeah, that farce. A _terrible_ thing! I went over on the set once, and that was enough. I mean, a scruffy little studio, one of those fly-by-night things. Lon Chaney—I wonder if he was sober enough to stand up! He had _big_ problems. And Carradine (an ugly-looking mutt)... They all drank like thirsty fish.

> I don't think Lugosi really cared about having a non-speaking part. I really don't—he got a thousand dollars for it.

Hope came to know Bela's passionate dislikes, such as cats ("He _hated_ cats!"), Boris Karloff ("He _loathed_ Karloff!"), and the Gabor sisters ("He said they were three tramps!"). But she also saw his Old World charm, his kindness to autograph seekers, his courtesy to her friends:

> With the women, he was very "gal-lant." My girlfriends just adored him, because—oh, God! They got their hands kissed—he was all

sweetness and light. When he wasn't drinking, he was very nice. And when he was with my friends, he was always nice, drunk or sober. Always.

"I don't think I ever saw Lugosi when he wasn't acting," said Hope. "I think it was just ingrained in him. And all actors play the same role. They're the world's greatest." There were other serious, traumatic complexities in the marriage. (For Hope's complete perspective, watch for *Lugosi's Last Days*, a forthcoming definitive book by Bela's friend Richard Sheffield and Lugosi scholar *extraordinaire* Gary Don Rhodes.)

Summer 1956. The first anniversary neared. There was the disastrous *The Black Sleep* personal appearance tour. Hope, Bela, and Richard Sheffield attended their last movie together—*Moby Dick*, at the Hollywood Pantages. ("Lugosi hated it," said Hope. "I think he resented seeing youthful Gregory Peck. I really do."). Ed Wood was shooting parts of what he would unleash upon the world in 1959 as *Plan 9 from Outer Space*, with some of Lugosi's footage (as the mute "Ghoul Man") reportedly filmed only days before his death. And, shortly before his death, Lugosi awoke in the middle of the night (after a bout of heavy drinking) and announced to Hope that Karloff was waiting for him in the next room.

He was profoundly frightened of death. And, as Hope learned much later, Lugosi had a secret: He was planing to divorce Hope, and sign a new will (cutting her from his inheritance) on Friday, August 17, 1956.

"Fate intervened, as it always does for me," said Hope; Bela Lugosi died the evening of August 16, 1956.

It was Thursday night—I got paid on Thursdays—and I got home, with all the damn yogurt and canned papaya (God, he loved canned papaya!). I was putting everything away, and I was debating with myself (I knew he was in the bedroom)—should I put the fish on or not?

Well, I went in the bedroom. He was stretched out on the bed, and he looked funny. I thought, "I wonder if he's dead?" and I patted him all over—he seemed to be all nice and toasty warm. He must have just died. Death never bothers me. I've had so many people around me die that it didn't bother me, but I wanted to make damn sure before I called somebody. If I got people in there, and he wasn't really dead—just drunk—he'd be mad as a hornet!

So I asked the woman next door. "No, God, no!"—she didn't want to look at anything that might be dead. So I went up and got the landlord—he didn't mind looking at the dead things. So he came down and said, "Yeah, I think so."

Bela Lugosi had died around 6:45 p.m. of a coronary occlusion. He was 73 years old. Hope found the Count Dracula of her fantasies on the bed, in his underwear, and hardly in a state befitting an icon. For all her irreverence about her famous husband, Hope was very sensitive about how Bela Lugosi would be seen by the authorities:

Aged actor Bela Lugosi was relegated to the sidelines for 1956's *The Black Sleep*. Here, Akim Tamiroff gets the juicy dialogue.

> I said to the landlord, "Well, let's put the liquor bottles away, shall we, before we call the police or anybody."

Hope met with the detectives, the morticians, and the coroner's staff before going to spend the night at a girlfriend's, to escape the press. She totally refuted the legend that Lugosi died while reading Ed Wood's script *The Final Curtain*. ("Oh, that's a lot of feathers!... The only thing he had anywhere near him was a bottle.")

The Strother Chapel of the old Utter-McKinley Mortuary, 6240 Hollywood Boulevard, hosted the funeral rites. (The building later became a theater, and just recently was torn down to accommodate the subway.) The mortician was a crony of Bela's, and Hope had expected special treatment. "Yeah, sure!" she sarcastically recalled. Her friend Phyllis had to loan her the money for the coffin.

> Lugosi and I'd had dinner a couple times with his friend at the mortuary. I wasn't too thrilled eating a meal with a couple of stiffs stretched out on the floor below. As things turned out, I wished that mortician had been one of them.

The funeral—"a very weird funeral," in Hope's words—took place Saturday afternoon, August 18, 1956. Hope had vivid memories of the problems getting a priest for

Dracula's final bride—Hope Lininger Lugosi.

the Catholic rites ("For a time, no priest would come! Lugosi had been married five times! *Please*!"); the Hungarian violinist; the mourning Tor Johnson ("He blubbered like it was going out of style"); and the pictures taken of the body, adorned in Dracula cape and costume:

They were taking pictures right and left of Lugosi in the casket. I don't have one to this day; don't ask me where they all disappeared. I know I gave one to Pat Delaney. She sent it to her son, who was stationed in Germany, and when he opened the envelope, he almost dropped dead!

Bela Lugosi was buried in Holy Cross Cemetery, in Culver City, next to Dixie Lee, Bing Crosby's first wife (Crosby has since joined them). Bela's ex-wife Lillian paid for the grave site and funeral service. Hope shared the tiny estate—totaling about $2900—with Bela, Jr.

"Life went on," said Hope.

Hope never remarried. Contrary to legend, she did not give away all of Bela's belongings to a famous collector(s); however, a full account of what Hope saved, sold, and gave away would require more space than is available here.

In 1957, Hope granted an interview to the *National Inquirer*. "Afraid of *him*? He was afraid of *me*!" said Hope, hamming it up for the reporter, claiming she was a witch and mocking her late husband. Once again, there was apparent method in her madness. It was her way of scaring off the curious; her way of hiding the hurt she had suffered in her year with this moody, tempestuous, deeply unhappy man.

She avoided publicity. She worked in Los Angeles and San Francisco. In 1976, Robert Cremer's book *Lugosi: The Man Behind the Cape*, was published with an Introduction by Bela, Jr. and a running commentary by ex-wife Lillian. (By then, Lillian was the widow of actor Brian Donlevy, to whom she was married from 1966 to 1972; Lillian Lugosi Donlevy died in 1981.) The family-authorized book was published without any input from Hope. Included, however, was a report from a social worker, who had visited Bela during his last marriage:

> When he related the story of his separation and divorce from his last wife (Lillian), he cried constantly. He became more upset when I tried to make a comment and snapped at me to be quiet. He said that he was unable to work because of physical problems, but remarked that his wife does not concern him with financial responsibilities. The patient was amused by his (current) wife's willingness to marry him under those circumstances. He said that she received so little from their relationship that there must be something wrong with her. Patient was bitter about his advanced age and seemed to be unable to cope with it.

Also in 1976, Hope moved to Hawaii, and worked in the leper hospital on Molokai.

> I loved the leper colony. We had loads of fun! The lepers all had money, and we'd go to a nice restaurant. I remember one leper who had very little of his fingers left. It never bothered him—if the waitress didn't cut up his meat for him, we did. If anybody looked like he was staring, we knew it was a tourist and told him to go suck a duck!

"Lugosi would have hated Landau..." thought Hope Lugosi.

By the time I contacted her in 1993, Hope Lugosi was retired, living alone in a modest apartment in Honolulu. Although her name was listed along with Bela, Jr.'s in the famous lawsuit with Universal over Lugosi's likeness, Hope made no attempt to profit. She tried to hide from fans, researchers, and memorabilia hunters. She loved to read, and would slyly tell me how she beat the Honolulu heat by relaxing in her apartment stripped nude.

"You won't believe this," she exclaimed in the midst of one telephone conversation, "but I haven't got a stitch on!"

In 1994, Tim Burton's *Ed Wood* came to theaters. Hope Lugosi was not characterized in the film, nor was there any mention of her existence—which was just the way she wanted it. Hope attended with her friend, Will Hoover, reporter for the Honolulu *Advertiser* newspaper, agreeing to an interview and posing for a newspaper photographer outside the Varsity Theatre. She enjoyed the film, but she naturally had her irreverent reservations—including some for Martin Landau, whose portrayal of Lugosi won him great acclaim and an Oscar.

She wrote to me:

Lugosi would have hated Landau for representing him as an old, ugly, foul-mouthed has-been. I disliked that language in *Ed Wood*, too. Lugosi never said a small "damn" around me or my friends; nor did Ed Wood or any of the others that I knew. I'm glad the Academy cut Landau off in his acceptance speech at the Awards. He's too long-winded, never knew Lugosi, and he should have said "Thank you" and bowed out!

Hope did acquiesce to one bit of notoriety in the wake of *Ed Wood*: she appeared in a flash clip, identified as "Mrs. Bela Lugosi," in a Halloween Pizza Hut commercial. She agreed to do it only after being assured it would only be shown in Hawaii.

Hope's end came quite quickly, from liver cancer. Bela Lugosi had been reportedly terrified of death: "...death doesn't hold the curse for me it did for him," Hope had said 40 years ago. Charles Heard, who spent some time with Hope during her last days, remembers that she faced death quietly and stoically, grateful to the last for her friends.

Her note on her last Christmas card to me had seemed a bit emotional. Now I knew why.

She left the hospital, going home to her apartment and books. Death came about five o'clock in the morning on April Fool's Day—a fact Hope would have enjoyed. (She also would probably have appreciated that she died in 1997—the 100th anniversary of the publication of *Dracula*.) She was 78 years old.

Hope Lugosi was cremated, and the ashes buried on Molokai.

A thousand miles of Pacific Ocean separate the graves of the last Mrs. Bela Lugosi and her demonic idol. In the fanciful Hollywood of 1997, one can only anticipate the rumors that the ghosts of Bela and Hope tandemly haunt the old apartment on Harold Way—reportedly now occupied by Chicanos with absolutely no interest in the apartment's Hollywood history.

After her death, I realized that I, too, would be haunted by the tag line of Chuck Moses' 1988 interview: Hope's words, "Open the window." Yes, it was probably just another example of her macabre sense of humor. But more nagging were the reasons behind that humor.

Hope Lugosi was a woman whose dream had become a nightmare. The Count Dracula she beheld on screen in 1931 was a heartbreaking (if noble) wreckage, wracked by age, divorce, drug addiction, alcoholism, and Hollywood apathy on the night she married him in 1955. He had accepted her love, her idolatry, her financial support, all the while believing there was "something wrong with her," pining for his previous wife, and—almost certainly, at least by the end of the marriage—not loving her.

It was a bizarre, doomed, and terribly sad marriage.

Yet behind all the grim jokes and salty cynicism, it was evident that Hope had—and did—always love him, and the Dracula ideal he represented to her. Even in his miserable last year, the old magic, the quality that has made Bela Lugosi so beloved a star today, would flare up and spark; Hope had seen it and shared in it. I think that in her own private way, Hope Lininger Lugosi was glad she had fulfilled the destiny she'd selected, pursued—and suffered: to be the last Bride of Dracula. As she told me:

> All my friends found his continental suavity and manner enchanting. He never failed to treat guests with the greatest of courtesy. Rest assured that you, and all the people now interested in him, would have loved to have met him—and he would have treated you like princes.

While most people instantly picture actor Bela Lugosi when thinking of Count Dracula, the part has been essayed by many distinguished players. Stoker, a frustrated play-wright at heart, set out to create a villain in the classic mold, and, with Dracula, fash-ioned a character that has evolved to classic status. Dracula is now one of the many challenges an actor must face in a career of interpreting the classics, along with Ham-let, Sherlock Holmes, and Prospero.

To many Dracula aficionados, it is not the classic Lugosi delineation that fasci-nates, but that of the gaunt, Shakespearean actor John Carradine. Though this fine actor in the barnstorming tradition never tackled the role in a quality vehicle, he is still remembered for the chilly suavity he brought to the role.

For the first time, the contributions of Lugosi and Carradine to the Dracula mythos are measured side-by-side by film critic and historian Gregory William Mank. A suc-cessful regional actor himself, Mank brings a performer's perspective to this battle of the blood-suckers.
—Bob Madison

Clash of the Draculas:
Bela Lugosi vs. John Carradine
by Gregory William Mank

> ...He would just look at me, and it would scare me into behaving. Because I thought of him as my father, I was not frightened of him as a horror man in the theatrical sense (although all my young friends would hide behind the theater seats when we went to see his movies).
> —Bela Lugosi, Jr. in his preface to *Lugosi: The Man Behind the Cape*, by Robert Cremer (1976)

> ...I remember a recurrent dream that scared the hell out of me: my daddy, dressed up in a Dracula cape and a black hat, coming at me on a red tricycle with wings.
> —David Carradine, in his memoir *Endless Highway* (1995)

During the Golden Age of Hollywood Horror, 1931 to 1948, three actors officially portrayed Count Dracula under the broken battlements of Universal City, California: Bela Lugosi, Lon Chaney, Jr., and John Carradine.

The recurring question among horror film buffs is: who gave the greatest performance?

CARL LAEMMLE *presents*

DRACULA

UNIVERSAL PICTURE

Bela Lugosi created an undead sexual predator; John Carradine would later make the Count even more romantic.

Well, forgive me for instantly ruling out young Lon, whose porcine, piggy-eyed Count of 1943's *Son of Dracula* looks like he just sucked the blood of an ox. (A *slow* ox, at that!)

It would seem that the true Vampire King, of course, would be Lugosi. After all, Lugosi's *Dracula* of 1931 created the horror film genre, and every subsequent entry in this genre owes a debt to both Lugosi and the film. His performance, as a Valentino from Hell, is truly magic and transcends any conventional mode of criticism. It has magnificence and poetry and classical power, and, come 1948 and *Abbott and Costello Meet Frankenstein*, Lugosi was back once more as the Count, to bring the curtain down officially on a magical era. Meanwhile, the actor played undead in MGM's 1935 *Mark of the Vampire* (as "Count Mora") and Columbia's 1944 *The Return of the Vampire* (as "Armand Tesla").

Yet Dracula, by any other name, was still Dracula. The years of legal battles between Bela Lugosi, Jr. and Universal Studios over the Lugosi likeness in Dracula merchandise would surely point toward Lugosi's coronation. And the touchingly macabre touch of Bela being buried at Holy Cross Cemetery in 1956, wearing his Dracula cape, would seem to award him the honor by poetics alone, even without the resume.

Yet one of the curiosities of the now quite magnificent Lugosi legend is the fact that there are serious film researchers and scholars who select John Carradine's Dracula of the Universal "monster rallies," 1944's *House of Frankenstein* and 1945's *House of Dracula*, as the true Vampire King. While none question Karloff's supremacy as the screen's greatest Frankenstein Monster of Hollywood's Golden Age (or any other age!), Lugosi's supreme cinema achievement comes under fire by some revisionist scholars as second best.

Indeed, for many fans, while Lugosi's Dracula may be Valentino from Hell, Carradine's Count—in his stylishly cocked top hat, flowing cape and satanic flair—is Lucifer Incarnate.

Of course it's a silly argument. Carradine's Dracula of the *House* pictures is almost a guest star, just one of the goblins, along with Chaney's Wolf Man, Glenn Strange's Frankenstein Monster, and the assorted mad doctors and hunchbacks. Yet—Carradine's Count truly does have a magic all his own....

So, the questions are:

Why did Carradine win the role of Dracula over Lugosi in *House of Frankenstein* and *House of Dracula*?

What qualities of his portrayal truly compete with Lugosi's legendary delineation?

Who's likely to wear ultimately the crown of King of Hollywood's Golden Age vampires?

Onward and upward—to discuss the phenomenon of Lugosi vs. Carradine.

The fall of 1930, while Bela Lugosi was filming *Dracula*, must have been a wonderfully satisfying time in his life. The proud actor must have come home each evening to his house at 1146 N. Hudson Avenue in Hollywood, aware of the history he was making on the Universal soundstages. True, the salary was only $500 per week; true, Tod Browning was a seemingly burned-out wreck of a director. And one imagines that Lugosi was probably aware that, as he practiced his on-the-set ritual—posing before a soundstage mirror, throwing his cape over his shoulder, and shouting "I *AM* DRACULA!" at his reflection—that co-stars David Manners and Helen Chandler were giggling at him.

It mattered little. He was giving a performance that he'd perfected on the Broadway stage and on tour; a portrayal that was his moment in time. Even today, Lugosi's Dracula has an aura of an actor fulfilling destiny.

It's odd, too, what time has done to Lugosi's Count; the "flaws" pointed out by so many writers are actually points in its favor. The theatrical poses and posturings—the slow, heavily-accented Transylvania delivery, by a man not yet fully accustomed to English—all serve to make Lugosi's Count a glamorously evil legend.

In a sense, the Lugosi vs. Carradine clash begins here—for Carradine always claimed that he was one of the final candidates (Conrad Veidt, Paul Muni, and Ian Keith were among the others) Universal had considered as Lugosi's competition for Dracula. Today, few historians take this claim seriously (any more than they do Carradine's tale that he had tested for the Monster role in *Frankenstein*).

February 12, 1931: *Dracula* opens at New York City's Roxy Theatre. "Bela Lugosi is Count Dracula and gives a brilliant portrayal" (*Billboard*)—"He's simply grand" (*New York Daily News*). Bela Lugosi was a now a star of melodramas and scare pictures: Dr. Mirakle in *Murders in the Rue Morgue*—Murder Legendre in *White Zombie*—vengeful Vitus Werdegast in *The Black Cat*, with Karloff. It was "Dear Boris," who, of course, had played the Monster in Universal's 1931 *Frankenstein*, originally slated for Bela—and who, as Hollywood fate would have it, had eclipsed Lugosi.

Gloria Holden burns a wax figure of Bela Lugosi; his chances of playing the role in a serious sequel would also melt away. *Dracula's Daughter* **(1936)**

Yet Lugosi remained, if Horror Star Number Two, at least Hollywood Vampire Number One. Ironically, come early 1935, as Karloff was at Universal reprising the Monster in *Bride of Frankenstein*, directed by *Frankenstein*'s James Whale, Lugosi was at MGM, back in his cape in *Mark of the Vampire*, directed by *Dracula*'s Tod Browning. Metro-Goldwyn-Mayer Studios was sacristy of Jean Harlow's platinum wig and Clark Gable's false teeth, so it's not too surprising that it presents fake vampires: Bela as "Count Mora" (Universal had copyright over the name "Dracula") and Carroll Borland as his vampire daughter "Luna," creating an icon as the long-haired succubus-in-shroud. Although revealed in the climax to be actors posing as vampires, their presence was the saving grace of this incredibly erratic joint remake of Browning's 1927 Lon Chaney vehicle *London After Midnight* and *Dracula*. Its major legacy is Borland's eventual inspiration of such figures as Morticia Addams, Vampira, and Elvira.

Once again, Lugosi could go home, now to 2835 Westshire Drive, atop a hill below the HOLLYWOODLAND sign, and enjoy his glory. His salary had risen, although hardly to what he now was worth. His fee for *Dracula* had been $3500; his salary for *Mark of the Vampire*: about $5000.

Plans for Bela to revive the Count in *Dracula's Daughter* (1936) fell through in a storm of censorship hassles and rewrites which reduced Dracula to a wax dummy cremated by the title vamp (Gloria Holden). Bela showed up for a few publicity shots and took home $4000 (more than his sum for the Dracula!) for time he'd relinquished preparing for his non-appearance.

Years passed. Bela Lugosi rode the crazy roller coaster of his movie stardom, creating such classic characters at Universal as Poe-obsessed Dr. Vollin of *The Raven*

(1935). So horrifying was Lugosi's *Raven* that Britain banned horror films. It was only after a two-year absence from movie screens that he came back as bearded, broken-necked old Ygor of *Son of Frankenstein* (1939). He reprised this wonderful villain in *The Ghost of Frankenstein* (1942).

January 1943. Bela was 60 years old, and had his wife Lillian, four-year-old Bela, Jr., and his "Dracula House" at 10841 Whipple Street in North Hollywood for comfort when Universal finally shot *Son of Dracula*—with Lon Chaney, Jr. in the cape. It was just another stop for Lon, who already had played the Wolf Man, the Frankenstein Monster, and the Mummy as Universal's "master character creator" of the 1940s.

Actually, Chaney could have been worse; director Robert Siodmak worked wonders with him, keeping his dialogue limited and making him a powerful, almost barbaric presence. Yet brawny "Aw-you-don't-understand" Chaney is ultimately miscast as the aristocratic vampire. In addition, the spotlight really falls on Katherine, the southern belle vampire, played by Louise Allbritton in a black wig and Vera West shroud, stealing the show as the Delilah to Chaney's hoodwinked, cuckolded Samson of a vampire.

Universal had insulted Bela, but Columbia came to the rescue: in late summer of 1943, as Bela was starring in a Hollywood stage engagement of *Arsenic and Old Lace* by night, he labored at Columbia by day in *The Return of the Vampire*. This ghoulishly atmospheric, strangely underrated chiller, directed by Lew (*The Raven*) Landers, flanked the star with a lovely heroine (Nina Foch, who today remembers the none-too-delightful fumes of the sulphur water Bela so enjoyed), a lady Van Helsing–type (Frieda Inescort), and even a talking werewolf (Matt Willis). Bela looked a bit aged and stiff at moments in this film, but overall he was splendidly evil, enjoying a blood-and-thunder demise in which he was not only staked—but melted in the bright morning sunlight. His vampire was called Armand Tesla. However, when *The Return of the Vampire* opened at New York City's Rialto in late January 1944, the *New York World-Telegram* headlined its review, "ANY WAY YOU SLICE IT, IT'S STILL DRACULA":

> Rialto patrons can cringe in their seats through another romp with Old Man Dracula the next couple of weeks with *The Return of the Vampire*. He is not called Dracula this time—but what's the difference, Dracula or Tesla? It's still Bela Lugosi soaring around and biting people on the neck.

By now a legend, Bela still wasn't paid like one. His fee for *The Return of the Vampire* was $3500—the same amount he'd earned for the 1931 *Dracula*.

Meanwhile Boris Karloff was about to end his *Arsenic and Old Lace* bonanza, as mad Jonathan Brewster of the original 1941 Broadway production and the national company. Universal was fantasizing a "monster rally" for his return.

As early as June 7, 1943 (two months before Columbia began shooting *The Return of the Vampire*, and six months before Karloff's tour ended), *The Hollywood Reporter* hawked a Universal project entitled *Chamber of Horrors*, with roles envisioned for Karloff, Chaney, Peter Lorre, Claude Rains, George Zucco, Lionel Atwill, Henry Hull—and Bela Lugosi. (This story, probably nothing more than a publicist's fantasy, is a vision that has had fans of the classic horror films drooling for decades!) Presumably, this *Chamber of Horrors* would have a crypt reserved for Lugosi as Count Dracula.

Over the next 10 months, *Chamber of Horrors* became *Destiny*, then *The Devil's Brood*—all the while fated to be released as *House of Frankenstein*. The pipe-dream casting of Lorre, Rains, and Hull fell through—and so did the inclusion of Bela Lugosi as Dracula.

Enter—with flourish, naturally—John Carradine. The great, gaunt, basso-voiced character actor of John Ford's *The Prisoner of Shark Island*, *Stagecoach*, and *The Grapes of Wrath* would portray Dracula in *House of Frankenstein*, as well as Universal's 1945 follow-up, *House of Dracula*.

Why?

> DRACULA—The role holds a curse greater than Hamlet! Give the audience Richard III, Othello, The Merchant of Venice and what will they remember? A Vampyre!
>
> —John Carradine, in his posthumously published Introduction to the *House of Dracula Filmbook* (MagicImage Publishing, 1993)

"I am a HAM!" rejoiced John Carradine during the era of *House of Frankenstein*. Fresh from a fall 1943 tour of "John Carradine and his Shakespeare Players" (with the producer/director/sole owner also starring as Hamlet, Shylock, and alternately Othello and Iago), Carradine was back in the movies. He lived at Hollywood's Garden of Allah, the long-gone colony of little Mediterranean-style villas surrounding the pool shaped like the Black Sea. He dressed in slouch hat, cloak, and cane, chain-smoking long, Russian cigarettes, looking, acting, and sounding like a 19th-century matinee idol. At night, Carradine would hit the bistros, bellowing Shakespeare, flanked by his blond lover Sonia, his Ophelia from his stage *Hamlet*, and who (very scandalously, for the era) lived with him at the Garden of Allah. (She would eventually marry him and give birth to sons Christopher, Keith, and Robert.) His was a strange, fun but almost masochistic flamboyance; a bizarre desire to win infamy as Hollywood's Shakespearean screwball.

He was also a magnificent actor—and he was Universal's new Count Dracula.

For years, historians have conjectured as to why John Carradine won over Bela Lugosi for Dracula in *House of Frankenstein*. Some of the reasons given:

•Carradine, in 1944, was a major Hollywood character player. *Time* magazine had reported Carradine's stage triumph as Hamlet in San Francisco; and, of course, he was no stranger to Universal City by now, having starred in *Captive Wild Woman* (1943), *The Mummy's Ghost*, and *The Invisible Man's Revenge* (both 1944).

•While Carradine was "in the loop" at Universal, Lugosi was out of it—ever since his disastrous turn as the Monster in Universal's 1943 *Frankenstein Meets the Wolf Man*. While it was the studio's post-production editing (removal of the Monster's dialogue and references to his blindness) that truly ruined the performance, Universal supposedly blamed Lugosi—and left him to the none-too-tender mercies of Monogram. (How ironic: in the fall of 1943, Carradine had financed his Shakespearean company via Monogram's *Return of the Ape Man* and *Voodoo Man*—in support of Lugosi.)

•It appeared the question might have been answered definitively when Paul Malvern, producer of both *House of Frankenstein* and *House of Dracula*, wrote a Foreword to the 1993 MagicImage *House of Dracula Filmbook*. "I know the first thing that you are

Actor Carradine had much at stake when he first played Dracula in *House of Frankenstein* (1944).

wondering," wrote Malvern in his Introduction (packaged by the book's editor, Phil Riley). "Why didn't Bela Lugosi play Dracula in my two monster films?" Malvern proceeded to supply only sketchy reasons: "...he (Lugosi) probably was working at a different studio—Lugosi was making pictures over at Monogram..." Malvern implied that he, as producer, preferred Carradine ("If there was someone that I thought would be better in the part I would win out!").

Film history seems to establish that Carradine was simply Universal's new, number one choice for the vampire king. However, a new question has arisen: could John Carradine have won the Dracula role only by default—because Bela Lugosi was otherwise employed?

A little background...

In his excellent article *The Road to Las Vegas: Bela Lugosi in American Theatre* in *Cult Movies* (#11), Frank J. Dello Stritto provides detailed coverage of Lugosi's stage work, including an itinerary of his exhausting, four-month, 33-city tour of the play *Arsenic and Old Lace*. Boris Karloff left the company in January of 1944, after three years on Broadway and national tour; Lugosi (who had played Jonathan on stage in San Francisco and Hollywood in 1943) promptly took over for Boris in Oklahoma City. Dello Stritto wrote how the tour was on its last legs; how Lugosi had to spend some "cold February nights sleeping in train stations"; how he "quickly shed 11 pounds and grew abrupt with interviewers." However the tour was (in Dello Stritto's words) "an

Carradine's Dracula had all the style and flair of a master stage magician.

unqualified triumph" for Lugosi. Indeed, in some cities, the play grossed more than it had with Karloff in the cast. Karloff probably didn't mind. He was an original investor in *Arsenic and Old Lace*, and Lugosi's triumph in the play could only fatten Boris' wallet. Karloff was in Hollywood, with a new Universal deluxe star contract: two films in 12 weeks for $60,000. On April 1, 1944, he completed two-thirds of the deal as he finished *The Climax*, boasting Susanna Foster and Technicolor; on April 4, he began earning the final $20,000 and working the last four weeks on *The Devil's Brood*, Universal's proposed monster rally, fated to be released as *House of Frankenstein*.

Universal built the whole schedule around Karloff's contract: a 30-day shoot, to last from April 4 through May 8, 1944, under Erle C. Kenton's direction.

So—did Universal page Lugosi (originally announced in trade paper notices) for *House of Frankenstein*, only to learn that the star of the studio's 1931 *Dracula* was spending frigid nights in East Coast train stations? Did Lugosi enter negotiations for *House of Frankenstein*—only to find out that the *Arsenic* tour (which ended in June) was long enough to keep him from returning to Hollywood for the Dracula episode (which was shot April 27 through May 8)?

Did Lugosi have a tantrum when he learned that the shooting dates couldn't be pushed back, since the whole film was blueprinted around Karloff's contract?

The overview of available facts supports the belief that Carradine was Universal's only choice. Yet one wonders. And it's an eye-opener to look at Universal's budget for *House of Frankenstein*, and see John Carradine's salary: $3500 per week, with a two-week guarantee; a total of $7000—exactly double what Universal had paid Lugosi for the 1931 *Dracula*; exactly double what Columbia had paid Bela for 1944's *The Return of the Vampire*.

But beyond the conjectures and salary checks is the performance.

House of Frankenstein is almost more three-ring circus than horror movie: Karloff serving as ringmaster, while Lon Chaney's Wolf Man, Glenn Strange's Frankenstein Monster, and Carradine's Count cavort for the crowd. Though J. Carrol Naish's heart-broken hunchback Daniel provides true pathos, the film is a carnival, almost in the same rococo style of the gaudily-painted "Chamber of Horrors" wagon that Karloff pirates from George Zucco. The chase scene, with Lionel Atwill's Inspector leading a cavalry of gendarmes after Dracula; the wonderful special effects; Elena Verdugo's Gypsy dance—all combine to create an atmosphere almost as much Barnum & Bailey as Universal Horror.

As Dracula, John Carradine, in his top hat and cape, evokes a Shakespearean actor gone to seed, reduced to a sad, lonely, and strikingly evil carnival magician. It was close to Carradine's own professional situation (hoping to premiere his "John Carradine and his Shakespeare Players" on Broadway for the Bard's April 23 birthday, he was doing *House of Frankenstein* instead), and nicely complements this big top of a horror movie.

But there's more.

In my opinion, the scenes played between Carradine and Anne Gwynne are among the most sexy shot in 1940s Hollywood. The vignette in which Carradine gives Anne his Dracula ring—his profile almost touching hers—their voices soft, whispering, passionate—his fervent, "I will come for you before the dawn—" This is the Devil seducing a 1944 apple-cheeked, all-American bride, and there's a sexy, crazy, macabre chemistry between the two actors. Anne Gwynne told Michael Fitzgerald she felt she had done some of her finest acting in *House of Frankenstein*, and she is excellent as she slinks and sighs her way from pretty ingenue to vampire's love slave. It's a wonderfully erotic episode.

Now, the question: could Bela Lugosi have matched the sexual allure that 38-year-old Carradine had given Dracula in *House of Frankenstein*? Or had the 61-year-old Hungarian already solidified into the stiff, iconic figure of his later career?

Of course, it's ridiculous to think of Lugosi failing as Dracula. And in *The Return of the Vampire*, he'd done a pretty good job of leering at Nina Foch. Still—it's a bit tough to imagine Lugosi oomphing with Anne Gwynne; a little challenging to imagine the puffy, gray Lugosi of 1944 riding atop the coach in that big chase scene; a slight stretch to conjure up Lugosi playing the Dracula-caught-in-the-rays-of-the-sun scene in the same limber, gut-wrenching style as Carradine.

John Carradine—sly, showy, spidery—seems to fit the sideshow ambiance of *House of Frankenstein*, and also plays beautifully with Anne Gwynne. He made his own impact in the role, so vividly that it's hard (for me) to imagine even Bela Lugosi—in these circumstances—improving upon him.

Carradine surely got a kick out of adding Dracula to his resume of Hollywood villains. But one doubts seriously if he felt the kind of moment-in-time glow that Lugosi had enjoyed while shooting *Dracula*. *House of Frankenstein*, Universal's yuletide gift to horror disciples, opened at Hollywood's Hawaii Theatre December 22, 1944, just one of the 11 releases Carradine graced in 1944.

Of course, no self-respecting critics of the war years would have dared seriously evaluate Carradine's Dracula performance; they were too busy deifying Greer Garson. Horror almost never received serious critical examination, and, even if it did, Carradine's Dracula in *House of Frankenstein* appeared in only the first part of an episodic picture. Yet, as decades passed, horror researchers and scholars would make their own judgments. In *Midnight Marquee* #49, John Parnum, editor of the late-lamented magazine *Cinemacabre*, wrote of John Carradine and *House of Frankenstein*:

> ...Carradine's thin frame seemed more appropriate as one of the undead. And his deep, resonant Shakespearean trained voice was decidedly more mesmerizing than Lugosi's stilted rote delivery of Americanized Hungarianese and Chaney's Hollywood histrionics—For many, Carradine remains the Dracula of choice, despite his supporting role status.

My personal reaction: is Carradine's Dracula in *House of Frankenstein* a fascinating performance?

Yes.

Is it a full-blooded challenge to Lugosi's 1931 *Dracula*?

No.

In September of 1945—almost a year-and-a-half after Universal had begun shooting *House of Frankenstein—House of Dracula* started production. Trade papers had rumored since early 1945 that Lugosi would play Dracula in Universal's next monster rally. Early in September of 1945, Lionel Atwill and Bela completed RKO's *Genius at Work* (Atwill as a master criminal known as "The Cobra," Lugosi as his servant). Later that month, Atwill went into Universal's *House of Dracula* as Inspector Holtz while Lugosi was not invited. Dracula once again belonged to Carradine, who joined Chaney's Wolf Man, Strange's Monster, Jane Adams' hunchbacked nurse, Skelton Knaggs' village grotesque, and Onslow Stevens' Mad Doctor, all under Erle C. Kenton's direction once again.

Carradine remained a very impressive Count—especially in his candlelight seduction of blonde Martha O'Driscoll as she played *Moonlight Sonata* at the piano. Universal shot Carradine's Dracula scenes first, leaving the actor free to start Monogram's *The Face of Marble* as *House of Dracula* went on for several more weeks' shooting. (There was one sensitive area for Carradine who, by now, had married Sonia. In his book *Maria, Marlene, and Me*, actor/critic Dean Goodman, a member of Carradine's 1943 Shakespearean company, wrote that Sonia had been "involved in an affair" with Onslow Stevens before becoming involved with Carradine. Could John have used this as "motivation" in the episode in which he pollutes Stevens' blood and makes him a Jekyll/Hyde madman?)

At any rate, *House of Dracula* was New York City's most incongruous Christmas attraction as it opened at the Rialto Theatre December 21, 1945. Forty-five years later researchers/film historians Michael Brunas, John Brunas, and Tom Weaver, in their milestone book *Universal Horrors*, would write:

> Carradine's remains the best Dracula, easily outshining the ossified
> Lugosi as well as Christopher Lee's red-eyed acrobat.

Universal apparently, shockingly forgot about Lugosi's link with Dracula. When Universal-International blueprinted *Abbott and Costello Meet Frankenstein* (1948), the studio originally considered Ian Keith for Dracula—presumably on the basis of his "Ormand Murks" in Republic's *Valley of the Zombies* (1946) and/or his having been a top candidate for the part in 1930. (One account claims the producers thought that the Hungarian was dead.) Lugosi ultimately got the part, and finally at respectable terms ($2000 per week, and originally set for four weeks and a day). He recreated the role with evil majesty; Charles T. Barton directed, and the film was a box office smash. Of course, Bela's Dracula of *Abbott and Costello Meet Frankenstein*, still wonderful, was a far cry from the sexy, Valentino-like, slow-speaking incubus of the original. The actor had aged into a stout, slick gent, albeit with enough wicked allure to seduce Lenore Aubert believably, dominate the film totally, and reclaim the role of Dracula definitively.

Yet I wonder (again): if John Carradine had not been busy in New York theatre at the time, would the studio have paged Carradine for the role—and ignored both Ian Keith and Bela Lugosi?

Bela Lugosi never played Dracula onscreen again. Yet the association was always there, throughout the late marital woes, the comeback wishes, and even his drug addic-

Like Lugosi, Carradine was never able to completely close the door on his Dracula portrayals.

tion, which, Dracula-like, drained the actor's life away. Lugosi wore the cape to the 1953 Hollywood premiere of *House of Wax* (along with a "gorilla" on a leash), in those pitiful clips from *Plan 9 from Outer Space*, and—on August 18, 1956—to his grave.

The role of Dracula became part of the Gothic downfall of John Carradine, too, along with the heavy drinking, the broken marriages, and the low-budget movies. Indeed, he would pick *Billy the Kid Versus Dracula* (1966) as the worst of his 200-plus films ("Who wouldn't?" he pondered). He was Dracula again (in a cage) in Mexico's 1967 *Las Vampiras*. He delivered the line he'd added in his later stage appearances in Dracula: "If I am alive, what am I doing here? On the other hand, if I'm dead, why do I have to wee-wee?"—in 1978's *Nocturna*. By now Carradine was gnarled, shrunken, hands pitifully deformed by arthritis: he was a sad wreckage of a Dracula. Perhaps Carradine's finest late-in-life evocation of the vampire was the April 17, 1977 *McCloud Meets Dracula* with Carradine as a famed vampire actor who turns out to be the real thing. It featured a clip from *House of Frankenstein*—and was filmed at Universal City.

John Carradine died November 27, 1988, in Milan; there was a Hollywood funeral, with all the Carradine sons present. There was no Dracula cape for the dead Carradine, but the funeral had its ghoulish aspect nonetheless. David Carradine wrote in his book *Endless Highway* that after the funeral

> ...we carted the coffin over to our house and opened it up. I looked down at him and the undertaker had put a demonic, artificial grin on his face—like nothing I had ever see him do in real life, except in a

138

Lugosi eyes a midnight snack in the original 1931 *Dracula*.

horror film. I reached out and, using the sculptural skills I had learned from him, I remodeled his face to be more naturally him. Then I poured half a bottle of J&B Scotch (his favorite) down his throat and we had a wake.

Since John Carradine had participated (as a civilian) in the 1941 California coastal defense system, he received a burial at sea, in the Catalina Channel, complete with a flag-draped coffin, guns firing and a bugler playing taps.

The debates as to who's the best vampire will wage forever: an argument that's visceral, emotional, and with no hope for resolution. In writing this story, I'm reminded how very much I admire both Lugosi and Carradine, and their very different interpretations.

Really and truly, however, it is completely safe to say that, in the world of pop culture, basic film history, and the mass myth pool of the popular imagination, Bela Lugosi will always be *the* Count Dracula.

My personal preference? It's probably obvious; for all my admiration of Carradine, I champion the Lugosi portrayal. There are various reasons, but one which struck me in writing this chapter was how much Lugosi *wanted* to be the best Dracula; his love for the role, his obsessive identification with it, his even wearing his cape to the grave. Perhaps John Carradine (who so deeply and futilely had wished people had remembered him as a great stage Hamlet) sensed this desire on Lugosi's part. Never the world's most humble man, Carradine personally announced that Lugosi was the supreme Count Dracula.

"His was the better vampire," said John Carradine of Bela Lugosi. "He had a fine pair of eyes."

Who Would Win? Dracula or...

A favorite pastime among children has been the fabulous Monster Test of Strength.

Surely you've done it yourself ...

The best way to describe this particular game is to recall a moment in Rob Reiner's wonderfully moving *Stand By Me* (1986), based on Stephen King's short story, *The Body*. In a scene that had millions of Baby Boomers smiling in self-recognition, one boy asks another: "Who's stronger? Superman or Mighty Mouse?" (My favorite question in this particular game was provided by my then 10-year-old brother David who then pondered: "Who's stronger, Spider-Man or Nero Wolfe?")

Speculation on the powers and abilities of movie monsters has been a pastime with children long before Frankenstein's Monster first battled the Wolf Man, and continues to this day. Universal Studios was quick to throw Count Dracula into the ring when they had Bela Lugosi thrash Lon Chaney, Jr.'s Wolf Man through a particularly remote and gloomy castle at the conclusion of *Abbot and Costello Meet Frankenstein*. Dracula transforms into a bat—a spectacular effect done with animation—only to be grabbed by the Wolf Man, both of them falling into the raging sea below. That particular bout has been called a draw by most experts.

After meeting and wrestling a score of monsters in various Mexican films, Dracula returned for round two with the Wolf Man in the absurd *Dr. Terror's Gallery of Horrors* (1967), where the lycanthrope took him down for the Count.

The idea reached its apotheosis in 1971's ridiculous *Dracula vs. Frankenstein*. The work of the late director Al Adamson, *Dracula vs. Frankenstein* also, sadly, marks the final film appearances of both J. Carrol Naish and Lon Chaney, Jr. Zandor Vorkov (an actor who had never been seen before or since) delivers a truly wretched performance as Dracula. Adamson added an echo to Vorkov's voice to give it a "sinister" quality, but the actual effect is to have the actor seem as if he dubbed his lines from the center of the Holland Tunnel. He is also equipped with a ring that shoots some kind of death ray, which was probably Adamson's attempt to delude kids into thinking they were watching a Godzilla film as well.

The major victory for the character comes at the confrontation at the film's climax, as Dracula squares off against the Frankenstein Monster. Happily, the Transylvanian Titan literally rips the Lightning Leatherneck to shreds.

While the film is barely watchable, the stunning poster art for *Dracula vs. Frankenstein* was done by comic strip great Gray Morrow. Morrow, who continues to draw the syndicated *Tarzan* strip, remembers that Adamson believed poster art to be more frightening when rich with dripping blood. To this day, Morrow remembers Adamson admonishing him, "Add more drip, Gray! Add more drip!"

Adamson's tragic end was like something from one of his own lurid films. His decapitated body was found hidden under the floor of his secluded home, the victim of a horrific murder. A contractor named Fred Fulford, who had been living and working at Adamson's home, was charged with the crime.

He must have seen *Dracula vs. Frankenstein*.

—Bob Madison

Woody Allen on the Dracula Legend

Suddenly he knows the sun is down. Like an angel of hell, he rises swiftly, and changing into a bat, flies pell-mell to the cottage of his tantalizing victims.

"Why, Count Dracula, what a nice surprise," the baker's wife says, opening the door to admit him. (He has once again assumed human form, as he enters their home, charmingly concealing his rapacious goal.)

"What brings you here so early?" the baker asks.

"Our dinner date," the Count answers. "I hope I haven't made an error. You did invite me for tonight, didn't you?"

"Yes, tonight, but that's not for seven hours."

"Pardon me?" Dracula queries, looking around the room puzzled.

"Or did you come by to watch the eclipse with us?"

"Eclipse?"

"Yes. Today's the total eclipse."

"What?"

"A few moments of darkness from noon until two minutes after. Look out the window."

"Uh-oh—I'm in big trouble."

—Woody Allen, from *Getting Even*

The faces of Dracula and his vampiric horde are ever-changing. Though unable to cast a reflection himself, Dracula quite often is the mirror image of ourselves and the world in which we live.

Dracula and vampires continued to evolve in the 1940s, drifting further away from the image created by Stoker and the re-vamped Count of Deane, Balderston, and Lugosi. The roots of today's vampire kaleidoscope—constantly shifting in such films as The Hunger *(1983),* Near Dark *(1987), and* Nadja *(1994), and the works of Chelsea Quinn Yarbro, Fred Saberhagen and Anne Rice—can be traced back to the war years.*

In The Vampire Strikes Back!*, author Frank Dello Stritto shows us the subtle ways in which Dracula responded to the changing American landscape. A keen critic of genre films, Dello Stritto is a regular contributor to* Cult Movies *magazine.*
—Bob Madison

The Vampire Strikes Back!
by Frank Dello Stritto

Movie vampires now arise from every class, lifestyle, gender, country, age group, and era. In today's cinema they can be tragic or fiendish, as likely to be good guys as bad guys.

Such diversity is a rather recent development. Offbeat vampire characterizations have always been on the fringes of the genre, but only became commonplace in the 1970s. Only after 1979, when three quite different Draculas appeared almost simultaneously (*Nosferatu, Love at First Bite,* and *Dracula*), did wild variation and experimentation come to dominate vampire films.

The dramatic and mythic potential of vampires has always been too broad for any single portrayal or personality to encompass. The question is not why such diversity arose, but why it took so long in coming. Since Bela Lugosi's 1931 performance, actors playing vampires have strained against this classic Gothic stereotype. Lugosi's mythmaking performance kept the vampire pretty much within the Lugosi persona for a quarter century. Due to legal technicalities, Universal had no copyright on the character, but no studio challenged its sole use to "Dracula" as a character or film title until 1957, perhaps coincidentally within a year of Lugosi's death.

Film writers either celebrate or condemn Lugosi's performance, but his hold on the part is undeniable. David Thomson writes in 1975's *A Biographical Dictionary of the Cinema* (reprinted in 1994 as *A Biographical Dictionary of Film*):

> He could be frightening in a way that other actors in horror never achieved... His Dracula was an original that the cinema never attempted to match.

But David Pirie argues in 1977's *The Vampire Cinema*:

> Lugosi's Dracula-style left no room for development—there was no direction it could take except that of self parody... as a personality, as a phenomenon, as a star, he was remarkable. As an influence on the emergent horror film, struggling for freedom from stage melodrama, he was disastrous.

Through the 1930s only a handful of vampire movies followed in *Dracula*'s wake. Carlos Villarias, Universal's Spanish Dracula, was instructed to mimic Lugosi; otherwise all the decade's vampires deviate from his stereotype. *The Vampire Bat* (1933) has no vampire, though Dwight Frye virtually repeats his Renfield role from *Dracula*. Danish-made (1931) *Vampyr*'s fiend is an elderly woman, more witch than vampire. In 1935's *Condemned to Live,* dormant vampirism awakens in a meek, middle-aged man on the eve of his wedding. He is the screen's first sympathetic vampire. A year later came the second in *Dracula's Daughter*.

For various reasons—limited distribution or popular acceptance, waning audience interest in the genre, pressure from censors—none of these films had any lasting impact on the popular image of vampires. After *Dracula*, the most financially successful vampire film of the decade is MGM's *Mark of the Vampire* (1935). The "vampires" are frauds, but they are straight from *Dracula*, led by Lugosi himself, superb but already bordering on self-parody.

When Dracula's mantle passed to actor Christopher Lee—again only a short time after Lugosi died—filmmakers were already looking to more innovative vampires. Movie vampires in the late 1950s range from coeds to cowboys, but the classic Gothic image still prevailed. That Lee became so identified with the role amidst such competition is a tribute to the frequency of his performances. His reign saw German Robles, Barbara Steele, Robert Quarry, Ingrid Pitt, and William Marshall all appearing as vampires in multiple films. Like Lee, all of them play caped Gothic fiends. Each had distinctive traits, but none strayed too far from the classic movie Dracula.

Likewise 1979's three Draculas—Klaus Kinski, George Hamilton, and Frank Langella—are definitely in the classic mold. But their Counts furthered strained and satired stereotypes defined by Lugosi and Lee, and ushered in the revolution in vampire portrayals of the 1980s.

Today's diversity in vampire portrayals really finds its roots in an overlooked two-year surge during World War II. After *Dracula's Daughter*, no vampire film appeared until 1943. That drought saw numerous appearances by Dracula's fellow monsters at Universal—three by Frankenstein's Monster and two each by the Wolf Man, the Mummy, and the Invisible Man. Many other monsters and madmen appeared as well, but no vampires.

Then from 1943 to 1945 came *Dead Men Walk, Son of Dracula, The Return of the Vampire, House of Frankenstein, The Vampire's Ghost*, and *House of Dracula*.

Six vampire films in three years is hardly a deluge by modern standards, but they represent almost half the vampire films made from 1931 to 1956!

Some of their important roles are played by virtual unknowns—John Abbott, Louise Allbritton, Matt Willis, Onslow Stevens—but they also starred some of the most celebrated players in horror film as well: Lugosi, John Carradine, Lon Chaney, George

Zucco, Boris Karloff, Dwight Frye, Lionel Atwill. The six films mostly follow the classic mold, but the variations are obvious and the escape from Dracula's Gothic shadow appeared well underway. Four quite different stories from 1946—*Isle of the Dead, The Face of Marble, Devil Bat's Daughter,* and *Valley of the Zombies*—employ some vampire lore and trappings but none of them were a traditional vampire film.

This revisionism of the vampire myth might have gained momentum, but the changing world scene moved faster. With the end of World War II, horror films abruptly fell out of fashion and vampires were all but forgotten. After 1945 and until Lugosi's death in 1956, only two vampires appeared in English language films; both in comedies and both played by Lugosi—Count Dracula in *Abbott and Costello Meet Frankenstein*, and Von Housen, yet another fraud, in *Mother Riley Meets the Vampire*. When Hammer's Christopher Lee revived the subgenre in the late 1950s, he basically picked up where Lugosi left off. Not until the 1980s would the classic caped, Gothic fiend refined by playwrights Deane and Balderston and actor Bela Lugosi cease to dominate vampire portrayals.

The vampire lore of ages past—the "real" traditional vampire, usually involves a corpse returning from its grave to attack its family. It is corruption from within, both on individual and familial levels. The vampire films of 1943-1945 experiment with the vampire's origins, motives, and victims. The first two vampire films after Hollywood's long neglect stumble onto the pre-Byron tradition of the Undead as homegrown.

Dead Men Walk—released February 1943 by PRC

> He was my brother, yet he always seemed an alien soul, even in childhood. I believe he hated me all his life. After he returned from India, Elwyn was like a man obsessed by a demon. Nothing was sacred to him. He had nothing but contempt for all that decent men hold dear. His mind became a black and evil thing, probing into perverted knowledge of ancient sorcery and demonology.
> —Lloyd Clayton (George Zucco) describing his dead but not yet departed brother Elwyn (also George Zucco)

Dead Men Walk is to the 1940s what *Condemned to Live* is to the 1930s—the lowest-budgeted, least technically competent, but most interesting vampire story of the decade. *Dead Men Walk* is rightfully obscure, and without horror film icons George Zucco and Dwight Frye, it would be even more so. Yet buried in its mediocrity is a potentially complex story of a family attacked by one of its own.

After a brief prologue of the Devil lecturing we "creatures of the light" about our "puny conceit," *Dead Men Walk* moves to the funeral service for Elwyn Clayton in a small rural town. "His hands are stained with the blood of the innocent and his unspeakable sorceries," decries Kate, one of the "mourners." Kate's precarious mental state is the result of "the shocking death of her granddaughter last year." Details of the child's death are never given, but Kate clearly blames Elwyn. Though apparently unstable, she emerges as the only one of the townspeople to thwart the vampire.

Hints drop that Elwyn may not have fallen to his death but may have been pushed. When his servant Zolarr (Frye) confronts Lloyd, the "good" brother scarcely denies the accusation. "No one will ever believe that," is his only reply. Soon, Elwyn rises from his grave:

> By the power of Shi-Tan, dark lord of the abyss, I live. I am not yet strong, but the power has been given me to draw everlasting life from the veins of the living. They will give me the blood of their hearts, while I destroy them.

This vampire returns from the dead not against his will but through his own mastery of a "perverted knowledge of ancient sorcery and demonology." Dracula never hints that he serves a higher force, but Elwyn faithfully follows some dark master. Late in the film, Elwyn prays before his altar:

> Oh, mighty lord of the abyss—your servant bows in eternal obedience to your will. The time has come when I must destroy all those who stand in our way.

"Eternal obedience" does not stop Elwyn from seeking vengeance on Lloyd, his brother and his murderer. As soon as Elwyn revives he confronts Lloyd:

> You took it upon yourself to sit in judgment of me and destroy my mortal span of life. You'll know I'm no intangible figment of your imagination when you feel the weight of my hatred. Your life will be a torment. I'll strip you of everything you hold dear, before I drag you down to a sordid death—Gayle was an easy hypnotic subject and I would make her my disciple. And to save her from being initiated into the dark mysteries, the eminently respectable Dr. Clayton stooped to murder—but you failed. By the power of those I serve, my life is indestructible, eternally sustained by the life I take from others. I'll take life from Gayle—slowly. You'll see her life ebb day by day and be powerless to save her.

Gayle, the heroine, is Lloyd's beloved niece. He is quite close to her, and a blood tie between them is almost certain. She often calls him "Uncle Lloyd," but never refers to Elwyn as her uncle, or as anything. As Lloyd's brother, Elwyn thus targets either his own daughter or his niece as victim and instrument of revenge. Most discussions of *Dead Men Walk* assume that Lloyd and Elwyn are twins since both are played by Zucco. Yet the actor's make-up strives to differentiate the characters—Lloyd has a full head of hair and a rather fleshy face; Elwyn is bald and gaunt. It's quite unlikely that only one identical twin would inherit the baldness gene. If the men are twins, then this tight family unit is even tighter, and Elwyn's plans for Gayle all the more damning.

Dead Men Walk gives no further clue to Elwyn's true kinship to Gayle. In the censorship environment of the time it could certainly go no further. MGM's watchdogs prevented the incestuous relationship planned for the vampires in 1935's *Mark of the Vampire* from reaching the screen. *Dead Men Walk* does warn that something very foul is afoot. In the prologue, the Devil boasts of "dark enshrouded regions of evil," "frightened whispers," "the spawn of hell," "the unholy communion." Lloyd speaks of

Vampire slave Dwight Frye ministers to a new undead master, George Zucco, in *Dead Men Walk* (1943).

"blasphemy" and "perverted knowledge." Kate also fumes of "unspeakable sorceries." Are we to believe that Elwyn had incestuous designs on Gayle? It is a question left only to our imaginations.

Immediately after Lloyd's encounter with Elwyn, Gayle shows the typical symptoms of movie vampire victims. Though Lloyd knows exactly what's happening, he is frozen in inaction. He so denies the truth that he looks for some medical reason for Gayle's anemia. His behavior sparks David, Gayle's fiancé, to suspect that Lloyd is the culprit. And he may be a culprit, or at least an accomplice, for standing by as his "other self" attacks his niece. Or he may be unable to accept that his murder of his own brother only spawned an even greater horror. Does Lloyd see Elwyn's return as retribution for his own sin? Even before Elwyn's reappearance, Lloyd shows ambivalent feelings about him. When David comments after the funeral that Elwyn must have been insane, Lloyd immediately defends his brother. As Lloyd works through his inner demons, he leaves poor Kate to battle the vampire. Zolarr murders her, increasing Lloyd's share of guilt. The story only ends when Lloyd resolves his indecision and tracks down the hiding place of Elwyn's coffin. Their death struggle starts a fire as the sun rises. Both brothers and Zolarr die.

Almost none of the story's potential reaches the screen. Most of the acting is poor; the staging and continuity are worse. Lloyd's denial and self-doubt seem only a plot inconsistency, and not shields for conflicting drives. While film critics and historians pan *Dead Men Walk*, even some of the harshest commentaries note the dramatic potential of the story. The plot serves up fratricide, child murder (Kate's granddaughter), and, quite plainly, incest (father/daughter or uncle/niece). In the 1940s, perhaps the only films to get such suggestions past the censors had to be trashily made or superbly cunning. *Dead Men Walk* is certainly not the latter.

Dwight Frye, shortly before his death, repeats his Renfield performance from *Dracula*. The role of Zolarr affords him little, and he gets no opportunity to recapture or build on his famous characterization. The only first rate aspect of *Dead Men Walk* is George Zucco's over-the-top portrayal of Elwyn Clayton. Elwyn is not a typical Zucco villain. Zucco's forte was incisive, sinister understatement; his eyes would ignite with passion as he coolly unveiled diabolical plans. He plays Elwyn with a sustained zest that dominates all his scenes. If Lugosi's vampire is something of a lounge lizard, Zucco's is a dirty old man. Lugosi always brought a blatant sexuality to his vampires, and his characters are usually intended to look younger than the actor himself. Elwyn—balding, graying, and sunken facial features—looks at least as old as Zucco's 57 years.

Yet, Elwyn is far livelier than any other character in the film. The combination of age and energy makes the villainous Elwyn an unsettling fusion of opposites, especially when contrasted to his low-key, lethargic brother. Often in modern vampire stories, rising as the undead is not only a return, but a rejuvenation, an eroticization. Until recently, films usually reserved that experience for women victims of vampires. In this dismal little film, with a plotline dripping with unrealized promise, Zucco gives an interpretation far ahead of its time.

Son of Dracula—released November 1943 by Universal

> Her case was different. Her background was—morbid. She had gone overboard on the subject of the supernatural, black magic and the like—and I rather believe that Miss Caldwell made the transition from choice—Don't forget the girl was morbid, that often means thanotophobia—fear of death. And Alucard could promise her eternal life.
> —Dr. Brewster (Frank Craven) and Prof. Lazlo (J. Edward
> Bromberg) discussing Katherine Caldwell (Louise Allbritton)

Universal's *Son of Dracula*—the Count's first appearance on film since 1931—might better have been called *Bride of Dracula*. Katherine Caldwell, heiress to the Dark Oaks plantation deep in the American south, drives the plot. Katherine schemes to lure Dracula (Lon Chaney) to Dark Oaks, dispose of her father to inherit his mansion, marry Dracula to become a vampire, and then replace him with Frank Stanley (Robert Paige), the man she really loves. She almost succeeds, but Frank destroys her rather than become undead—or "immortal," a term Katherine prefers. Dracula himself, masquerading as Count Alucard, is only a pawn in her plan.

Dead Men Walk and *Son of Dracula* were filmed during World War II when the familiar Stoker tale of invasion by an evil foreigner would have fit the times. But both stories present evil from within. These domestic demons have gone abroad to master, not study, the dark arts. We learn in *Dead Men Walk* that Elwyn Clayton traveled to

Lon Chaney, Jr. muscles his way into a roadshow production of *Our Town*. *Son of Dracula* (1943)

India to study "perverted knowledge of ancient sorcery and demonology." As *Son of Dracula* opens, Katherine has returned from Hungary with a gypsy witch, Queen Zimba, in tow. In Hungary she also met Dracula and arranges for his visit to Dark Oaks. Dracula eliminates Zimba immediately on his arrival, about all he does in the movie that Katherine has not planned for him.

Fiendish Katherine, like fiendish Elwyn, emerges not in the anonymity of a large, swarming city, but in a rural, isolated town. Everyone knows everyone around Dark Oaks, and elements of Wilder's *Our Town* are omnipresent. The embodiment of this quaint, inbred community is Harry Brewster, local doctor and protector of family values: the story's relentless opponent of evil. When suspicions about Alucard first begin, Brewster boasts, "He can't stay in town without my knowing it." Wrapped in self-righteous solemnity, Brewster breaks first into Dark Oaks' guest house and then into the mansion's basement long before any misdeeds justify such snooping. Hearing that Katherine will wed her strange visitor, Brewster files an insanity complaint against her. Even the local judge, himself part of the ol' boy network, finds Brewster's legal case laughable. Brewster is not alone in his attempts to expel Katherine's unwanted outsider. Before Alucard arrives, Frank, Katherine's doting fiancé, investigates the Count through the Hungarian embassy (who have never heard of him); meanwhile Brewster contacts Prof. Lazlo, a specialist in Hungarian history (who certainly has).

Neither *Dead Men Walk* nor *Son of Dracula* are the overt xenophobic parables that might be expected of 1943, but they are curious, confused reaffirmations of American isolationism. As armies of Americans mobilized to go abroad, the films warn of the notions that might return with them. Anticipating the Red Scare of a few years later, Dracula himself echoes the warning, but like the real monsters then overrunning Europe, he is more concerned with ethnic than ideological purity. On their wedding night he tells Katherine why he left Transylvania, apparently to him a land of mongrels:

> My land is dry and desolate. The soil is red with the blood of 100 races. There is no life left there. Here, you have a young and vital race.

Thus, though inbreeding may occasionally produce abominations like Katherine or Elwyn, it's outsiders and their ideas that lead to destruction. Dracula repeats his case to Lazlo, "I am here because this is a young and virile race, not dry and decaying like ours." Lazlo agrees, but blames Dracula, not "the blood of 100 races." Neither is inclined to debate the question.

Criticism of *Son of Dracula* usually focuses on Lon Chaney's portrayal of Count Dracula, and justifiably so. The actor retains the formal-wear of Deane, Balderston, and Lugosi, but returns to the part something of the savagery of Stoker. Its concept is very difficult to portray as written. It affords an actor limited opportunities for the vampire; once introduced, he is seldom seen.

After the success of *The Wolf Man* Universal tapped Chaney to play its monsters, regardless of how the parts suited him. As Dracula, and as Frankenstein's Monster a year earlier, Chaney seems hamstrung. He comes alive in the closing scenes of both films to give rousing finales to his performances, but for most of the films he seems daunted by the specters of Lugosi and Karloff. James Twitchell in *Dreadful Pleasures* tracks Chaney's problems as Dracula to his basic screen persona:

> Lon Chaney, Jr. looked like the perpetual son, and he could act like one in his Wolfman (sic) roles, but Dracula is anything but a child—he is only a parent, more specifically, only the father.

In addition, all-American Chaney is completely unconvincing as a foreigner. Yet he faced a bigger problem than persona or accent—Dracula the character is as drastically miscast in *Son of Dracula* as Chaney the actor. This vampire is superficially close to Stoker's villain, but he is ultimately less a blood-drinking fiend than a repressed romantic, manipulated by Katherine. She clearly has him in her power—Alucard keeps all his promises to her (killing her father, marrying her, transforming her to a vampire) and shares all of his secrets, including the hiding place of his coffin. Alucard's destruction happens only because he never protects himself against her. He may even love Katherine. On their wedding night he tells her:

> As I have told you my dear, ours will be a different life, without material needs. A life that will last through eternity.

Modern revisions of Dracula often cast the vampire as a doomed lover, something quite at odds with Stoker. Here a romantic side to the character is suggested. But only just, for Dracula is neither played nor intended to be sympathetic. Chaney, left adrift with a part half traditional and half innovative, cannot pull off a credible performance.

Katherine and Dracula marry; he carries his bride across their threshold and after those few romantic words moves to take her blood—make her a vampire as she has planned. But jilted Frank arrives and shoots Dracula. The bullets pass through him and strike down Katherine. She slumps to floor, as Frank flees. When next seen she is indeed undead. How does Katherine become a vampire? Does Dracula bite her after she is shot, or does she die of the bullet wounds and, like Elwyn Clayton, return through her own evil desire—perhaps with a little help from Dracula? Katherine later states, "Through [Dracula] I attained immortality," but exactly what happens at Dark Oaks after Frank leaves is not explained. If the shots killed her, Dracula's bite could not bring her back; but however her initiation is achieved, Dracula is detained at Dark Oaks long enough for Frank to escape. By the time Dracula catches him, Frank has reached a church cemetery whose crucifixes protect him.

Female vampires were no strangers to the screen in 1943. In 1931 Dracula had three "wives" and had transformed Lucy (who may still be roaming London as the film ends). *Vampyr*'s fiend in 1931 is elderly Marguerite Chopin; *Mark of the Vampire* in 1935 had Luna; 1936 brought *Dracula's Daughter*. Katherine, like Marguerite, is a monarch; an unrepentant source of evil rather than a victim of it, a female vampire who will have slaves rather than be one. Her plan to eliminate her husband is unchanged after her transformation. On the night after her conversion, she unveils her plans for Dracula to Frank:

> I don't love him, Frank. I never did—Count Alucard is immortal. Through him I attained immortality. Through me you will do the same. And we will spend eternity together—You have no choice. I've taken the first step while you were sleeping... Isn't eternity together better than a few years of ordinary life?—There's one thing you must do while you are in your present form—destroy Dracula.

Katherine's weakness is that she cannot conceive that Frank will not follow her—evil can never comprehend good. With the information she gives him, he does indeed destroy Dracula, but Frank destroys her also.

Katherine Caldwell, the movies' first aggressive, domineering female vampire, is the choice role in *Son of Dracula*. In the 1940s, female predators easily attracted censorship attention. Whether actress Louise Allbritton or the studio decided to play it safe is unknown, but Allbritton's vampire is only adequate. A wasted opportunity is Katherine's return from the grave. Except for a slightly paler shade of make-up, the character is unchanged. Allbritton never achieves mystery or sensuality. Her Katherine, both alive and undead, is cold and aloof, and never makes much lasting impression.

Son of Dracula has a lot in its favor—original story, atmospheric filming, imaginative special effects, and good supporting cast. Some magnetism in its central characters might have made it a classic.

The Return of the Vampire—released January 1944 by Columbia

> Andreas: You! You have no power over me. That was ended many years ago. I'm no longer your slave. Dr. Ainsley has cleansed me of all the evil forced upon me. You can't bring it back! You can't—I won't let you. I won't!
> Tesla: You're a fool, Andreas. A complete, utter fool. Your fate is to be what you are, as mine is to be what I am—your master. Come here.
> Andreas: I won't. I—(transformation into werewolf begins)
> Tesla: Look at me, Andreas. Look at me. Andreas, come here.
> Andreas: Master, you have come back!

Dracula, as an adaptation of Bram Stoker's novel or Deane and Balderston's play, has been filmed at least a dozen times. But no true sequel has ever been made—the closest is probably George Hamilton's spoof, *Love at First Bite*. Dracula as a recurring film character is like James Bond or Sherlock Holmes—each follow-up story is a new adventure rather than the continuation of a saga. The original Dracula—Stoker's or Lugosi's—really has no saga to continue. Frankenstein's Monster searches for a friend or a father; Kharis the Mummy quests for his lost love Ananka; the Wolf Man seeks release from his curse. But Dracula's death brings closure to his story.

Not quite. One twist in the 1931 *Dracula* leaves on opening for an evolving tale. As David Skal notes in *Hollywood Gothic*:

> Exactly why Tod Browning decided to have Dracula attack Renfield is unclear—the script called for the vampire women to do the deed—but consciously or unconsciously he tapped directly into Stoker's subtext, and the film takes on a decidedly homoerotic tone. Renfield is the only character in the film who actually undergoes any change or development; the real "story" is Renfield's tragic, unrequited love for the Count.

Interpretations of Stoker's subtext abound, but Columbia Pictures in 1943 used what Skal calls "the real story" to construct an unauthorized sequel to *Dracula*. In the 1931 film, as in Stoker's novel, the pivotal confrontation is between the vampire and the scientist. In this "sequel," it is between the vampire and his rebelling disciple. Blatant infringement on Universal's sovereignty is avoided by jumbling character names and plot details. But *The Return of the Vampire* picks up where 1931's *Dracula* ends, and even casts Bela Lugosi as the vampire; not Dracula but Armand Tesla, an 18th-

Though named Armand Tesla, Bela Lugosi was still Dracula in 1944's *The Return of the Vampire*.

century Rumanian occultist who returns from his grave. Renfield is renamed Andreas and made a werewolf—though Renfield indeed may have been a werewolf of sorts, for he howled with the wolves at night. Prof. Van Helsing and Dr. Seward become Prof. Saunders and Lady Jane Ainsley. Like Seward, Lady Jane runs a sanitarium near London.

In the film Andreas (Renfield) survives Tesla's (Dracula's) destruction. For years Andreas remains under the care of Saunders (Van Helsing) and Ainsley (Seward), slowly and painfully recovering from Tesla's domination. Twenty-three years later Tesla is strong enough to will Saunders' death and escape from his grave. (Although Saunders was already elderly when he killed Tesla—this vampire's curse lacks teeth!) He reclaims Andreas and seduces Saunders' granddaughter Nikki. He calls her to become his vampire bride. Andreas is wounded as they escape:

> Andreas: Help me, master, I am hurt.
> Tesla: What is that to me?
> Andreas: But I'll die—you must not let that happen, master. You promised me life eternal—like yours, forever.
> Tesla: I no longer need you, Andreas. Your usefulness is over.
> Andreas: You must not say that, master!
> Tesla: Get away from me, idiot. Get back to that corner. Remain there to die.

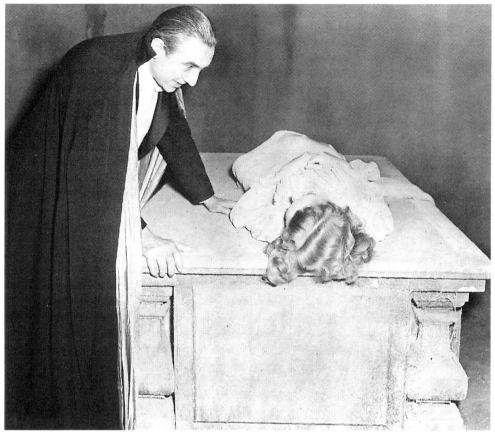

Armand Tesla (Bela "Dracula" Lugosi) makes trouble in war-torn London.

In the corner of the crypt, Andreas finds a crucifix and remembers Ainsley's words:

> You are saved, Andreas, because I have taught you the meaning of
> goodness. You hold it now locked tightly in your heart, and nothing
> evil can ever stand against it again. Always remember that goodness
> is the strongest force in the world, and that all evil cannot prevail against
> it. Remember that and you will be strong...strong... strong.

Andreas recovers his human form and confronts Tesla:

> For years I've lived in terror of you. I'd wake up screaming in the
> night because I'd thought you had come back. I was your slave again
> because I forgot what Dr. Ainsley had taught me, but now that is over.
> I'm going to destroy you forever.

Andreas forces Tesla into the sunlight, drives a stake into him, and Andreas dies of
his wounds and exertions.

Columbia introduced a few elements that superficially differentiate Tesla's tale from
Dracula's. *Son of Dracula* continually reminds us that Dracula is Hungarian; so *Return*

of the Vampire often repeats that Tesla is Rumanian. Previous vampire movies sidestep the basic implausibility of a Gothic vampire by ignoring the external world; Stoker avoids it by giving Dracula a very low profile once in London. *Return of the Vampire* blatantly makes Tesla a metaphor for the modern world's evils. He is first destroyed at the end of one World War, and revives with the outbreak of the next. Tesla's story would never unfold but for German air attacks during World War II. His body is unearthed by a bombing of London, and is unstaked by a clean-up team. He takes the identity of an escaped refugee from Europe (again, xenophobia follows the vampire). A second air raid stops Ainsley from following Nikki. A third one erupts as Andreas finally confronts Tesla.

Any masquerade that *Return of the Vampire* is anything but a continuation of *Dracula* is futile with Bela Lugosi playing Tesla in full Dracula costume of evening clothes and high collar cape. But Tesla is not a duplicate of the 1931 Count. Tesla is quite business-like whereas Dracula often seemed amused by the newness of his surroundings. Gone is Dracula's slow, overly deliberate elocution, replaced by a rather abrupt speaking style. Also gone are Dracula's ambiguous attempts at charm and wit. Tesla is quite unlikely to drop such wonderful comments as "I never drink—wine," or "To die, to be truly dead; that must be glorious!" At the very least Dracula always struck his English hosts as a bit odd. In Stoker's original novel, Van Helsing tells us that the newly arrived vampire is like a child, and will become more dangerous as he assimilates his new land and its customs. Tesla is that Dracula—more at home in England, more comfortable speaking English. Dracula hid in gloomy Carfax Abbey but Tesla takes rooms at a gentlemen's club, and even holds court at Lady Jane's gala reception. Tesla is the crueler, the more arrogant fiend, and Lugosi is still the classic, demonic vampire. Age (Lugosi was then 61) and ill health show on the actor, but the cape work, the voice, and body language are all superb.

For all of Lugosi's vampires (real ones, not the charlatans he plays in *Mark of the Vampire* and *Mother Riley Meets the Vampire*), the first objective is to recruit a male slave. His vampire films are thus open to some homoerotic interpretation. The situation follows all the Draculas, who prefer victims from their own gender. *Dracula's Daughter* is famous for its strong suggestions of lesbianism. Alucard's only victims in *Son of Dracula* are male—Katherine's father and Tommy, a young boy. Likewise in *House of Frankenstein* and *House of Dracula*, Dracula only takes the blood of men. The Count in 1931's *Dracula* takes Renfield and an entire crew of sailors before turning to his first female victim. Of all his victims, male or female, only with Renfield does he have any "relationship," albeit lopsided. Dracula is distant and commanding; Renfield veers from crippling anguish to abject rapture on anticipating sundown and his master's return.

Matt Willis as Andreas, *Return of the Vampire*'s key role, falls far short of Frye's classic performance. His werewolf make-up, avoiding conflict with Universal's copyrights for its Wolf Man, is often criticized as looking more like a cuddly dog than a wolf. But Willis plays the werewolf almost as a puppy, literally frisking at his master's feet. Willis' werewolf may not look much like Chaney's Wolf Man; but the actors' marked facial resemblance, without make-up, may not be coincidental and may have figured in Willis' getting the role.

Lugosi's Dracula at last meets the Wolf Man in *Abbott and Costello Meet Frankenstein* (1948). Dracula again seeks a slave (Frankenstein's Monster), and again this aristocratic vampire is thwarted by a manic-depressive werewolf. With modest suspension of disbelief over minor details, *Dracula, Return of the Vampire,* and *Abbott and Costello Meet Frankenstein* can be viewed as an unintended, accidental trilogy of Dracula's death struggle with his slave. In the saga Renfield, Andreas, and Talbot become a single evolving character who progresses through the series from victim to rebel to crusader. With each transition Renfield/Andreas/Talbot grows in physical stature, and his journey from enslavement to empowerment is mirrored in his deepening kinship to wolves. First he howls with them; then he becomes one on his master's command; then he transforms independently of Dracula and through that transformation destroys his nemesis. His wolfish traits strengthen as Dracula's diminish—by the end of the trilogy, the vampire shows no hint of the lupine powers he possessed at its outset. Renfield/Andreas/Talbot can never quite shed his "tragic, unrequited love" for the vampire, and the zeal to derail Dracula's final scheme may be that of a lover scorned, or a son neglected. Farfetched no doubt—but *Abbott and Costello Meet Frankenstein* tells nothing of what drives Talbot to prevent Dracula's reviving and enslaving the Monster. Dracula's intent is quite clear, for he himself tells us that:

> This time the Monster must have no will of his own. No fiendish intellect to oppose his master.

In the finale the Wolf Man, in a laboratory filled with potential victims, singles out Dracula to attack—Universal's version of the legend requires that "the werewolf instinctively seeks to kill the thing it loves best." The last image of the two monsters before they disappear forever is almost a romantic cliché—the Wolf Man leaps from a balcony to snare Dracula in bat form. He clutches the bat to his bosom as both fall to their deaths. The series of classic Universal horror films begin a first encounter (1931) and end with a last embrace (1948).

House of Frankenstein—released December 1944 by Universal

> Niemann: Do you expect your patrons to believe that the skeleton you show them is really that of Count Dracula?
> Lampini: I, Lampini, took it—pardon me, borrowed it—from the cellar of Dracula's castle in the Carpathian mountains. With my own two hands I spread upon the floor of its coffin a layer of soil taken from its birthplace. So that by proxy, shall we say, the skeleton of his earth bound spirit might lie at peace within his grave.
> Niemann: Until the withdrawal of the wooden stake from his heart would set Dracula free again, to satisfy his unholy appetite for blood.

Lugosi's vampire is one of films' definitive satanic portrayals. His interpretation could never evolve Dracula into a sympathetic figure. Until 1944, no real alternative to the Lugosi Dracula existed. Ralph Morgan in 1935's *Condemned to Live* and Gloria Holden in *Dracula's Daughter* play vampires as tragically afflicted rather than hellspawned. Neither influenced the popular image of vampires. Lon Chaney in *Son of Dracula* never quite achieves terror or pathos. The emergence of a sympathetic Dracula begins subtly with his vignette in *House of Frankenstein*. Subtly because this Dracula, played by John Carradine, never gives voice to his plight like later screen vampires (including Carradine in *House of Dracula*). Carradine's portrayal taps into the self-realization that *The Vampire Film* considers the force propelling the vampire to tragedy, for it is only "lack of self-consciousness that keeps him from despair, from the existential anguish." Lugosi's Dracula is energetic and aggressive; Carradine's is reflective and re-signed. In their seduction scenes, Lugosi *takes* the girl; Carradine *receives* her.

Dracula is only an aside to the main plot of *House of Frankenstein*, which revolves around the Wolf Man and a mad doctor's plan to revive Frankenstein's Monster. Yet the vampire gets quite a build-up. Boris Karloff and George Zucco, as mad doctor Niemann and chamber of horrors impresario Lampini, quickly summarize the vampire legend. Niemann, after disposing of Lampini, continues with a spirited lecture to Lampini's audience (which includes Lionel Atwill), describing how Dracula, if freed, would "feed hideously upon the living whose veins pulsate with warm and vibrant blood." Dracula's resurrection comes when Niemann pries the stake from the vampire's skeleton.

Dracula is quite a contrast to his introduction. Like Chaney, Carradine's Dracula straddles the play's conception of the character, melding that with the mustached, older Count found in Stoker. But whereas Chaney is the forceful brute

Poster art for this monster rally was much like circus advertising.

that Stoker imagined, Carradine is Stoker's antithesis—introspective, soft-spoken, elegant. As his body materializes, he gasps in a birth pain while Niemann holds the stake threateningly over his heart. Thus Dracula enters not all-powerful but quite helpless.

His gaze is every bit as mesmerizing as Lugosi's—not with diabolical intent but with eerie blend of haunting and haunted. He escapes his coffin only by agreeing to settle Niemann's score with an old enemy.

Dracula's taking of Rita (Anne Gwynne) remains one of the most unusual vampire seductions in film. Chaney probably looks and acts more like the Stoker Dracula than any actor who has attempted the part—and Stoker's concept as written is very difficult to portray. It affords an actor limited opportunities, for the vampire, once introduced, is seldom seen. Again, as in *Son of Dracula*, the Vampire King is treated more as a phenomenon than an actual personage. In *House of Frankenstein*, the notion is planted, as it is in *The Vampire's Ghost* and *House of Dracula,* that the vampire may not consciously choose his victims. Carradine completes the seduction with great charm:

> Dracula: You admire my ring?
> Rita: When I look at it, I see glimpses of a strange world—a world of people who are dead and yet alive.
> Dracula: It is the place from which I've just returned.
> Rita: It frightens me.
> Dracula: Wear it. It will drive away your fear.
> Rita: It's too large.
> Dracula: It will become smaller.
> Rita: No, I'm afraid. Take it back.
> Dracula: It is the bond that links us together.
> Rita: I see your world more clearly now. I am no longer afraid.
> Dracula: I will come for you before the dawn.

Rita falls under his spell. The vampire completes his mission for Niemann by killing her father-in-law, and races with her to reach his coffin before dawn. Lingering with Rita is his destruction. He is pursued not for murder, but for her abduction. Dracula's exit is as brilliant as his entrance. The sun's rays cut down him down just as he reaches the coffin, and he crumbles into a skeleton. Rita returns to a husband who never suspects that she, not Dracula, instigated the misadventure almost against the vampire's will.

Lugosi's and Carradine's Draculas represent polar opposites of awareness. Lugosi's Dracula is self-fulfilling and never reflects on his actions; Carradine's is aware of the evil he performs but is moved by a power stronger than himself. Carradine late in his career graciously called Lugosi the better vampire—but actually any comparison is futile. Preference between them is purely a matter of taste. They are entirely different monsters sharing only the same name, and neither shares more than a surface resemblance to Stoker's Vampire King.

The Vampire's Ghost—released May 1945 by Republic

> There is no rest for me. The path of time is curved upon itself like a circle, without beginning, without end. I must follow it forever. I cannot die. I cannot rest. I cannot rest. I cannot rest.
> —Webb Fallon (John Abbott)

The ascent of the sympathetic vampire continues in *The Vampire Ghost*, one of the more distinctive efforts from low-budget producer Republic Pictures.   What Dracula feels in *House of Frankenstein* is verbalized by this movie's vampire, Webb Fallon. Fallon does not so much bemoan his curse as recite it. He gives no hint of satisfaction or remorse in his many ruminations. Fallon owes as much to the Ancient Mariner as Dracula, for he often reflects on his fate:

> Years ago, there was a young woman—I caused her death. Since that time I have been under a curse, the curse of the Undead. Young people like you and Julie—I destroy them. I cannot die. I live on and on, destroying peace and happiness—You can't fight me. I have walked the earth for four hundred years. I have learned things that no human being can ever know. No man is strong enough to fight me.

Thus this vampire's curse is not undeath itself, but repeating through eternity his original sin. In life he somehow killed an innocent woman, and in undeath he must do so again and again. Loquacious Fallon reflects on the notion further. Near the end of the film, as he is about to complete his conquest of Julie, he tells her helpless fiancé, Roy:

> This has all happened before. It will all happen again, no matter where I go, until the end of time.

No lamentation, no hint of suffering in his voice, even when he tells the story's holy man, Father Gilchrist:

> Fate sometimes leads a man down strange pathways. Sometimes things drive a man regardless of his will, things that may even tear his soul.

Fallon becomes only slightly more animated when he croons to Julie,

> A man may follow that path forever if he chooses. He need not walk alone. We could walk that path together, Julie. We could visit worlds no human has ever seen.

Julie is totally in his power when Fallon promises such delights, so his musing is hardly for her benefit. It's also at odds with his curse to repeat endlessly his crime of destroying young lovers. The statement is a peek into Fallon's lonely soul, his hope that each new conquest will be his last. But his curse permits no such peace. Fallon survives only as a detached observer to his own unending existence, truly moved by a power not himself. His will and his actions are separate entities. Whether quelling a brawl in his sleazy cafe, gambling with his unruly clientele, trekking through jungles, or charming women and the local authorities, Fallon maintains an unearthly, weary serenity. Tomorrow holds no surprises for him.

John Abbott's performance as the soft-spoken, imperturbable Fallon is exactly the interpretation needed to hold together a film which, despite the intrigue of its script, has all the shortcomings of a quickie production. In avoiding direct grabs at the viewer's sympathy or loathing, Abbott's Fallon commands an ambiguity the character could not otherwise attain. Like the dreadful *Dead Men Walk*, *The Vampire's Ghost* falls short of the promise of its story and its star. Some bravado from Abbott might have yielded a more memorable portrayal, but the story requires a seductive evil, working ever closer to his victims before he strikes.

The Vampire Film hails *The Vampire's Ghost* as a landmark not only for its portrayal of an overtly sympathetic vampire but its departure from Universal's Dracula legend. Deviations from tradition are many and obvious. Instead of an Eastern European traveling west, Fallon is an Englishman in Africa. He need only wear dark glasses to move freely in the daylight. He sleeps at night, not daytime, and in a bed, not a coffin. Fallon need only keep a small box of soil from his grave close by. He is quite a sound sleeper, for he does not waken when two native carriers steal into his tent to confirm their suspicions and discuss what to do over his sleeping form. Just as Chaney and Carradine go beyond Deane and Balderston to Stoker for inspiration, *The Vampire's Ghost* goes beyond Stoker to Polidori's "The Vampyre" (1816) from which it lifts whole sequences and plot devices. Chief among these is the restorative powers of the moon. "The jungles are deep and full of secrets," waxes Fallon in the prologue, "and the moon that lights them is still a mystic moon." Even the film's main concession to standard lore—Fallon casts no reflection in a mirror—sets it apart from Universal. Universal's three Draculas of the 1940s (Chaney in *Son of Dracula*, Carradine in *House of Frankenstein* and Lugosi in *Abbott and Costello Meet Frankenstein*) are all seen in mirrors; though in *House of Dracula* the studio returns to the gimmick.

Darkness, shadows, and Gothic trappings typical of vampire films are replaced here with stark light in a jungle setting—a trading post upriver near plantations in central Africa. Like all men in the film, Fallon wears white. The sole exception is Father Gilchrist. Gilchrist's black frock is so incongruous to the locale that the contrast might have been intentional. For such a low-budget film the use and interplay of dark and light are easily over analyzed, but *The Vampire's Ghost* is still the only vampire film with a white monster feeding primarily on blacks. The Draculas prefer to stay within their own genders; Fallon prefers to cross racial lines. "Africa, where men have not forgotten the evil they learned at the dawn of time," Fallon tells us. "I always come back to Africa." He plans to make missionary Julie his bride and also takes two other white victims, Barratt and Lisa, in revenge for cheating him. But his basic feeding stock is the native Bakundans. Even Lisa is much darker than any other white in Bakunda and is probably intended to be of mixed blood. In 1940s Hollywood race was at least as delicate a topic as sex, and miscegenation as taboo as homosexuality or incest. Vampires alone among monsters have physical intimacy with their victims; until the late 1950s their feedings were rarely shown, and certainly not interracial attacks. Therefore, the viewer is only told of attacks on villagers and plantation workers. The premise of the plot is the growing civil unrest in the vampire's wake. Through most of the story, the whites who rule Bakunda are clueless about the killings; the blacks who "have not forgotten the evil they learned at the dawn of time" soon know the culprit's identity and seek to destroy him.

Fallon's only explicit attack on a black victim comes in the film's prologue. A white hand opens a door to reveal a sleeping black woman. She awakens, screams, then disappears in shadow. A bold scene for restrictions of the times, especially since the victim shows a bit of cleavage (the only cleavage in any of the six 1943-1945 films). Still Republic hedges its bets. The victim is rather light-skinned; and being in the prologue, the scene could be easily be excised for distribution of the film in sensitive markets. Some prints of the film replace the black woman's murder with Barratt's (and repeat that same shadowy scene of Barratt's murder later in context). This less provocative version aired on television in the New York area in the 1960s, where *The Vampire's Ghost* popped up often on Saturday afternoons.

Rhona Berenstein's 1996 *Attack of the Leading Ladies!* treats "jungle films" as a major subgenre of horror. Basically, in Berenstein's thesis, Hollywood horror films deal with anxieties imbedded in gender-roles; "jungle films" bring into that recipe racial fears. *The Vampire's Ghost* probably probes these ideas as much as any 1940s film of its type cared or dared.

Many critics can not get beyond the film's low production qualities. The direction, except for a few scenes, is unimaginative. Only Roy Barcroft (Barratt) and Adele Mara (Lisa) are more than adequate, and plot inconsistencies abound. Through most of the film Fallon "reads" the ceaseless drums as well as any native; yet in a long sequence at the story's close the natives track him with drums while he remains ignorant of the obvious warnings. Caribbean, African, European, and Eastern superstitions are blended without much care, and this plotline is very confusing on whether Fallon's victims stay dead or return from their graves. Whatever its shortcomings, *The Vampire's Ghost* remains a unique rending of the vampire legend, an imaginative deviation from the Dracula stereotype, and an important advance in portrayals of sympathetic vampires.

House of Dracula—released December 1945 by Universal

You see before you a man who has lived for centuries, kept alive by the blood of innocent people—That's why I've come to you—to seek release from a curse of misery and horror against which I am powerless to fight alone
—Dracula (John Carradine) to Dr. Franz Edelman (Onslow Stevens)

House of Frankenstein's script allows a range of interpretations of Dracula. John Carradine plays a refined gentleman, and portrays the vampire as a tragic figure. In *House of Dracula* the dialogue and plot now suit the performance. Dracula describes himself as "powerless" and desires "release from a curse of misery and horror." He acknowledges for the first time that his victims are "innocent." Though filmed within a year of *House of Frankenstein,* Dracula seems older and rather frail in this second film. He's philosophical, and perhaps more anemic. Edelman takes the Count as a patient, but sternly dictates the conditions. The vampire quietly accepts. This Dracula seems world-weary and past his prime.

Edelman traces Dracula's curse and possible cure to a "peculiar parasite" in his blood, and proposes treatments, which include blood transfusions. Dracula's cure is progressing when the vampire himself undermines it. Nor can he resist seducing Edelman's assistant Miliza (Martha Driscoll). Universal often recycled dialogue in its horror films, and Miliza's entrapment borrows much from Rita's in *House of Frankenstein.* Still, the scene is Dracula's best in the film:

Miliza: I've never heard this music before, yet I'm playing it.
Dracula: You're creating it—for me.
Miliza: It frightens me.
Dracula: It's beautiful. It's the music of the world from which I come.

Miliza: It makes me see strange things—people who are dead yet they
are alive.
Dracula: Mine is a world without material needs.
Miliza: It calls to me, but I'm afraid.
Dracula: The fear will pass as the music becomes fixed in your mind.
It will make you long to be there.

During his next treatment, Dracula injects his own blood into Edelman, no doubt to enslave him. Edelman destroys Dracula before the possession overtakes him. Why does Dracula ruin his one chance of escaping a "curse of misery and horror"? The vampire cannot control his own desires. As Kirk Schneider points out in 1993's *Horror and the Holy*, Dracula could easily overwhelm the world of the living on its own terms, as anything from philosopher to physicist to romantic poet. He possesses knowledge and experience denied to ordinary humans, but he cannot control his hunger. This Dracula can scarcely select his own victims. He cannot help but attempt Miliza's seduction and Edelman's domination. Infected Edelman himself explains the compulsion to Lawrence Talbot (like *House of Frankenstein*, this film also features the Wolf Man and Frankenstein's Monster):

> Because you've suffered the tortures I am going through now, you of all people will understand what I am going to say. In trying to perform a miracle of medical science, I've failed. My blood has been contaminated by the blood of Dracula. My soul and mind have been seized by a nameless horror—a lust!

Stevens' raving, maniacal Edelman hardly seems inspired by Carradine's civilized, restrained Dracula. One of several ironic touches that *House of Dracula* fails to exploit is that Edelman himself predicts what he will become. In the story's opening, when Dracula asks if he believes in vampires, Edelman dismisses the supernatural, but adds,

> Cases have been recorded in which the victims, driven by some abnormal urge, actually believe the blood of other people necessary to keep alive, and become psychopathic killers in order to obtain it. This probably upsets their metabolism, induces fixations and lustful appetites.

Thus Edelman describes his own fate—he takes on some vampire traits, and transforms to a psychopathic killer fixated on reviving the Monster. Here, *House of Dracula* borrows a subtle idea from the 1931 *Dracula*. When Dracula first meets Renfield, the vampire muses on blood ("the blood is the life"), spiders and flies ("the spider spinning his web for the unwary fly"), and wolves ("listen to them—the children of the night"). Later under Dracula's spell Renfield becomes obsessed with exactly those images. In *House of Dracula*, the irony is more elegant, in that the victim himself foresees his own horrible fate.

As in *House of Frankenstein,* Dracula is destroyed early in *House of Dracula*, and the central story becomes Edelman's struggle against Dracula's curse. When first afflicted the doctor has visions of reviving the Monster and strangling his doting assistant Nina. At the close of the movie his fiendish self realizes both dark wishes. The good Edelman befriends Talbot and cures him of his werewolf curse, but Talbot sees the doctor in a mad fit kill a villager. Edelman, returned to sanity, begs for Talbot's silence, pleading for time to complete his great humanitarian work. Then, the doctor says, he will take his own life, and makes Talbot promise to kill him if he is unable to commit suicide. Later, as the police close in on the doctor's laboratory, the again demonic Edelman screams at Talbot, "I hate people who break their promises!" Is this actually the good Edelman speaking, reminding Talbot of his second vow? Talbot keeps his

oath and shoots the doctor, who smiles in gratitude as he dies. Soon the laboratory, including the revived Monster, erupts in flames. It's a blessing that Edelman's body is consumed by fire—otherwise, according to vampire legend, he might rise as one of the Undead; this time with Frankenstein's Monster to do his bidding. Dracula must have liked the notion, for he returns in *Abbott and Costello Meet Frankenstein* to recruit the Monster himself.

Quasi-Vampires

Edelman's quasi-vampire is more a harbinger than an inspiration for the four quasi-vampire films of 1945-46. Though no vampire appears in *Isle of the Dead, The Face of Marble*, *Devil Bat's Daughter*, or *Valley of the Zombies*, they are included in tallies of vampire films for the various features of the legends they employ. *Face of Marble* has a mad doctor (John Carradine) reviving the dead, who return as phantom-like beings. One of them is his dog, which slaughters cattle and drinks their blood. *Devil Bat's Daughter* is a sequel to 1940's *The Devil Bat*, whose mad doctor (Bela Lugosi) creates giant bats to attack his enemies. The sequel strives to be a psychological thriller: the innocent heroine (the original mad doctor's daughter) is driven to believe she is an insane killer, perhaps with a supernatural curse. *Valley of the Zombies* has a psychotic undertaker (Ian Keith) who believes he lives by blood transfusions. He is hardly super-

natural, for the police gun him down in the finale. These films have all the problems of low-budget quickies like *Dead Men Walk* and *The Vampire's Ghost*.

Isle of the Dead, one of the last of Val Lewton's suggestive horror films for RKO, is the only film of this 1945-46 quartet of any quality. A general (Boris Karloff) is determined to protect a small Greek island of refugees from a plague sweeping over them and from a legendary vampire-like creature that may be in their midst. Duty grows to obsession and then to mania until the general himself falls to the plague. No vampire is ever seen, and the only "monster" is the general. Perhaps the film is a bit too low-key and talky, but focusing on the quirks of the vampire hunter rather the vampire is a novel approach—pun intended, for even Stoker's Professor Van Helsing himself is a bit eccentric.

Despite the overall quality of these films, filmmakers obviously had come to see the vampire as a fictional device they could mold to their wishes. But 1946 saw the demand for horror films collapse. Even before World War II ended, market saturation and dwindling quality and originality were driving horror into eclipse.

Presumably, post-war audiences had little appetite for the traditional horrors. As posed by *The Vampire Cinema,* "the destructive capacity of a dinner-suited East European could only seem patently feeble" after Hitler and Hiroshima. Not until the late 1950s would film makers in Mexico and England spearhead a resurgence in Gothic horror. Until then few vampires appeared; in English-speaking movies only two— *Abbott and Costello Meet Frankenstein* and *Mother Riley Meets the Vampire*. Bela Lugosi starred in both, showcasing his distinctive style. The wonderful deviations from his interpretation forged by Carradine, Zucco, John Abbott, and Chaney were forgotten until the television generation revived them.

Bela Lugosi seldom got what he wanted, but often what he wished. In a 1933 interview, Lugosi waxed poetic on the joys of his native Hungary:

> ...All the great character parts are played by four or five different players. Each competes with the other. Each plays the part in accordance with his own concept. And the audience is just as much interested in the actor's conception of the role than (sic) it's interested in the play itself.

In the vampire films produced in Hollywood from 1943 to 1945, that's exactly what occurred. Lugosi and Zucco give excellent renditions of unholy fiends; Carradine and Abbott opt for sympathetic characters with varying degrees of malice; Chaney, attempting a blend of tragic figure and Stoker's vampire, strives for both extremes. From Zucco's no-hold-barred energy to Abbott's almost superhuman restraint, the actors' interpretations run the gamut of styles. Supporting them are Louise Allbritton as the first American vampire and the first aggressive female vampire, Dwight Frye trying to reprise his classic Renfield, Matt Willis expanding Renfield's part in the Dracula saga, and Onslow Stevens as a fiend part vampire and part Jekyll and Hyde. These vampires and their kith and kin come mainly from Eastern Europe, but also India, Africa, England, and rural America. Within the censorship environment of the era, the characters embody rather boldly a spectrum of sexual and social tensions and taboos. A generation would pass before such diversity in screen vampires would be seen again.

Even by today's standards of innovation and experimentation, their six films are an impressive collection.

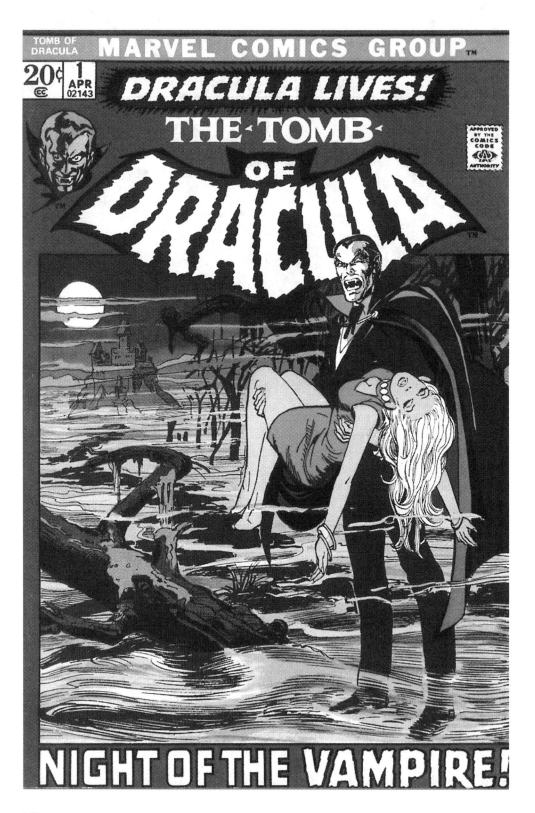

Long the stuff of nightmares, Dracula is also popular with children. When not eating Dracula breakfast cereal (Count Chocula), or seeing him on Saturday morning televi- sion on such shows as Scooby Doo-Where Are You?, *playing with vampire model kits and Dracula toys, or mimicking the Count on* Sesame Street, *children can be found reading about him in the most successful medium ever created for young people: comic books.*

Dracula's dark and bloody adventures are perfectly matched with the four-color comic pages, and as the age of comic readers increased over the years, the Vampire King's adventures have become more adult. Today, it is possible to read the violent adventures of Vlad Tepes, or the starkly pornographic adventures of Dracula in hell, or pass along to children a Dracula-ized version of Daffy Duck or the popular Disney characters.

Comics are, along with motion pictures, one of America's greatest indigenous art forms. Dracula has always been an honored guest in the New World, and Dracula's adventures in the comics are as responsible for formulating our visions of the undead Count as are motion pictures.

Author Rickey L. Shanklin is especially suited to tracking the Vampire King's comic book career. A former book reviewer for the Baltimore News-American, *Shanklin turned his journalistic experience to creating a newspaper of his own, devoted exclusively to reviews of books and movies,* Between the Covers. *He is also the author of several celebrated Dracula comics, starting with his monumental* Blood of the Innocent, *which pitted Stoker's Dracula against real-life monster, Jack the Ripper.*
—Bob Madison

Fangs for the Funny Books: Or, Dracula in the Comics
by Rickey L. Shanklin

As with most cultural changes of the 20th century, Dracula was there at the beginning.

There have been vampires in the comics almost as long as there have been comics. In 1939, Batman battled vampires in *Detective Comics* #31-32; three years later, it was Captain America's turn as he faced a Japanese scientist whose serum induced a scien- tific vampirism. In 1948, Rulah, the Jungle Goddess, ran across a tribe of lycanthropic vampires.

Vampires appeared frequently in horror comics of the day, but it wasn't until 1951 that Count Dracula made an appearance by name: in *Suspense* #7, published by Atlas Comics, in a story entitled "Dracula Lives!" The following year, Atlas (now Marvel

After pitting Dracula against the other monsters on film, Universal Pictures duplicated the process in comic books.

Comics) published a story featuring Dracula's son in *Mystic* #17; and Superior published *Journey into Fear* #8, with a story/character called "Tracula."

In 1953, however, things changed.

The initial copyright term of 28 years on Bram Stoker's 1897 novel *Dracula* had been renewed in 1925 for another 28 years, bringing the literary character to 1953... and public domain! Classics Illustrated, the leader in "literary adaptations" (and a sort of illustrated cliff notes for millions of school children), passed on adapting *Dracula*, leaving the field wide open for Avon Periodicals to publish *Eerie* #12 in 1953, featuring a book-length adaptation—and cover!—of *Dracula*.

But the menace of Dracula could not long be endured, and the lid on his four-color coffin was about to be slammed shut again! In 1954, Atlas squeaked by with *Journey into Unknown Worlds* #29, with a story entitled "Of Royal Blood." And then all hell broke loose!

The 1950s are fondly remembered for a lot of things: fast cars, Elvis, cycles, rock 'n roll, and grade-B sci-fi flicks among them. But it was also a decade of fear and paranoia. The Cold War escalated daily, the Red Menace spread pervasively throughout society (or so we were led to believe), and our friend the atom grew ever more sinister. This was a fertile ground indeed for opportunists and political hatchet-men.

Enter a villain blacker than the Transylvanian Count: Dr. Fredric Wertham, a name that still strikes terror in the hearts of pop culturists and comic book buffs to this day. With the publication of his influential *Seduction of the Innocent* (a condensed version had appeared earlier in *The Ladies Home Journal*), he fueled the United States Subcommittee hearings on Juvenile Delinquency, leading to the creation of the Comics Code Authority. Influenced largely by Wertham—who worked exclusively on anecdote, hearsay, and outright fabrication—a concerned United States government suddenly saw simple comic books as the source of the nation's problems, blaming them for everything from widespread crime to sex mania to creeping Communism.

Aimed at cleaning up comic books read by children (and adults) nationwide, the Comics Code ended the spate of horror, crime, and "good girl art" comics that constituted much of the market. (This was, however, a godsend for the superhero titles that were to emerge—and flourish!—again.)

Wertham sought out and destroyed monsters in the comics with all the zealous monomania of Dr. Van Helsing. Laying the Vampire King to rest once more... it would be fully eight years before Dracula would be resurrected in comics.

Dell Comics, publisher of *Mickey Mouse*, *Popeye*, *Little Orphan Annie*, *Tarzan*, *Raggedy Ann*, and hundreds of photo-cover Western comics, had never succumbed to the lure of the lucrative horror/crime market in the 1940s and 1950s, so there had been no reason for them to join the Comics Code Authority when it was formed. Now, free of its constraints, they published *Dracula* (#1) in 1962. Featuring Count Dracula and several supporting characters from the novel, it was not an adaptation of Stoker's novel or a movie version, but it apparently touched an exposed nerve with several very determined publishers.

In 1964, DC's *Jerry Lewis Comics* #83 featured Count Drinkula; and Gold Key Comics (part of Dell), published *The Munsters* #1, which, powered by the Monster Boom gripping the country, would run for 16 issues. Dracula found his way into *Mad Magazine* (#85), and Warren Publications released a black-and-white, magazine-sized horror comic reminiscent of the E. C. Picto-Fiction titles of the fifties: *Creepy* #1. Featuring top-notch illustrators of the period, *Creepy* was a seminal influence on the field, demonstrating the sales potential of such well-written subject matter. Along with sister publication *Famous Monsters of Filmland*, *Creepy* was joined the same year by *Famous Films* #2, a fusion of the two magazines. *Famous Films* #2 featured a fumetti style photo-novel adaptation of *Horror of Dracula* and *Curse of Frankenstein*, with word balloons and sound effects superimposed over black-and-white stills. (*Horror of Party Beach* had been the first such effort.) The experiment proved to be a failure.

In 1965, *The Adventures of Bob Hope* #95 introduces Dr. Van Pyre, a high school principal that would appear for almost three years in the DC comic; *Famous Monsters of Filmland* adapted *Horror of Dracula* for a comics section in issue #32; Dracula got *Sick* in #41; and *Creepy* #8 published "Coffin of Dracula" part one. (Part two appeared the following year in *Creepy* #9.)

Erie publications began a line of black-and-white comic magazines the following year, featuring generally awful stories reprinted from the 1940s and 1950s. Titles included *Classic Horror Tales*, *Horror Tales*, *Tales from the Tomb*, *Tales of Voodoo*, *Terror Tales,* and *Weird*. Most sported lurid cover paintings of torture, decomposing flesh, and general mayhem. The line (mercifully) ended in 1978.

A banner year for Dracula, 1966 finds him in *Herbie* #20 from ACG, another humorous appearance. Dracula's character appears in "The Impressionist" in *Twilight Zone* #66 from Gold Key, who also publishes *Flintstones* #33 "The Flintstones meet Frankenstein and Dracula." In an attempt to ride the "bat" craze—Adam West's *Batman* is the number one hit on television—Dell releases *Dracula* #2. (Actually, "escapes" better defines it...) Dracula dons new duds, and makes the super-hero scene for 3 issues... stunningly stylized by coloring-book artist Tony Tallarico. (In truth, the only thing worse than the art is the writing on this attempt.)

Pyramid Books, meanwhile, published Christopher Lee's *Treasury of Terror*, a paperback collection of black-and-white horror stories... including "Dracula's Guest"; and Ballantine Books releases *Dracula*, another paperback. This one, illustrated by Al McWilliams, adapts the original novel with style, and is well-written throughout.

Eerie (*Creepy*'s new sister magazine) ushers in 1967 with a Dracula story in issue #11, and Dell releases *Mad Monster Party*, based on the Rankin-Bass animated hit film. Over at Gold Key, *Ripley's Believe It or Not* #4 features "The Vampires."

Dracula sleeps through 1968, and as we land on the moon (in 1969), *Dark Shadows* #1 is published by Gold Key, three years after its television debut. Like most Gold Key comics, the art is only adequate and the stories are somewhat reserved. The magazine *For Monsters Only* (#7) features a humorous Dracula tale, and Cousin Creepy is joined by his sexy sister, *Vampirella*. Vampi, as she is known, hails from Drakulon, and arrives thirsty... and half naked! (No wonder her magazine ran 115 issues... and she still has an ongoing comic!) *Vampirella* was an instant hit, sporting spectacular covers (the cover of the first issue is by the legendary Frank Frazetta) and much better than average scripts.

Psycho #1 is introduced in 1970, another black-and-white horror magazine, this one from Skywald Publishing. (Dracula appears in the first issue, his only 1970 appearance.) Unlike the early Warren stories, Skywald's scripting is often bizarre to the point of outlandish, relying heavily on shock value and over-emphatic verbiage.

The Comics Code Authority, now horribly out-of-date by 1971, is revised to allow traditional monsters. The flood-gates now open. Marvel introduces Morbius, the Living Vampire, in *Amazing Spider-Man* #101. (Morbius is to become a staple character in the Marvel Universe, encountering many of their characters and even achieving his

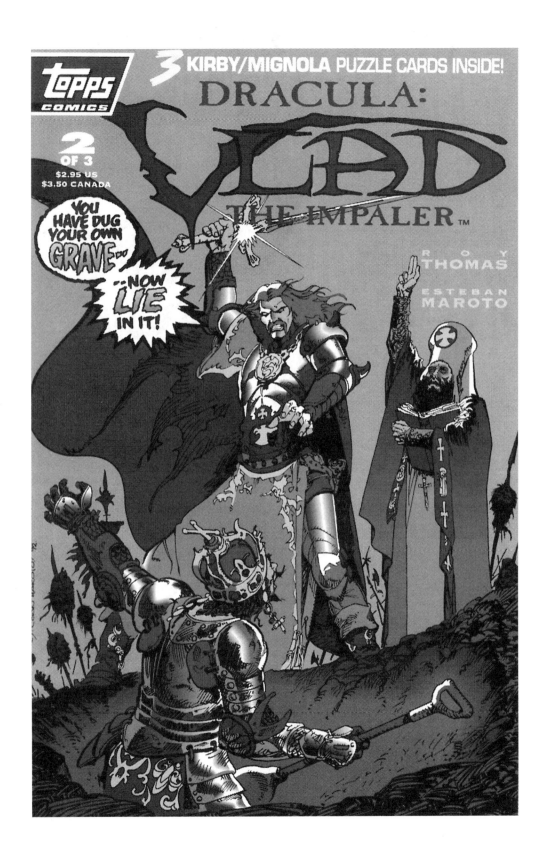

02187

With *Dracula Lives!*, **the vampire king joined the ranks of black-and-white comic magazine characters.**

own title!) Gold Key introduces Baron Tibor (another vampire) in *Mystery Comics Digest* #4. *Superman's Pal, Jimmy Olsen* introduces Dragorin, and even *National Lampoon* gets into the act with its wicked Dragula, about a gay vampire who can turn into a French poodle!

Dracula comes to the United States from Spain in 1972. Twelve oversize color magazines entitled *Dracula* are published in Spain; republished in London by New English Library (and also as *Dracula Annual*), issues #1-6 arrive in the U.S. as a single

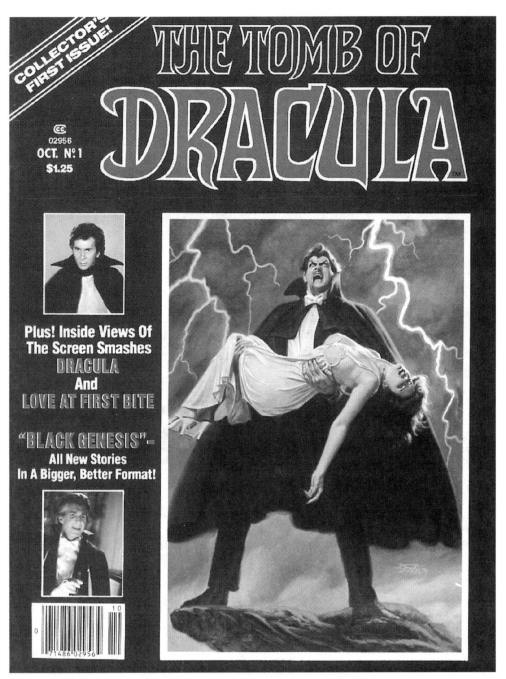

Dracula was a frequent guest at newsstands in the vampire-rich 1970s.

volume published by Warren. The same year, *The Monster Times* #1 is released, featuring an adaptation of 1922's *Nosferatu* by Berni Wrightson. (Not new to the character, Berni—and other artists—had often featured Dracula in fanzine stories and illustrations.) Marvel pokes fun at *Blacula* in *Spoof* #4, and releases *Tomb of Dracula* #1.

Originally planned as a black-and-white magazine, *Tomb of Dracula* became the longest-running Dracula comic ever. The Dracula character owes his visage to gaunt actor Jack Palance, and Marv Wolfman's writing made this series the yardstick against

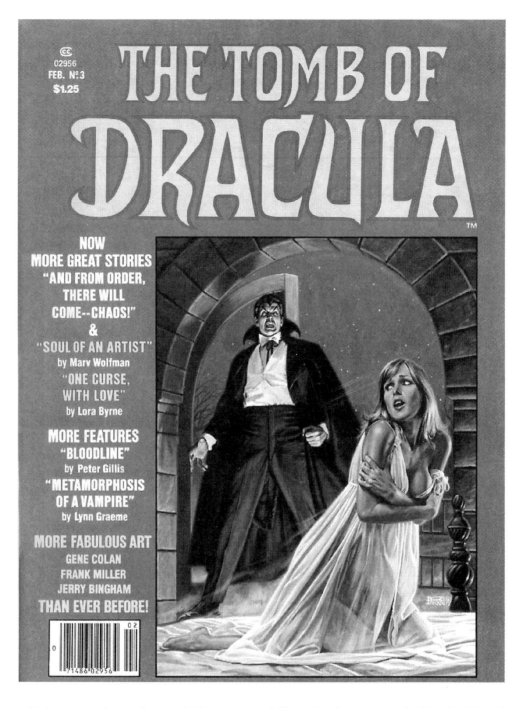

which many other series would be measured. Dracula also appears in *Psycho* #9 and *Psycho Annual* #1 from Skywald.

Comics published in 1973 included an unauthorized *Blacula* comic (printed in black, white, and red); *The Frankenstein Monster* #7 and 8 (from Marvel); *The Occult Files of Dr. Spektor* #5 from Gold Key; DC's *Prez* #4 ("Vampire in the White House"... with Dracula attacking the country's first teen-age president); *The Many Ghosts of Doctor Graves* #44 from Charlton, featuring Dracula's cousin; and DC's *Weird War Tales* #18 featuring "Captain Dracula"... in name only!

Pendulum Press released yet another black-and-white adaptation of the novel (a good one, nonetheless), and the magazines were filled with royal blood. Marvel published the first issues of *Dracula Lives!* and *Vampire Tales*, both black-and-white magazines. Marvel's black-and-whites (including *Tales of the Zombie*) generally were quite well-written, with gray wash tones accomplishing what color provided in their regular line; their standards remained high throughout the run.

Dracula appeared in *Eerie* #'s 46, 47, and 50; Skywald's *Nightmare* featured Dracula in issue #19, and on the cover of #15, while *Psycho* featured the Count in issues #14 and 16. Skywald also issued *Scream* #1, a special Dracula issue.

Dracula's biggest year of the decade was undoubtedly 1974. Beginning with a humorous story, "Fangs for the Memory" in *Arrgh!* #1 (Marvel), and the first appearance of Count Duckula in *Daffy Duck* #92 from Gold Key, "Dracula" joined Scooby Doo in Gold Key's 25th issue of *Scooby Doo—Where Are You?* Pyramid Books got another joking jab to the jugular with *Vampire Jokes & Cartoons*. The magazines were also busy, with Dracula's daughter, Lilith, appearing in Marvel's *Vampire Tales* #6 and *Dracula Lives!* #10; Skywald featured Count Dracula in *Nightmare* #21, the *1974 Nightmare Yearbook*, *Psycho* #'s 19 and 21, and another original story in *Scream* #10. Over at Warren, *Vampirella* #39 featured several Dracula stories. In the color comics, there was *Mystery Comics Digest* #17 and *The Occult Files of Dr. Spektor* #8 ("Dracula's Vampire Legion") from Gold Key; and *Weird Mystery Tales* #14 (DC).

At Marvel Comics, Dracula was a star, making appearances in *Giant-Size Spider-Man* #1, followed by *Giant-Size Chillers* #1 (whose name changed to *Giant-Size Dracula* with issue #2), and *Werewolf by Night* #15 (finishing up a story begun in *Tomb of Dracula*).

By 1975, the horror craze had about run its course. Marvel's *Tomb of Dracula* continued (it would eventually end in 1979), and Power Records issued a comic/record set starring Dracula (from *Tomb of Dracula* #2). A single issue of *Fright* (with the origin of the *Son of Dracula*) appeared from Atlas/Seaboard, an upstart company founded by Stan Lee's brother. (Marvel and DC would soon squash this competitor by glutting already-crowded newsstand comic racks with additional titles, thereby making shelf space unavailable to the unproven newcomer!) Both *Dracula Lives!* and *Vampire Tales* would end in 1975, along with *Scream, Nightmare,* and *Psycho.* A year after *Tomb of Dracula*'s demise, DC's *I, Vampire* would begin in *House of Mystery* #290, running through most issues until #312. (The title character, however, was Andrew Bennett, not Dracula.)

In 1973, I sent a manuscript to then-editor Marv Wolfman at *Dracula Lives!* for an eight-page story entitled "Two Faces of Death." I was asked to expand the story to 16 pages, but in the interim the cancellation of Marvel's black-and-white horror line was announced. Except for the remainder of his days at Marvel, Dracula virtually disappeared from the comics field for the next decade.

In 1982, Count Dracula got the hots for Storm in *Uncanny X-Men Annual* #6, marking a rare appearance of the character during his "retirement" from the field. This successful interaction between the King Vampire and super-heroes would lead to many more such encounters in the years to come as Marvel sought new and different ways to exploit their characters.

It was during this 10-year span that I met Mark Wheatley and Marc Hempel. The original eight-page story I had sent to *Dracula Lives!* (now expanded to 16 pages)

piqued their interest, and together we began a collaboration that eventually made its way to DC Comics as a proposed graphic novel. But while DC was considering the proposal, an unexpected player entered the field. Warp Graphics, who had been publishing the wildly popular Elfquest series, was looking for something different to add to their line.

Our proposal, now titled *Blood of the Innocent*, struck a chord... and the original eight-page black-and-white story expanded to a four-issue full-color mini-series! Published in 1985, *Blood of the Innocent* resurrected the noble Count in the first weekly comic book ever sold in the United States (Will Eisner's *Spirit* had been a newspaper insert). With painted covers by Marc Hempel (perhaps best known for his *Sandman* series), the series featured Count Dracula's feud with Jack the Ripper in 1888 London. The interior art was penciled by Marc Hempel (based on photographs and drawings of the personalities and locales featured in the storyline) and inked and painted by Mark Wheatley (who also co-wrote the final script).

Carefully researched, the series remained faithful to the details concerning Jack the Ripper's bloody reign of terror, and served as a prequel (of sorts) to Stoker's novel, *Dracula*. A bit of a Ripperologist, I chose Prince Albert Victor, Duke of Clarence, as the identity of Jack the Ripper. After all, what better nemesis for a Count than the heir to the throne of England? With an introduction by renowned horror-writer Robert Bloch (who had been a favorite writer of mine as well as a regular correspondent), the series had grown into far more than I had ever imagined.

The following year, 1986, Warp Graphics Annual featured a follow-up story to the *Blood of the Innocent* series. Also that year, Showcase Comics released *Cryptic Tales* #1, featuring Count Dracula. With the birth of independent comic publishers around the country, Dracula—and his fellow bloodsuckers—was about to receive the red carpet treatment.

In 1987, Apple Press published the first issue of my *Blood of Dracula* series. Three stories ran in each issue, two of which were continuing storylines. "Count Dracula" was Hammeresque in design, set in Bukovina near the turn of the century. It featured comely damsels, vampire slayers, a Burgomeister, and all the other trappings found in a good Hammer yarn. (In later issues, with the addition of artist Mike McCarthy, the series evolved into something akin to a cross between *Andy Warhol's Dracula* and *Doc Strangebrew's Travelling Odditorium & Sideshow!*)

Set 300 years in the future, "Dracula 2199" found the Count more than a little out of his element. In a world dominated by superscience and artificial blood, Dracula found more than vampire-hunters to worry about! Establishing himself as a deity, Dracula feeds on the blood of his followers while amassing an army to reclaim his throne.

The third series was "Death Dreams of Dracula," in which Dracula's spirit interacts with the dreams (and nightmares) of Ed Gein, Melvin Purvis, Lady Maclain, SS Commanders, Ambrose Bierce, and even the population at ground-zero Hiroshima!

Two issues of *Blood of Dracula* were published in '87, and the series ran for 19 issues.

Marvel's four-issue mini-series, *Blood*, appeared in 1988, along with the first issue of Now Comics' *Fright Night*, based on the popular Tom Holland movie. Apple's *Blood of Dracula* continued through #8, but it was the publication of another black-and-white comic, one featuring no vampires at all, that really started things rolling. James O'Barr's first issue of *The Crow*, from Caliber Press, was published with little fanfare. It was not an overnight success (in fact, hundreds of copies not given out at the 1988 San Diego Comic Con were discarded!), but grew slowly by word-of-mouth. Soon, with back-issues commanding premium prices, fans were clamoring for copies of the obscure, semiautobiographical, comic-noir series. Dealing with death, love lost, and ultimate justice, the series widened the market for more grim, dark titles. And who better to join the fray than that grim and dark prince, Dracula?

The floodgates reopen in 1989. Morbius, the Living Vampire, returns to the Marvel universe in *Dr. Strange* #10, and issues #14-18 feature the return of the rest of their vampires in "The Vampiric Verses"; Eternity Comics begins reprinting the old Skywald *Dracula* stories in *Vampyres*, and they issue another adaptation of the Bram Stoker novel in *Dracula* #1-4 (both *Vampyres* and *Dracula* are subsequently reissued as trade paperback collections); Pioneer debuts *Vegas Knights*, with Dracula battling ninjas!; and Dark Horse publishes a one-shot sci-fi vampire comic by French artist Druillet titled *Nosferatu*. *Blood of Dracula* issues #9-15 appear (beginning with issue #14, "Death Dreams" is replaced by "The Lost Frankenstein Pages" by Berni Wrightson; #15 contains a stereo flexi-disc). The biggest event of the year, however, is the beginning of Innovation Comics' adaptation of the Anne Rice novel, *The Vampire Lestat*. With painted art throughout, the 12-issue series marks the beginning of a long collaboration between the writer and Innovation.

Following up on their success with *The Vampire Lestat*, 1990 sees another Anne Rice novel adapted into comics: *The Mummy*. Also that year, Innovation releases *The Vampire Companion*, an Anne Rice interview/preview comic. *Nathan Impaler, Monster Hunter* goes after Dracula (from Night Realm Comics); Marv Wolfman introduces *R.I.P.*, a TSR Comics Module; Eternity adapts "Dracula's Guest" as *Dracula: Lady in the Tomb*; and Eclipse Comics publishes an adaptation of Richard Matheson's novel, *I Am Legend*. (This black-and-white adaptation is far more faithful to Matheson's novel than either *The Omega Man* with Charlton Heston or *The Last Man on Earth* with Vincent Price.) Issues #16-18 of *Blood of Dracula* are published (#17 with a new Berni Wrightson cover), and Apple enters the super-hero market with *The Bat* #1. Published to take advantage of the release of the first Tim Burton *Batman* movie, *The Bat* features a crime-fighter who obtains Count Dracula's ring to aid him in his war on crime. But the ring, even as it grants him the power he desires, begins to corrupt his soul. In the end, he removes the ring at the cost of his own life. (No further issues were published, however, because DC Comics felt that the character infringed on their trademarked "bat" man.)

Marvel's legendary *Tomb of Dracula* returned with a four-issue miniseries in 1991, but falls short of its former greatness. The storyline was weak, and the art seemed uninspired this time around. (The covers were especially poor.) Innovation launches three new painted comic adaptations: *Queen of the Damned* and the long-awaited *Interview with the Vampire* from Anne Rice, and a new *Dark Shadows* series to tie-in with the new TV series with Ben Cross.

Vampirella (her magazine canceled in 1983 and revived for a single issue in 1988) returns in *Vampirella: Morning in America*, a Dark Horse/Harris four-issue mini-series. The final issue of *Blood of Dracula* is published (#19), leading into a new four-issue *Death Dreams of Dracula* series. Apple also publishes *Vampiric Jihad* (a collection of Dracula 2199 stories) and two issues of *Big Bad Blood of Dracula* featuring "Dracula meets Cadavera." (Also in these issues: "A Chronology of Dracula from 1430 to 2200,"

COMIC SHOP NEWS

278

BRAM STOKER'S
DRACULA

It was inevitable that one bat-man would meet the other; the cover of DC's masterful *Red Rain*.

and the 1970 Berni Wrightson Dracula classic "StakeOut.") Other comics for 1991 include *Ghosts of Dracula* from Eternity; *Little Dracula* from Harvey; an adaptation of the F. W. Murnau film *Nosferatu* from Caliber/Tome; *Subspecies* (a movie tie-in) from Eternity; *Spider: Reign of the Vampire King* from Eclipse (based on the pulp super-hero); *Nosferatu: Plague of Terror* (Millennium); and *Blood Junkies on Capitol Hill* (vamPACs?) from Eternity.

The release of Francis Ford Coppola's 1992 film, *Bram Stoker's Dracula*, finds Topps publishing a four-part film adaptation; a *Dracula: Vlad, the Impaler* comic; the *Dracula Chronicles*; the *Frankenstein-Dracula War*; and even *Dracula vs. Zorro*! Reprinting old *Tomb of Dracula* issues, Marvel releases *Savage Return of Dracula* #1, the *Wedding of Dracula* #1 and *Requiem for Dracula* #1. Marvel also releases *Nightstalkers* #1 and *X-Men vs. Dracula* #1 (reprinting *X-Men Annual* #6). DC has *Scarlett*, a super-hero vampiress, and *Vampirella* still refuses to die, back for a five-issue Harris series (later collected into a trade paperback). Apple releases *Death Dreams of Dracula* #4 (the final issue), and two issues of the X-rated *Dracula in Hell* (chronicling young Vlad's ascension to power at the fabled Scholomance in a crescendo of gore and sexual excess!). Eclipse publishes *Blood is the Harvest*, while Darque Studios release *Christian Dark* #1. Following the success of Innovation's Anne Rice adaptations, Malibu begins adapting Brian Lumley's *Necroscope* and *Vamphyri!* novels, featuring the bloodthirsty Baron Ferenczy.

In 1993 the vampire series *Vigil* begins (from London Night Studios), followed in 1994 by *Renfield* (Caliber) and *Rune* (Malibu). Marvel issues *Spider-Man vs. Dracula* #1 (reprinting *Giant-Size Spider-Man* #1) and *The Silver Surfer vs. Dracula* (which reprints *Tomb of Dracula* #50, and other material). DC Comics releases the first issue of *Vamps*, the all-girl vampire series (and a good one, too!) and Harris releases *Vengeance of Vampirella* #1... which is still available at comic and specialty stores. (This undying interest makes *Vampirella* the longest-running vampire comic, with about another half dozen graphic novels and trade paperback collections not mentioned here. Add to this a very limited edition statue, a plastic model kit from Aurora, posters, and the *Vampirella Classics* series, which reprints her early stories.)

A character similar to Vampi, DesNoir (fangs and figure again!) emerged from Jim Balent and Ed Polgardy's *From the Darkness* series some years back. In addition to her comic books, there was also a limited edition statue of the character offered for sale.

In underground comix, we had *Jerry, the Vampire*. There was even a comic titled *What if...Wolverine Was Lord of the Vampires?* in which Wolverine beheads the Count and usurps the vampire lord's throne!

The British Halls of Hammer—House of Horror magazine regularly featured excellent comic adaptations of various Hammer films; Japan gave us *Vampire Hunter D* and *Vampire Princess Miyu*; and there are countless Dracula comics from Italy, Mexico, France, and the rest of the world.

Over the last three years, Vampirella has teamed up with Shadowhawk (from Image) and DC's Catwoman. And with the continued success of the series of *Batman* movies, it was inevitable that the two greatest "Bat-Men" in pop culture would square off.

Count Dracula battled Batman in DC's Elseworlds graphic novel, *Red Rain*. A brilliant reimagining of both legends, *Red Rain* has DC's Dark Knight becoming a vampire to grapple with his most fearsome nemesis ever: Dracula!

Bram Stoker's Burial of the Rats was published by Roger Corman's Cosmic Comics and there was even a 3-D Dracula comic from 3-D Zone (and *To Die For in 3-D* from Blackthorne). There was a sequel to the original novel from Adventure/Malibu (*Dracula: The Suicide Club*), *Dracula's Daughter* got her own comic, and *Dracula, the Impaler* was published by Comax. *Daffy Duck's Duckula* got his own book along with *Carmilla* and *Draculina*. Add to the list *Young Dracula*, the *Vampire's Kiss*, *Night's Children*... and *Children of the Night*. Did I mention *Scarlet in Gaslight* (with Houdini!), *Return of the Impaler*, and *Scare Tactics*? Dark Horse even published a *Universal Studios Monsters: Dracula*, featuring a Dracula that bore an uncanny resemblance to Bela Lugosi. Acid Rain Studios published *Naked Fangs, Vampire Vixens, Vampire Swimsuits*, and others. Both *Wetworks* and *Spawn* feature vampires regularly, and vampires have appeared in *Bloodshot* and *Shadowman* from Valiant Comics.

With the success of their Vertigo line (due, largely, to the popularity of *Sandman*), DC Comics has been at the forefront with good vampire comics over the last year or so. *Preacher* continues to be one of the best reads around (though definitely not for the kiddies), along with *Dhampire* by Nancy Collins. Another subsidiary of DC, Helix, released *The Black Lamb* by Tim Truman, this series featuring a kind of vampire Lone Ranger, out to preserve and protect the innocent (monsters) while hunting and destroying those who prey on humankind.

Is the list complete? Not by a long shot! Ever elusive, shifting shape and visage, Dracula continues to stalk the four-colored pages. Dracula's influence on the comics is too pervasive, too widespread for any listing to be comprehensive.

But the point I think, is indisputable: Dracula has been in the comics for nearly 50 years, and will be part of the medium as long as children and adults cluster round illustrated stories.

As long as there are comics, Dracula, the *original* Bat-Man, will be in them!

UNIVERSAL PICTURES
PRESENTS

DRACULA

ALL PLASTIC ASSEMBLY KIT

The Very Model of a Modern Major Movie Monster

In 1962, Aurora Plastics of Hempstead, Long Island, brought Dracula into the homes of millions of monster-hungry kids.

It was then, during the height of the "Monster Craze" that swept the young people of America, that Aurora created its now-legendary line of monster model kits. With these nine-inch monster models, America's youth could own their own favorite movie monster in effigy, fully painted, or glow-in-the-dark, and place them proudly on their night tables, bookshelves, or windowsills. Dracula was joined by a whole gamut of creature features: Frankenstein's Monster, the Wolf Man, the Phantom of the Opera, the Hunchback of Notre Dame, King Kong, the Creature from the Black Lagoon, and Mr. Hyde. The striking box cover art for the model kits was done by James Bama, who also painted the now-legendary covers for the Bantam paperback reissues of the Doc Savage novels.

Later editions of the model kit featured a brief biography of the King Vampire on the instruction sheet. It was a neat addition to Dracula lore.

Closely modeled on Bela Lugosi's Dracula for Universal pictures, the figurine came complete with display stand: a creepy dead tree and vampire bats. (These were bats identical to those in Aurora's Batman model kit.) Once built, kids gleefully destroyed Dracula with firecrackers, burnt him down to a smoldering pool of molten goo in backyard funeral pyres, or chucked him playfully from windows, only to buy and build him once more, proving that Dracula was indeed eternal and undying. It's unlikely most kids would've been so destructive had they known the eventual value of these kits: today, an unbuilt Dracula kit in its original box can fetch as much as $500!

Later, Aurora wisely capitalized on the twin passions of vampires and hot rods with the creation of Dracula's Dragster. (Other cars in this dance macabre of monster and machinery were Frankenstein's Flivver and the Mummy's Chariot.)

There has been a major renaissance in model kits over the past decade, which has seen the rise in many privately produced "garage kits." Garage kits are usually sculpted, manufactured, and sold by the same individual, most often without official sanction or license from copyright owners. A trip to any one of the hundreds of "monster conventions" held nationwide each year can yield a bundle of new Dracula figures, many of them expertly crafted and produced, and miles away from the simple model kits of cherished childhood.

—Bob Madison

Halloween is Dracula Night...

A 1992 study revealed that Dracula was the most popular Halloween costume ever. The reasons for his popularity on this, the monster's holiday, are easy to decipher.

First, Dracula has always been the most popular of the classic Gothic characters. The image of the pale-faced European in evening clothes (invented by Hamilton Deane and John L. Balderston for the stage play) has come to mean "Dracula" throughout the world. A rented tux (or your Dad's old suit), a cape of black felt, a menacing look, and *voila!*

Ben Cooper, one of the leaders in children's Halloween costumes, created an amusing Dracula costume, and there are several unauthorized Dracula masks in the visage of actor Bela Lugosi. Dick Smith's *Do-It-Yourself Monster Make-Up Book* (1965), a magazine one-shot from Warren Publications, opened with a do-at-home vampire make-up.

But aside from the ease with which it is possible to assume the vampire's role, it is also *fun.* Disguising ourselves as Dracula allows us to comfortably explore the dark side of our natures and our sexual personas, even if for one night a year.

The historic Halloween parade in New York City's Greenwich Village features more than its share of vampires, both in and out of costume. (New York is also home to scores of blood fetishists, who engage in a Dracula masquerade all year.) And the Cathedral of St. John the Divine, the world's largest Gothic cathedral, hosts a Halloween spectacle every year, usually including a screening of *Nosferatu* to a live organ accompaniment. The Cathedral's Monster Procession, which ends the celebration, includes some of the finest Dracula and vampire costumes ever created.

Dracula becomes a television staple those last few weeks in October, and magic and novelty stores sell papier mache coffins, inflatable giant bats, and plastic vampire fangs. Television and radio talk shows regularly feature vampire content, and local newspapers interview such vampire authors as Chelsea Quinn Yarbro and Fred Saberhagen.

Dracula has truly put the bite on Halloween, making the holiday his own. Judd Hirsch's Dracula—crowned King of the Monsters—had to negotiate with Mariette Hartley's witch to get Halloween going for 1979's *The Halloween That Almost Wasn't*, and three Dracula clones sang back-up for Tim Burton's affectionate Halloween-Christmas tribute, *The Nightmare Before Christmas.*

When making an appearance at this year's Halloween party, remember Dracula. It's a role to sink your teeth in.

—Bob Madison

The Don Post Dracula Mask

Children across America were able to *become* Dracula when Don Post released his first ever Dracula mask in 1964. Modeled vaguely on actor Bela Lugosi, the mask followed on the heels of Post's first commercially successful mask, Frankenstein's Monster, who first lumbered onto the latex scene in 1948.

Dracula's visage was re-vamped in 1966 when Post unleashed his Deluxe Series of masks. These masks, also known as the Calendar Masks thanks to a striking full-color calendar featuring Post's work, are extremely valuable today and are actively sought by collectors. Its scarcity and artistry have elevated prices for the mask, which originally retailed at $30, to more than $500.

Post's Deluxe Dracula mask bears an even greater resemblance to Lugosi, and had the briefest production run of the entire series due to litigation by Lugosi's heirs against Universal Studios.

Post added another version of Dracula to his repertoire when he created the Grandpa Munster mask in 1964, part of a series of masks based on television's *The Munsters.*

Post's masks stamped the imaginations of Americans who grew up during the "Monster Boom" of the late 1950s through early 1970s. When the Lugosi Dracula mask was no longer available, young vampire enthusiasts were able to buy a stunning reproduction of Nosferatu, as embodied by silent-screen player Max Schreck, which was now comfortably in the public domain. I had a Nosferatu mask during my boyhood in the early '70s and I can attest that, with a dark suit and stiff walk, the transformation was complete.

Post's legacy lives on. Don Post Studios is now run by his son, Don Post, Jr., and continues to produce masks inspired by fantastic films. They have moved away from the classic monsters of the Universal movies, and now produce hundreds of monster and horror masks featuring such characters as Yoda from the *Star Wars* films, Margaret Hamilton from *The Wizard of Oz,* and the beasts from *Gremlins.*

Oddly enough, the best-selling mask in the company's history is the undead visage of actor Tor Johnson!

—Bob Madison

Dracula continues to evolve with each passing decade, meaning different things to new generations.

As thrill-hungry baby boomers flocked to movie houses in the 1950s and 1960s, eager to be terrified, England's Hammer Film Productions decided to fill that market demand with new Technicolor reinterpretations of the classic Gothic monsters.

Soon after reviving the Frankenstein Monster in The Curse of Frankenstein, *Hammer's Bray Studios became the new stomping grounds of not only Dr. Frankenstein, but the Mummy, a werewolf, the Phantom of the Opera, and assorted zombies.*

And, of course, Count Dracula.

Christopher Lee became the actor most frequently associated with Dracula for the rock-and-roll generation, and his colorful B-movies became standard fare at drive-ins around the country. The most financially successful of the bunch, 1968's Dracula Has Risen From the Grave, *featured a deliciously campy ad campaign to lure the youth market, and a savagely gory finale with Lee impaled on a silver cross to keep them in their seats.*

While Hammer's Dracula films rapidly lost their foothold in the popular imagination during the heated revival of interest in Dracula in all branches of the media in the 1970s, they are still fondly remembered by many who grew up with them.

Author Gary Svehla is, of course, publisher and editor of Midnight Marquee, *one of the premiere magazines examining horror and fantasy films. His line of Midnight Marquee books, co-edited and published with his wife, Susan, strive to make some of the best critical essays regarding genre films available to movie fans everywhere.*

A devoted enthusiast of Hammer Films, Gary here outlines their many contributions to the cinema of Dracula.

—Bob Madison

Hammer Films and the Resurrection of Dracula
by Gary J. Svehla

When Hammer Film Productions introduced *Horror of Dracula* (*Dracula*, in England) to American film audiences during the summer of 1958, a new era of Dracula and vampire cinema was upon us.

Or was it?

Both general movie aficionados and horror film fanatics are quick to jump into two camps concerning the supremacy of individual screen Draculas, most selecting either

Bela Lugosi, who single-handedly created the popular conception of a "horror movie star," and Christopher Lee, who frequently essayed the Dracula role for Hammer Films.

The Lugosi supporters cite his European elegance and aristocratic demeanor, his deliberately delivered dialogue, his suave veneer, and his subtle animal magnetism. Actor Lugosi still remains the popular conception of the Count in the American consciousness, starring in what Universal Pictures called "the strangest passion the world has ever known." And although steeped in wonderfully Gothic surroundings (the "broken battlements" of his Transylvanian castle are a masterpiece of set design), Lugosi's vampire remained sexy: more than 90 percent of the actor's fan mail came from women. His Dracula was proof that vampires were frightening *and* attractive. "They wanted to know if I only wanted maiden's blood," the actor later recalled. And while tastes in what is and isn't attractive have changed, Lugosi's peculiar charm introduced the element of sensuality missing from Stoker's hoary creation.

Christopher Lee's Count primed his sexual pump with gushes of sensual magnetism and animal savagery. In his brief scenes at the beginning of *Horror of Dracula*, he quickly turns from bland aristocrat to demonic fiend. While Universal Studio's ad campaign suggested that "he [Dracula] kisses with crimson lips," Hammer showed us those blood-smeared chops in glorious Technicolor, close-up and bestial. As Lugosi slowly lunged for his victim's throat with a furtive sexuality, Lee's approach was more seductive and erotic, at first tenderly nuzzling his female victim's face and neck before barring his fangs and digging in for the kill.

To be honest, both interpretations of Dracula are surprisingly much more similar than has been suggested in the annals of film criticism. Neither actor closely adheres to Stoker's original concept of the vampire, and neither actor has starred in a film that can legitimately be called a definitive adaptation of the novel. However, both actors are elegantly European, cultured and dangerous, albeit in their own individual ways.

When Lugosi's Count pays a visit to his eventual victims in the privacy of their opera box seats, or when he greets the overwhelmed Renfield (Dwight Frye) at Castle Dracula, Lugosi always exudes a disquieting old world charm.

Lee plays a similar scene when greeting Jonathan Harker (John Van Eyssen) to his castle, and though he has less dialogue than Lugosi, he is an equally attentive host. And while Lee's barbaric, hissing attack upon Jonathan Harker in the library is more visceral than anything in Lugosi's *Dracula*, Lugosi does indeed display his predatory nature when Renfield cuts his finger on a paper clip. His creepy slow crawl forward, arm outstretched, maniacal smile on his face, reveals the blood-loving beast underneath the veneer of the composed Count.

But even more revealing is Dracula's quick anger upon looking into Van Helsing's (Edward Van Sloan) mirrored cigarette box. When the vampire's nemesis tricks the Count into revealing his vampirism (by lack of reflection), Lugosi responds with a hateful, feral look of fury.

The most apparent differences between the interpretations of Lugosi and Lee are found in their body language and movement. Since Lugosi's Count is a creature of stately deliberation, it would be impossible for Lugosi to create the frenetic energy that Lee displays at the climax of *Horror of Dracula*. In that film's well-remembered climax, Dracula and Van Helsing (Peter Cushing) settle their dispute in a ferocious bout of hand-to-hand combat. Such exertions seem beyond Lugosi's Dracula, who creeps and floats as though he were starring in an opera whose musical rhythms dictate his move-

Dracula (Christopher Lee) awakens to a new age of sex and violence in 1958's *Horror of Dracula.*

ment. Christopher Lee's Count is more the cornered wolf whose guttural wails and biting, clawing brutality echoes his need to survive at any cost.

Yet in spite of these and other differences, both interpretations of Count Dracula are ultimately similar in the following ways: both are romantic figures whose interests lie with the female of the species, both are of patently aristocratic stock, both can generate a false charm to disarm victims, and both are unrepentant monsters hiding under a surface of cultured European breeding.

For far too long Dracula buffs have been trying to separate Christopher Lee and Bela Lugosi into opposite points of the compass, stressing the differences in their interpretations in an effort to paint one actor as being superior in the role to the other. Myself, I disagree with many film historians and favor Christopher Lee's visceral performance over Lugosi's theatrical interpretation of the Count. While Lugosi's performance is *different,* it's every bit as good, and I have no fault over those critics who favor Lugosi's performance.

It is the frequency of Lee's Dracula performances on film that has also helped him put his individual stamp upon the role. Lugosi played Dracula in 1931 and did not repeat the role again onscreen until 1948 when he appeared in the comic spoof, *Abbott and Costello Meet Frankenstein,* despite more than two decades of stage appearances in the role too numerous to chronicle in these pages.

But Christopher Lee created Hammer's Dracula franchise, which allowed him to essay the role in seven films: *Horror of Dracula, Dracula—Prince of Darkness, Dracula*

189

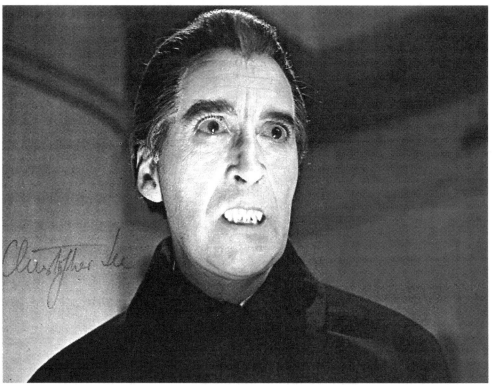

No actor in movie history has portrayed the evil Count as many times on the screen as Christopher Lee.

Has Risen from the Grave, Taste the Blood of Dracula, Scars of Dracula, Dracula A.D. 1972, and *Satanic Rites of Dracula* (*Count Dracula and his Vampire Bride* in the U.S.). Whether or not one views Christopher Lee's performance as superior or inferior to Bela Lugosi's, the fact remains that no actor in movie history has portrayed the evil Count as many times on the screen. (Lee did his own riffs on *Abbott and Costello Meet Franken-stein* when he parodied his Dracula portrayal in *Uncle Was A Vampire* and *Dracula Father and Son*. He also worked outside Hammer to appear in director Jess Franco's abysmal *Count Dracula*.)

This is the first major accomplishment that Hammer Film Productions added to the evolution of Dracula cinema: the concept that the infamous anti-hero could headline a cinematic franchise and carry the audience simply on the basis of Christopher Lee's image, name, and box office appeal. To a new generation of horror movie fans, Chris-topher Lee *was* Count Dracula, and Hammer the new home of Gothic cinema. Even though the early Hammer Dracula films most successfully stand the test of time, espe-cially the first, *Horror of Dracula* (considered by many to be Hammer's masterpiece), *Brides of Dracula,* and *Dracula—Prince of Darkness* are superior productions as well. The subsequent sequels grow less and less ambitious: *Taste the Blood of Dracula* is the last entry worthy of serious critical attention, while *Scars of Dracula, Dracula A.D. 1972*, and *Satanic Rites of Dracula* not only tarnish the reputation of Hammer Films, but drag Stoker's creation to new lows.

Despite the eventual degeneration of the series, Hammer's *Horror of Dracula* is pivotal to the history of Dracula films for bringing the subtext of Tod Browning's film into stark relief: the perversity of vampirism and the all-consuming seduction of evil.

Lee finds accommodations for another guest at Castle Dracula.

Bela Lugosi's Dracula looked and acted evil, and while he appears dominantly handsome outside of Carfax Abbey, the persistence of his evil both repels and attracts. However, Christopher Lee's unconventional good looks go beyond the similar virtues which Lugosi brought to the cinematic table. Lee's Count is openly sensual and erotic, and his two female victims are eager to be savaged by their dark and bloody seducer. First the youthful and virginal Lucy (Carol Marsh) is slowly sapped of her energy as she longingly looks beyond the bay windows as the autumn leaves rustle and blow past. Her breathing becomes forced and rhythmic, her bosom heaves up and down, as her blatant sexual urges await satisfaction at the mouth of Dracula. Her naked passion leads to a nocturnal visit from the dreaded Count. Soon the undead Lucy's sexual abandon reaches greater perversity as she stalks children, becoming a vampiric child molester. The vampire's all-consuming sexuality even extends to incest: Lucy attempts a nightgown-clad seduction of Holmwood (Michael Gough), her own brother, who initially resists. Fortunately he is rescued by the hidden Van Helsing as she attempts to "kiss" her brother's vulnerable throat.

Interestingly enough, Hammer's latter-day entries in the erotic vampire sweepstakes—*The Vampire Lovers, Lust for a Vampire*, and *Twins of Evil*—which are much more blatant and soft-core in their sexuality, fail to generate the erotic perverse intensity inherent in these earlier, more subtle Hammer entries. These 1970s Hammer films are much more titillating upon a surface viewing, but their cheap eroticism lacks the intensity and artistic expression displayed in these earlier Gothic films.

Christopher Lee remains sinisterly mute in *Dracula—Prince of Darkness* (1966).

Later in *Horror of Dracula*, Holmwood's wife Mina (Melissa Stribling) becomes the latest "bride" of Dracula, hiding the Count's coffin in the cellar of her own home. Wearing high collars or scarves to hide the mark of Dracula "kiss," Mina's smirks and smiles cannot deny the hidden satisfactions which she has encountered as willing victim of Dracula. Her cold, aloof, and dogmatic husband Arthur seems passionless and pallid compared to her nocturnal lover, a sexual outlet that Mina obviously needs. In such an interesting romantic triangle, Mina seems so much more alive during her necrophilic "affair" with Dracula than with her cold-fish husband. In this Victorian world view, Dracula's romantic power is the root-cause of his menace. If sex is anti-social and evil, then the sexless Van Helsing's zeal to eradicate such a blatant sexual monster makes him a worthy opponent of the sexually active vampire king. Here *Horror of Dracula* anticipates the spate of "slasher" films in the 1970s and 1980s, where sexual release is often met with physical punishment and violent death. In this mythic vision created by Hammer, vampirism is akin to sexual experimentation... and to be stopped at any cost! By repeatedly making vampirism both sexual and dangerous—as seen first in Stoker's text and later in Universal's *Dracula's Daughter*—Hammer has underlined an important part of Dracula cinema.

Even though Stoker created much of the accepted lore concerning vampires—that a vampire must sleep in consecrated soil, that a vampire casts no reflection in a mirror, and that a vampire may be destroyed by a wooden stake through the heart—Hammer dramatically recast those rules by portraying vampirism as a cult or a perverted reli-

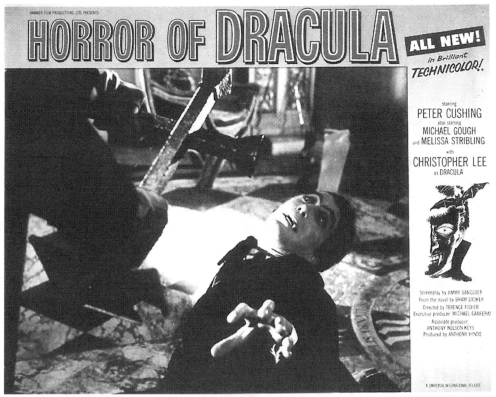

HAMMER FILM PRODUCTIONS, LTD. PRESENTS

HORROR OF DRACULA

ALL NEW!
in Brilliant
TECHNICOLOR!

starring
PETER CUSHING
also starring
MICHAEL GOUGH
and MELISSA STRIBLING
with
CHRISTOPHER LEE
as DRACULA

Screenplay by JIMMY SANGSTER
From the novel by BRAM STOKER
Directed by TERENCE FISHER
Executive producer MICHAEL CARRERAS
Associate producer
ANTHONY NELSON KEYS
Produced by ANTHONY HINDS

A UNIVERSAL INTERNATIONAL RELEASE

Advertising for *Horror of Dracula* emphasized the additions of Cushing, Lee, and Technicolor.

gious sect. In the capable hands of Hammer's scenarists (mainly Jimmy Sangster and Anthony Hinds/John Elder), the "new rules" of vampirism resulted in a Religion of the Undead.

This is another major contribution that Hammer made to Dracula cinema: a radically new way to perceive vampirism. The concept was best explored in Hammer's *The Kiss of the Vampire*, whereby the vampires, under leader Dr. Ravna (Noel Willman), were actually a cult whose members, during their ceremonial meetings, wore white robes and initiated new members into vampirism. Such an undead cult was merely hinted at in Hammer's *Horror of Dracula,* and its successful sequel, *The Brides of Dracula*, as Peter Cushing's Van Helsing speaks frequently about "the cult of the undead." Later, the vampire cult idea could be found in both *Vampire Circus* and *Captain Kronos: Vampire Hunter.*

In these, and other vampire films, Hammer, like Universal, focused upon the anemic, strength-sapping illnesses of the otherwise healthy and young female victims of vampirism. Their energies and spirits are sapped by some unseen malady; eventually, the victims die a slow, tragic death, their energies only returning when they rise from their graves. It is in these sequences especially that Hammer infused "new blood" into the genre. These reanimated corpses, now seductively dressed and burning with renewed energy and sensual power, roam the woods and graveyards by night, searching out new victims for blasphemous sexual crimes.

Hammer also liked to paint religious paraphernalia in bold, symbolic colors. In the classic Universal films a vampire would snarl and flee from the appearance of the small

193

Veronica Carlson sends birthday wishes to Dracula buffs everywhere.

crucifix on a chain; in Hammer's world, a larger, silver cross would be held outstretched like the Holy Grail, forcing the condemned vampire to squirm and slowly back away in agony. Sometimes, the vampire would vanquish its tormentor, and stare down the cross-wielding crusader. Harking back to Stoker's novel, Hammer had religious symbols burn impressions into the flesh of vampires touched by them. Such fear and loathing would be registered by orgasmic breathing, a heaving of breasts, and ultimately screams of pain as the flesh was burned by this symbol of good. In the hands of Hammer's directors and writers, vampire hunters wielded huge crucifixes and large stakes, perhaps too blatantly phallic, all the more visually symbolic of their goodness in fighting the disease of vampirism.

The reanimated seductress would then be lured back into her unholy resting place, back into her crypt, back into her coffin, where only the knowledgeable vampire slayer could bring peace to the tormented victim of the undead. The horror of vampirism for Hammer, like Stoker before them, is best manifested as a voluptuous, wanton lust in the female of the species. Thus, when Van Helsing drives a wooden stake through the shrieking vampire's heart, vivid crimson spurting as the wooden shaft is buried deep in the vampire's chest, the sexual subtexts that drive both novel and film adaptations are consummated. Finally, after turning away from all this bloodletting, the camera would inevitably return to the face of the vampire, now in peaceful repose, having been freed from the vampire's sexual hunger through a "cleansing" act of brutal sexual healing.

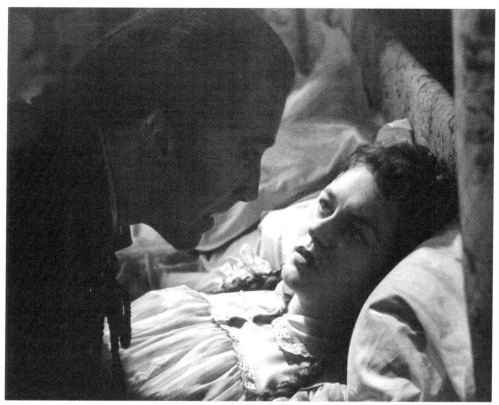

Christopher Lee emphasizes sensuality in *Horror of Dracula* (1958).

Such horrific stakings, blood spurtings, and peaceful redemptions would be repeated in such Hammer films as *Brides of Dracula, Kiss of the Vampire,* and *Dracula—Prince of Darkness.* These sequences powerfully demonstrate the mythic, ritualistic, and religious dogma which Hammer created around its interpretation of vampirism. And to reinforce the concept of vampirism as a perverted cult or unholy religion, Van Helsing was soon replaced in the Hammer series by actual men of the cloth, including such clerics as Father Sandor (Andrew Keir) in the monastery-set *Dracula—Prince of Darkness* and the Monsignor (Rupert Davies) from *Dracula Has Risen from the Grave.*

Hammer chose to illustrate the battle of good against evil with imagery more overtly religious than anything found in the Universal films. The vampire myth was revised in *Dracula Has Risen from the Grave* to include the proviso that a vampire can only be killed by a wooden stake if its attacker is a true believer in God and manages to say a prayer before Dracula pulls out the bloody toothpick.

Finally, the early Hammer films offered the lush Technicolor photography of cinematographer Jack Asher and others, aided in a large part by the budget-minded yet inspired production design by Bernard Robinson. With the use of color, Hammer established that lush hues and Gothic horror can go hand-in-hand. In the 1950s to early 1960s, Technicolor photography was at its artistic peak, and *Horror of Dracula* and *Brides of Dracula* remain as examples of Hammer's most inspired use of color photography, perhaps the most creative in the history of horror cinema.

Universal was fortunate in having the genius of German-born Karl Freund to create the look of *Dracula* in all its monochromatic splendor, and the set design for Lugosi's

Associated British-Pathe Ltd present A Hammer Film Production
"DRACULA—PRINCE OF DARKNESS"
STARRING   (X)
CHRISTOPHER LEE
BARBARA SHELLEY   ANDREW KEIR
TECHNISCOPE (R)   TECHNICOLOR (R)
RELEASED THROUGH WARNER-PATHE DISTRIBUTORS LTD

Christopher Lee was the first actor to bring Stoker's "vampire wedding" to movie screens.

Transylvania castle remains the most dazzling ever recorded in a horror film. Hammer, however, dared to add color and period detail to its horror Gothics, employing a veneer of Victorianism more consistently than Universal.

Horror of Dracula—though it is difficult to convince people who never saw the film theatrically—is a totally different film when viewed in its original Technicolor. Its later reissues (both on video cassette and laser disc), in more muted Eastmancolor, rob the film of much of its splendor. In its original form, the deep saturated hues and tones of Castle Dracula's interiors are awe-inspiring.

Hammer changed the look of horror films when it lensed *Horror of Dracula* in rich primary colors. Even the drops of blood that fall upon the crypt inscription of "Dracula" during the opening credits are literally redder than red. Universal successfully proved that Gothic films do not have to depict reality, but rather suggest an alternate world of light and shadow. The Gothics of Hammer were no more natural than Universal's, but they used a more colorful palette to illustrate its unnatural world.

Reality isn't the goal of Christopher Lee's horrific entrance during the library sequence in *Horror of Dracula*—his fangs bared in depraved intensity, blood smeared all over his mouth and face—just stark terror. Director Terence Fisher and cinematographer Jack Asher ably accomplish their goal—to bring scares back to the horror film and the Baby Boomers that wanted them.

Even in the more subtle sequences of *Horror of Dracula*, with the daylight fading and autumn leaves blowing wildly just outside of large French windows, a somber mood is generated through inspired color photography.

For the climactic struggle between Dracula and Van Helsing, Hammer set designers decorated Dracula's study with knickknacks, globes, shelves, and antique furniture, creating a setting both ancient and evil. Against this backdrop, the color photography makes Dracula all the more frightening in his funeral clothes and black cape, appearing like the Devil incarnate. Cushing's Van Helsing dives for the curtains to reveal the first rays of sunlight, again abetted by superb color lensing, creating such an impact as the image of sunlight—so white, so pure—contrasting the dark evil that the black-caped Dracula represents. Dracula's graying, decomposing flesh slowly turns to ash, eventually blowing away with a cleansing breeze, leaving only his ring within the colorful astrological circle painted onto the floor. Again, such a contrast would not be nearly as effective if filmed in black and white: the key sequences in Hammer's films were created and designed to take advantage of color photography.

Finally, while Hammer continued the already hallowed tradition of turning away from Stoker's novel, it also avoided the stagy elements of the Hamilton Deane–John L. Balderston play. *Horror of Dracula* is not the definitive interpretation of Stoker's novel, nor does it try to be. But by parting from the text of the play, the Hammer film avoids the talky, stage-bound quality that hobbles the Lugosi film. Jimmy Sangster's tight screenplay manages to keep the action moving at a brisk clip while never losing an opportunity to maintain a high level of scares. Characters are sketched quickly, but never caricatured, and events speed forward with an internal logic sometimes missing from Stoker's novel. For speed, economy of narrative, and story momentum, *Horror of Dracula* remains the best of the Dracula movies.

As Sangster states in his autobiography *Do You Want It Good or Tuesday?* (Midnight Marquee Press, 1997): "In the novel, Dracula came to England by sea. There was no way that Hammer was going to go for that... so we settled for a journey on a horse-drawn carriage, crossing a border manned by one customs-immigration official. That they could shoot in the grounds of Bray Studios." And just as he did with *The Curse of Frankenstein* a year earlier, Sangster fashioned his screenplay around Hammer's resources, providing a showcase for their abilities. Sangster did manage to use some of the novel's many characters—Jonathan Harker, Mina Murray, Lucy Westenra, Arthur Holmwood—but pared away many of their relationships and personal histories. Sangster's 82-minute movie script instead concentrated on the Gothic implications of bringing to life a monstrous, undead Vampire King who thirsts and lusts for human blood. "The terrifying lover who died yet lived... the blood in his veins once flowed through hers!" declared the ads for the American release.

It is amazing to think that Jimmy Sangster only made £750 (or $1200 at today's current rate of exchange) for writing *Horror of Dracula*, the unofficial Hammer masterpiece. In his autobiography, Jimmy Sangster writes: "Okay, so it was a pretty good movie... But masterpiece! Come on!"

Mr. Sangster's legions of fans beg to differ.

Like Stoker's novel, Sangster's Dracula is the focal point of attention even though he is mostly offstage. Actor Christopher Lee only appears onscreen for a total of some seven minutes, yet he remains the catalyst for the film's action. He also completely reshaped and recast the Lugosi persona to create his own interpretation. By appearing in six additional Hammer productions, he became the omnipresent Dracula of the Baby Boomer generation. Freely acknowledging Lee's many limitations as an actor, it cannot be disputed that his performance in *Horror of Dracula* is a classic in its own right.

More so than Lugosi, Lee's Count Dracula is a terribly flawed anti-hero. However, just as soon as the audience comes to sense the loneliness inherent in the state of vampirism, his feral demonism breaks through; Dracula becomes the cornered beast who will gladly kill rather than be killed. And thus emerges both the sad Byronic hero and the insidious, seductive fiend, all housed within the character of Count Dracula, onscreen for less than 10 minutes in this 82-minute film.

Jimmy Sangster's script reserves its main focus for the athletic, monomaniacal vampire hunter Dr. Van Helsing, for once not portrayed as an elderly savant. Sangster casts Van Helsing as Dracula's sole nemesis, rather than the leader of a band of vampire hunters found in Stoker's novel, and the tension between these two adversaries creates the dramatic core of the movie. Sangster's pulse-pounding ending provides a truly dramatic confrontation between Van Helsing and Count Dracula, something missing from *every* earlier movie version. And this climax, even today, remains a treasure.

Hammer Film Productions of England never had the resources available at Universal Pictures, lacking the American studio's money, top-drawer performers, and Hollywood's masterful technicians. However, with *Horror of Dracula* Hammer had a vision. Limited by a low budget, hampered by a restrictive censor board, and hoping to repeat the lucky financial success of their earlier *The Curse of Frankenstein*, Hammer happened to combine a screenwriter of immense creativity, a director who understood the dramatic tension inherent in horror films, a cinematographer who was a master of Technicolor photography, a production designer who could perform miracles on a limited budget, and two acting talents who each found his niche in modern genre films. Against all odds, *Horror of Dracula* became a landmark film, one that became much more than just a remake, but a film that redefined the expectations of cinematic Gothic horror to become the trendsetter for all subsequent Dracula films to be produced for the next two decades.

Horror of Dracula is a classic horror film, and Christopher Lee's performance as Dracula is a revitalization of the character. The question is not whether his performance is better than Lugosi's, for Bela Lugosi's identification with the role is too complete and encompassing for any actor to do more than offer variations upon its theme. But Hammer and *Horror of Dracula* redefined the vampire-Dracula cinema for Baby Boomers, cutting new creative trails through unknown terrain, a terrain that is waiting yet to be further explored by a new generation of horror film and Dracula aficionados.

Composer James Bernard tenders birthday greetings to the vampire king.

Sex appeal is a vital component of Dracula's popularity.

Much of the sex in Stoker's novel—Harker's encounter with the vampire brides, or Mina's bloody tryst with Dracula, for instance—is of a decidedly unconventional stripe. It is this whiff of dangerous and kinky sex that has powered much of the myth from generation to generation.

One would imagine that, in these liberated times, the sexual allure of the vampire had run out of gas. But that is patently not the case. Anne Rice's extraordinarily successful vampire series is openly erotic—and largely homosexual, to boot. The Romance was a strong component of television's Gothic Romance, Dark Shadows, *and today amateur "vampires" drink the blood of willing victims in a decidedly kinky, and dangerous, sexual underground.*

The predatory sexuality of Dracula's nature is the key to his vampirism. He is the one monster that seduces, his victims coming to him lovingly. It is the duality of the vampire's kiss—both sensual and repugnant—that is behind all of Dracula's libidinous lurking.

Author Randy Vest is a reporter for People *magazine, to which he also contributes CD reviews. A professional singer-actor, Vest has trod the boards in some 30 plays and musicals, lurked in the background of many films and TV soap operas, and worked as a stand-in for John Lithgow and Ken Howard. Randy dedicates this chapter to his beloved sister and niece, Kathy and Trista Pierce, his favorite companions in a darkened movie theater; his Dad, the late Dale Vest, who took him to his first Hammer film (a midnight showing of* Horror of Dracula) *and always encouraged his journalistic career; his Mom, the late Kay Vest, from whom he learned an early love of movies; and childhood pal Jimmy Hayes, with whom he devoured each and every issue of* Famous Monsters of Filmland *magazine, sharing all things dark and sensual.*
—Bob Madison

Sex and Eroticism From Dracula and His Brood

by Randy Vest

When *serious* movie buffs talk about sex and eroticism in the cinema, discussion doesn't automatically spring to the horror and fantasy genres. Some might recall smoldering stuff like Paul Newman pursuing Patricia Neal in *Hud* or that lingering kiss between Steve McQueen and Faye Dunaway in *The Thomas Crown Affair*. Then there are the infamous *noir* pairings like Kathleen Turner and William Hurt in *Body Heat* or Jessica Lange and Jack Nicholson eating more than dinner on the kitchen table in *The Postman Always Rings Twice*.

Bela Lugosi's Dracula and the women in his life. *Dracula* **(1931)**

But carnal desires for the undead? You bet your sweet bones! The trail of sex and blood is a lengthy one, and this chapter can't hope to be all-inclusive by covering every one of the dozens upon dozens of Dracula and vampire films that have contained the stuff that wet dreams are made of. But here's an attempt to chronicle just some of the heated moments involving some very cold characters in seven decades of Dracula-related cinema.

Early Erotica

Let's start at the very beginning (as perky Julie Andrews once sang in *The Sound of Music*; a classic spoonful of sugar that many musical haters probably consider to be as horrific as anything from Bram Stoker's pen). Well... not the *very* beginning but pretty close to it. The year is 1931 and Bela Lugosi is giving the Hungarian eyeball to svelte blondie Helen Chandler in the now-dated, dreary Universal Pictures classic *Dracula*. In fact, in the fast-paced, hectic environment in which we now live, this stagy snorer offers little to keep the viewer's more prurient interests aroused, save for the comparatively mild erotic aspects of the relationship between Count Dracula (Lugosi) and the two ladies in his "life": the saucy Lucy (Frances Dade), and his hoped-for eternal mate, Mina (Chandler). The first taste of erotica comes early on in the film when we see Dracula's three brides dressed in long, white negligees that are hardly revealing in any sense of the word. (This was 1931, after all.) Slowly they advance on a prone Renfield (Dwight Frye). Enter Drac, who waves the ladies away, and does the biting honors

Lupita Tovar recoils from the cross after losing her "virginity" to the Count in 1931's Spanish version of *Dracula*.

himself (off camera, of course). This interesting bit of homoeroticism predated the downright kinky *Dracula's Daughter*, which we'll discuss in a moment, and was so obliquely gay even for the period that it cannot compare to the blatant male eroticism further down the cinematic road.

Things pick up a bit after Dracula meets Lucy and, playing the voyeur, watches from the sidewalk as she (at her bedroom window) removes part of her upper garment while preparing for bed. He does go inside for his personal kind of nightcap but the scene fades before we see any teeth-to-throat contact. Things get a bit more heated later on when Lucy, dressed only in her negligee and under Dracula's spell, meets him on the fog-shrouded lawn of the estate and disappears into his embrace as he engulfs her in the folds of his all-encompassing cape. Perhaps the more active imaginations of 1931 viewers brought more to this scene than just a nip on the neck. It certainly is open to the interpretation of a feverish mind.

Mina later confesses to Van Helsing (Edward Van Sloan) and the others how Dracula's influence over her took hold. "He [Dracula] came to me. He opened a vein in his arm... and he made me drink." Kinky? It gets kinkier. How about a little pedophilia thrown in for good measure? Lucy (now one of the undead) begins preying on little girls. According to the local newspaper, the "lady in white" promised the victim chocolates, enticed her to a secluded spot, and there bit her slightly in the throat. (Again, like all the other erotically charged material in this film, off stage.)

Of course, compared to the simultaneously shot Spanish version of *Dracula*, some of this looks mighty tame indeed. The brides of Dracula that director George Melford filmed during the evening and wee hours of the morning with an all-Spanish cast (on the same sets used by director Tod Browning for his daytime-hours-shot version) are seen just as briefly as the English brides but they leave a much more lasting impression. These gals mean business. Renfield (Pablo Alvarez Rubio) has the goods and they want what he's got. Compared to their bemused, timid, emaciated-looking American counterparts (David J. Skal, in his 1990 tome, *Hollywood Gothic*, likened them to "zombie schoolmarms"), these beauties sport long, flowing hair and more revealing gowns. In this version, the Latin ladies do the honors on Renfield's neck themselves. And then there's the under-the-influence heroine Eva (Lupita Tovar) who, in the English subtitles of the video tape, tells her worried fiancé Juan Harker (Argentinean actor Barry Norton), "I felt very weak, as if I had lost my virginity." She does lose a good part of her nightie later on. As Miss Tovar tells home video viewers in a pre-feature interview, "The wardrobe was different. The dresses that Helen Chandler wore were all covered up. What they gave me were big [gesturing to her bosom] décolletage, you know, what you would call sexy. I wasn't even aware of it." By way of further explanation, Tovar offers, "Latins have a different way of expressing ourselves, you know. We're very emotional. And the American people were kind of subdued."

Obviously. In comparison to Mina's hypnotic fixation on Jonathan's (David Manners) throat in the American version, Tovar's Eva literally goes for Juan's jugular. We actually see Eva's teeth bite into his neck. And Lucia (Carmen Guerrero) is preying on the little girls (off camera) in much the same way as the American Lucy is. As for Dracula himself, Carlos Villarias—reportedly the only member of the Spanish cast allowed to view the dailies of Browning's version and encouraged to emulate Lugosi—gives us much of the same over the top, play-it-to-the-very-last-row-in-case-they-can't-see performance that Lugosi brought to his Count, infusing it with very little subtle sexuality. Ultimately, Villarias' execution of the role is as heavy-handed (or should we say heavy-ha*m*ded?) in its own way as Lugosi's.

A much subtler bloodsucker was essayed by Gloria Holden in *Dracula's Daughter* (1936) in which she starred as the Count's unholy offspring who has a taste for the tender throats of young ladies as opposed to those of men. Director Lambert Hillyer and Universal Pictures don't try to disguise the character's lesbian leanings and, in fact, one of the taglines in *Daughter*'s original ads screamed, "Save the women of London from *Dracula's Daughter!*"

The following dialogue exchange was featured in the 1995 documentary, *The Celluloid Closet*, based on Vito Russo's 1981 book that discussed the representation of gays and lesbians in the cinema. The scene in question involves the mysterious Countess Marya Zaleska (Holden) and a young, desperate woman named Lili (Nan Grey), whom Zaleska's servant Sandor (Irving Pichel) has saved from suicide and, with the promise of shelter, has brought back to the Countess, ostensibly to be her next art subject. It soon becomes obvious that the Countess is panting rather than painting as Lili, at the Countess' request, removes her blouse. The Countess, who has secretly watched her disrobe, eyes Lili hungrily as she appears from behind the screen, bare-shouldered.

Lili: Why are you looking at me that way? Won't I do?

Countess: Yes. You'll do very well indeed. [Holding up her ring] Do you like jewels Lili? This is very old and very beautiful.
Lili: [Becoming afraid] I don't think I'll pose tonight. I think I'll go if you don't mind. [The Countess advances on her] Please! Don't come any closer!

The last thing we hear from Lili is her terrified scream as the camera swings upward to a grotesque mask on the wall. (Haven't we all had nights like that?)

Dracula's Daughter is an early example of lesbianism in a vampire film and this scene was only a hint of the more permissively filmed encounters to come, which are discussed further on.

A Brief Breather and Time For a Cigarette

Overall, the few vampire flicks of the 1940s and early 1950s offer little in the form of erotic pleasures. Oh, there's a full-faced Lon Chaney, Jr. mesmerizing Louise Allbritton in *Son of Dracula* (1943) and Lenore Aubert succumbing to Lugosi's charms in *Abbott and Costello Meet Frankenstein* (1948), but the fang flicks of the era were pretty sexless (and fangless!) for the most part.

Hot Stuff From Hammer

Britain's Hammer Films came to the rescue in 1958 with their superb take on the vampire legend, *Horror of Dracula,* starring Christopher Lee as the undead Count and Peter

Cushing as his arch-nemesis Dr. Van Helsing. Suddenly, all of the erotic elements that had only been hinted at for over two decades were now in everyone's faces, changing the way eroticism would be portrayed in vampire movies for decades to come. This film almost single-handedly brought forth the sexual aspects inherent in the vampire myth to a horror film-starved public and a wholly new, sexy Count in the person of Lee. Michael Carreras, son of Hammer head James Carreras and a producer-director in his own right, elaborated for writer John Brosnan in his 1976 book, *The Horror People*: "The greatest difference between our Dracula and anybody else's was the sexual connotations. There was no real horror in it, the women were eager to be nipped by Dracula and I think that gave it a fresh look."

The 1950s audience, having become inundated with giant insects of every type and schlocky papier mache AIP monsters from filmmaker Roger Corman's cranium, were now treated to voluptuous ladies, spilling over the tops of their sheer negligees, awaiting the arrival of Dracula in breathless anticipation and vivid color. In more than one case, they became a seductive, snarling handmaiden of the Count, bent on drinking the blood of their male loved ones. Director Terence Fisher brought bats and babes to movie screens, and the vampire cinema is still recovering. Fisher elaborated on his erotic formula for writer Gary Parfitt in a 1973 interview for *Little Shoppe of Horrors* fanzine, saying:

> For its time, one had to skate over it [the sexual aspect] of course. There was a great permissiveness for writing in the theater, but not as much in the film world. Everything then in daily life had a pleasant and natural progression. One could only underline a little more. If one could hint at it or not even hint at. Now of course, it could be filmed with far more explicitness, if it has the element of justification.

As for Dracula's fangs being interpreted as phallic symbols, Fisher mused, "The basic meaning of the fangs in Dracula is interesting. You could trace them right back to the serpent in the Garden of Eden, couldn't you? The evil, the fangs of the serpent. There is an association of superstition."

Nearly 10 years earlier, Fisher talked about his film to interviewer Michel Caen for the French magazine *Midi-Minuit Fantastique* (translated by Ton Paans in 1985 for *Little Shoppe of Horrors*). "The scene in which Lucy [Carol Marsh] awaits Dracula is very effective. It could have been ludicrous, but I was very careful with that scene and did my best to make it look extremely graceful, almost dream-like. I tried to convey at the same time Lucy's passion for his embrace and her horror at the sight of him... attraction and repulsion at the same time. Very similar, in fact, to Mina's [Melissa Stribling] situation. When she returns from her nocturnal walk after her first encounter with the Count, she has a look on her face that is just unbelievable! She has undergone a veritable transformation. Her glowing face betrays an amorous revelation of an enormous magnitude."

Hammer's *The Brides of Dracula* (1960) is teeming with sexual undercurrents. Much has been written about the hothouse sexuality of this film, and it is not hard to see why. With its eerie echoes of Tennessee Williams' *Suddenly, Last Summer*, *Brides of Dracula* may be the most subversive of the Hammer films.

Yvonne Monlaur and Andree Melly prove burnt toast is better than burnt fingers in *The Brides of Dracula* **(1960)**

The Chateau Meinster houses a leg-manacled, fey, pretty-boy bloodsucker along with his sinister, latently lesbian nanny, and his suffocating, emotionally incestuous mother whom he eventually dispatches by sucking her blood and making her one of the undead. (Excuse me Dr. Van Helsing, may I have a word with you about my dysfunctional family?) And the lesbian content in exchanges like the one that takes place between pretty young Marianne (Yvonne Monlaur) and her now-undead roommate Gina (Andree Melly) are intriguing. With fangs bared and ample bosom heaving, Gina advances on the terrified, confused Marianne, hissing: "Marianne... my darling Marianne. You haven't forgotten your little Gina? Put your arms around me please, I want to kiss you Marianne. Please be kind to me. Say that you forgive me for letting him love me?"

Along with their mesmerizing 1964 classic *The Kiss of the Vampire*, which featured an orgiastic, legs-and-panties-in-the-air, climactic bat attack on a white-robed cult of blood enthusiasts, Hammer pulled in the pounds with six more Dracula titles (Christopher Lee again with bridgework in place) throughout the 1960s and early 1970s, each one sporting its own scenes of eroticism.

Dracula—Prince of Darkness (1966) showed Diana Kent (Suzan Farmer) drinking the Count's blood from an open vein in his chest while *Dracula Has Risen from the Grave* (1968) offered us Veronica Carlson as the virginal Maria who, as she loses her innocence to the Count's desires, chucks her dolly off the side of the bed as Drac sinks his teeth into her throat. (Subtle, huh?) *Taste the Blood of Dracula* (1970) is awash in sadism, incest, prostitutes, and other family entertainment while *Scars of Dracula* (1970) features glimpses of bare bottoms, a man's red bikini underwear (very rare in the 1800s, no?), and more sadism (Lee's Dracula punishing slave Patrick Troughton by branding him with a red hot weapon—no wonder the upper classes have servant problems!).

Scars of Dracula's director Roy Ward Baker confessed: "I do believe there is such a thing as obscenity though a lot of people say there isn't. But I don't mind eroticism and I don't mind pornography—as someone once said, nobody ever got killed by a tit." (He obviously hadn't seen Woody Allen's *Everything You Always Wanted to Know About Sex, But Were Afraid to Ask*).

By the time of Hammer's early 1970s excursions like *Dracula A.D. 1972*, *The Satanic Rites of Dracula* (complete with nude devil worshipping scenes), *Countess Dracula* (with scenes of blood bathing), and the delightfully depraved *Vampire Circus*, the mix of violence and nudity barely raised an eyebrow.

Lust and Laughs in the 1970s and 1980s

The vampire flicks of the 1970s and 1980s are a mixed bag of terror, titters, and titties, but definitely more sexually frank overall. *Count Yorga, Vampire* (1970) shows Yorga (Robert Quarry) attacking a young lovemaking couple in their parked van (it's surprising that the fey Yorga didn't bite the young man on the rump), while *House of Dark Shadows* (1970) has a vampiric Carolyn Stoddard (Nancy Barrett)—dressed in the usual lady vamp garb of sheer, low-cut negligee—supping at the throat of her pajama-clad boyfriend Todd (Donald Briscoe) in a stable loft. The delightful *Love at First Bite* (1979) finds neck-nipping George Hamilton stalking fashion model Susan St. James for laughs, and George Romero's hypnotic *Martin* (1978) features the disturbed title character (John Amplas) in a brutal rape/seduction/blood-drinking opening scene aboard a train, that is a deliciously disturbingly guilty pleasure.

Andy Warhol's Dracula (1974), directed by Paul Morrissey, is a grosser of a black comedy with an ailing Dracula (Udo Kier) invading Italy in search of the blood of virgins, which will restore his health. Staying at the faded estate of a once-wealthy family that boasts four "pure" daughters, Drac meets with disappointment as he samples the blood of two of them who, unbeknownst to him, happen to be very experienced in all things sexual. Experiencing food poisoning from "tainted" blood, the Count proceeds to retch the red stuff into a bathtub, a toilet, the floor, the walls, and just about right out of the viewing screen and into your lap, crying out in his heavily German-accented English: "Za blood of zeese who-ahs iss killing me!" (Yes, it's about as good as it sounds.)

A similar, yet even funnier pronunciation of the word "whores" is delivered by perennial Warhol favorite, New Yawk-accented Joe Dallesandro, who plays the estate's hunky gardener-handyman-stud muffin. At one point Dallesandro asks: "So what's he [Dracula] doin' witchu two who-ahs?"

Dallesandro sported quite the body beautiful in those days and it's on ample display here, along with the bods of Stefania Casini and Dominique Darel, who play the slutty daughters. This trio is responsible for some truly sexy couplings amidst all the violent, bizarre goings-on.

The year 1979 boasts memorably erotic throat threateners: John Badham's *Dracula* starring Frank Langella and Werner Herzog's *Nosferatu the Vampyre,* featuring Klaus Kinski in the title role. Actually, in the latter, Kinski's grotesque make-up (white face,

Amanda Bearse starred in the largely homoerotic *Fright Night* (1985).

long fingernails, and long, sharp, protruding front chompers) and bizarre costumes (he sports a cute little knitted cap in his first scene, looking for all the world like a decaying Disney dwarf), all but ensure a lack of erotic content. But there are a couple of surprises. Namely, 'ratu's seduction of a moaning Lucy (Isabelle Adjani), wherein he lifts her garment to admire her legs and then drinks her blood with his hand on her breast, and a scene where Harker (Bruno Ganz) cuts his thumb and hungrily sucks the blood from it.

In comparison to Kinski, Langella plays things a little closer to the cloak. Badham's excursion, however, could easily be retitled *The Hands of Dracula*, given the director's countless close-ups of the cast's hands. These shots are almost overshadowed by the close-ups of Langella's nervous, dancing pupils. Still, if you can get past a screenful of hands and eyes (and Langella's windblown, *Charlie's Angels*-esque mane), there's payoff in an extremely erotic dream-like sequence of entwined bodies, bats, and Bond girl-like silhouettes (and more hand close-ups!). It even offers another of those Lucy-supping-at-the-Count's-chest scenes. (Evidently there's a lot to be said for Langella's sex appeal in general, especially by middle-aged women. This writer's sister, a long-time Langella fan, opined that "those fangs can eat crackers in my bed anytime!")

But of all the erotic entries from the 1970s and 1980s, you can't do much better than *Daughters of Darkness* (1971), a beautifully photographed Belgian-French co-production directed by Harry Kumel. Sexually, this film has something for everyone—lesbians, S&M, bisexuality... and, oh yes, vampires! Look for a young, slim John

Karlen (Willie Loomis and Harvey Lacey on TV's *Dark Shadows* and *Cagney and Lacey*, respectively) cavorting nude in several scenes. And watch for some truly tantalizing seduction scenes between the beautiful Delphine Seyrig as the mysterious Countess Bathory and Danielle Ouimet as Karlen's bride.

Lipstick Lesbians

Besides the titillating scene in *The Brides of Dracula* and the same-sex seductions of *Daughters of Darkness* (both described above), other films about the undead deserve inclusion here for their sapphic content. Roger Vadim's *Blood and Roses* (1961), based on J. Sheridan Le Fanu's novel, *Carmilla*, must have cranked a few libidos in the largely repressed viewing audience of that era. Certainly the onscreen nuzzling of Elsa Martinelli by the possessed Annette Vadim during the course of this beautifully photographed cult classic had to have thrilled young audience members of every persuasion.

But leave it to Hammer Films to pull out all the stops (albeit with wildly uneven results) on the Carmilla/Mircalla/Marcilla legend with what has become known as the "Karnstein Trilogy"—*The Vampire Lovers* (1970), *Lust for a Vampire* (1971), and *Twins of Evil* (1972). Awash in flimsy nighties, full frontal nudity (top and bottom), and inappropriate pop songs (*Lust for a Vampire*'s "Strange Love" sung by the inimitable "Tracy"), the trio of films is a hodgepodge of flesh and fright that caters a little too obviously to heterosexual male fantasies even though *Lovers*' director Roy Ward Baker asserts: "From the beginning I was determined not to make an exploitation movie about lesbian vampires. I wasn't going to be 'funny' about the subject. It came off rather better than people expected simply because the characters were simply treated as lesbians and that was it."

Screenwriter Tudor Gates adds: "I felt that the thing to do was to bring Hammer Films up to the 1970s. So I deliberately threw in the nudes and the lesbians and all the rest of it. I believe it was the first time they'd done that."

Lust, the second in the series, is by far the most dramatically lacking of the three, but probably packs more prurient punch than the others given the parade of full frontal nudity on display and a scene of implied cunnilingus. Co-producer Harry Fine admits that the final product is an "explicitly melodramatic make-out movie."

Twins is the dramatic winner, and that isn't saying much. There is as much of an actual plotline on display as there is the flesh of former *Playboy* centerfold twins Madeleine and Mary Collinson, who romp through the film mostly in sheer nighties and revealing, low-cut gowns. No innocent Disney *Parent Trap* hijinx here, folks! And even though their religious fanatic uncle, Gustav Weil (Peter Cushing), warns them of the perils of evil and debauchery, naughty Frieda runs off to the castle of Count Karnstein (Damien Thomas), promptly becoming one of the undead and indulging in a main course of Breast of Village Girl for supper. *Bon appetit!*

The lesbian encounters in tooth cinema get more and more graphic in the 1980s and 1990s. One of the most notorious of the fanged-femme flicks is Tony Scott's *The Hunger* (1983) where Catherine Deneuve, as a centuries-old vampiress, sets her sights on a young doctor (Susan Sarandon). Raymond Murray's 1996 book *Images in the Dark: An Encyclopedia of Gay and Lesbian Film and Video* said the movie was "dripping with cinematic style and chic sexual intrigue... less vampire horror film and more a sensuous drama of lesbian attraction and desire."

Stephen Geoffreys is seduced into vampirism by older-man Chris Sarandon in 1985's *Fright Night*.

But all of this seems like mere beating around the bush by the time of the David Lynch–produced *Nadja* (1994), where we see the title character, who is Dracula's daughter (Elina Lowensohn), seducing a young married woman (Galaxy Craze) and coercing her to taste her own menstrual blood. It's a highly-charged scene that's placed amidst much arty photography and deadpan humor. (Fasten your seat belts! Peter Fonda is along for the bumpy ride as an aging, hippie-type Dr. Van Helsing.)

Fiendish Fangots

Which brings us to examples of male homoeroticism in vampire cinema. One of the hottest, hands down, has to be Neil Jordan's *Interview With the Vampire* (1994) with a screenplay (based on her novel) by Anne Rice, and starring Tom Cruise and Brad Pitt as undeads in love. Say what you will regarding the much-discussed book vs. film debate or the misguided casting of Tom Cruise; if male-to-male neck-chomping is your bag, then this flick's for you! And you don't have to wait long for the thrills; about 10 minutes into the film we see Lestat (Cruise) hungrily clamp onto the throat of Louis (Pitt) and soar skyward in a sensual, melodramatic clinch that would have given Scarlett and Rhett a run for their money. And later, the attraction between Louis and vampire Armand (Antonio Banderas) is so obvious—their lips, in one scene, are close enough to be able to sample each other's Chapstick—that you fully expect these jugular jawers to exchange gold bands and march down the aisle to some unholy nuptials.

The horror comedy *Fright Night* (1985), directed by Tom Holland, has a lot of homosexual content going on under its heterosexual surface. Vampire Jerry Dandrige (Chris Sarandon), along with his faithful handyman Billy Cole (Jonathan Stark), moves into—and begins putting the bite on—a quiet, suburban neighborhood. Cole, at one point, tells the police that Dandrige is his "roommate," and it looks like, for all intents and purposes, the pair are lovers. Living next door is horny teenager Charley Brewster who, in between spying on Dandrige's nocturnal activities and watching TV's *Fright Night* program, is usually trying to make out with girlfriend Amy Peterson (Amanda Bearse, who publicly came out as a lesbian some years later). Charley's pal Evil Ed (Stephen Geoffreys) is a nerdy, possibly-in-the-closet teen-ager who has one of the movie's most sensual and affecting scenes. Accosted by Dandrige in a deserted alley, a tearful Ed is seduced into joining the ranks of the undead with the following come-on:

> Dandrige: You don't have to be afraid of me. I know what it's like being different. They won't pick on you anymore, or beat you up. I'll see to that. All you have to do is take my hand. Here, Edward... take my hand.

With that, Dandrige extends his long talon-like fingers and pulls the kneeling Ed up into his caped embrace. (The erotic moment is shattered seconds later as Charley and Amy hear Ed's piercing scream in the distance.) Actor Geoffreys would later go on to star in all-male nudie-cutie films for the gay audience, showing off his best talents in *Hunk Hotel.*

Ulli Lommel's *Tenderness of the Wolves* (1973) stars Kurt Raab as a killer who preys on young boys, having sex with them before murdering them and drinking their blood. Based on the real-life case of Fritz Haarmann, a man who killed some 30 male youths after World War I, the movie is certainly not going to win any awards with GLAAD (Gays and Lesbians Against Anti-Defamation), but is a fascinating study and was the basis of an earlier movie, Fritz Lang's *M* starring Peter Lorre (as a heterosexually inclined snuffer) in 1931.

Once Bitten (1985) is one of those mindless heterosexual teen comedies that permeate the suburban cineplexes just about every season. Although Lauren Hutton (as the blood-seeking Countess) spends most of the movie trying to keep her breasts from falling out of cut-down-to-there evening wear, there is a homoerotic (albeit homophobic) scene involving the film's male lead, a pre-*Ace Ventura*, pre-*Mask* Jim Carrey as a teen-age virgin whose blood the Countess craves. Having already been bitten (on the inside of his thigh) by the undead femme fatale, Carrey has been acting mighty strange and his two buddies (Thomas Ballatore and Skip Lackey), fearing he's become an unwilling suckee, decide to do a visual exam of the suspected violated area in the school shower. Of course, mistaken intentions ensue and the other bathing jocks, who have glanced over to find Carrey being physically subdued by his chums (one grabbing him from behind, the other kneeling in front of him), are seen running from the stalls, yelling "Fags in the shower! Fag alert!" The next scene finds one of Carrey's chagrined buds, reputation ruined, lamenting the aborted flesh exam and, fearing that he and his bud might have liked it too much, wailing: "We're homos! We're rump rangers!" much to the amusement, undoubtedly, of insecure straight male teen-age moviegoers everywhere.

Grace Jones strikes a sultry pose from *Vamp*.

Take It to the Limit

XXX-rated excursions into the domain of the undead sport the slapdash, thrown-to-gether look that is the trademark of most porno flicks. Take, for example, *Gayracula* (1983) featuring a lead vampire (Tim Kramer) of the bleached-blonde California surfer dude variety who, near the beginning of the film, shows us that vampires sometimes opt for a more radical fashion sense by going au naturelle under their capes. Like the majority of explicit flicks, the film is awash in sub-amateurish acting, a mere hint of an actual script, and lousy production values. Still, it's amusing to see the eroticism inherent in the vampire legends taken to the absolute nth degree. In one scene, Kramer's ravenous bloodsucker drains a victim (Michael Christopher) of his blood by sinking his teeth into the guy's bum. But at least director Roger Earl seems to be a fan of the horror

Geena Davis vamps it up in *Transylvania 6-5000*.

genre, lifting portions of his music soundtrack from *Young Frankenstein* and Badham's *Dracula*.

Just as much of a mess is Taylor Hudson's *The Bite* (1993) with two male vampires as centuries-old lovers who actually sleep nude in the same coffin—this is a porno film, after all. Dillon Reid and blue movie vet Jon Vincent are the blood-lusting casket snoozers. The plot, like the acting, is negligible but there is some truly sensual neck-biting amidst all the by-the-numbers sex scenes.

The Naughty Nineties

Overblown and overwrought, *Bram Stoker's Dracula* (1992), directed by Francis Ford Coppola, might be filled with over-the-top performances, bad British accents, and some truly abysmal acting (can you say K-E-A-N-U?), but it's a lush affair cinematically and a sensual jackpot. You know you're entering some new "eeriotic" territory when, early-on, we see Mina Murray (Winona Ryder) coyly eyeing some sexually explicit drawings in the book, *Arabian Nights* ("Disgustingly awful," she sniffs). She and her friend Lucy Westenra (Sadie Frost) giggle in amazement over the various lovemaking positions shown in the artwork, and talk quickly turns to Mina's fiancé Jonathan Harker (Keanu Reeves) as Lucy teasingly asks, "Jonathan measures up, doesn't he?"

She could well query Dracula's three vampire brides who are making a meal of Harker over at Drac's digs in Transylvania. In one quite graphic scene, we see a bare-breasted bride materialize between Harker's trousered, but spread-eagled, legs. She is

Keanu Reeves stays *as* dinner in *Bram Stoker's Dracula* (1992).

joined by two other vamps who caress, kiss, and lick Harker's body as he writhes in a state of ecstasy-fright. The lead seductress ultimately chomps down on his groin, discovering the answer to Lucy's earlier question put to Mina. Unfortunately, this vamp's not one to bite and tell and we, ahem, get the short end of the stick.

By the way, Dracula himself (Gary Oldman) is no slouch in the sex department. His seduction of Mina is a keeper. It's the old "drink-the-blood-from-the-rip-in-my-chest" routine but his orgasmic sighs and moans as she does so suggests that he's losing more than plasma.

But Drac and his brides aside, we love Lucy, who ultimately ends up being almost as shocking, if not more so, than the lusting brides. When dashing Quincey P. Morris (handsome Bill Campbell) arrives at a party, Lucy throws herself at him and coos, "Oh, Quincey! Please let me touch it. It's sooooo big!" She then pulls a knife the size of Christopher Lee's ego out of Morris' sheath. And later, when she's lying underneath a hairy, beast-like Dracula and receiving his pounding, lustful thrusts in a nightmarish garden sequence, we play the voyeur along with a stunned Mina, who has arrived in time to witness the animalistic act.

All of these examples have been just a taste of the thrills those evil neck nibblers have been providing for decade after decade. And with the abundant supply of graphic nudity and sex scenes we've been treated to in the 1990s, one can only dare to imagine what's in store for us in post-millennium vampire cinema offerings. But if you should consider the time spent reading this chapter to be merely fanged foreplay or a case of *toothus interruptus*, then fly on out to your local video vault or cinema revival house and put the bite on a few of these films for some fast relief.

During the past 100 years, Dracula has seldom been out of the public eye. But the vampire redolent 1970s, more than any other decade, holds the most legitimate claim to the title "The Dracula Decade."

The 10 years heralded an explosion of interest in Stoker's Vampire King, with more film appearances than ever before, long runs on and off Broadway, and a demonic presence in books, comics, and television. Nothing like it has ever been seen before or since.

The many changes brought to the character during this decade are with us to this day: Dracula's romantic demeanor, his Byronic passion, the deep and abiding tie to his historical namesake, all find their roots in the 1970s.

Few people are better qualified to trace the Count's rising star during this time than Steve Vertlieb. Frequent journalist and film critic, Vertlieb was one of the principal writers of The Monster Times, *the finest publication of the 1970s dealing with horror films and fiction.*
—Bob Madison

Dracula in the 1970s: Prints of Darkness
by Steve Vertlieb

The most reassuring aspect of trends and cycles is that as one door closes, another one opens.

The same may be said of coffins.

As the mortuary door rusted shut on Hammer's Dracula movie cycle of the 1950s and 1960s, a breath of deliciously stagnant air was about to escape into the staid 1970s. In the interim, however, Hammer Films, the dominant producer of such films, was continuing to nail the lid on the market. While the quality of Hammer's gentle excursions into Dracula country had diminished, they still retained, you should excuse the expression, a stake in the genre.

Hammer had established itself in the mid 1950s as the horror capital of England, and was a major contender, along with Roger Corman's AIP, for the financial championship of the youthful horror film market. Beginning with the acclaimed first entry in their series of films featuring science-fiction hero Professor Quatermass in 1956's *The Creeping Unknown*, Hammer released a consistently excellent stream of horror and science fiction melodramas. In 1957 they struck gold with a plan to release a controversial remake of the 1931 Boris Karloff classic, *Frankenstein*. The "rub," however, was that the supposed remake would be updated to fit the sensibilities of a more liberated generation of film goers. Color would be added to lend realism to the series, along with generous doses of sex and violence.

It proved to be an unbeatable and potent recipe for box office success. The film was a sensation, and prurient interests had seldom been better satisfied.

The following year saw the release of Hammer's second monstrous remake. This time they turned their attention to Bram Stoker's immortal vampire, Dracula. *Horror of Dracula* reunited the creative team responsible for injecting new blood, so to speak, into the earlier *The Curse of Frankenstein*. Peter Cushing, the evil Baron in *Frankenstein*, this time played the vital Dr. Van Helsing, while the venerable monster himself crept out of the crypt once more as Christopher Lee became the new Dracula. This new incarnation of the undead aristocracy revitalized the genre and brought the anemic vampire richly back to life.

With a literate, crisp screenplay by Hammer veteran Jimmy Sangster, Lee's Dracula was frightening to behold: a fierce, powerful aberration whose fangs dripped blood while snarling his defiance in dangerous self-assuredness. Stalking his hapless victims to the thunderous rhythms of composer James Bernard's primal, passionate score, this was a savage predator who ripped out the throats of his prey like a ravenous wolf.

Lee and Sangster gleefully discarded the gentleman Count of previous films, replacing the civility of Bela Lugosi with the untamed fury of a wild, vicious animal. The stunning chase and unforgettable climax of this first Dracula pitted Van Helsing's grim, heroic determination against the centuries-old ferocity of the rabid vampire cornered in his den. It is, perhaps, the quintessential sequence in the repertoire of this small, once mighty independent studio.

As the 1960s drew to a close, Hammer was already in a major decline, its glory years sadly behind. There was still occasional brilliance, as witnessed by its final Quatermass outing, the breathtaking *Five Million Years to Earth* in 1967, but the fundamental essence of its creativity had ebbed. Its creative team largely dissipated, Hammer began to repeat itself in unflattering self-parody.

As a new decade was dawning, Hammer continued to release new excursions into the Dracula mythology, which usually proved little more than variations on an already exhausted theme. While the films themselves had dropped in quality, there were still moments of inspiration which allowed the disparate parts to elevate the films on the whole. Hammer's Dracula films became much like sex: when they were good, they were terrific, and when they were bad, they were still pretty good.

Hammer Productions entered the new decade in the fall of 1970 with the release of its fifth Dracula film, *Taste the Blood of Dracula,* on September 16. The film introduced the late Ralph Bates to the screen in the first of his horror film appearances at Hammer. It also starred Christopher Lee once again in the role he loved to hate, or, perhaps, hated to love. Increasingly dissatisfied with the growing mediocrity of his scripts, Lee voiced his displeasure at being typecast in a genre he had grown to loathe. Indeed, he threw open his arms to director Billy Wilder a year earlier and eagerly embraced the opportunity to portray Mycroft Homes in Wilder's bittersweet romantic comedy, *The Private Life of Sherlock Holmes*. In the role that Lee later described as his personal favorite, the actor seemed to joyously poke fun at his own stiffness and pomposity while enacting Mycroft as a humorless civil servant.

One must eat, however, and so Lee reluctantly donned the regal cape of Transylvania's favorite son once more, inviting audiences to taste the now somewhat anemic blood of his romantic alter ego, Count Dracula.

Christopher Lee looks at the bright side of his later Hammer films in *Taste the Blood of Dracula* **(1970).**

Taste the Blood of Dracula was a pallid offering indeed. Audiences delighted in Lee's overbearing presence as Dracula, but his moments onscreen were simply that, mere moments. The rest of the picture seemed lacking in atmosphere or interest; indeed, everyone in the cast appeared to walk through a strictly by-the-numbers script. The sets, costumes, and general atmosphere of the film were mostly first-class, as always, but Bram Stoker's demonic creation seemed mostly comatose at best. Peter Cushing, who elevated the status of any film with his presence, was sorely missed. *Taste the Blood of Dracula* simply failed to ignite sparks. Even in later years, when Hammer's Dracula series had degenerated still further, the presence of both Cushing and Lee assured audiences a degree of charm and romanticism. The absence of one or the other made the picture's shortcomings, like the Count's reflection (and, oft times, Lee's performances), all the more transparent. Dracula had risen again, but this was a grave endeavor for the Count who played second fiddle to his misbegotten disciples. The teen-aged daughter of one of his sworn enemies occupied more screen time than Lee, alluring and a lure for the downfall of her father and her friends. James Bernard, however, contributed one of his most exquisite scores to the picture, providing the few genuine moments of afterglow to an otherwise mediocre endeavor.

If its earlier effort featured little of the vampiric Count, Hammer's next foray into vampirism would obliterate him entirely.

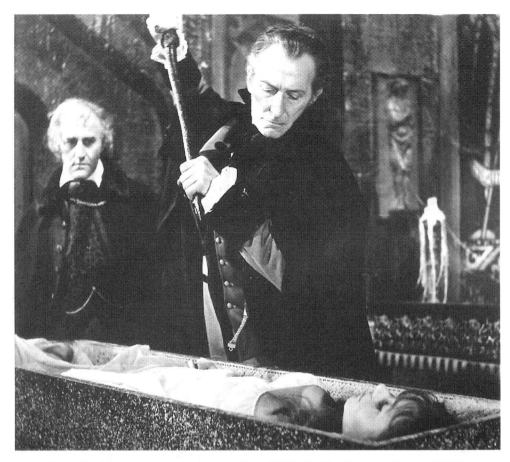

Peter Cushing aims for the heart of Ingrid Pitt in *The Vampire Lovers* (1970).

The Vampire Lovers, released later that fall, was yet another retelling of Sheridan Le Fanu's *Carmilla*. Filmed originally in 1931 by Carl Dreyer in France as *Vampyr*, in 1960 by Roger Vadim as *Et Mourir De Plaisir* (*Blood and Roses*), and once more as *Terror in the Crypt* in 1963, Fanu's 1871 story has had nearly as many incarnations as his Carmilla has identities. *The Vampire Lovers*, it should be noted, did not imply affection for the undead on behalf of filmgoers, rather, it pointed to the previously understated sexual preferences of these naughty little suckers... in this case, lesbianism.

Ingrid Pitt played the cultured daughter of a countess, given shelter by General Spielsdorf (Peter Cushing) and his family. Marcilla (Pitt) seduces and murders the general's niece and disappears into the night. Spielsdorf vows revenge, tracking Marcilla (now Carmilla) to her latest haunt, a sumptuous estate where she encounters a young girl with a sumptuous body. (Carmilla always liked quality.) Emma Morton (Madeline Smith) is lovely, innocent, and virginal, succumbing to the tutelage of her calculating vampire friend who delights in biting her, not on the throat, but on the tips of her nipples. (Whenever Hammer could tap into an adolescent sex fantasy, it would.)

Carmilla, it seems, is actually a survivor of the infamous vampiric family Karnstein, and is bent on sharing her horrific legacy with partners both willing and unwilling. The General ultimately tracks down the bloody ingenue, rendering her harmless by means of decapitation. Hammer had found a way to give the General "head."

The Vampire Lovers was, in the final analysis, a success. Sincerely acted and rich with generous helpings of stylish eroticism, the film managed to overcome the absence of a definitive male vampiric influence, as well as cheesy color and a release in America by the even cheesier AIP. Peter Cushing managed to lend solid, if brief, support while a shadowy figure on horseback may or may not have been Dracula himself.

The first year of the decade will be remembered as a veritable blood feast at Hammer. Before the end of 1970 the studio released its second Dracula film of the year, and its third vampire feature. It's been said that not even plastic surgery could have saved *Scars of Dracula* from its fate, but, despite its disastrous reputation (and some scathing observations by its star), the film is actually more interesting than the earlier *Taste the Blood of Dracula*.

Directed by Roy Ward Baker (*Five Million Years to Earth*), and with a lovely score by James Bernard, *Scars of Dracula* returned the unholy Count to his castle in the Transylvanian mountains and provided the series with one of its most unforgettable images: the sight of Count Dracula climbing the outer wall of his castle. The stunning imagery, inspired by Bram Stoker's novel, was exciting to behold and an unnerving reminder of the vampire's rodent-like persona. This was, after all, not an aristocratic royal, but a vile, detestable creature of the night.

If the remainder of the screenplay was routine, the film distinguished itself in these inspired moments, including a wholly surprising finale in which the vampire prince is destroyed by a brilliant bolt of lightning. *Scars of Dracula* was, despite its unwarranted reputation of mediocrity, a welcome return to the quality of the earlier films of the series.

A worthwhile candidate for derision was the studio's next excursion to the crypt, *Lust for a Vampire*. An unofficial remake of *The Vampire Lovers*, which had been released only a year earlier, *Lust* provided ample evidence that Hammer had simply run out of ideas.

The production was plagued by difficulties from the outset. Peter Cushing had been scheduled to star, but was forced to decline the assignment due to the illness of his beloved wife, Helen. Cushing was replaced by Ralph Bates, who took the role as a favor to the distraught Cushing. Director Jimmy Sangster became a last-minute replacement for Terence Fisher, who had broken his leg while drunk. (He must have read the script.)

Once again the terrible Karnstein family was wreaking havoc across the countryside in the person of their nubile daughter Carmilla (talk about juvenile delinquency!), cleverly changing her name this time to Mircalla. Perhaps Clark Kent's glasses might have made for a more effective disguise. The "lust" in the title told it all. Where *The Vampire Lovers* was erotic and suggestive, *Lust for a Vampire* was nearly pornographic. Star Yutte Stensgaard was selected for her twin abilities rather than for her sensibilities, and very attractive they were, too.

Sadly, however, she couldn't act. Nor could Mike Raven as Count Karnstein. Consequently, the film was an embarrassment for everyone concerned. For all of its notoriety and supposed titillation, the film is an incomparable bore.

Christopher Lee, after years of pleading for a chance to play Stoker's Dracula "as written," got his wish in director Jess Franco's multi-national production of *Count Dracula* (1970). It remains Lee's worst interpretation of the role... his acting so stiff as to give dead people a bad name. While Lee shoulders the lion's share of blame for this mess, fault must also be placed upon the indifferent (one is tempted to say nonexistent) direction of Franco, a thoroughly incompetent script, cheap and shoddy sets, an unbelievably bad score, and special effects that would not have been out of place in a grade school production of the play.

This "faithful" adaptation of Stoker's novel is anything but, and remains a major embarrassment to all involved. Most importantly, it proves that while Lee was an able vampire—and Dracula to a whole generation—a full-blooded portrayal of the role was completely out of this imposing, but limited, actor's range. His performance is utterly without charisma or resonance, and he preens about with an absurd sense of entitlement: Lee obviously felt the role was his even if he were sleepwalking through it.

Herbert Lom, usually suave and capable, brings nothing to Van Helsing. It is only Klaus Kinski, as Renfield, who actually delivers a performance. Kinski's depiction of lunacy is quite disturbing, and should've found a home in a better picture.

That *Count Dracula* is largely forgotten today is not surprising. What is surprising is that it was ever produced at all.

Hammer fared better with its next film. *Countess Dracula*, released in October 1972 in the U.S., was actually more a historical drama than a horror film. Based on the life and crimes of true-life villainess Elizabeth Bathory, the picture recounts the bloody eccentricities of the infamous "Blood Countess," who bathed in the blood of virgin women, and who was reputed to have murdered upwards of 650 people. Ingrid Pitt played the infamous Countess with customary relish as she discovered herself in a pickle over past and present indiscretions. While Bathory rivaled her male counterpart, Vlad the Impaler, for the sheer savagery of her brutality, this fictional Countess was somewhat more demure. Here, she embarks on her criminal career as an aged matriarch who discovers, quite by accident, that the blood of virgins, mixed with bath water and a little ginger ale on the side, is the magical elixir of youth.

Needless to say, the good Countess was never dirty again.

Distinguished British actor Nigel Green co-starred with Pitt as the loyal consort, Captain Dobi, in what, distressingly, proved to be his final performance. Critical reviews of the film were better than usual, but the public was indifferent to the Countess' charms. The picture premiered in England on the lower half of a double bill headlining *Hell's Belles*. Nigel Green took his own life on May 15, 1972, perhaps more from embarrassment than anything else.

Twins of Evil strolled down the Hammer aisle next in yet another variation of the already exhausted Carmilla theme. In this outing Peter Cushing appeared as a fanatical Puritan cult leader committed to eradicating the infestation of vampirism troubling his village. Count Karnstein has been borrowing from the village "library," a veritable treasure trove of nubile young virgins with whom he has his way. However, when the already unpleasant Count is drafted into service by the reincarnation of his undead, incestuous ancestor Mircalla, the Count's ugly demeanor becomes all the meaner. (If nothing else, *Twins of Evil* is a potent parable against extended family visits.)

Madeleine and Mary Collinson, real life twin sisters, appeared in both the film and a celebrated *Playboy* magazine pictorial designed to display their twin charms. The plot, in which one sister is infected with the vampire plague while her innocent sibling

Ingrid Pitt displays her charms in *Countess Dracula* (1972).

is unjustly mistaken for her, was a harbinger of the spate of "evil twin" television films in the 1980s. While Peter Cushing lent credibility to the well-traveled story, the film is remembered, somewhat unfairly, for its popular *Playboy* spread. Released in June of 1972 in America, the film has much to recommend it apart from its sensationalistic umbilical connection to Hugh Hefner.

As Hammer continued its uphill struggle to retain control of the declining horror market, a quiet revolution was taking place across America, where a modest made-for-television movie and a book on the historical Dracula were about to change the face of vampirism forever.

On January 11, 1972, the *ABC Movie of the Week* premiered what would become the most popular made-for-television movie in history (or at least the history of television).

The Night Stalker began, innocently enough, as a straight mystery concerning a murderer who drained his victim's blood, preying on strippers and prostitutes in Las Vegas. Assigned to cover the story for the Las Vegas *Daily News* is a former star reporter for the big New York newspapers, Carl Kolchak, recently fallen upon hard luck and hungrily searching for the story that will catapult him back into the big time. Kolchak quickly senses that there is significantly more to the story than has been admitted by the Las Vegas police department.

On the scent of a more provocative truth, Kolchak screams to the police that "this nut thinks he's a vampire." What neither the reporter or the viewing audience suspected at this point was that the "Vampire Killer" really was, in fact, a vampire.

As scripted by Richard Matheson, from an unpublishable first novel by Jeff Rice, whimsy is replaced by terror as both reporter and audience come to realize the unacceptable truth. Produced by Dan Curtis, who's vampire soap opera *Dark Shadows* had captivated viewers in the 1960s, *The Night Stalker* put together a powerhouse collaborative effort. Written by Matheson, whose credits include *The Incredible Shrinking Man, I Am Legend, Bid Time Return (Somewhere in Time)*, and various episodes of *The Twilight Zone*, and directed by veteran John Llewellyn Moxey, *The Night Stalker* starred the great Darren McGavin as the intrepid reporter. ABC's *The Night Stalker* took the country by storm. Filmed in 1971 as *The Kolchak Tapes*, and broadcast in early 1972, it was, up to its time, the highest rated made-for-television movie ever.

Character actor Barry Atwater was virtually unrecognizable as the ageless vampire, Janos Skorzeny, while Ralph Meeker, Carol Lynley, and Simon Oakland rounded out the impressive cast. Interestingly, not only Bram Stoker but Mickey Spillane seemed represented in the teleplay, for both Darren McGavin and Ralph Meeker had earlier portrayed Spillane's hard boiled sleuth, Mike Hammer. McGavin portrayed the detective for years in the popular CBS television series, while Meeker essayed the role in the cult classic *Kiss Me Deadly* (1955).

The Night Stalker was an altogether delightful mixture of comedy and chills. It went on to inspire a sequel, *The Night Strangler*, a still popular television series, and, by his own admission, Chris Carter's cult favorite, *The X-Files*. Carter was deeply influenced by Kolchak and set about creating a modern variation of *The Night Stalker*, combining both horror and comedy. Reportedly, Carter tried recently to persuade McGavin to reprise his characterization for an episode of *The X-Files*, but the aging actor preferred to leave well enough alone.

Dracula hit the bestseller lists in 1972 with Raymond McNally and Radu Florescu's masterful *In Search of Dracula*. This magnificent book traced the life of historical Dracula Vlad Tepes, detailing his many atrocities in a mixture of brilliant scholarship and lurid sensationalism.

The effect this book would have on the rest of this Dracula decade is impossible to measure: suddenly, the whole world was Vlad Tepes conscious, and Dracula had been given a new unlease on his unlife. Though Stoker makes the connection between his fictional vampire and the historical Dracula plain, it was almost as if McNally and Florescu re-invented the character, giving him a past and richness that he previously lacked. In their own, unique way, these two academics have been as responsible for the modern conception of Dracula as were playwrights Hamilton Deane and John L. Balderston, and the fruits of their scholarship started to influence the character immediately. Indeed, they are solely responsible for the resulting Dracula mania that swept the nation, and the films, books and plays it produced.

When the Marvel Comics Group introduced their stylish *Tomb of Dracula* comic and *Dracula Lives!* black-and-white magazine, stories of (or referring to) the historical Tepes were featured regularly. And in 1979's *Love At First Bite*, Susan St. James often refers to her elegantly undead suitor as "Vlad." The authors' influence is felt still, in the 1990s, with Francis Ford Coppola's *Bram Stoker's Dracula*.

More importantly, *In Search of Dracula* led to a vast revival of interest in things Dracula on Publishers Row, extending to the later, lesser, works of Leonard Wolf and Gabriel Ronay.

The genre received an additional transfusion in 1972 with the release of American International's *Blacula*. The studio had begun the decade in its usual lurid manner with *Count Yorga, Vampire*, a cheesy, yet occasionally frightening vampire film with Robert Quarry delivering a fine, understated performance as the Count. Subtlety was rarely the studio's forte, however, and Quarry's earnest effort was sadly overshadowed by the cheap look of the film.

With the growing prevalence of black exploitation films crowding the American market, it was a natural that someone might suggest a black horror film. Dimension Productions announced their entry into the genre with *Black Dracula*.

Deadlier than Dracula!
Dracula goes cool and funky with William Marshall's performance of *Blacula*.

While the film never proceeded beyond pre-production, it evidently inspired Power Productions to begin work on a similar production, *Blacula*. While *Blacula* seemed to suffer from the same cheapness of appearance that plagued most American International presentations, it was also blessed by the towering presence of actor William Marshall in the title role. A major influence on the American stage with an astonishingly rich voice rivaled only by Orson Welles, Paul Frees, and James Earl Jones, Marshall's very presence in the film elevated its stature tremendously.

A gifted actor, Marshall had endeared himself to television audiences five years earlier by appearing in a classic episode of *Star Trek*, "The Ultimate Computer." This December 1967 episode featured Marshall as a brilliant but tortured "mad" scientist,

Richard Daystrom, whose mental engrams have been imprinted in the circuits of an equally mad computer, M-5. So popular was Marshall's performance that references to his character, and the Daystrom Institute, named after him, continue to this day in various *Star Trek* incarnations.

At the actor's insistence, the script for *Blacula* was given a taste of racial significance. As Prince Mamuwalde, Marshall visits Castle Dracula in 1815 in search of support for an end to the European slave trade. (Politics have always made strange bedfellows.) Apparently unaware of the Count's unsavory reputation, he attempts to enlist the Count's help, only to be met by racial slurs, vampiric attack, and entombment. Dracula, played by actor Charles Macaulay, condemns Mamuwalde and his wife Luva (Vonette McGee) to a living death behind the walls of a hidden chamber in the castle. Luva will die a slow, horrible death, but the black prince, for his perceived arrogance, will suffer the unquenchable thirst of the living dead. He is dubbed Blacula by his host and walled up within the castle for 150 years, until inadvertently released by some gay interior decorators. (*Blacula*, it seems, cannot resist slurs and stereotypes of any kind: the film's two gay characters are two of the most outlandish creatures to ever scuttle out of the celluloid closet.)

Conceived and executed as a cheap exploitation film, the production was doomed to a tacky look, script, and direction. Not even the performance of a former Othello could save this misdirected venture from the proverbial fate worse than death—it is the film, and not Mamuwalde, that Dracula should have entombed. A sequel, *Scream, Blacula, Scream*, followed a year later. Mixing vampirism and voodoo, it was less successful than its predecessor. With lackluster direction by Bob Kelljan, who also lensed *Count Yorga, Vampire*, this new *Blacula* was anything but a scream. When asked about his working relationship with the director at a recent convention sponsored by The Horror & Fantasy Film Society (FANEX), Marshall seemed to have no recollection of him. Informed that Kelljan "directed" the second *Blacula* film, the actor responded with a terse "supposedly."

Dracula's friends and family members continued to proliferate throughout Europe and the British Isles. Hammer Films returned to the genre in 1972 with the release of *Vampire Circus*. Once again vampires set up shop in a middle European village, terrorizing women and children first, proving, of course, that chivalry is not dead... even if the women and children are. When the evil Count Mitterhouse (what is it with counts?) is finally cornered and impaled, he vows to return, a pale reflection of himself, and gain back his power by devouring the nourishing blood of others. Time passes while the accursed villagers suffer the slings and arrows of outrageous scripting. The village is soon consumed by some dread disease, and is ordered quarantine.

Astonishingly, a large and mysterious circus troupe manages to elude the city's protectors, arriving in town prepared, along with Mickey, Judy, and a barn, to put on a show. It isn't long before a series of mishaps begin to befall the beleaguered townspeople. Virgins, of course, are the meal of choice, or the first course. Other family members soon follow. The dreaded circus performers change into panthers and assorted fanged beasts at will, recalling the plot (but not the style, grace, or subtlety) of Val Lewton's *The Cat People*.

When the Count himself (Mitterhouse, not Dracula) finally returns to life, the future prosperity of the village of Schtettel is thrown seriously into doubt until a heroic young man traps the Count's head within the bow string of a crossbow, firing the fatal arrow that decapitates the unwelcome intruder.

They don't make movies like *Vampire Circus* anymore. We should be eternally grateful for small favors.

Dracula jointed the mod squad in late 1972, mixing sex, drugs, and rockin' vampires. One of the silliest, if not the worst of Hammer's Draculean excursions, *Dracula A.D. 1972* was an embarrassing amalgam of traditional and juvenile narrative that pitted the once noble aristocrat against modern day teeny-boppers. The boppers win and Dracula is (or should be) covered in shame.

On the plus side was the joyous reuniting of

Christopher Lee reaps yet another Hammer Films script.

Peter Cushing and Christopher Lee. As usual with their collaborations, it is the erstwhile Cushing who carries the proceedings. The highlight of the film remains the opening sequence, in which the two old enemies battle atop a careening coach. While both actors had obviously aged in the years following their initial confrontation in 1958, their obvious joy in playing opposite one another once more was infectious. The film takes place 100 years after the last rough-house between Dracula and Van Helsing (completely disregarding the Stoker timeline) in present-day London. There, Lorrimer Van Helsing seeks to protect his lovely granddaughter, Jessica (Stephanie Beacham), from the seduction of innocence. Dracula's descendent, Johnny Alucard (Christopher Neame), celebrates a black mass inside an abandoned church along with a group of terminally bored teen-agers, including Jessica and the luscious Caroline Munro, as Laura.

Growing apprehensive at the sobriety of the ceremony, the callow congregation escapes a vaguely perceived impending danger, leaving behind the foolish Laura, who comes to regret her decision (like much of the film's paying audience). Dracula returns to life and wisely attacks the voluptuous Laura, unfortunately eliminating Ms. Munro from the remainder of the film.

Like his illustrious ancestor, Lorrimer Van Helsing specializes in researching and investigating occult practices and begins to suspect that his grandfather's evil nemesis has returned to exact a personal revenge. Not surprisingly, Dracula's method of revenge involves transfusing Jessica's blood with his own, taking her as his vampire bride. Or something. When Jessica's boyfriend becomes a vampire and summons her to the desecrated churchyard at the Count's command, Van Helsing lies in wait, blinding Dracula with holy water and sending the disoriented vampire plunging into an open grave lined with carefully placed stakes.

Other than a few memorable sequences reuniting Cushing and Lee, such as the opening moments between the Count and the original Van Helsing, *Dracula A.D. 1972* is a miscalculated attempt to draw blood from a stoned generation. Poorly directed by Alan Gibson, ineptly lit and photographed by Dick Bush, and with abysmal music by Michael Vickers, *A.D. 1972* is easily the weakest, most ineffectual entry in the series.

And that's saying something.

Among the most eagerly anticipated events of the 1974 television season was the Dan Curtis production of *Dracula*. Heralded at the time as a definitive interpretation of the famous novel, there was a palpable excitement in the air when the CBS telefilm finally unspooled. (Its initial premiere was delayed during broadcasts of the Watergate hearings.)

The team responsible for *The Night Stalker*—producer Curtis and author Richard Matheson—here presented a streamlined version of Stoker's novel. Jack Palance, who had scored earlier with his portrayal in the Canadian Broadcasting System's production of *The Strange Case of Dr. Jekyll and Mr. Hyde*, played Dracula, bringing a brooding, Byronic romance to the role.

Unfortunately, the overall production is not nearly as good as Palance. Matheson's screenplay is unusually weak, and the supporting players, including Nigel Davenport and Simon Ward, are uninspired. Directed and photographed without the slightest hint of either creativity or imaginative style, this new *Dracula* seemingly accomplished an impossible dream: it made Stoker's Victorian nightmare a spectacular bore.

Though inadequate, Matheson's screenplay was the first to include the Count's past as Vlad Tepes in the wake of McNally and Florescu's *In Search of Dracula*, a nifty touch. Also, Matheson created the Dracula-searching-for-his-reincarnated-love subplot that was later appropriated by James V. Hart for 1992's *Bram Stoker's Dracula*. For all the problems of the later film, Hart's work is conspicuously better than Matheson's.

It's a shame that this version isn't better: with the combined talents of Palance, Curtis, and Matheson, this version of the venerable fright tale could have been a contender.

While cinema variations of the old vampire legends were rapidly deteriorating in quality, an unexpected love letter to Hollywood's Vampire King came seemingly out of nowhere.

In 1974 G.P. Putnam & Sons published Arthur Lennig's *The Count: The Life and Times of Bela "Dracula" Lugosi*. A warm, loving and extremely poignant examination of the career and tragic life of one of horror cinema's most celebrated players, Lennig's book managed to finally put Lugosi's career in perspective.

Dealing richly with Lugosi's matinee idol status in his native Hungary, his beginnings as a stranger in a strange land called Hollywood, his all-too-brief, yet dazzling stardom, and his untimely decline and fall into misery and drug addiction, Lennig's appreciation remains a revelation. It's unlikely that even the most callous reader could find himself unmoved or untouched by the story of Bela Lugosi, the horror and fantasy genre's first true star.

Lennig concludes... "So, on August 16, 1956, Lugosi, who had feigned death so many times during his career, would feign no more." And so Lugosi, dead 18 years at this time, returned once more from the grave to bring a momentary dignity back to the genre.

Bram Stoker's immortal literary creation was now under constant attack by satirists and well-meaning incompetents who continued, sadly, to assault his once terrifying countenance. Perhaps the most reprehensible ravishing of the Count came from modern history's most blatant purveyor of mediocrity, Andy Warhol, who produced a test tube rip-off of the classic novel, replete with repellent gore and tasteless pornography. Alternately known as *Blood For Dracula* and, unashamedly, *Andy Warhol's Dracula*, Paul Morrissey took a pathetic stab at directing with nonexistent style or clarity of vision. With an inept starring performance by Udo Keir and presented in 3-Dimension (two more than the film possessed), *Blood For Dracula* is a repugnant exercise in bloated self indulgence that is both regrettable and forgettable. Dracula had now been truly seduced and abandoned.

David Niven, having already played Ian Fleming's master spy James Bond in the broad satire *Casino Royale*, now essayed the role of Count Dracula in a decidedly minor spoof, *Vampira*. Also starring Teresa Graves, the original title *Vampirella* was changed due to possible copyright infringement of Warren Publications' comic magazine.

Neither *Vampira*, or the infamous Warhol *Blood For Dracula*, did much to resuscitate an increasingly anemic legend. A gifted light comedian, Niven was the only screen Dracula to have won an Oscar (for *Separate Tables*, 1958), until Jack Palance picked up his award for *City Slickers* (1991). Fortunately, this sorry film was not the end for Niven, who went on to a successful career as a memorist and novelist while occasionally appearing in quality films like *Death on the Nile*.

By comparison, Hammer Films' *Kronos*, released in America in June 1974 as *Captain Kronos: Vampire Hunter*, was a veritable breath of fresh air. Infused with boyish enthusiasm, *Kronos* was a swashbuckling adventure replete with swordplay, sorcery, sex, and vampirism... not necessarily in that order. Hampered by an undistinguished performance by awkward newcomer Horst Janson, *Kronos* was, nevertheless, an innocent fantasy that attempted to reinvent the vampire legend with new rules and regulatory guidelines. The sparkling beauty of Caroline Munro was also very much in evidence, a far more tasty morsel to envision than the earlier depravity of Udo Keir. Directed by Brian Clemens (of television's *The Avengers*), and featuring the music of Laurie Johnson (*First Men in the Moon*), the film may have been a trifle too experimental for its own good. Ultimately, its box office failure was yet another nail in Hammer's coffin.

Another failed experiment, Hammer's *The Satanic Rites of Dracula*, was released in England in January 1974. The film wouldn't see an American release until 1978, in an attempt to cash in on the success of Frank Langella's Broadway *Dracula*. *Satanic Rites* gained notoriety later as the film that transformed Dracula into Howard Hughes, as well as the long-overdue last appearance of Christopher Lee as the vampire prince.

In this telling, Count Dracula has at last tired of death on Earth and has decided to end the world, not only for himself, but, generously, for everyone else inhabiting the planet as well. He'll accomplish this task—no mean feat even for the Vampire King— by developing a deadly new strain of plague to eradicate the whole of humanity, thereby eliminating once and for all the annoying source of his needed blood supply. Disguised as business mogul D. D. Denham, Dracula has an unscrupulous scientist create a new strain of bubonic plague. As tycoon, Dracula has fully adapted to the lifestyles of the rich and infamous.

The film also generated some remarkably erotic and kinky imagery, including half-naked women shackled and chained in a hidden cellar. However, the most sexually arousing sequence involved a blatantly satanic ritual in which a willingly submissive young woman lay writhing naked upon an altar as drops of blood are spilt over her breasts, stomach, and exposed vagina. (Poor Peter Cushing was obviously more interested, at this point, in retirement money than anything else.) Finally she is stabbed in the heart with a large, ritualistic dagger brandished by the cult leader, bringing her exquisite torment to a climax with a shuddering scream.

When Jessica is abducted by Dracula's henchmen, Van Helsing follows to prevent the girl from becoming the monster's bride. (It's interesting that, after all the heartache they have caused him, Dracula would want to marry into the Van Helsing family.) After the expected conflagration, Van Helsing entangles the vampire in the vines of a hawthorn bush, driving a stake through the monster's heart.

Satanic Rites of Dracula was Christopher Lee's final go-round as Count Dracula. Lee was particularly lucky in his vow to never don the vampire's cape again—for no one ever asked him. It was also, sadly, the final on-camera teaming of Cushing and Lee in a Hammer production. For both men, it was the end of an era.

Although a failure, Hammer obviously wanted to continue with a modern series of Van Helsing adventures. Cushing's Lorrimer Van Helsing was fast becoming the Sherlock Holmes of the monster set, aided by his equally heroic granddaughter Jessica and her Scotland Yard crony. Joanna Lumley replaces Stephanie Beacham in this film, and she's absolutely fabulous. The whole enterprise had a very Sax Rohmer feel to it, and, if not for the presence of Dracula, might have made a worthwhile thriller!

Having merged with the fad for black exploitation films in *Blacula*, it was only natural that the emerging Kung Fu craze should also chop away at the vampire's legacy.

Easily the most bizarre addition to the Dracula legend by Hammer was *The Legend of the Seven Golden Vampires*, also known as *The Seven Brothers Meet Dracula*, and, *The Seven Brothers and Their One Sister Meet Dracula*. (I kid you not!)

It must have seemed an inspiration during the Kung Fu craze of the 1970s to combine the two genres, along with the great film studios of both England and Japan. Shaw Bros. eagerly accepted the offer to join with Hammer in producing the first martial arts Dracula film. Unfortunately for the two companies, it looked as though Matt Dillon was more adept at mastering martial arts than the seven brothers, who should have stayed home to sing, dance, and marry their seven brides.

Dracula was played by John Forbes-Robinson, who was, at best, an ineffectual Count. Of course, the little-known truth unearthed here was that Dracula, who had evidently tired of being a reclusive billionaire, had transformed himself into Kah, an Asian practitioner of occult rites. (Right.) Surely now the seven brothers would endure The Wrath of Kah.

Peter Cushing was enticed into portraying Van Helsing one last time, and if there is any joy to be found in this numbingly imbecilic enterprise, it is the enthusiasm this great actor brings to the part, combined with the wonderful music of Hammer's least appreciated genius, James Bernard.

Hammer's final horror effort was the moderately effective thriller, *To The Devil A Daughter*, based upon the novel by Dennis Wheatley, and featuring Christopher Lee as an evil, excommunicated priest who plans to offer up his godchild to the devil upon the attainment of her 18th birthday. An embarrassed Richard Widmark co-starred as an expert on occult practices, persuaded by the girl's father to save her from the awful satanic cult.

The film is best remembered for the much-advertised nudity of the deliciously nubile daughter of German actor Klaus Kinski. Nastassja Kinski, barely 18 years old in her first screen appearance, was the picture of virginal innocence. (What an actress!) Her nude scenes were captivating to say the least, but it was an inauspicious beginning to a solid body of dramatic work, and a tepid farewell, at best, to the Hammer House of Horror. (They would produce one more film, a remake of Hitchcock's *The Lady Vanishes*. Though no patch on the original, 1979's *Lady* was a respectable swan song for the studio.)

After the release in America of *To The Devil A Daughter* in July 1976, vampires in general and Dracula in particular appeared dead in the running water, but all that was about to change dramatically. In the annals of motion pictures the year 1939 is universally acknowledged as the single greatest year of important releases in the history of the industry. Similarly, the year 1977 was about to emerge as the pivotal turning point for Bram Stoker's Prince of Darkness.

The year began innocuously enough with an episode of NBC-TV's *McCloud*, starring Dennis Weaver. One of the recurring shows on the *NBC Sunday Mystery Movie* (the others included *Columbo*, *McCoy*, and *Quincy*), the April 17 program was a bizarre episode entitled *McCloud Meets Dracula*. Here, transplanted cowboy hero Marshall McCloud is confronted by a baffling series of murders that appear to be vampire related. Universal's premier vampire of the 1940s, John Carradine, was reincarnated as Loren Belasco, an eccentric horror movie actor who believes himself the descendent of the historical Dracula. (A name with a more than passing similarity to Bela Lugosi's actual last name, Blasko.)

Diana Muldaur co-starred in the episode, along with Tom Snyder, appearing as himself, interviewing Bela-sco on *The Tomorrow Show*. Carradine-Belasco recounts his career for Snyder to the accompaniment of film clips from *House of Dracula* and *House of Frankenstein*, in which he portrayed his infamous ancestor. In the end, Belasco is revealed as the actual murderer (surprise!). Following a rooftop chase (where Carradine is extensively doubled), the actor jumps from the roof like a bat outta hell and vanishes from sight. Appropriately enough, a bat outta hell appears where Belasco disappeared and flies off into the sunset.

For the production a magnificent painting of Carradine as the Count was created by the artists at Universal, which reappeared some years later on the wall of horror film television host Roddy McDowall in *Fright Night*.

Thirty years after the creation of Bram Stoker's literary masterpiece, *Dracula*, Hamilton Deane, the son of one of Stoker's boyhood chums, decided to translate the novel to the London stage. An actor and playwright, Deane's theatrical version debuted at the Grand Theater in Derby in 1925, later arriving London's West end in February 1927 after years on tour. It would run for 391 performances before taking to the road again, where it seemed indestructible.

Deane often appeared in these productions as Van Helsing. So potent was the resurgence of interest in *Dracula* that American producer-publisher Horace Liveright imported the successful play to the New York stage, where it opened at the Fulton Theater on October 5. Rewritten almost completely by John L. Balderston, who later co-authored the screenplays of *Bride of Frankenstein* and *Gone With the Wind*, the Deane-Balderston version of *Dracula* gave the world its popular conception of the character.

It would also give the role its most legendary interpreter: a then little-known Hungarian actor named Bela Lugosi. Lugosi would recreate his stage role four years later in Universal Pictures' movie version of *Dracula*, simultaneously ruining his career and achieving a perverse type of immortality.

The New York engagement of the play ran for 261 performances and then enjoyed huge success on the road. And the rest, as they say, is history.

But history has an uncanny way of repeating itself. It was 50 years later

One of Edward Gorey's masterful sketches... now a popular postcard.

Edward Gorey's evocative second act curtain for Broadway's *Dracula* (1971).

almost to the day, on October 20, 1977, that a new production of *Dracula* opened in Broadway's Martin Beck Theater. Directed by Dennis Rosa, and with celebrated scenery and costumes designed by artist Edward Gorey, this enormously popular revival starred the gifted and romantic actor Frank Langella as the Count. Langella would enjoy somewhat modified success several years later in a similarly inspired revival of William Gillette's *Sherlock Holmes* for the Williamstown Theater, but it was this witty production of Dracula that all too briefly elevated this sensitive actor to star status.

Dracula, the Vampire Play enjoyed newfound success on the New York stage and generated numerous road companies across the country.

Count Dracula lived again.

Soon after Dracula's Broadway success, the blood-thirsty Count made his way down to New York's Greenwich Village. There, at the Cherry Lane Theater, Dracula settled in for a long run with *The Passion of Dracula*, by Bob Hall and David Richmond. This nifty adaptation of Stoker's novel featured Christopher Birnau as the Count, and a spectacular man-to-bat transformation effect that put its Broadway counterpart to shame.

The Passion of Dracula is well remembered by theater goers, and gave serious competition to its Broadway rival. So popular was the production, in fact, that Birnau's Dracula appeared regularly with Paxton Whitehead, then appearing as Sherlock Holmes on Broadway's *Crucifer of Blood*, in local Sizzler's Steak House commercials. It was not the first time the Great Detective and the Vampire King met during the decade: the literary Holmes and Dracula crossed swords in both *The Holmes-Dracula File* and *The Adventure of the Sanguinary Count*.

One of the most interesting (and persistent) rumors of the decade was the talk surrounding the never-produced *Sherlock Holmes and the Prince of Darkness*. With Jack Palance slated to repeat his role as Dracula and former *Prisoner* Patrick McGoohan as Sherlock Holmes, the film promised to be a delight to fans of both classic characters. Sadly, it never came to pass.

Something must have been in the air in 1977, for soon the BBC, in conjunction with America's Public Television, broadcast its own version of Bram Stoker's novel. *Count Dracula*, as scripted by Gerald Savory and directed by Philip Saville, would quickly become (and remain) the definitive interpretation of the famous novel.

The casting of the title character, as so often had occurred in the past, would lean more toward a romantic leading man or matinee idol. French actor Louis Jourdan, who scored so well for MGM in *Madame Bovary* with Jennifer Jones in 1949, for Universal with *Letter From An Unknown Woman* with Joan Fontaine in 1948, and again at MGM with *Gigi* in 1958, was cast as that man from Transylvania.

His Count was suave, debonair, and lethal. Appearing with Jourdan were Bosco Hogan as Jonathan Harker, Judy Bowker as Mina (later the heroine in Ray Harryhausen's *Clash of the Titans*), Susan Penhaligon as Lucy, Jack Sheperd as Renfield (a standout), and Frank Finlay as Van Helsing. Finlay's performance in the role may be the most compelling ever enacted, or, at least, is in a dead heat with the redoubtable Peter Cushing. Finlay later turned the tables on himself as scientist turned vampire in Tobe Hooper's epic science fiction drama, *Lifeforce* (1985).

Dramatist Gerald Savory had been drawn to the novel *Dracula* ever since 1920 when, as an 11-year-old boy, he and his brother read the novel aloud with two other children and their mothers, varying the dramatic styles as both families were vacationing in Folkstone, England for the Easter holidays. Savory's mother, an actress and leading lady of the period, was rather prim and proper in the reading of her chapters. Her friend, an actress as well, was more animated and expressive in her performance, chilling the children's blood with nightmarish renderings. More than 50 years after that memorable vacation, the writer fulfilled a lifelong ambition: to turn his favorite novel into a literate television play.

Additionally, he turned the teleplay into a novel, published the same year in England by Corgi Books. In the book's preface he writes: "Above all, I believe that both the television version and the following pages will give a very clear idea of what first, rather surprisingly, stuck in my schoolboy mind and which is the core of the original novel—the struggle between good and evil. Whatever Count Dracula represents—Satan, beast, or virulent disease—Professor Van Helsing lays it on the line. 'Evil will not disappear just because we disapprove of it. We must fight.'"

This production of *Dracula* has been praised for the past 20 years for both its literacy and fidelity to Stoker's novel. Its settings and set pieces remain startling, effective, and evocative. For much of the film, Stoker's disquieting narrative is brought spectacularly to life. At Castle Dracula, Harker is unnerved while shaving as Dracula enters the room and casts no reflection in the small mirror. The Count mocks him by placing his fingers upon the glass surface, reflecting not even a shadow. Nonchalantly dropping the mirror from his castle window, he admonishes his guest, warning him that "mirrors are stupid things... you shouldn't trust them."

Later, Harker peers out of the window of his bed chamber where he sees Dracula crawling face down across the castle wall, flopping his legs and belly like some monstrous winged rodent. Now convinced that his life is in deadly peril, the solicitor himself climbs the castle wall and descends dangerously into the deserted courtyard. There he enters another room, the Count's burial chamber. The vault is lined with large, black coffins... with Dracula sleeping serenely inside one of them.

As Harker lifts a shovel to smash the body of his host, Dracula turns to meet his gaze, untroubled by the threat. His eyes burning red, his cheeks bloated and gorged, he smiles as Harker runs screaming from the crypt.

This moody, atmospheric production remains the high point of Dracula cinema, and is a tribute to the creative genius of Bram Stoker.

Television continued its illicit love affair with motion pictures when NBC attempted to resurrect the movie serial, or chapter play. *Cliffhangers*, like the *NBC Mystery Movie*, rotated several story lines, but this time to minimal effect. This short-lived series might have benefited from the use of cliff notes to elucidate its dishearteningly large cemetery plot holes.

Based upon the chapter plays that dominated the Saturday matinees from the silent days well into the 1950s, *Cliffhangers* was a half-hearted enterprise wholly lacking in either quality or conviction. Each episode ended with the lives or chastity of its principal characters in peril. Without Pauline, however, the cliffhangers were without interest or excitement and seldom, if ever, over the edge.

One of the continuing stories, *The Return of Dracula*, starred Michael Nouri as the ageless count, posing as an attractive college professor in an urban campus community. Sporting a blow-dried 'do and bedroom eyes, Nouri was a Dracula for the polyester, disco age.

Interestingly, when *Cliffhangers* was canceled, the writers brought closure to the Dracula storyline and none of the others. Cured of his blood addiction, Dracula is left alive in anticipation of love and the ensuing Reagan years.

Germany's Golden Age of Film produced the first screen translation of Dracula with the release of UFA's unauthorized *Nosferatu, Eine Symponie Des Grauens* (*A Symphony of Terror*) in 1922. Starring Max Schreck, whose name is the German word for "terror," *Nosferatu*'s reputation has continued to grow over the years, and it is now ranked among the true classics of silent cinema.

As Dracula (named Orlock for copyright reasons), Schreck was truly ghastly, the visage of an upright, white rat. While the adaptation was not legally sanctioned by the Stoker estate—and nearly hounded out of existence by Stoker's widow—it remains the most horrifying of the many versions of Dracula. As directed by F. W. Murnau, *Nosferatu* was truly a symphony of terror.

In 1979, German director Werner Herzog remade the film, starring the actor who, three years earlier, had given the devil his daughter, Klaus Kinski. (Kinski is also the only film actor to have essayed both the roles of Renfield and Dracula.) Though Kinski's make-up closely copied the original Schreck conception, Herzog was careful to create an art film and not a horror movie. Herzog actually shot two versions of his epic, one in German and one in English; neither is good. Twentieth Century-Fox had hoped to

Klaus Kinski as the walking pestilence that is *Nosferatu* (1979).

score a big hit with the English version, but later deemed it unreleasable. Instead, it shipped the German version to art houses, where it received scant attention.

Much of the imagery in Herzog's film is captivating, but the finished piece remains an effort without soul. It retains the best aspects of the earlier film's look, but none of its passion or integrity.

The decade closed with two of the most interesting representations of Dracula on film.

After 10 years of Dracula films, it was time for an affectionate valentine to the world's favorite vampire.

Starring George Hamilton, in a performance that merges Bela Lugosi with leading man chic, *Love At First Bite* was the most successful comedy of 1979. With Arte Johnson as Renfield, Susan Saint James as the love interest, and Richard Benjamin as Van Helsing's descendent (a psychiatrist, Van Helsing has changed his last name to Rosenberg "for professional reasons"), the film was produced on a shoestring and raked in millions.

Hamilton was never better, never more likable, than in *Love At First Bite*. It heralded a minor renaissance of his career, and led to another spin on that *other* ageless romantic idol in *Zorro: The Gay Blade* (1981).

At the core of this sweetly funny and romantic film was the isolation of Dracula—here an arch romantic—from the cold rationalism of the modern world. Looking for a love that transcends time and place, it is Dracula who becomes heroic and 20th-century man that is monstrous. Kicked out of his Transylvania castle by the Communists, mis-

ドラキュラ都へ行く

カラー作品／アメリカ映画

日本ヘラルド映画

Herald

understood and abused by contemporary New York, cast adrift by changes in social conventions, Hamilton's Dracula become a figure from a desperately missed past, a matinee idol that embodies a more adventurous, more romantic world.

While Hamilton's film was in production at Fox, Universal was taking the same theme of a romantic, lovelorn Dracula much more literally for its own film.

Since Frank Langella scored such a tremendous hit with his Broadway *Dracula*, it was only natural that Universal (home of Bela Lugosi's 1931 Dracula) would plan a remake.

In July 1979, just months after the release of both Werner Herzog's *Nosferatu* and Stan Dragoti's *Love At First Bite*, the second screen version of the Deane-Balderston

ドラキュラ都へ行く

Dracula opened in theaters nationwide. Frank Langella donned the vampire's cloak once again, hoping his Broadway triumph would translate into big screen box office. The cultured, elegantly beautiful Kate Nelligan played Lucy (actually Mina; the film makers switched the character's names), and gifted scene-stealer Donald Pleasence played Dr. Seward. In what was a much-anticipated stroke of casting, Lord Laurence Olivier, the most respected actor of the century, was signed to portray Van Helsing.

Frank Langella became Dracula for the blow-dried decade with 1979's *Dracula*.

Perhaps because of the manner in which the character was written, or perhaps due to Olivier's growing health problems and advancing age, the actor played Van Helsing as a weak, ineffectual old man. His Van Helsing was no match for the virile, romantic vampire as embodied by the delightful Langella.

Dracula is Langella's film all the way. He manages to bring romance, terror, strength, and compassion to the role... his is a Dracula to savor. Langella's work in this film has often been dismissed by horror movie fans who cannot appreciate a performance that is bigger than its genre. That's a shame, for with Langella, the role of Dracula finally took on classical proportions.

Langella is abetted by fine production values and stylish direction by John Badham. As Dracula is at last destroyed, his body dangling lifelessly in the wind, the pure essence of his dreamlike nobility escapes unfettered into the breeze, where his soul can attain a joyous peace. It is an unexpectedly lovely moment made all the more unforgettable by the faintly swelling echo of composer John Williams' haunting score... the wondrous echo of an immortal literary creation that continues to haunt both our dreams and our imaginations.

It was a beautiful image upon which to end this, the Dracula Decade.

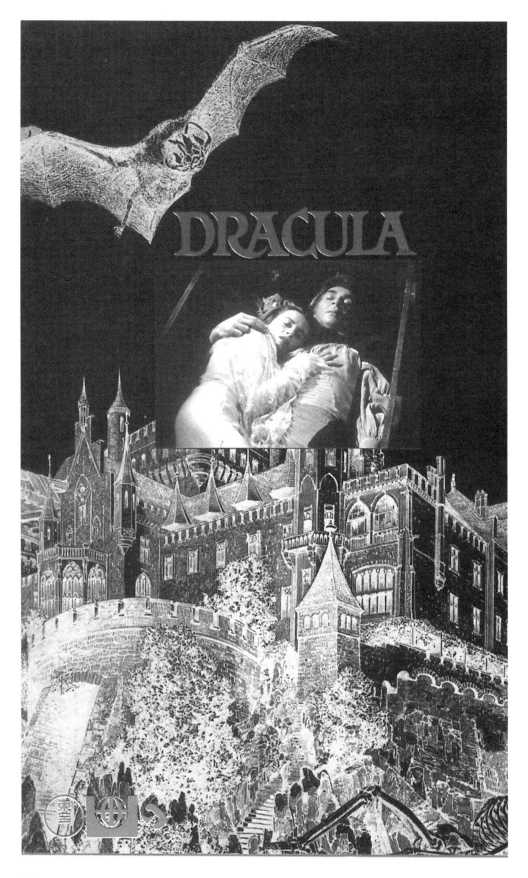

In this interview prepared exclusively for this volume, film director John Badham discusses the genesis of his 1979 film, Dracula.

Considered by many, including this editor, to be the finest movie version of the Dracula myth, Badham's film followed in the wake of the celebrated 1977 Broadway revival of the Hamilton Deane–John L. Balderston play.

Universal, in a move that eerily paralleled Hollywood history nearly 50 years earlier, lured the Broadway Dracula *to its motion picture soundstage. Though Frank Langella's interpretation of Stoker's vampire was a radical departure from Bela Lugosi's performance, both have made significant contributions to the Dracula myth. While Lugosi gave the world the face and voice most identified with the King Vampire, Langella made his evil attractive.*

That was exactly what director Badham had in mind, as you will see here.

The interview was conducted by author and horror film historian Tom Weaver. A contributing editor to Fangoria *magazine, the* Wall Street Journal *for horror-film mavens, Mr. Weaver has written more than 10 books, including* They Fought in the Creature Features *and* Poverty Row Horrors.

—Bob Madison

The Vampire's Return: John Badham on the Making of *Dracula*

an interview by Tom Weaver

How did you first become involved with Dracula*?*

I had gone to New York to see Frank Langella in the Broadway production of *Dracula*. Frank was someone who I'd known from the Williamstown Theater Festival [in Williamstown, Massachusetts] for many years. Both he and I had spent time there prior to *Dracula*, in our growing-up-in-theater days. Anyway, I had heard that he was in a wonderful production of *Dracula* in New York and went to see it. Universal Studios, who I was in business with at the time, had the rights to the play since they had made the Bela Lugosi *Dracula* back in 1931. That film was based on the very same play that Langella was doing. Because of the play's success, Universal was interested in doing a remake.

Once they decided to go ahead with it, the question then became, what sort of approach to take with this? How should we do it? The Broadway approach was to play it sort of in a campy fashion, with some *wonderful*, delightful, whimsical sets by artist Edward Gorey. There were black-and-white line drawings for the sets. For example, the books and bookcases were just drawings on canvas, and it all looked like an Edward Gorey sketch. Well, I didn't think that was going to work for a *movie*, which is so

Director John Badham during the making of 1979's *Dracula*.

realistic in nature. You might be able to make it work if you were *only* on the inside and *only* doing interiors, but we knew we wanted to open *Dracula* up with lots of exteriors. So the choice was made to go back to the Bram Stoker novel... re-examine it... try to approach it freshly, as though it had not been done before... and see what was in the novel that perhaps had never even been touched. We also wanted to take advantage of Frank Langella's very good looks and that kind of romantic quality that he was capable of bringing to the part. We wanted to approach it in a very romantic way.

And that's the approach you and W. D. Richter brought to the script.

Yes. I had brought him in, feeling that he would be very, very good at adapting the novel. His approach was to (a) examine the novel, but then (b) to go back and look at the play by John Balderston and Hamilton Deane and make sure that we didn't leave out bits that people had come to dearly love. You get complaints if you don't do lines like "I never drink *dot dot dot* wine" [*laughs*], so there was that little bit of mixing back and forth. But of course when we looked at the Stoker novel, we found all *kinds* of wonderful material that had not really been done—images of Dracula not only as a bat, but as a wolf, as wind, and as fog, or his ability to crawl down the side of a building head-first, like a lizard. These kind of images would be quite spectacular.

As part of your preparation, did you read the novel, or watch any of the old movies?

I certainly re-read the novel and worked at it carefully with Richter. And he and I together ran many, many, *many* versions of *Dracula*. At the time, there were something like 75 vampire films that we tracked down. A large number of them were from Spanish-speaking countries, because they seemed to have a particular fascination for the subject matter. We looked at *Andy Warhol's Dracula* [1974] and the various Hammer films with Christopher Lee... anything we could get our hands on, just to see what people were doing. We hoped to avoid some of the pitfalls that they had fallen into, and also not repeat something that *we* might think was very clever, but suddenly discover later that it had already been done before. There was a lot of research and, of course, it was a great deal of fun. Many of these movies are fun even if they're sort of campy... and of dubious taste.

Do you happen to remember which film, or films, you were most impressed by?

Well, I remember being very fascinated by *Andy Warhol's Dracula*, which was directed by Paul Morrissey, because it took such a wonderful, modern approach to Dracula. It had him driving around Italy in an old limousine, chauffeured by Renfield [*laughs*]! Renfield *always* pops up, in *all* of these incarnations. They were in search of *wirgin* blood, and they had run out of *wirgins* in Europe and now had gone to Italy thinking that, because it's a Catholic country, there would be *lots* of *wirgins* there. It gets funnier and funnier—I don't know *why* this should be funny, but it *is*! It was so outrageous, the whole idea.

Out of all the old versions, my favorite by far is the silent Nosferatu.

Nosferatu is *quite* good. In fact, there was even a remake done around the time that we did ours [Werner Herzog's *Nosferatu*, 1979]. I went to see it with great trepidation, because the imagery was *so* powerful in the trailers and the ads. I didn't care for the results as much as I liked the trailers. The imagery in the *original Nosferatu* is, needless to say, just quite, quite amazing.

When you made Dracula, *your feature credits to date were* The Bingo Long Traveling All-Stars and Motor Kings *and* Saturday Night Fever. *Did you encounter anybody along the line who had reservations about whether you were the right guy to direct* Dracula? *Did you ask yourself at any point, "Am I the right guy for a movie like this?"*

Well, I had just had the very good fortune to have a *huge* hit in *Saturday Night Fever*, and so people were inclined to have a lot of faith in me. And I was interested in the subject matter—it was a great change of pace. I had done a great number of episodes of Rod Serling's *Night Gallery* when I was doing television. I worked on that series right from its very inception, from the *pilot*, and I was also its associate producer. So that kind of stuff I enjoy and had a lot of fun working with, so something like *Dracula* was terrific for me.

Your real casting coup was, of course, Laurence Olivier as Van Helsing.

We were excited by the idea of getting Laurence Olivier from the beginning. The fact that he was *up* for it, and the fact that he had fun *doing* it, was very exciting for everybody concerned. He had been quite ill, and had terrible cancers and so on that were at least under control if not in remission at the time of *Dracula*. He was not nearly as frail as he had been when he did *A Little Romance* (1979) for [director] George Roy Hill. I remember he had to ride a bicycle in *A Little Romance*, and that was just a huge problem for them... how they were going to get Lord Olivier to ride a bicycle when he was too frail to bring it off? But they did it, thanks to the fact that Olivier had an *amazing* double who he worked with, a guy you could shoot very, very close on for a lot of physical things. He could pass for Olivier, and I was able to make good use of him quite a bit as well. (His name was Harry; his last name I would like to tell you, but it escapes me at the moment.) As ill as Olivier was and as cognizant of his limitations as he was, it still annoyed him a *lot*—*that* he had to rely on Harry. And, if he *thought* he had a possibility of being able to do something, he *wanted* to try it.

For instance?

At one point I had a scene with Olivier running down a hallway of the insane asylum, coming up to an open cell door and discovering that a child has been attacked by Dracula in the middle of the night and is lying dead on the floor. So he's got to come *running* down this hallway and look in. I said, "I guess maybe we should ask Harry if he wants to do this," and Olivier said, "No, no. I want to do it, I want to try it. I can *do* it!" I said, "All right, let's rehearse it. Go ahead." And he came down the hallway, and it was *so* slow. *So-o-o* slow. He got to the doorway and he looked up at me and he just had this sad look on his face, and he said, "Well... I guess we should call Harry ..." I felt like [*makes a crying sound*] *but* he just couldn't get the pace out of it that we needed.

Was he always the first choice for that role?

I believe so, yes. I remember, in our very earliest discussions with Ned Tannen, who was president of Universal Pictures at the time, there was talk of how great it would be if we could get Olivier.

According to one of the Olivier biographies, he was paid a million dollars to co-star in Dracula, *and he could only work for a few hours in the middle of each day. Does that sound right?*

Lots of those "biographers" don't even *talk* to the people they're writing about... you know how *that* works. A million dollars? I don't think so. I was not the producer so I didn't have the budget in hand, but I don't think that was right. I might believe $750,000, but not a million. As for working only for a few hours a day, one of the *nice* things about working in England is that they generally tend to work shorter hours than here. A 10-hour day would be the norm in England, whereas we have a tendency to

Billboard at Times Square for Badham's *Dracula*. It was, at the time, the world's largest film advertisement.

stretch it out to 12 hours and exhaust everybody! So we would always try to give him the most generous call we could, as late in the morning as possible. But I seem to remember that he was there eight or nine hours fairly regularly. We always had on the set a fairly large easy chair and a big ottoman so he could put his feet up, because he had something like phlebitis and he needed to keep his feet up and stay rested. Everybody had such respect for him and *liked* him so much, and he was such a nice man, that you just went out of your way to do things for him and to make sure that he was okay. But I don't think that we had to baby him in any extreme kind of way. Certainly if I was through with him at two-thirty or three in the afternoon, I'd say, "Get him out of here. Let him go home." But he was very determined to do the most professional job, and would hang in there to the bitter end if he were needed for anything. We were shooting in January and February, and it was *pretty chilly* out there [*laughs*]. His circulation was not the best, so he would get particularly cold, and we were always moving him quickly back into the trailer, keeping him in where he could stay warm.

In one of the scenes that we were doing outside in a park, Kate Nelligan is heading for Carfax in a little horse and wagon along beside a lake; Olivier stops her and pleads with her *not* to go up there. She had a whip in her hand, and she was supposed to come down and *whip* him across the face. I know *that's* not going fly, that we're not going to whip Lord Olivier across the face, but I could make it look just as bad by having her hit him with the whip on the shoulder, or something like that. In the rehearsal, she came down with just the most tentative *tap* upon his shoulder. I remember him saying, "No! Hit me. Hit me!" And so she came down a little harder, and he said, "No! Come *on*! Let's *go*!" I mean, he wouldn't stop until she really laid into it. I don't think she could have hurt him—he had on the thickest overcoat and so on. But he just knew that it wouldn't look any good unless she really laid into it. She couldn't hurt him but, still, she was terrified.

What was your relationship with him like? Was he directable?

Oh, he was *very*, very directable; English actors are, *thank God*. They are the most flexible. If you said, "Please do this on your head," they *might* think you were crazy (and you in fact might be), but, by God, they'll *try* it, they'll start balancing on their head for you. American actors are not *nearly* so cooperative. They want to question everything, especially the stars: [*in a whiny voice*] "Why do we have to do *this*? Why do we have to do *that?*" But English actors *want* to give the director what he wants.

Reportedly Olivier took you off to the side one day and told you that if he couldn't deliver a prayer in Dutch or Latin rather than in English, he would call a press conference and denounce the movie.

In the *broadest* strokes, this story is true. Here's what really happened: That dialogue was written [in the script] in English, and I think it might have been indicated that he was to speak it in Latin. ("In the name of the Father and the Son and the Holy Ghost, I consecrate this earth," something like that.) In rehearsal he said to me, "Can I do it in Dutch?" and I said, "Sure. Oh, sure, okay, fine!" He was learning a Dutch accent, and he wanted to speak the prayer in Dutch. The night before we shot, I thought, "Oh, boy, what if nobody understands what he's saying? *Yikes*! Well," I said to myself, "I *told* him he could do it in Dutch, so that's okay, we'll do it in Dutch, but *m-a-y-b-e* I better get a take in English, just in case." So we get to that point in the day and it's about, oh, 15 minutes before lunch, which of course is a sacred thing in the movie business—all kinds of meal penalties are invoked once you work into the lunch hour. It gets to be a nervous time, you want to finish the work you're doing. So we do the take in Dutch and that's fine, and then I go over and I say, "Sir, would you mind, could we do one take in English just in case we have a problem?" And he says, "No, absolutely not. No, it *has* to be in Dutch." I say, "Well, I'm just... *nervous* about it, nervous that people won't understand." He says, "No, it's *heretical* to pray in a language that's not your own." Well [*laughs*], I had not heard this particular bit of theological doctrine! We're now up to something like three minutes to one o'clock, or whenever lunch hour was, just right on top of it. I ask a third time and he says, "Oh, all right, let's do it."

He didn't have to tell *me* twice—I turn around and say, "Okay, let's go! Come on, let's roll the camera! Hurry up." But as I'm waiting to put the slate in, I think to myself, "Oh, sure. I know what he's going to do. He's going to give it some kind of half-hearted reading, and then look at me and say, 'That's it.' It'll be some kind of half-baked thing that I can't use, but he'll say that he *did* it." *That's* what I'm anticipating, but he does it and it's *perfect*. You could not *ask* for it to be better, it was just as good as though that was the way it always had been intended to be done and that he was totally in favor of it. So I say, "Cut, print, everybody go to lunch," everybody's out the door and we made it. *Whew*, big relief!

But then he waves at me and he says, "Young man ..." (You could still call me "young man" at that point.) "Young man, come over here." I come over and he says, "I just want you to know *you are not using* the take we just did." I say, "Oh, why is that?" He says, "I only did it because I didn't want to embarrass you in front of the crew. If you use it, I will call a press conference and tell everyone that you have *lied* to me." It bears the amplification, because he was very, very concerned about *my* image of the crew, and that him saying he wouldn't do something would cause loss of face for me. And he was very considerate of that. (And I was extremely appreciative of it!)

And did you need that take in English?

No, we didn't, everybody understood it just fine. I could have avoided this whole thing by not being neurotic about it. It worked out just fine.

What was his relationship with Langella like? Did they get along well?

Yes, they got along very well. Everyone got along extremely well with him—it was hard *not* to. He was extremely pleasant, he was having a good time, and there was no reason for *any*body to be the least bit upset with him. The hardest thing *for me* was dealing with him initially; I was just totally intimidated by him. But he went out of his way to put me at ease. I would say, "Sir, we're going to do ..." and he would say, "Call me *Larry*, dear boy, *Larry!*" I'd go, "Uhhh... yes sir," and again he'd say, "Call me Larry!" Finally I just said to him, "You know, this is very hard for me because the first movie I *ever saw* was *Henry V* [1945] in London, right at the end of the War. It was the first movie my mother ever took me to. It's very *hard* for me to call you Larry!" [*Laughs*]

Cut to four months later, as we are at the end of the movie and one of the last things that I'm doing with Olivier is in the bowels of the ship, with him pinned to the wall by a stake that Dracula has driven through his body, impaling him to the bulkhead of the ship. He's hanging there, dying, and I'm getting a close-up of this. Langella told me later that he was sitting outside the set listening to what was going on, waiting for Olivier to be done so that he could say good-bye to him. (It was Olivier's last day.) And Langella overheard the following exchange: "All right, you're dying, you're dying, your head's going down. Okay, your eyes are closing, your eyes... Oh, for God's *sake*, Larry, close your *mouth!*"

So you had become so at-ease with him that ...

So at-ease that I'm going, "Oh, for God's *sake*, Larry, close your *mouth!*"

On the original Universal Dracula, *Lugosi supposedly stayed in character, tended to be aloof, tended to be kind of mysterious. What was Langella like on the set of your picture?*

Well, he also tends to be somewhat like that. He generally stays apart from people, he's very concerned about his work and very professional and sort of "elevated above the fray," if you will. It's always a little bit tough working with him... he's not your buddy, this is somebody who's just there to do an extremely professional job and he's going to make sure that it comes out the way *he* wants it to come out. He's got very strong ideas and he's very bright and very talented.

In an interview he said he was trying to find "the soft underbelly" of Dracula.

Looking for the softer side, the romantic side, the *vulnerable* bits. Yes, he *was* looking for all of that, and I think he did have a handle on it.

Langella's Dracula was a creature of romance.

But he was also very menacing when he wanted to be.

Oh, yes, absolutely. Frank has *great*, great, great strength on stage and on film, he's just got a tremendous amount of power.

Whose idea was it to shoot in England?

I think that was always our idea; I remember Walter Mirisch and I talking about it from the get-go. The landscapes there are just wonderful, and it's just so easy... I mean, you just cannot *find* a bad shot. It's so easy to find the locations you need, and everybody speaks the language. I guess we could have gone exploring into Eastern Europe or something like that, but since the novel is written in the north of England, we went to the real locations described in the book and then proceeded to try to put things together that would be like those. We shot in Cornwall, which is in the southwest of England... at St. Michael's Mount, which is at the very, very tip of Penzance. (It's a castle-monastery that has a sister building, Mont-Saint-Michel, just off the Normandy coast in France.)

Now some lord lives in St. Michael's Mount, and we used that for the exterior for Dracula's castle.

What about Dr. Seward's asylum?

That was to the north of Cornwall, at the birthplace of King Arthur, Tintagel, where we found a particularly grotesque building that would work for the insane asylum. It was a hotel, but not a very attractive one. It was a rather grotesque Gothic pile, and we knew it would work just great. It was not our first choice, however: our first choice was a place in a little town called Mevagissey. In a rainstorm one afternoon, the line producer and I saw this hotel, a *wonderfully* ugly and grotesque 19th-century building, just *truly* horrid-looking. We said, "Oh, what a *great* insane asylum!" In that part of England, a lot of these resort hotels close down for five or six months out of the year because the weather is *so* bad that, from October to March, they're just out of business. (There are force-ten gales down there—just horrible!) We were going to be shooting in October or November down there and that would work out great, because the hotels closed down and they would probably let us work there. So I'm running around this hotel with my camera, shooting photographs of it in this rainstorm, while the line producer goes in to find the owner. I come in from the rain dripping wet and he's got the owner in tow—it's a little old lady, white hair, very, very British, and he's telling her what he wants to do. And she looks at him and says, "Absolutely *not. No way.*" He tells her that we will pay nice money and we will keep their staff going and how good it will be for them, and she *will not budge.* He's quite, quite charming, and he couldn't move her the slightest bit. Well, apparently what had happened was *in 1934*, 44 years previously, Olivia de Havilland and Errol Flynn had come to Mevagissey to make a film, and they were going to use the exterior of this building. And this lady informed us that *all* the people of Mevagissey had come out and tramped her flower garden [*laughs*]— *and* she was not about to have the same thing happen again! So we were sent packing, tails between our legs!

Did the weather turn out to be a problem?

No, actually, it turned out to be just fine. In fact, we had to *create* rainstorms because we didn't have enough [real ones].

Why were Mina's and Lucy's character names switched?

I can't quite remember. Maybe Richter and I felt like Mina was a dopey name and that Lucy was kind of a *nice* name [*laughs*], so we were rearranging it slightly!

Was Walter Mirisch around? Did he have much input?

Walter was *very* much a hands-on producer. He and his brother Marvin were there, and one or the other of them was *always* on-site with me and available. (Unlike many of the producers of today, who you don't meet until the preview. I mean, you *might* meet them the day you make the deal, and the next time you see them is a year later at the preview.) The Mirisch family believed that the producer's job is to be there and to help and to be *producing.* Their knowledge of motion pictures is vast and their skill at dealing with people was terrific.

Was their input any good?

Yes, it was always quite good, although we did have a funny conversation about one scene toward the end of the movie. Dracula is running around deep down in the basement of the castle, escaping from people, and Walter said, "You can't have this scene!" I asked him, "Why not?" and he said, "It's *daytime.*" I said, "So ...?", and he said [*sputtering*], "Well, well—vampires can't run *around* in the daytime!" I said, "Walter... we're talking about *vampires.* This is *bull*shit! We can have them do whatever we *want!*" [*Laughs*] I said, "Now, just think for a minute, Walter: it's always light somewhere on Earth, right?" He said, "Yes." And I went on: "Where it's light and where it's dark is constantly changing. So it's not a matter of being in a place where it happens to be dark. If you're a vampire, you just have to be out of the direct sun. *That* would seem to be the operating principle of this legend." Look at it this way: when Dracula gets in his coffin, he's down in a dark place, out of the light. And he can't go out into the direct light or he's in trouble. So we had to write dialogue into the script to say, "It is always light *somewhere* on Earth. The trick is to stay *out* of it!" But I just had to laugh, because Walter had taken it so seriously. *My* attitude was, if we ran into a situation that caused us some kind of a problem, we'd just make up a new rule to go along with it.

Can you think of another example of that?

When Olivier goes in search of his daughter Mina [Janine Duvitski], who he thinks may have turned into a vampire, he goes down into some mine tunnels. There are bats flying over him and rats running under his feet, and in the script he trips and falls down, and the cross that he is carrying to ward off a vampire falls into a puddle where it can't be seen. As he is patting his hand around in this puddle trying to put his hand on the cross, in that puddle we see the reflection of feet coming up, and the camera uses that as an excuse to come onto the actual feet themselves and finally tilt up onto Mina, who is standing there looking god-awful. We line up this shot and the cameraman is going to a lot of trouble to get the reflection to work right and so on, and the assistant director tells me right as we were ready to shoot, "We can't *do* this. There's a reflection here, and vampires don't reflect." Well, we have now put so much time and effort into this shot (which is really terrific, a nifty shot) that I look up at him and I go, "We're gonna shoot it anyway! I don't care!" I was so cranked up for it that I just wasn't going to ignore it [*laughs*]—I was in a state of advanced denial over the thing!

We go ahead and shoot the scene and it's terrific. Later, as we're into previews, somebody says, "You can't *do* this. It's a reflection." I looked at them—by now I had a couple of months to think about this—and with the straightest face I could muster, I said, "Oh, no, it's okay in this particular case. Normally vampires don't reflect unless we are looking at *holy* water. You see, the cross has fallen in and made it holy water, and what we see is the vestigial remains of her lost soul." And they all went, "Ohhhhhh! Ohhhhhh, *I* see!" [*Laughs*] My God, it was even put into the press kit... it became one of the "Rules About Vampires"!

Donald Pleasence plays Dr. Seward as sort of a quack, sort of a repulsive character. Whose idea was that?

Well, I guess Walter Mirisch and I have to be blamed for that. Donald was great fun, he was one of the great upstagers in acting history. He was just terrific fun to work with because he was just so playful and enjoyable to have on the set. He came to me during rehearsal and said, "Would you mind if I had a small brown paper bag that I carry around, that has some little hard candies in it?" I said, "Oh, sure, okay, that'll be fine." Well, little did I know what I was agreeing to: he used this as an *upstaging tool*. At either the beginning of a line of dialogue or more usually at the end of a line of dialogue, he would pop some little candy into his mouth, sort of forcing the editor to stay with him before cutting away. You would stay with him for "the business," you were *always* paying attention to what was going on with those candies. And he was sticking them in other people's faces, offering them around and so on, making quite a big deal out of it. In one scene, he and Olivier were having this tearful good-bye, and Olivier was saying something that I couldn't quite make out. When we were doing the post-synchronized dialogue, I asked Olivier to replace this *if* he could remember what it was that he said—I didn't have any idea. He said, "I was saying, 'Keep it.'" I said, "What do you mean, 'Keep it?'" He said, "Look. Look what's going on the screen." And what I could now see, once I understood, was that Donald was sticking these damn candies right up into Olivier's face during a tearful good-bye scene [*laughs*]! Olivier had a-hold of Donald's hand by the wrist and was pushing it down below the camera, saying, "Keep it! Keep it!"

Maurice Binder, your visual consultant—what did he contribute?

Maurice had done a lot of the titles for the James Bond pictures, and he and I started talking about the love scene with Dracula and Lucy. I wanted to do something really special there—I had something in mind, but I wasn't quite sure *what*! What we eventually came up with was probably the first use of lasers in film, where we filmed them making love against this background of The Who's laser, that we borrowed from the rock band The Who. They used it for their shows, and we could only use it on Sunday. So we shot the footage with Dracula and Lucy, on a Sunday, against this laser—which was something I had been experimenting with on *Saturday Night Fever*, but had not been able to use. On *Saturday Night Fever* the laser was just too big and heavy and cumbersome and you couldn't get it around, and we needed to take it to a *disco*. That was like forget-it time! But when you had smoke and all that stuff going through the laser beams, it was pretty fabulous, and looked really, *really* nice. So that's what we came up with for *Dracula*. Maurice took that footage and he shot some additional footage of all the other things you see in that montage, and basically *created* it. I just let him go off on his own, and that's pretty much his editing and creation.

In that scene Dracula and Lucy are mostly seen in silhouette. Is it Langella and Kate Nelligan we're seeing there?

It's Langella and Kate Nelligan 99 percent of the time. I think there's a couple of close shots in there, like a hand running across a leg or something, that I'm *pretty* sure are inserts that Maurice did.

I believe this was the first version of Dracula with significant special effects. The other versions had little or nothing, except maybe a bat bouncing up and down on the end of a wire.

Generally that was because these movies were done so cheaply. The state of special effects, even (in 1979) when *this* picture was done, was still pretty simple—nothing

Badham's *Dracula* was the first version with significant special effects.

we did was really, really elaborate. We just used a lot of ingenuity. But there were a lot of special effects compared to the Lugosi *Dracula*, which is simple to the *extreme*.

Talk a little about your impressions of the Lugosi Dracula.

I thought that it was... clunky, but that the presence of Lugosi made it *work*. I understand that at the time there was a great deal of fear at Universal about making it too frightening, and lots of things that probably were really interesting (such as Dracula getting out of the coffin and coming through the window and so on) they just cut away in their efforts to tone it down. [Director] Tod Browning was a wonderful filmmaker when you see a film like *Freaks* [1932], but *Dracula* doesn't seem to be up to that same kind of effort.

Were you leaving the door open for a sequel by letting the bat fly away at the end of the movie?

Everyone in the world thought that *except for the director*. The director was the only *fool* who thought, "Gee, it's kind of open-ended. Isn't it fun that, after all this, they didn't really *get* him? Isn't that interesting? It leaves questions in your mind. Is she carrying his baby? Is *she* really a vampire?"—because she's got this little smile on her face. *I* was thinking of all these interpretations; and then people started saying, "Oh! Looks like a sequel here!" I would grind my teeth, because it was the last thing in my mind. But it's quite obvious to me now how you'd read that.

What's the best scene in the movie?

I think the best sequence is about an hour into it: it encompasses that scene with Olivier coming into the cemetery, climbing down into the mine and finding his daughter and killing her, followed by the love scene between Dracula and Lucy. I think there's about a 15-minute sequence in there that really works (for *my* taste). When I gave a keynote address to the (God help me!) Count Dracula Society at their annual luncheon, that was the part I chose to run because I thought that it worked the best. It had the idea of the movie condensed into that 15 minutes—you had the romanticism of it and the scariness of it. It was also Stephen King's favorite moment. I don't think he cared for the movie, but he did say that he really liked that scene with Olivier discovering his daughter.

Why "God help me, the Count Dracula Society"? Were they a bunch of oddballs?

Oh, they're the sweetest people in the world—but they *are* unusual. They're basically very nice people who just have fun with that kind of stuff. The fact that some of them show up wearing a cape, or extreme make-up, is just the fun of it... it makes you kind of appreciate how much fun movies *can be.*

There are scenes in the Dracula laserdisc that are look almost black-and-white. In fact, a friend of mine tried to take his back to the store, and the clerk told him that was the way the discs were made.

And the guy is right! The guy in the store was not just trying to get out of having to refund the money, he was telling the truth. I had wanted to do the film in a very severe color limitation, as close to black-and-white as I could get. I was thinking about John Huston's *Moby Dick* (1956) and some of *Oliver!* (1968) where they had done a really good kind of black-and-white effect. But I was told that the only lab that could currently do that was in Red China—the Technicolor lab that used to do that had sold all of its three-strip equipment to Red China. So we did the best we could under the circumstances. But when we went to this new video format a couple of years ago, to redo the original laserdisc they had done, I was told they had more control over what they could do with the color. So we experimented with it, and that's what we came up with.

How is the laserdisc different from what we saw in the movies in 1979?

What you saw in the theater had a very warm *golden* color. We limited the color in the art direction by trying to make things in lots of blacks, whites, and grays.

Twenty years later, rate your own movie. Talk about what's good and... maybe what's not.

Well, I *know* we could have done much better with the effects and with the make-up—I thought we just did a so-so job on it. By make-up, I'm talking about Langella decomposing at the end, and the undead Mina. For Mina I wanted stuff that was much more terrifying, and it wound up being tamed down because the actress was allergic and couldn't really take much. But I'm not sure what more to say about it... it's like talking about your children! You sort of know all of their weak points and strong points and things like that, but it's kind of hard to talk about them.

Draculas for the past 20 years have all walked in Langella's shadow.

The first time I saw it, it struck me that it was trying to please everybody. Sometimes it was stately and romantic for "the gals," and at other times, like when it got gory, it seemed like it was made for "the guys." It seemed designed to alternately please, *and then* turn off, *half the audience.*

That's possible. Probably my taste is a little more catholic, and I liked the scary parts *and* the erotic parts. I certainly got a lot of people saying to me [*in a breathless voice*], "Boy, thanks for makin' that movie. I had a great *date* that night!" [*Laughs*] And yet I had this idea that evil often comes in extremely attractive forms. Anybody can usually resist evil that is in a very *un*attractive form—if Bela Lugosi walks in the room, or Nosferatu walks in the room, *you* know to get the hell out of there. If Frank Langella walks in the room, you go, "Oh, boy, I'll hang around!" Drugs, alcohol, *many* things are in that same kind of Langella-like form: they're very seductive, they're very attractive, and you're kind of *drawn in* by them. That is evil at its *most successful*, evil that is able to be attractive. That was our take on this: we were seeing the results of evil as well as its attractive side. Whether or not we were successful, that's your opinion, and whatever you like, it's okay, I have to accept it. But that's what I was trying to work with. It might be too esoteric a thought, but it was my governing idea.

Dracula's Birthday Parties

The 100th anniversary of the publication of *Dracula* was met with celebrations nationwide.

New York City played host to The Dracula Centennial: The Aesthetic of Fear, a conference held from March 21-23 at New York University. Among the guests were Stephen Jay Gould, author of *Bully for the Brontosaurus*, Joyce Carol Oates, the distinguished author of *American Appetites* and *Black Water*, and the world's best-selling author, Stephen King. An adaptation of the novel done as a concert performance started the festivities.

The Museum of Modern Art presented a special series of films to packed houses in conjunction with the festival called CinemaDracula.

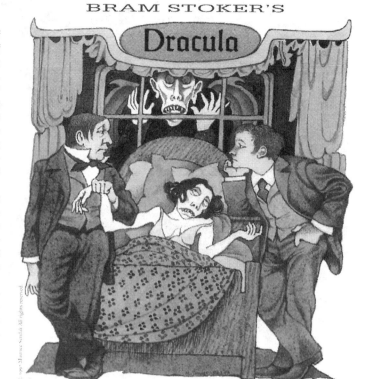

BRAM STOKER'S

Dracula

A CENTENNIAL EXHIBITION
AT THE ROSENBACH MUSEUM & LIBRARY

EXHIBITION CATALOG

Many rare and celebrated films, such as *Jonathan* (1970) and George Romero's *Martin* (1976), along with the expected lesser films, such as 1969's *Taste the Blood of Dracula* and 1979's *Nosferatu*, were seen on a theater screen for the first time in decades. New York area Dracula and vampire buffs stayed with the double and triple features scheduled in the series late into the night.

Dracula '97 was held in Los Angeles, from August 14 -17, and must rate as the largest Dracula celebration in history. With something for serious scholars, movie buffs, and Dracula and vampire fetishists, as well as people interested in the Gothic music scene, Dracula '97 strove to present the total Dracula experience. Chelsea Quinn Yarbro, author of the fantastically successful series of books about vampire Rakoczy, comte de Saint-Germain, was one of the organizers of the event.

The Rosenbach Museum and Library in Philadelphia was the site of Bram Stoker's Dracula: A Centennial Exhibition, which opened on April 13, 1997. This wonderful archive contains the original notes Bram Stoker made while planning his vampire masterpiece, and had those papers, along with memorabilia from Stoker's life and career as manager of the Lyceum Theatre (including souvenirs from his several visits to Philadelphia in that capacity), on display. Also on display was Stoker's original typed draft, which had never been previously seen on the East Coast. The exhibit opened with a reception and lecture featuring authors David J. Skal (*Hollywood Gothic*) and Nina Auerbach (*Our Vampires, Ourselves*), two of the most respected authorities on everything Dracula.

The most delightful artifact of the Rosenbach exhibit was not something from their archives, but rather a graphic created for the exhibit itself. Famed children's book author Maurice Sendak (*Where the Wild Things Are*) created a special art print and poster to commemorate Dracula's anniversary and the Rosenbach exhibit. Done with all the skill and whimsy that have made him beloved by generations of children, Sendak creates a very *Nosferatu*-like Dracula, who hovers over a rapidly fading Lucy. Suitors Holmwood (here looking somewhat like Oscar Wilde) and Arthur appear more interested in each other than anything else, and share a longing gaze.

—Bob Madison

Vampires entered the "real" world in 1972 with The Night Stalker, *a dazzling film that (at the time) garnered the highest ratings of any made-for-television movie ever. This film took the vampire out of a mythical middle Europe and placed him in a setting both recognizable and distinctly American: contemporary Las Vegas.*

The vampire myth was changed forever.

The success of The Night Stalker *was readily apparent—spawning a sequel film and a television series—but its influence was more subtle. Its incredible popularity helped jump-start the vampire and Dracula craze of the 1970s, and the film's contemporary edge made vampires more accessible (and acceptable) to an audience that had been immune to the monster's Continental charm.*

Also, despite the waning box office returns of the Hammer Dracula films, it proved that vampires could still be big business with audiences. Thanks to The Night Stalker, *Dracula was free to break once more into the American mainstream, resulting in a feast of blood for 1970s audiences.*

Director John Llewellyn Moxey, the man behind The Night Stalker's *camera, had a prolific career in television, including the pilots for* Ghost Story *and* Charlie's Angels. *He was also the man behind one of the most stylish, fiendish and frightening modern horror films,* Horror Hotel. *Shot in 1959,* Horror Hotel *has an atmosphere, pacing and a grisly verve sadly lacking in most other British horror productions of that era. Once seen, it is never forgotten.*

John Llewellyn Moxey is currently living in retirement in Washington state. He was interviewed exclusively for this volume by author and genre film expert Tom Weaver.
—Bob Madison

Night Stalking: An Interview With John Llewellyn Moxey
an interview by Tom Weaver

How old were you when you first knew you wanted to work in films?

I visited some studios in England when I was about 12 years old, and I was absolutely captivated by the whole business of movie making. I said to the people who had taken me to the studio, "I'm going to work here." And sure enough, I later worked on that very stage in that very studio. It was a small independent studio in Walton-on-Thames called Nettlefold. That's how it started.

What was your first job in the industry?

I started in the cutting room, and then I became an assistant director and did a little bit of acting, in movies and quite a lot of theater. Most of my film acting was in stuff that the general public never saw—I took parts in training films for the services. Occasionally I had other jobs; once during a slump in the British film industry, I cleaned windows at the Piccadilly Hotel [*laughs*]! Which at least was a very *elite* place to clean windows! But I *had* to pay the rent, you know.

Then I became interested in television. Some friends who were already in television got me into TV, and then ultimately I became a director at the BBC. Eventually I found myself bouncing backwards and forwards between film and television. I think the first feature I did was *City of the Dead* [American title: *Horror Hotel*] with Christopher Lee.

Did you think a horror movie would get you off to a good start as a feature director?

Let me put it this way: the horror genre was something that always interested me. I enjoy horror movies and I enjoy entertaining people, and I think horror movies have a certain element of entertainment which I enjoy putting across to an audience. I believe that you have to leave a lot to the audience's imagination because you can never be quite as horrific as what people can dream up in their minds. That's what we did with *Horror Hotel*, we tried to *suggest* some of it.

The cast is an interesting mix of "new" people like Venetia Stevenson and Dennis Lotis and old-timers like Patricia Jessel and Valentine Dyall.

Yes, it *was* a mixture, and that's really what we *went* for, to put some well-known "horror faces" (if you like!) in there, to mix in with the new people. Dennis Lotis hadn't really made a lot of pictures at that time, he was pretty new to it. He was really a singer, but a *name* in England at that time. He really *was* good in it—in fact, I didn't think there were very many weak performances in it. Patricia Jessel and Valentine Dyall, of course, didn't really live up to their "horror image"—they were both very amusing people, and fun to work with. They treated me like a small boy at times [*laughs*], but they were very obliging, and did what I asked. And Christopher Lee I've known for some time—I had worked with him before this, when I was an assistant director. He and I knew each other and were friends, and he was very helpful and very good.

The sleeve of Lee's robes is on fire in his last scene. Did it take any coaxing to get him to do that?

No, he was an experienced guy and we had good special effects people. He knew the technique we were going to use, and it was very carefully planned so that he would not get hurt. Some of the others in that scene, the ones who were completely engulfed in flames—some of them were dummies and some of them were stunt people who were dressed for the fire scene.

Horror Hotel *really looks like a picture that everybody put a little bit of extra effort into.*

Oh, absolutely. *Absolutely.* I think, without blowing my own trumpet, I had the knack of getting people happily to work together. (And, luckily, happily to work with *me*.) I always think that directing is a love affair between you and the crew and the cast, and I think, because people *like* each other, they do their best for each other. That was so with *Horror Hotel*—*everybody* tried to do their very best.

It's so much better than any of the Hammer films that were being made around that same time. Have you seen enough of those to have an opinion?

[*Disdainfully*] Yes, *I* know the Hammer films. One thing we *didn't* want to do was to make a Hammer film!

Why do you say that?

Well, we wanted to make something *better*, we wanted to make something with a little *class*, and I think that we went a long way towards it.

How were Hammer's films viewed by movie makers in England?

They were... Look, I don't want to be *rude* to anybody. They did what they set out to do. Whether I wanted to emulate them is another matter! But Hammer made a lot of money, I'm sure, with those pictures.

Why did you make the move from England to America?

David Susskind asked me to direct one of his television specials, *Dial M for Murder* (1967) with Laurence Harvey. I did three for him: *Dial M for Murder, A Hatful of Rain* ... and then there's one we don't speak of [*laughs*]! [Moxey refers to the notorious 1968 TV version of *Laura* with George Sanders and Lee Bouvier.] We would rehearse the casts in New York and then fly them back to England, where we'd have a week's preparation and then we'd tape the show over a couple of days in a British television studio.

But what made you decide to permanently relocate?

Without going into too many details, I'd had a personal tragedy in my life and I wanted to get out of England for a bit. I didn't know what my plans were at the time, and David Susskind said, "Why don't you go to California and work there?" Somebody at Universal had seen some film that I had made—I don't know which one it was—but the next thing I knew, I was under contract to Universal and I worked there for a bit. That's how I started my career in California; then I just liked it so much I *stayed*.

How did The Night Stalker *come your way?*

I forget how Dan Curtis and I got teamed up on that one, to tell you the truth. I was sent the script and I remember reading it on the beach in Malibu and thinking this was a wonderful story—and the *next* thing was, we were making it! But how it got to me, I don't altogether remember. It may have been through *Horror Hotel*—*that* may have been seen by somebody.

What was Dan Curtis like to work for?

I *liked* Dan. Dan wanted to be a director himself (and later *became* a director), but he didn't really interfere. He was very full of helpful hints and everything, and we were good friends. We also had a lot of fun together "off-camera," so to speak—we spent a lot of time in each other's company. He was an interesting man.

Darren McGavin's hard-nosed reporter made vampires acceptable to modern viewers.

Did you get to meet either of the writers, Jeff Rice, who wrote the original story, or Richard Matheson, who wrote the teleplay?

Oh, yes, Jeff and I knew each other and worked a lot together. He was a sort of withdrawn gentleman, but a clever man with a great idea. Richard Matheson—well, I don't want to get into *that* story too much. There *was* a problem, and—let's put it this way—Dan and I *did* steer that script quite heavily.

What was shot first, the Las Vegas scenes or the bulk of the movie at Samuel Goldwyn Studios?

We went to Las Vegas first, and we were there probably not more than a week. It was quite fun, because we worked in a casino, and we had Barry Atwater walking around looking like a vampire in the middle of Las Vegas—that was quite interesting. Actually, not many people took a bit of notice of him! Well, it's a *joke* when you think about it: a vampire in Las Vegas? What else *is* there? They're *all* vampires in Las Vegas [*laughs*]! So it had a certain undercurrent of humor, I think, the whole *idea*. Darren McGavin and I became good friends. He is (a) a very nice person, and (b) a very talented man. And he's fun to work with—and it's nice to work with friends. When you work with friends, it saves a lot of heartaches sometimes. He was very helpful and

Scenes from *The Night Stalker* were often evocative of the comedy classic *The Front Page*.

a very interesting actor—I liked his work. And he was *ideally* cast. This was, I think, probably one of the best things I'd seen him do at that time. He's always done good things, but that part happened to have fit him like a glove. He brings a certain something to the parts that he takes.

His performance is a big part of the reason The Night Stalker *is so good.*

Absolutely. That and a *very* good script—it was an innovative and clever storyline. Once a director has *that*, you haven't got to fight the story. That was a good storyline with some well-drawn characters. And we had a great cast—Dan Curtis, who knew more American actors than *I* did, was very helpful in putting together a really great cast. Dan was a prime mover in bringing these first-rate people together, and *everybody* fit in their particular role perfectly. It was a *well*-cast picture.

The chemistry—or the sparks, I guess I should say—between Darren McGavin and Simon Oakland were terrific.

Yes, that was fun. Those newspaper office scenes were *great*, and (of course) McGavin and Simon Oakland were very friendly off-camera. We didn't *have* any internal fighting. You know something? I would say I've *never* had a bad "scene" on a movie between the casts and myself, or between members of the cast. We always had a

Modern man and ancient superstition clash in *The Night Stalker*.

good time. Oh! The only problem we did have was, I made a film in England called *Foxhole in Cairo* [1961] and the two ladies in that really *hated* each other. They had a fight scene, and when it was over, we had a real problem separating 'em [*laughs*]!

Memories of Barry Atwater, who played the vampire?

Oh, poor old Barry! The contact lenses he wore were a problem—he did suffer through that. We had a doctor on the set all the time, making sure that he didn't damage his eyes. He was a very good actor, and there he was playing this speechless character. But he was magnificent—he took on the job whole-heartedly and he was enthusiastic to make it a success, and he worked very hard at doing that. We all thought we were working on something special, and I think we were all very excited to get the film made in the best way possible, get it done and get it out there, because we felt that we had a great success among us.

Some of the fight scenes in Night Stalker *are still exciting today—you had a great team of stuntmen working with you.*

Oh, yes, I had a wonderful stunt crowd. There was one magnificent moment outside a hospital where a motorbike slides toward the camera. Well, the bike came too far. I was standing there, and I had to jump over the bike as it swept through—I remember *that* very well! Dick Ziker was the stunt coordinator and he did an excellent job. He always insured that every safety precaution was taken, and nobody was hurt making this picture. And we did some quite hairy stunts! Dick Ziker was also Barry Atwater's stunt double.

The music is another big part of what makes Night Stalker *so good.*

Yes, it was an *excellent* score! I knew Robert Cobert well; we worked together on another picture, too, I think one of David Susskind's. He was very inventive and very *intuitive* to what the film required.

Why did you start using your middle name Llewellyn?

When I was living on the beach in Malibu, I knew somebody who was a numerologist and he said, "If you used your middle name, it would be better for you." And so I used it.

Was The Night Stalker *one of the first movies you used your full name on?*

Yes. Maybe the guy was right [*laughs*]!

The Night Stalker *was the highest-rated TV movie, and only three movies had gotten bigger ratings—*Ben-Hur, The Bridge on the River Kwai *and* The Birds.

And if we hadn't had *Brian's Song* [1970] against us, I believe we would have won an Emmy or two. (I like to *think* that, anyway!)

Why was it the ratings success that it was?

It was very well-publicized by ABC—the promotion of it was well-handled. And there was a certain titillation (as I said) about there being a vampire in Las Vegas. It tickled the imagination to read about the film, and luckily when people started watching it, they *stuck* with it. And it *built*.

Why weren't you asked to direct The Night Strangler, *the sequel?*

Well, as I said, Dan Curtis wanted to become a director, and so *he* directed it. I wish for *his* sake he'd had a better script than he did.

There's nothing wrong with the script of The Night Strangler *except that it's a remake of* The Night Stalker.

It's *very* derivative. Then when the TV series *Kolchak: The Night Stalker* came along, they wanted me to direct some episodes. Universal and I had quite a go-round about it—one of the VIPs at Universal tried to get me to come and do it, he called me several times about it, and Darren did too. I didn't want to do it because I didn't agree that it would *make* a TV series, I didn't think that the premise would work. You *can't* have a vampire-of-the-week, and it also wasn't like *The X-Files*. I just felt that the very way it was going to be tackled wouldn't stand up. And having made the movie, which *was* a success, I didn't really want to go on and do something which I didn't have a feeling would be equally successful.

Did the huge success of The Night Stalker *have a positive effect on your career?*

Yes, it did. Looking back, I probably didn't take great advantage of it as I should have. But it certainly didn't do me any harm [*laughs*]!

Finished with vampires, hapless Kolchak faced a slew of lesser monsters.

The only "harm" that I can possibly see is that it seems to have typecast you as a director of TV horror and suspense movies.

It was either after *The House That Wouldn't Die* [1970] for Aaron Spelling or *Night Stalker* that somebody in *Variety* or *The* [*Hollywood*] *Reporter* wrote that my directing reminded him of James Whale, he called me "a latter-day James Whale." Which to me was quite interesting, because I think James Whale's *Frankenstein* was magnificent. So, yes, people thought of me as a horror film director. At the time that genre of picture was very popular and everybody was making 'em. Aaron Spelling, for instance; I did two for him with Barbara Stanwyck (*The House That Wouldn't Die* and *A Taste of Evil*, 1971), which were both sort of like horror pictures.

When did you retire from the picture business?

When I'd done *enough*, really. The field became more attuned to younger people, and I felt it was time to step down. I moved up to Washington because I once made a picture in Vancouver and I liked Puget Sound, and I thought, "Well, one day, maybe when I retire, I'll come live up here and do some boating"—which is what I do.

I'm grateful that I was able to work on such a wide spectrum of movies—that's something I've *always* been grateful for. I was always very pleased to have been able to work in television. My early directing days at the BBC was a great learning experience—to have worked in the days of "steam television" [live TV] was a great learning ground. It taught you a lot about editing because it was *instant*, you had to do it there and then. I've seen both *sides* of it, both television and movies, from the days when we looked through the viewfinder of a television camera and the image was upside-down, to working with the most modern Panavision equipment in movies. The technical side of it interests me, too, cinematography-wise and everything like that, so I'm glad that I've had the experience of working through sort of a broad spectrum of technical improvements. I've worked with some wonderful crews—magnificent crews—and great casts, very, very friendly people. I'm grateful to have had these experiences in my life.

Dracula comes in many guises. His evil is unending, eternal, always with us. Even when not dressed in evening clothes and cape, he is still there, wearing some other disguise to lull us into a false security before he strikes out at us.

When many people think of the 1980s and its yuppie culture, they hear vampires cackling in the distance. As government and big business drained an already depleted public dry, a whole new type of vampire—a business-suited parasite who sucks the money and life from corporations and employees—came into being.

Few films examined the vampiric resonances of the 1980s better than The Vampire's Kiss. *But as Gary Don Rhodes makes clear, Stoker was there before us, as he often was, pointing the way of the vampire and putting him into context for us 100 years before the fact.*

Gary Don Rhodes is one of the most respected film scholars on the contemporary scene. With his monumental Lugosi: His Life in Films, on Stage, and in the Hearts of Horror Lovers, *Rhodes has simply written the best book ever on Hollywood's Vampire King. He is also a documentary producer, whose biographical films have appeared on The Learning Channel and public television.*
—Bob Madison

The Vampire's Kiss: Echoes of Bram Stoker in the 1980s
by Gary Don Rhodes

> "... the horror overcame me, and I sank down unconscious."
> —Jonathan Harker in Bram Stoker's novel *Dracula* (1897)

> "I got a little upset at the office."
> —Peter Loew in Robert Bierman's film *Vampire's Kiss* (1989)

Readers still wonder how consciously Bram Stoker infused *Dracula* with its teeming undercurrents. Was Stoker, after all is said and done, a canny observer of the Victorian world scene, making thinly veiled comments on a variety of factors contemporary to the novel's creation? Or was the novelist, as was more likely the case, unconsciously revealing his innermost obsessions and sexual fears?

The world of Stoker's *Dracula* was symptomatic of various concerns of late 19th-century England, including Victorian sexual politics, venereal disease, the paradigmatic shift from religion toward science, technological advances, the influx of Easterners to Western Europe, and the inherent problems of capitalism. Stoker's work teems with the terrors of a world that was both changing and locked in the iron grip of the past.

After sharing a century with the Dracula persona, the question of Stoker's motives becomes less important. The astounding fact is perhaps that the Stoker creation, in both more recent cinematic remakes and vampire films in general, continues to hold a firm grip on the mainstream imagination, even as other subgenres of horror have lost their appeal.

Contemporary American culture is now post-Darwinian. For example, the mad scientist, such a fixture of American genre films from the 1920s through the 1950s, has all but disappeared from the cinematic landscape. The mad scientist has little relevance to modern America, just as, say, the apocalyptic vision of George Romero–style zombies is less threatening in a post–Cold War environment.

Dracula and similarly-caped vampires have stamped 20th-century culture with their own vampire's kiss. The very tradition that Stoker set in motion with his novel offers an elasticity of possibilities not present in either stories of mad scientists, manifestations of ghosts, zombie films, or tales of radiation-created monsters. The Stoker-style vampire possesses a ready ability to adapt to all manner of cultural, psychological, technological, and economical concerns. While most of the significant vampire films of the 1980s, for example, do not deal explicitly with Dracula, Stoker's Vampire King is always visible just below the surface, powering these new visions of vampirism the same way Stoker's obsessions powered his own novel.

In American society of the 1980s, a "just wanna have fun" attitude and an emphasis on youth culture collided with the reality of AIDS, while the illusionary nature of the Reagan recovery became apparent in the stock market slump of 1987, Irangate, and the Savings and Loan scandals. Emphasis on high-tech industries and defense spending brought the yuppie into existence, and America's growing conservatism transformed "liberal" into an almost dirty word. Borrowing money, on an individual basis or as a nation, soared to new heights, highlighting both the possibilities and frailties of capitalism. These challenges and problems did not go unnoticed by the public at large; indeed, these very concerns made an incredible commercial success out of such documentary films as Michael Moore's *Roger and Me*, which pinpointed these difficulties and aired them publicly at movie theaters.

The vampire tale proved immediately capable of adapting to this particular cultural environment, just as it had in prior decades. If reality did not yet bite in Winona Ryder and Generation-X style, the vampire film of the 1980s did. *The Hunger*, *Once Bitten*, *Buffy the Vampire Slayer*, *Vamp*, *The Lost Boys*... all of these films posited the vampire in such a way as to address the era's various interests and concerns, much as Stoker did in his time. And, as the decade moved to a close, the oft-overlooked but particularly insightful *The Vampire's Kiss*, a black comedy with Nicolas Cage, addressed most of the major concerns of the 1980s.

The 1980s themselves began on the crest of a late-1970s Dracula movie mania. John Badham's stylish *Dracula* with Frank Langella, Stan Dragoti's sendup of the character in *Love at First Bite* with George Hamilton, and Werner Herzog's remake of F. W. Murnau's *Nosferatu* with Klaus Kinski, all appeared within months of each other in 1979. All of three of these films drew their inspiration from the past, while the vampire films of the next decade would stand firmly rooted in the present. The two American films were both strongly indebted to the Bela Lugosi tradition of stage and screen, while the Herzog film was, if not an exact remake of 1922's *Nosferatu*, at the least a mirror image of the classic German silent.

Roddy McDowall as horror host Peter Vincent in Tom Holland's affectionate valentine to vampires and the boys who love them, *Fright Night* (1985).

"Where is the lair of the suspected creature of the night?"
—Peter Vincent (Roddy McDowall) in *Fright Night* (1985)

Most vampires of the 1980s, whatever debt they owe to Stoker, markedly shifted away from the long-standing traditions of vampire cinema. This is not to suggest that the makers of films like *The Hunger*, *The Lost Boys*, or *Vampire's Kiss* were unaware of their cinematic forefathers. Indeed, Universal Pictures' conception of the vampire is so prevalent, so entrenched into every aspect of modern culture, that it would be impossible to be oblivious. The Bauhaus tune *Bela Lugosi's Dead*—with lyrics invoking the coffins, bats, and blood of both the Hungarian actor and Stoker—allows *The Hunger* to pay tribute to the past in a subtle way, while *Vampire's Kiss* finds Nicolas Cage watching *Nosferatu* on late-night television.

Director Tom Holland's *Fright Night* (1985) gave particular attention to the Stoker tradition, with references to earlier vampire films and actors like Bela Lugosi in abundance. Though the bulk of the plot concerns teens Charley Brewster (William Ragsdale) and Amy Peterson (Amanda Bearse), *Fright Night* even goes so far as to feature Roddy McDowall as a washed-up vampire film actor, Peter Vincent, named in affectionate tribute to horror film icons Peter Cushing and Vincent Price. At one point, Vincent may well be voicing the thoughts of actors Cushing and Price when he laments the status of the 1980s horror film: "Nobody wants to see vampires anymore. All they want to see

David Bowie and Catherine Denueve as Euro-trash vampires in *The Hunger* (1983).

is some demented madman running around in a ski mask hacking up young virgins." In reality, *Fright Night* itself paved the way not just for a sequel (1988's *Fright Night Part 2*), but also for a number of subsequent vampire comedies that emphasized teens and the youth culture of the eighties.

Only months after *Fright Night*, Howard Storm's *Once Bitten* hit theaters. "The Countess" (Lauren Hutton), a bonafide vampire, chases high schooler Mark Kendall (a pre-*Mask* Jim Carrey), accomplishing few laughs and basically no memorable moments. *The New York Times* (Nov. 15, 1985) felt sure it was "no funnier among the undead than it is among the living." Joel Schumacher's *The Lost Boys* (1987) also centered on the young, achieving a stylish look and helping to popularize actor Kiefer Sutherland. As with *Once Bitten*, however, the film received little love from critics. *Variety*, for example, believed it "panders to the basest instincts and is hokey even on its own ludicrous terms. At 92 minutes, it still seems to last all night long." More of these films followed as the decade continued, including the interesting *My Best Friend Is a Vampire* (1988) and the lesser *Teen Vamp* (1989).

My Best Friend Is a Vampire, staring Robert Sean Leonard before he joined the *Dead Poets Society*, is a rather apt metaphor for the acceptance of homosexuality in the post-Stonewall age. Most of the film's running time deals with Leonard's acceptance of his own vampiric "alternate lifestyle," convincing his parents and friends that he's "still the same," and finally winning over stake-wielding fanatics (the parallel to the Christian right is especially apt). Though a modest little film, the gay cues are unmistakable, and it's interesting to wonder what gay teens made of it.

One of the more unusual vampire films of the period remains Tony Scott's *The Hunger* (1983) starring Catherine Denueve and David Bowie. Both portray vampires, though Bowie's life-force begins to fade and he begins to age rapidly. Vampirism for him has become something akin to a blood disease, and here the film eerily anticipates the growing awareness of AIDS in the early-to-mid 1980s. Scott's film features strong performances and a beautiful look, though it too left many popular critics cold. The *National Review* (June 24, 1983) believed *The Hunger* was "most interesting for its utter lack of sense... looks like an extended commercial for Calvin Klein jeans." *Variety* (April 27, 1983) called the film "all visual and aural flash, although... [it] possesses a certain perverse appeal." The trades oscillated back and forth from judging the film "chic trash" to an "insidiously intriguing vampire tale."

What critics did not realize at the time (and would not, until Francis Ford Coppola's *Bram Stoker's Dracula* did it for them), was that the link between vampirism and AIDS was a strong one, and that as awareness of this new "blood disease" grew, so would the interest in vampires. As always, vampires were the honored guests at a new danse macabre, helping usher a significant part of an entire American generation into the grave.

Other vampire films of the period dealt with other concerns of the 1980s' culture. *Pure Blood* (1983) featured a business tycoon that literally needed the blood of others to survive, a wicked comment on growing yuppyism. *I Married a Vampire* (1984) featured a vamp who takes revenge on all those whose greed—a major vice of the decade—have made her life miserable. And the vampire of Gerard Ciccoritti's *Graveyard Shift* (1987) scout the big city for fresh blood by working as a cab driver; the film could have been subtitled *The Underclass Bites Back*.

As the decade moved to a close, most all of the concerns dealt with in the 1980s vampire films coalesced into *Vampire's Kiss*, a dry black comedy. Director Robert Bierman, who had previously directed the HBO film *Apology*, and 24-year-old actor Nicolas Cage teamed to create an unusual and provocative vampire film. The skilled cinematography of Stefan Czapsky and the haunting score of composer Colin Towns helped further the film's stylish edge. Scripted by Joseph Minion, author of *After Hours* (1985), the film was shot in New York City. Though it was not embraced by the mass public and received limited distribution, *Vampire's Kiss* is replete with echoes of Bram Stoker's novel that resonate alongside the concerns of the 1980s.

It fact, it could be argued that *Vampire's Kiss* is the 1980s comment on, and reaction to, Stoker's masterpiece. Every element of the film carefully reflects some aspect of *Dracula*, as if questions of sex and class were batted back-and-forth between their respective centuries like a cultural tennis ball.

Vampire's Kiss tells the story of young literary agent Peter Loew (Cage), a perfect example of the decade's arid yuppie culture. During one of his many one-night stands, a bat flies into the room and interrupts his liaison with Jackie (Kasi Lemmons). Later, he tells his analyst, Dr. Glaser (Elizabeth Ashley), of the arousal he felt from fighting off the bat. He has already told her of his aversions to his various female friends. "I wanted her the same as always," he confesses of one, immediately adding: "I wanted her to disappear. I wanted her to be the hell out of there... and she got the hell out of there."

The bat episode marks the beginning of his descent into an alternate reality. The next day at work, he scrutinizes the legs of his secretary Alva (Maria Conchita Alonso) before looking out of his office window to notice a woman named Rachel (Jennifer Beals) buying a hot dog. Though he does actually meet her, Peter imagines that he has

Vampire wannabe Nicolas Cage sinks deeper into madness.

taken her home, and that she is a real vampire who bites him on the neck. Loew avoids other women as his imaginary liaison pitches him deeper into delusion. One morning, for example, he lets Rachel into his shower; but as he opens the curtain, no one steps in. Nonetheless, he holds a conversation with himself as if an actual entity, vampire or otherwise, was there. When the film does show us his imaginary vampire, she makes clear to him that she is the only one who can put him out of his misery.

As he loses his grip on reality, he attempts to exercise greater control at his office, terrorizing Alva by making her spend day after day searching for a missing but relatively unimportant literary contract. Their conflict builds to a moment when Loew tries to convince Alva to shoot him. Instead, she faints amid his threats of rape, and Loew is left to kill himself. He's unaware her gun is loaded with blanks, and, after firing it inside his own mouth, he's further convinced of his status as the undead.

He resorts to sunglasses for protection from the daylight and turns his sofa into a makeshift, yuppie-style coffin. As his teeth have yet to become fangs, Loew purchases a plastic pair at a novelty store. With these he kills and drinks the blood from a pigeon purloined from a nearby park. Later, after murdering a real woman and being dumped by the imaginary Rachel, Peter returns to his apartment. Alva's brother, who believes Peter has raped his secretary sister, appears and forces a stake into his chest.

Of the character, Nicolas Cage told *American Film* (June 1989), "He has this certain accent and tone of voice, the 'Continental bullshit accent' I call it, that he uses to help make up for his own insecurities that he's not a writer, he's a literary agent. I've seen people behave that way, and I've always found it to be a big front, as though they were hiding something very vulnerable inside themselves."

While Maria Conchita Alonso remains memorable as the tormented secretary, Cage does transform the film into a tour-de-force for his over-the-top acting style. His overt motions and intense, almost obsessive attempt to become the character drew comparisons at the time to Robert De Niro. In one scene that illustrated Loew's psychological descent, Cage even insisted on actually eating a live cockroach on camera, promptly washing his mouth out with vodka when the cameras stopped rolling.

"The script originally called for it to be [raw] eggs," Cage explained to *American Film*, "but I didn't think that was shocking enough. So I asked if they could wrangle up a cockroach, a New York-style cockroach. But when I arrived on the set the next day and saw the size of the cockroach, it really blew my mind. Actually, they wrangled up three cockroaches, but we got it in two takes. I wound up feeling kind of sorry for them."

> "[Lucy's] teeth, in the dim, uncertain light, seemed longer and sharper than they had been in the morning. In particular, by some trick of the light, the canine teeth looked longer and sharper than the rest."
> —Dr. Seward's Diary, 20 September

The imaginary Rachel exhibits her teeth at Loew's apartment. The film makes clear he did meet the "real" Rachel at a club, but never illustrates that she really accompanied him back to his apartment. Instead, it is an imaginary Rachel who takes control of him sexually. She bites him, but—as she is merely a fantasy—she is gone the next morning. He tries to serve her coffee, though he almost shakes the cup from its saucer when he realizes there is no one in his bed. He does place a bandage on his neck near his jugular vein, but only after having cut himself shaving.

The vampire women of Stoker's novel possess a potent sexuality that both attracts and repels the male characters. Jonathan Harker writes of Dracula's brides in his diary on May 16, "All three had brilliant white teeth, that shone like pearls against the ruby of their voluptuous lips," or, "... I could hear the churning sound of her tongue as it licked her teeth and lips... I could feel the... hard dents of two sharp teeth, just touching and pausing [at my throat]."

Myths abound in different cultures of the sexual monster, the *vagina dentata*. Such myths posit the woman as castrator, and many depictions invoke images of female genitalia bearing teeth. The imagery of a hellish mouth—a black hole that threatens to chew and swallow its prey—made a conspicuous return during the Reagan decade. This imagery appears in many vampire films, with Amanda Bearse in *Fright Night* (when she reaches full vampire status) and Catherine Deneuve in *The Hunger* (especially in the close-ups of her mouth) being two of the more obvious examples. The blood on these and other female vampires' lips (including Jennifer Beals') represents the blood of a now-castrated male.

There is nothing new in this imagery, invoking innumerable texts and films, including the "vamp" of the early 20th-century cinema. It also takes us back to Stoker and Lucy Westenra. After she becomes a vampire and is caught returning from her search for blood, Van Helsing, Dr. Seward, and Arthur Holmwood ambush her at her tomb. Lucy advances toward Arthur, "with outstretched arms and a wanton smile... with a languorous, voluptuous grace." She says, "Come to me, Arthur. Leave these others and come to me. My arms are hungry for you. Come, and we can rest together. Come, my husband, come!" These words are spoken in "diabolically sweet" tones, which had—in another *vagina dentata* reference—"something of the tingling of glass when struck" in them. The sound peals through the brains of the other men present, threatening madness.

The 1980s vampire is replete with this kind of imagery. For example, *The Hunger* offers an extreme close-up of Denueve's mouth and teeth, which fill the entire screen. Another case in point is Grace Jones, who portrayed the vampire Katrina in Richard Wenk's *Vamp*. Even the staid *New York Times* (July 25, 1986) believed, "there are a few brief scenes in which, transformed into a misshapen monster with clustered columns of teeth, she is truly terrifying." Most notable perhaps is actress Amanda Bearse, who—as Amy in *Fright Night*—briefly transforms into a vampire with a particularly large mouth and enormous, jagged teeth, easily the best remembered scene from the film. The proliferation of female vampires in the 1980s, bearing teeth and seeking male victims, highlights the *dentata*'s return.

Jennifer Beals as the vampiric Rachel in *Vampire's Kiss* is yet another example of this mythology. Baring her teeth, she even informs Peter, "You're like me now" after his believed initiation into vampirism. This can easily be taken as a comparison between her femininity and his now-castrated body. The film invokes the *dentata* in yet another way as well; Medusa references, which the film makes in the "Rattlesnake Hills" contract, are a part of this tradition of female castracite. Peter's obsession over the contract and his nervous affliction when the story's writer phones him are the result of this subtle injection of the Medusa.

Eventually, Loew's fears drive him to a stage where—despite whatever desires he holds—copulation is no longer possible; his psychological problems have led, as his very name has always suggested, to a state of impotence. As a result of his fears of feminine sexuality, he cannot physically have intercourse. The film catalogues other metaphors for impotence: when he takes Alva's gun and shoots it, the weapon is merely full of blanks, or when Peter asks his analyst, "What could be easier?" regarding how one files literary contracts, emphasizing *"You just put it in!"* The movie almost parodies its own subtext; at times Cage adopts the stiff, phallic walk of actor Max Schreck in *Nosferatu*.

Even still, he cannot grow fangs, and touches his short canines in surprise at their minimal length. He is reduced to buying a pair of "cheapie plastic" Halloween teeth. After using them on the neck of a victim whom he actually kills, Peter gleefully tells the imaginary Rachel, "I can do it. I know I can do it now." She replies in disgust, "Peter, you're so pathetic." Later, as he takes a long stake and places it at his groin as an intentional phallic sign, Loew screams at an imaginary female date, *"Leave me the fuck alone!"* And when he cannot construct his story of what's going wrong, Dr. Glaser even advises him (as he sits near a statuette of a fertility god), "Just spit it out, Peter." At this stage, Loew is not unlike Dr. Seward's description of Arthur Holmwood in Stoker: "Poor fellow! He looked desperately sad and broken; even his stalwart manhood seemed to have shrunk somewhat under the strain of his much-tried emotions."

"Maybe I should see a shrink."
—Peter Loew moments before his death

Another important aspect of the film is Loew's psychoanalyst, Dr. Glaser. Unlike Abraham Van Helsing in Stoker's novel, she is vastly unaware of what is occurring. His drift into psychosis and madness go unnoticed by her in their sessions, and thus the

Cage's performance drew on the pervasive feelings of dislocation in the 1980s. *Vampire's Kiss* **(1989)**

film makes a curious comment on the "science" of psychoanalysis. "I think your profession is entirely bogus... entirely, in my opinion," Peter says at an imaginary meeting with her. Certainly Minion's script pokes fun at the profession, but at the same time it begs for a psychoanalytic interpretation.

Like Stoker's *Dracula*, sex is the engine that drives *Vampire's Kiss*. Sex and the vampire are irrevocably linked, with blood and semen commingled in the unconscious mind. Many theorists have pointed out that the vampire films of the 1980s and 1990s were an extension of the fear of AIDS. This explanation certainly has merit; indeed, a film like *Bram Stoker's Dracula* (1992) makes an implicit but conscious parallel between the blood diseases of the 19th-century and AIDS. Certainly one could argue that even those vampire films that do not actively try to invoke a discussion of AIDS are still connected to it, with their subtlety indicative of the often repressed status of AIDS in the mindset of everyday American life. Even still, Beirman's film is teeming with other subtexts as well.

Despite its overt attention to sexuality, *Vampire's Kiss* does explore many other issues that exist within Stoker's novel. The "modern" world and its technology, for example, become major concerns in both works. In Stoker, the phonograph and typewriter help record memories that prove helpful in destroying the vampire. The *Demeter* brings Dracula to London by sea, with its name invoking the myths of the Goddess of the earth that acts as a nightly womb for the Count. When he flees back to the East, however, he travels on the *Czarina Catherine*, named for the leader who attempted to bring technology to Russia. As he moves by ship, the band of vampire hunters intent on killing him move by train, using the telegraph as a means of keeping track of the vampire's vessel.

Cage's vampire-psycho fits well into the American corporate culture in *Vampire's Kiss*.

Stoker's Dracula is also a capitalist. If he has old money, it is as Harker describes "gold of all kinds, Roman, and British, and Austrian, and Hungarian, and Greek and Turkish money." Though the East from which he comes is certainly not an economically capitalistic environment, it is a whirlpool of different races, and while there the Count shows no discrimination in his tastes. And, most importantly, the Count's immigration to England—a bastion of capitalism in an industrialized late 19th century—is itself a capitalist enterprise. Along with highlighting the real estate work of Jonathan Harker and Peter Hawkins, Stoker even deems Lucy Westenra's vampiric enterprise as a "career," with the single word invoking for 19th and 20th century readers a vision of an economic endeavor in a capitalist environment.

> "Oh Christ. Oh Christ. Where am I? Where am I? It's... It's...
> Whe... Where am I? Oh Chr... Christ. Where am I?
> Oh, oh, I've become one of them... a vampire!
> Oh God... oh. Oh God, where am I?"
> —Peter Loew looking into a bathroom mirror.

Critic Pauline Kael said of *Vampire's Kiss*, "It may be the first vampire movie in which the modern office building replaces the castle as the site of torture and degradation. ... And [Cage's character] is somehow a plausible part of the singles' nightlife and Manhattan street world." And Peter Loew factors into this modern world as an example of the yuppie decade, whose own mindset of reality—whether through the frailty of the stock market in 1987 or the dubious nature of the "Reagan recovery" or Savings and Loan scandals—is almost as fragile as his own.

The difficulties of this world, of course, were compounded by rapid advances in technology and emphasis on corporate business and making money. For example, Peter makes his threat of firing Alva equal to the threat of raping her. "Unemployment," he screams. "Can you live with that?" And, in perhaps the film's most trite moment, one of Peter's acquaintances is describing a financial investment to yet a third person; after describing the plan's interest payment, he is questioned, "Who would be interested?"

Given this viewpoint, we might suggest an extension of Kael's comment. If the modern office building replaces the castle in *Vampire's Kiss*, the actual vampire at work is the modern city and modern yuppie ethics, sucking the mental health and vitality out of a character like Peter Loew. When he falls at one stage and drops his loaf of French bread, it's not at the site of just any crucifix, but one that is a bright and modern neon. And, just as modern communication pervades Stoker's novel, the phone in *Vampire's Kiss* becomes important. More than once he attempts to call his analyst, and, after buying his plastic teeth, a phone booth he uses to contact her becomes one of the last vestiges of reality that he recognizes.

At times, Peter blames his difficulties on a lack of love. His cabby claims "there is work, and there is love, am I right?," but white-collar work and a singles' nightlife is all that Peter has known. "I never found the right woman, that's all. I just never found the right woman," he believes. The imaginary Rachel—constructed as she is in Peter's mind—places great emphasis on having him say he loves her. But at the same time this also scares him. While waiting to order at a restaurant, for instance, he becomes violently upset while overhearing one woman talk about a marriage proposal and promptly leaves.

Peter also knows his fangs have not grown and he has not changed into a bat; however, he does lose the ability to see himself in mirrors. His reflection is really there, but his inability to see it marks his lack of identity in the urban environment. "Extremely anti-social behavior," the imaginary Rachel says of him at their last meeting. He says he loves her in response, and immediately vomits. At an imaginary session with his analyst, he cites love as the cure to all his ills.

"I don't really see this movie as a vampire film,," Cage remarked to *American Film*, hitting on this same issue. "I see it more as a black comedy about a man who is going out of his mind because of a lack of love—loneliness being the reason."

This lack of identity and subsequent resort to oneself places Peter Loew in the position of both "vampire," as it's his mind that generates the imaginary Rachel, and victim, complete with vampire bite/razor cut. Again this hearkens back to Stoker, who portrays a trapped Jonathan Harker in much the same way. It is Harker at Dracula's castle who fears he "is the only living soul within the place." While shaving in front of a mirror, he feels Dracula's hand on his shoulder, which amazes him as "the reflection of the glass covered the whole room." Harker alone is in the mirror. We can read these moments as the two characters being one, or, as examples of a doubling not very different than that of Loew and Rachel. Only days later in the novel, Dracula mimics Harker to the degree that he imitates his appearance. "It was a new shock to me to find that he had on the suit of clothes which I had worn whilst traveling here...," Harker writes in his diary on June 17.

The element of time is an important factor in both works as well. For Jonathan Harker, it is the very mark of civilization. The further East he travels, the less crucial time seems to be. "It seems to me that the further East you go the more unpunctual are the trains," he writes in his diary on May 3. "What ought they to be in China." And, shortly before he is to meet the carriage Dracula has sent for him, his driver looks at his watch and says "an hour less than the time." The driver immediately wishes to move on to Bukovina, but then the speed of Dracula's own carriage ("Denn die Todten reiten schnell"/"For the dead travel fast") stops him.

As Peter Loew seems to realize, time is a key signifier of his own civilization. With regard to the missing contract, he terrorizes secretary Alva in her attempt to find it. "Now it's fucking Tuesday, and I don't see it here on my desk," he yells. When she finally does discover the missing paperwork, Peter simply repeats "too late" to her, acting more as a commentary on his own mental condition as anything else. He pleads for his analyst to meet with him as soon as possible, even though he doesn't make it to the meeting. He sets his alarm before climbing into his makeshift coffin. As he loses touch with reality, the only element of time he understands is the difference between day and night, due centrally to his knowledge of the Stoker tradition. "Christ! This is the end!" he screams as he turns a corner on a New York street and finds the morning sun staring him in the face.

Both *Dracula* and *Vampire's Kiss* also place a great emphasis on writing and the writing process. Letters, diaries, transcripts of cylinder phonograph recordings, newspaper clippings... Stoker places much importance on the written word. This is how his characters tell their stories and how they construct themselves; it is how the past is reconstructed and how the future is planned. Indeed, it's even the manner by which characters construct themselves, as when Harker—writing by candlelight in Castle Dracula—imagines himself as a young maiden woman. "Here I am," he writes in his diary on May 15, "sitting at a little oak table where in old times possibly some fair lady sat to pen, with much thought and many blushes, her ill-spelt love-letter, and writing in my diary in shorthand all that has happened since I closed it last."

In the case of Peter Loew, however, writing is a major aspect of his downfall. His life revolves around the writing process; he is, after all, an important member of a large literary agency. He is near authors on a daily basis; he speaks with them on the phone. But he himself is not a writer. During one of his imagined meetings with the Jennifer Beals vampire, he imagines that she calls him a "literary genius." In reality, he has difficulty in telling his own story to his analyst. On one occasion, he gives up and walks out after a failed attempt to recount what happened when the bat appeared in his room. During another session, he grows progressively violent in his tone while reciting the alphabet, moving rapidly from "A, B, C" and bringing himself to an heated and animated "Z." In this regard, he is most like Dracula himself, who exists only through the recorded words of others.

The overall events of *Vampire's Kiss* are necessary in helping us reconstruct what's really happening. Innumerable clues help move us toward an accurate evaluation; for example, the cross-cutting between a panhandler on the subway singing *Beautiful Dreamer* and Peter violently destroying his apartment as he drifts further and further into the world of the vampire he has dreamed/imagined. But an edge of ambiguity marks the film, especially on a first viewing. This extends to the degree that its difficult to finally determine whether or not he really is becoming a vampire.

To *American Film*, Cage offered the view that "he's as real a vampire as vampires can be, in the sense that if a man thinks he's a vampire and actually bites a woman on the neck and sucks her blood, I guess that makes him a vampire, even though he doesn't turn into a wolf at night or have fangs." *New Statesman and Society* went so far as to mention, "It matters not whether Loew is a real vampire—it is enough that he believes himself to be one."

Pauline Kael at the *New Yorker* explained (June 13, 1989), "The Hemdale people, who backed the film, made cuts—especially in Loew's sessions with his therapist—and, from reports of people who saw the director's version, key material was removed." As *New York* magazine review explained (June 19, 1989), "*The Post*'s David Edelstein, who saw the movie in an earlier version, claims that the emotional roots of Peter's dilemma were a lot clearer before the studio, Hemdale, began recutting the movie. But I found that the confusion [regarding the reality of Peter's vampirism] didn't destroy my great pleasure in *Vampire's Kiss*."

This confusion is exactly where *Vampire's Kiss* builds its most extensive, if not most subtle and implicit, connection to Stoker's novel. The film finds Loew creating an account of what is occurring for himself, as well as constructing an account for his analyst. Secretary Alva attempts her own account. None of these are correct, and the film places pressure on the viewer to determine if an exact or faithful story of an event is possible, or if we are left to deal only with possible versions of a history that is at its heart unknowable.

Stoker's *Dracula* forces this same question upon the reader, though—embodied most strongly as it is in the character Mr. Swales, who is overlooked in most film versions of the novel. Mina's journal of August 1 records her and Lucy Westenra's meeting with Swales, the old man at the harbor. He makes an extensive case for the unreliability and falsity of stories and accounts as he attacks the written words on tombstones:

"It makes me ireful to think o' them. Why, it's them that, not content with printin' lies on paper an' preachin' them out of the pulpits, does want to be cuttin' them on the tombstones. Look here all round you in what airt ye will; all them steans, holdin' up their heads as well as they can out of their pride, is scant—simply tumblin' down with the weight o' the lies wrote on them, 'Here lies the body' or 'Sacred to the memory' wrote on all of them, an' yet in night half of them there bean't no bodies at all; an' the memories of them bean't cared a pinch of snuff about, much less sacred. Lies all of them, notin' but lics of one kind or another!... The whole thing be only lies... How will it please their relatives to know that lies is wrote over [the tombstones], and that everybody in the place knows that they be lies?"

What Swales questions can be used as an indictment against the reliability and truthfulness of every fact, memory, and story in the Stoker novel, built as it is on the very subjective accounts of characters, rather than, say, the omniscient and all-knowing narrator that might be indicative of much realistic fiction of the 19th-century. From this perspective, by the end of the novel a reader can question everything that occurs in it, including whether Dracula—the one character who never constructs a story, but is constructed by others in their individual accounts—ever really existed at all.

For *Vampire's Kiss*, this means that the question is not whether the supernatural is really at play, causing an uncertain hesitation in the viewer. Instead, it means a confrontation with the reality of accounts. It's less whether Peter Loew is reliable to himself or his analyst, but whether he even has the ability to express an objective account of *any* event. This confusion marks the film to a stronger degree than any other quality, drawing audiences into a world of uncertainty, just as Swales does to readers in Stoker, and everyone is forced to in the daily subjectivity of "real life." Though such confusion

Nicolas Cage's performance in *Vampire's Kiss* continues to unnerve viewers nearly a decade later.

is an uncomfortable world view to encounter, Kael is correct to believe it does not destroy the pleasure of the film; indeed, on repeat viewings, it creates it.

Critical reviews of the film itself were mixed, with many at a loss to even place the film within a specific genre. On one end, even while acknowledging the film's faults, *New York* magazine called the film "one of the few accomplished and original American movies released this year." However, *Variety* (Sept. 21, 1988) believed that "... audiences are likely to become confused about the character's predicament.... Pic might have worked as a horror comedy or as a case study psychological drama. This hybrid is unlikely to please fans of either genre."

Variety also noted another difficulty the film was up against; Hemdale found difficulty getting a distribution deal for *Vampire's Kiss*. And, as one reviewer believed, "it's not difficult to see why. Other than as a cult item at midnight, confused pic has limited commercial possibilities, due to muddled script and another eccentric performance from Cage."

Despite its lack of general acceptance, *Vampire's Kiss* anticipated also the American vampire films of the 1990s, which examined sex and sexuality, disease, urban America, capitalism, and technology. The prevalence of the Stoker image persisted, but morphed to the changing realities of American culture and its members. *Bram Stoker's Dracula* (1992), *Buffy the Vampire Slayer* (1992), *The Addiction* (1995), *Nadja* (1994), *Dracula: Dead and Loving It* (1995), and *Vampire in Brooklyn* (1995) all, to greater or lesser extents, owe a debt to Stoker's creation.

The 1980s vampire films that led to those of the 1990s, however, feature signs of the Stoker tradition, even if both the name and character Dracula were missing. While these films readily exhibit their specific ties to the eighties culture, an examination of a movie like *Vampire's Kiss* allows us to reveal the vital subtexts that pulsed through Stoker's novel *Dracula*. Echoes of his novel and the Dracula persona he created resonate through such films... echoes that are still heard after an entire century.

Nicolas Cage Remembers *Vampire's Kiss*...

I have very distinct memories of *Vampire's Kiss*. It was something of a "turning point" picture for me, and I find that echoes of that performance keep creeping up into my later work. There is a little of my *Vampire's Kiss* performance to be found in *Face/Off*, and I think the experience of the earlier, independent film has allowed me to feel comfortable taking chances with my other acting.

The project came to me because a friend of mine had read the script and suggested I take a look at it. My agent gave it to me to read and I flipped out over it, and saw it as a perfect opportunity to explore some of the avenues I wanted to take in my work.

I have been a long-time buff of German Expressionism, and that whole stylized mode of acting. *Vampire's Kiss* was a chance for me to work off some of the Expressionist fantasies that I've harbored since seeing some of the classic silents like *The Cabinet of Dr. Caligari* and *Nosferatu*.

Motion picture acting is currently in a very "natural" and "realistic" stage, so I was excited by the opportunity to inject some of this Expressionist flavor into a modern film. Acting is a style and a craft, and I thought that most contemporary performances are natural, sometimes at the expense of the surreal or abstract. *Vampire's Kiss* was a unique chance to take my acting down a different direction by tailoring a performance grounded in Expressionism in a 1980s movie. As the character in the film grows more insane, I was able to play him in a more stylized, Expressionist manner. I was also able to incorporate a little Max Schreck, the actor in the silent *Nosferatu*, into the performance.

Reading it, I took it as a story of a man who was losing his mind through loneliness, and his own inability to experience love. It was this lack of love, plus the kind of loneliness and isolation that is so abundant in the contemporary world, that drove him over the edge. And because of his vampire fantasy, he starts feeding his way down the food chain, finally committing the ultimate, lunatic act when he kills someone.

Outside of my love of Expressionism, I had no particular interest in the vampire genre. I was interested in the Max Schreck performance specifically, but I was also intrigued by the work of his contemporaries: people like Emil Jannings and Werner Krauss and Conrad Veidt. I've always felt that the Dracula story is one that is a tale of love and exile, passion and redemption. Francis Ford Coppola did what is perhaps the ultimate take on that theme with *Bram Stoker's Dracula*, which I think also works so well because of its high level of stylization.

Vampire's Kiss moves away from the Dracula tradition in that it is less about romance and more of a case history. Both are about tortured souls, but *Vampire's Kiss* is more about what the lack of love would do to a man's state of mind.

One of the things I still hear about is the scene where I eat the cockroach. It was truly a terrible day for me... I didn't particularly want to do it, but thought it was a good business decision. Special effects did not have to create a fake bug for me to eat, and it also helped bring some attention to the film. Today, audiences mostly react to a few million dollars worth of special effects and not much else, and I like to think that we managed to make them jump in their seats with no special effects at all.

It was my hope that *Vampire's Kiss* would be a movie that would be remembered. I think it's worked out that way. It surprised everyone, because the film had a lot going against it. Hemdale put me in a silly cape and fangs for the video box, ignoring a brilliant design that let the audience know it wasn't just a schlocky, vampire picture. And, being an independent film, it didn't get the distribution that the larger pictures got. Today, I think people are more open minded about what it is: a black comedy about a man that is losing his mind.

I did a lot of my most experimental work with *Vampire's Kiss*. It gave me the foundation to experiment. Independent films are a lot like laboratories, and you can experiment there in ways you can't in a larger film. In a big budget movie, like *Face/Off*, you always have to be careful of what you can and can't do. I felt very secure about the work in retrospect, and am very happy to keep drawing on elements of that earlier work today.

I wouldn't say no to doing another vampire film, but it would have to have a great director and a great script. I'm open-minded to anything as long as it's first rate and allows me to grow as an actor.

—Nicolas Cage

Dracula in the 1990s: Dead and Loving It
by Bob Madison

Dracula has rested uneasily during the decade of his centennial. As he did in Stoker's novel, the Vampire King has preserved and marshaled his strength, waiting for the opportunity to strike anew.

That opportunity has come several times in the 1990s. As I write this, I'm flying 38,000 feet over the United States, waiting to meet with other Dracula supplicants at *Dracula '97*, the century-in-the-making celebration of all things Dracula. The event is merely the culmination of, not only 100 years of Dracula and vampire entertainment, but a decade devoted to the undead.

The Dracula and vampire touchstones of recent years have been Francis Ford Coppola's ambitious 1992 retelling of Stoker's novel, *Bram Stoker's Dracula*. Its success helped move along Neil Jordan's equally ambitious adaptation of Anne Rice's bestseller, *Interview With the Vampire* in 1994. Finally, Mel Brooks helped put the whole thing into focus with his dead-on parody of Dracula and vampire films, *Dracula: Dead and Loving It*.

Though these films are covered throughout portions of the present volume, it is only appropriate that we pause here to take a closer look at the 1990s triptych of vampiric delights.

Bram Stoker's Dracula

Perhaps only a filmmaker with the clout and audacity of Francis Ford Coppola could have designed and created this, one of the finest, most cinematic adaptations of Stoker's novel.

Coppola's thesis was that *Dracula* was as old as cinema itself, and the director incorporates many stylistic and special effects techniques that date back to the earliest days of movie-making. In one interesting digression from the source novel, Dracula actually takes Mina to the cinematograph, there to enjoy the new scientific marvel of motion pictures.

"Astounding," Gary Oldman's Dracula says, impressed. "There are no limits to science."

Count Dracula (Gary Oldman) and Mina (Winona Ryder) clinch in *Bram Stoker's Dracula* (1992).

"Science," sniffs Mina, played by Winona Ryder. "Do you think Madame Curie would invite such comparisons?"

Perhaps not, but Coppola's argument is a valid one. Dracula's undying appeal can be attributed in equal measures to Stoker's novel, and to that indigenously American art form: the motion picture. And Coppola's film is a delight for film buffs, including

Bill Campbell Remembers *Bram Stoker's Dracula*

I had just done *The Rocketeer*, and I came to read for the part of Jonathan Harker. Francis liked me for the role, but it eventually went to Keanu Reeves. So he gave me Quincey, because it's a heroic part, and it was good for me to do.

I read the novel first, then the whole cast went and spent a week at Coppola's place before shooting began, reading the book. We sat around a table and read the novel aloud,

Bill Campbell as cowboy Quincey Morris (far left), paying last respects to Lucy Westenra (Sadie Frost).

reading it in character. They were really good people to work with. Anthony Hopkins, Richard Grant, Sadie Frost, they were all down to earth and a pleasure to be with.

I found I really *liked* Quincey. It was a good part, and it was also the first time that the man who killed Dracula in the book also killed him in the movie! I got a handle on the Texas accent when I called some people there that my father knows. I especially liked playing a cowboy; I'm from Virginia and did a lot of riding when I was a boy.

I had a full beard when I came into read for the part. Being a rough-and-tumble cowboy, I thought Quincey needed facial hair. I begged Francis please to let me keep my beard. He looked me over and said, "I don't know. I figure Quincey to be a clean cut all-American guy."

I offered to shave my beard off in stages and let him see how he felt about it. I kept shaving bits of it off, and when I got down to the last stage, he told me to take it all off.

Another reason I wanted to keep my beard was that I can't stand to have appliances on my face. Wearing a fake mustache is like having a popsicle stick glued to your face. When I went to him on the first day of shooting—*some 50 minutes before I was supposed to shoot my first scene*—he looked at me for a minute and said: "You were right! Go make it happen!"

I raced to the make-up guy and he was flabbergasted, he hadn't worked it through. He quickly improvised something, and I thought it looked pretty good in the end.

There were a couple of interesting things that happened to me during the making of the film. One of them happened when we were shooting the fight scene in Dracula's courtyard at the climax. The guy who was playing the Gypsy that stabbed me was actually the president of the Oakland chapter of the Hell's Angels. During the fight I punched him in the face by accident. I was a little nervous about that—you don't punch one of the Hell's Angels and walk away lightly. Fortunately, he was an affable kind of guy and he just laughed it off.

The other incident was really interesting. I think the neatest moment for me on the set was when we were shooting the sequence on the train. In the film, we were going across Europe to head Dracula off at the pass. The interior of the train was really well tricked out in period detail. The camera was behind me, and I was looking into the rest of the train, from the camera's perspective. Outside of the window I couldn't see anything that wasn't done in period design. Extras dressed as peasants huddled outside and the steam from the train was coming up with the snow in the background and so forth.

Francis had this method of playing the music for the movie over the speaker system before a take—he'd do it quite often. Right before the take Francis surprised us at the last moment by having a conductor with a thick European accent yell out "All aboard!" As he helped some of the villagers into the train—at that moment I had this intense feeling of being absolutely *in* the novel. The feeling wasn't more than just a few seconds long, but is was a moment of being absolutely *in* the book. And that for me was one of the really great moments of being part of the film.

If I have any regrets at all, I guess it's over the end sequence. We didn't have a close-up of Quincey when he killed Dracula scripted. On the set, though, we figured that when I plunged the knife into Dracula, we should have some kind of reaction shot. We did shoot a take, I thought it was kind of necessary because you see what Quincey thinks while killing Dracula, but it didn't make it to the final cut.

—Bill Campbell

Dracula menaces Jonathan Harker in one of the creepier moments of *Bram Stoker's Dracula*.

James V. Hart Remembers *Bram Stoker's Dracula*

Since the early 1970s I had been eager to do a version of *Dracula* that was faithful to Stoker's original novel. The book *Dracula* had just never been adapted for the screen the way it should have been, and I wanted to see it done right.

I enlisted the aide of champion Dracula scholar Leonard Wolf, and we joined forces on the project. We couldn't get anybody to pay attention to *Dracula*. We had gone to Universal to convince them to do a big screen, David Lean type epic film. I had this vision that encompassed the scope of this great, sprawling 19th-century novel, but they didn't see it. I guess they thought *Dracula* had already been done.

When Frank Langella revived interest in the character with the opening the Balderston-Deane play on Broadway, it just made me want to do it more. Nobody had captured the character's sexual magnetism the way Langella had at the Martin Beck Theater... and that approach was the one that I think really worked. In reading the novel, there is a strong, erotic, sexual energy to Stoker's work, and that was the energy that powered the thing.

Langella's opening night was an incredible evening, and the house was packed with people from all over the place. Little old ladies from Queens, people from Texas, Californians—it was just this huge cross section of people.

Langella's Dracula was witty, seductive, grave, powerful, frightening... it was no wonder that, when he stepped into a room, women were attracted to him. But the real coup of the evening was the Act One curtain. In the play he comes in to seduce Lucy in his silk shirt, and she's there in a silvery, 1930s nightgown. He opens up his chest and raises Lucy up to him and she swoons. He brings her to his chest, and then slow fade to black and curtain.

The audience sat there, stunned. Then when they collected themselves, applause, applause, applause. And I'll never forget the four or five ladies sitting in front of me. Out-of-towners, you know the "big hair" ladies that could've come from anywhere, and they just sat there talking about what they had just seen. And one lady turned to another and said: "I'd rather spend one night with Dracula dead, then the rest of my life with husband alive."

And that, more than anything, underscored for me the power Dracula had over women... an awakening of the sexual energy that they had buried or forgotten. That moment, that night, convinced me that *Dracula* should be a women's film, that the key was the female characters, and not the men. I think Stoker wrote out his own fears of unbridled female sexual energy, which is why all those Victorian guys were so stiff and uptight about what happened to their women. So women were the essential key to the picture, especially now.

I didn't think women had the power on screen in the 1970s that they do now, and I think *Bram Stoker's Dracula* could only have happened in this age of empowered women. But it's all there in

Stoker—our society and our mores and our trends had caught up with what Stoker had unleashed 100 years ago. Stoker was way ahead of his time.

I still can't figure out how anyone can read the novel, and then go back to the play and think that's *Dracula*. Once you sit and read the novel, you see it's not only a horror tale, but an action adventure piece, a mystery, a chase with a great climax... and I think the sweep and the size of it scared people away. It's an epic, it's huge. Traditionally, filmmakers kept going back to the play as a way of making it smaller, more claustrophobic. But that's not Stoker: he's sprawling and larger-than-life, with this great confrontation of the armies of darkness trying to get to the castle, and a small band of dedicated avengers on Dracula's trail. How do you adapt a horror novel that ends like a John Ford Western? (I was actually criticized in a newspaper from my own home town of Fort Worth for including Quincey, a Texan with a bowie knife! They wondered: how dare I throw a cowboy with a bowie knife into this 19th-century novel! They never read the book!)

Another factor in getting the film produced was that Dracula is more pertinent today than ever before. Look at music, night life, fashion, the whole obsession with vampires in literature and television and films. But what's more interesting is that our concepts of good and evil have "grayed up"...

Vlad Dracula, warrior prince (Gary Oldman) in *Bram Stoker's Dracula.*

they're no longer black and white. That's because the church has failed to deliver on its promises .. and has failed consistently. The church is the most hypocritical institution on this planet—just read the papers and you'll find it's constantly involved in some kind of scandal. So, right now, Dracula presents an interesting alternative: an eternal life that does not require faith, but that can start right here and now. There are no worries in vampirism, and you can walk around fearless. Dracula and vampires are the dark alternative to a failed morality system.

In doing the screenplay, my whole goal was to present him as a full-bodied, complex human being who went to war with God, and who was later redeemed and saved at the end. A man who was redeemed by love. There're a lot of soulless people out there, because there is nothing to redeem them. In the end, Dracula is really one of the lucky ones, because Mina's great love for him brought him redemption.

Francis Ford Coppola did an extraordinary job; he took what I did in the first draft and created a Dracula that we had never seen before. The film brought a whole new level of empathy and appreciation to Dracula... making him a very contemporary character.

Bram Stoker's Dracula is also very contemporary for its comments on the AIDS crisis. Francis picked up on my idea of cursing someone with your tainted blood, and making a moral decision on that. I had lost my brother to AIDS, and we all wanted to make some kind of conscious statement on the crisis.

When Dracula comes to Mina in her room, she knows the consequences, and that they were irreversible. Dracula knew that he could kill her through his sexual greed, that he would kill her with the disease his blood carried. And this Dracula had the moral conviction to want to deny that and not condemn her. I wanted the "vampire wedding" scene to play that way, because so many of our family members and so many of our friends in the arts are gone because of AIDS. I thought this *Dracula* had to deal with that issue... and this blood exchange is as unforgivable as not using a condom and thinking you're invulnerable. Everybody involved in the film wanted that scene to play, even though some studio people wanted to cut or shorten it. Francis and Gary worked to keep it intact, and it's one of the most powerful scenes in the film.

Now that it's over, I think Francis made a fine film. A lot of people would take issue over whether or not it's the definitive *Dracula*. People either loved it or hated it; there was very little middle ground. I think Francis Ford Coppola is the only director who could've brought that kind of vision to the screen and pulled it off. It's like grand opera and nobody else—not Spielberg, Robert Zemeckis, nobody—could've made that film like Francis did. I think it will stand up as one of Coppola's most respected works, along with *Apocalypse Now* and the *Godfather* films. Everybody was very protective of that screenplay, and I'm very proud of it.

—James V. Hart

generous dollops of Stoker's tale along with interesting inclusions of elements of everything from F. W. Murnau's 1922 classic *Nosferatu* and Karl Freund's memorable *The Mummy* (1932). And while the sweeping, epic screenplay by James V. Hart sometimes fudges the exact particulars of the novel, in terms of incident and continuity it is the closest adaptation of Stoker ever committed to film.

An added bonus is the inclusion of a prologue featuring the historical Dracula, the result of much of the ground-breaking Dracula research by such scholars as Leonard Wolf, Raymond McNally, and Radu Florescu. How much of an inspiration this petty dictator and despot had on Bram Stoker's creative process is open for debate (probably not much at all), but the "historical" Dracula, Vlad Tepes, has become something of a cottage industry for Transylvania tourism and academics. Talk about the "real" Dracula has been freely bandied about during any discussion of Dracula ever since the publication of McNally and Florescu's 1972 *In Search of Dracula*, and to finally have this real-life monster on celluloid is an added treat.

Dracula buffs are also treated to the inclusion of Stoker's Texan, Quincey P. Morris. Stoker loved Americans and cowboys, and it is here, in the New World, that Dracula's legend has been forever vampirically preserved on film. Quincey's ascent into the movie myth is long overdue.

Surely the discussion of any Dracula film comes down to the performance of the monster itself. In that respect, Gary Oldman does not disappoint—his Dracula may well become a benchmark by which future actors are measured. Oldman seems to have studied the work of previous Draculas and taken the best elements of their performances, merging them somehow into a unified whole that works wonderfully. Mixing the otherworldly menace (and voice) of Lugosi with the aggressive, animal qualities of Palance, and the seductive, lady-killer charm of Frank Langella, Oldman presents viewers with the most multi-faceted portrayal of the character attempted thus far. This is a Dracula for connoisseurs.

Most of the cast do not measure up to Oldman's creepy mastery. Newcomer Sadie Frost was magnificent as the victimized Lucy, and Bill Campbell, Cary Elwes, and Richard E. Grant acquit themselves well as her trio of suitors: Morris, Holmwood, and Seward. Tom Waits as Renfield and Keanu Reeves as Jonathan Harker are both weak, but, surprisingly, it is Anthony Hopkins who disappoints the most, with his wild, woolly and completely unfocused performance as Dr. Van Helsing.

Is Coppola's *Bram Stoker's Dracula* the definitive version? No, nor can any film ever be. Stoker's text is so rich, so invulnerable to even the most complete of adapters, that it will always be ripe for interpretation. Half of the fun is watching people try.

Interview With the Vampire

The hothouse mix of romance, Southern Gothic, and homoeroticism that was Anne Rice's best-selling *Interview With the Vampire* had defied the best intentions of moviemakers for years. Everyone from John Travolta to Cher had once been mentioned as a possible Lestat (the only Hollywood luminary seemingly unconsidered was Benji), and a workable screenplay seemed beyond the powers of even Anne Rice herself.

So it was with a mixture of elation and trepidation that her legion of loyal and vocal readers went to Neil Jordan's film version, starring Tom Cruise as Lestat and Brad Pitt as his suitor, Louis.

Brad Pitt as Louis in *Interview With the Vampire*.

The event did not prove to be worth the wait. The gay subtext that powered most of the action is completely missing from Jordan's film version, making superfluous the vampire adoption efforts of this unconventional couple. (Kirsten Dunst, as their vampire child, Claudia, delivers the film's sole competent performance.) Cruise comes off badly as Lestat, a role completely beyond his corn-fed, all-American boy image. Director Jordan made the mistake of allowing Pitt to provide the film's voice-over narration, a built-in assurance that viewers would sleep through the bulk of its padded 120-plus minutes.

Antonio Banderas, usually darkly sexy and capable, seems mostly asleep under his Morticia Addams fright wig. Most viewers shared his tired response, as Pitt did his best with a vapid script to portray the self-hatred and anguish caused by the alternate vampire lifestyle. (Rice's novel may have been aptly subtitled *Queer and Loathing*.)

All of this is a great shame. Rice's novel has all the essentials for a great movie: a trio of intriguing main characters, scope both epic and historical, and a rich and fruity subtext. In the years to come a more capable and courageous film may be made of her material, but until then, this interview is most significant for what was left unsaid.

Dracula: Dead and Loving It

Writer-director Mel Brooks has the one essential necessary to all great parodists: affection for his material.

Brooks has been a fan of the great movie monsters since his earliest boyhood. It was that affection that helped inform 1974's *Young Frankenstein*, which ranks alongside *Abbott and Costello Meet Frankenstein* as the best of the horror comedies.

It was only natural that Brooks would turn his attention to Stoker's Vampire King during the vampire-rich 1990s. Tapping actor and physical comedian Leslie Nielsen for the title role, Brooks managed to poke gentle fun at Tod Browning's 1931 classic, vampire icon Bela Lugosi, Stoker's novel, John Badham's version with Frank Langella, and Francis Ford Coppola's more operatic excesses... indeed, it seems the only significant vampire reference Brooks missed is 1972's *Blacula*.

Unlike his earlier *Young Frankenstein, Dracula: Dead and Loving It* is no classic. However, there is much to savor for the Dracula buff, and Peter MacNichol's dead-on impersonation of Dwight Frye is worth the price of admission alone. (This author nearly had a stroke during the afternoon tea party sequence MacNichol played with Harvey Korman's Dr. Seward.) Brooks lends able support as Dr. Van Helsing ("Remind me to put down newspaper the next time," he says after Lucy has been staked by Jonathan), and Steven Weber is fine as a modern day David Manners.

Wisely, Brooks realizes that our favorite bogeymen have no real power over us unless we can occasionally laugh at them.

The Millenneum and Beyond

The future of Stoker's Vampire King will be hotly debated during Dracula '97. Held in Los Angeles at the Westin Hotel, and featuring panels and presentations from some of the finest Dracula scholars alive today (including several contributors to the present volume), the conference will attract an international audience. In attendance will be such diverse groups as a delegation of Gypsy dancers from Transylvania and academics from some of the nation's finest schools; film critics and vampire-movie stars (two, Carla Laemmle and Lupita Tovar, go back as far as Universal's 1931 *Dracula*); pale teens into Gothic music and the generation raised on *Shock Theater*; real-life blood fetishists, and a troupe of players from the Grand Guingol. All are now making their way to Los Angeles with a purpose, much the same way that Stoker's Count made his deliberate way to London.

Would it be possible to break the time barrier and travel through the decades, what would Stoker find more astonishing? That his literary creation has not only survived

100 years, but is the center of such slavish devotion, or that the world he knew of hansom cabs and gaslight and fog has been replaced by one of jet planes, cyberspace, home computers, and AIDS?

Probably both in equal measures.

In this final decade of the 20th-century, Dracula's shadow darkens the popular imagination as never before. It is appropriate that his anniversary decade has been such a busy one for him. The 1990s has seen the ascendancy of Stoker's penny dreadful to classic novel status, and the legend continues to be interpreted and reinterpreted in ways significant to contemporary audiences. Mel Brooks may well have written the Vampire King's epitaph—*dead and loving it.*

As the millennium approaches, Dracula's powers show no signs of waning. The dark promises he made a century ago are more seductive than ever, and we, his ever-eager victims, continue to invite him to dine.

But what is the secret of the Count's hold over us? Why do we, so far removed from the supernatural by the marvels of a technological and scientific age, return again and again to the dark and dangerous revenant of Stoker's imagination?

The answer lies in Dracula's fantastic ability to change with the times. The Dracula that attracts a convention center of supplicants today is not solely the monstrous ogre of Stoker, but a character that continues to shift and morph as time and fashion dictate. Ironically, Stoker's vampire is much like a house of mirrors: but because he cannot cast a reflection of his own, it is our selves, our fears, and our longings that we glimpse in the darkened glass. Dracula is the monster that everyone knows, but who will forever be different things to different people. Every decade has recreated Stoker's monster to meet its own conventions of both the dangerous and the romantic. Whether re-conceived in 1920s Germany as a creeping pestilence or as a figure of sensuality and romance in the sexually liberated America of the 1970s, the one certainty about Dracula is that he will continue to *change*.

Given this gift for reinvention, it is not surprising that Dracula survives today. No, the amazing thing about Dracula is what he was and what he has become. Stoker conceived of the character as an atavistic ape-man, a throw-back to the time of Attila the Hun. But the name Dracula now conjures an ever-widening variety of mental images, including everything from a predatory aristocrat in evening dress to a walking metaphor for the AIDS virus. Indeed, the 1990s has offered an amazing diversity of Dracula and vampire imagery, and is almost a reflection of the preceding century in microcosm.

A quick thumbing-through of Dracula's portrait gallery reveals that we have spent the past century white-washing Dracula's reputation. Stoker was not unaware of the early Byronic tradition of vampires best exemplified by Lord Ruthven, he simply chose to ignore it. His Dracula was no seducer, no ladies man, no tragic lover. Stoker's Dracula was a creature of shadows, a monster briefly sketched in the opening chapters—complete with protruding fangs, hairy palms, and rancid breath—and then quickly removed from the action. Missing from the bulk of the remaining pages, drawn with little more than shadows, Stoker leaves his readers needing more of the Vampire King.

And so, the 1990s has gone, as previous decades have, in search of Dracula.

What will Dracula's disciples find in Los Angeles, in the anniversary year of 1997? The answer will change with each individual, but as Americans peer into Dracula's unreflecting mirror, my guess is the image reflected back will simply be ourselves.

Something special is usually reserved for a volume's afterword, and that's what we have here for you now.

David J. Skal is the outstanding Dracula scholar of this century. His book, Hollywood Gothic, *is the single most essential volume on Dracula after Stoker's original novel, a witty and informative feat of scholarship that has put this Dracula century in perspective.*

David's quest for Dracula proves the vampire's victims run to all types, and the hold of his undead embrace can last a lifetime. Most Dracula buffs can pinpoint the exact moment they felt that frission, that indefinable something that let them know that they were party to a great and mysterious secret, a secret to which the Transylvanian Count held the key.

That frisson is the secret of Dracula's undying appeal: he is the shadowy catalyst leading to our unknown selves, the master of life's two great mysteries, sex and death. Every generation remakes Dracula, and, in doing so, reveals itself.

David Skal's other books include V Is for Vampire, The Monster Show *and* Dark Carnival: The Secret World of Tod Browning—Hollywood's Master of the Macabre. *He has also written critically acclaimed episodes of A&E's Biography on the lives of Bela Lugosi, Boris Karloff, and Lon Chaney, Jr.*
—Bob Madison

Afterword—Him and Me: A Personal Slice of the Dracula Century

by David J. Skal

This is the true story of how I decided to become a vampire, but finally settled for a more fulfilling life as Dracula's helper.

A few weeks before Halloween 1962, when I was 10 years old, the threatened prank of the season wasn't toilet-papered fences, but the deployment of nuclear warheads, aimed at the American mainland from Cuba. I had been looking forward to growing up, but President Kennedy's grim announcements on television strongly indicated that this might not be in the cards. While waiting for my untimely incineration, I went to the library and pored over the pictures of fallout shelters in magazines. The people inside them looked like ordinary suburbanites, but more monastic. They sat calmly among their stockpiles of rations, listened to radios for instructions, or lay in motionless repose on minimalist cots, staring at the bare walls. The fallout shelter was a lot like a crypt, where people existed in a strange half-life poised precariously between consumer nirvana and nuclear oblivion. They were something like vampires, I realized, atomic-age undeath shielding itself from a nasty nuclear sun. In other books I found graphic pictures of atomic bomb survivors. They, too, looked like the living dead—walking, rotting corpses. It was possible that everyone I knew in Garfield Heights, Ohio, might look just like this, or worse, in the very near future.

The October issue of *Boys Life* magazine had come in the mail with a full page color advertisement dripping with its own kind of death anxiety: Aurora Plastics' model kits of the Wolf Man, Frankenstein, and Dracula, now available for 98 cents. I was fascinated by the illustrations, especially the steely, piercing gaze of the Count. He was all about control and survival at a time in which I felt in control of nothing and unlikely to survive.

We didn't have a fallout shelter, but I liked the idea of not having to die. I actually knew very little about vampires, except that they wore fancy clothes, drank your blood, and that they, if kept out of the sun, could live forever. My very first exposure to Dracula was a skit on the *Carol Burnett Show*, in which Durward Kirby played the Count, lurking in the closets of a suburban home. Early on, I was puzzled that Dracula was always considered a monster, but didn't look like other monsters. He looked like some kind of magician or ringmaster. Nevertheless, he was the monster that always interested me the most.

Part of the attraction came from youthful laziness. Dracula was an easy costume to do for Halloween, much easier than the other monsters. All you needed was some white powder, an eyebrow pencil, plastic fangs, and Vaseline in your hair. While the missile crisis unfolded, I started working on my Halloween costume. I didn't have "real" vampire fangs, so I used those goofy wax teeth you used to be able to buy at the candy counter for a penny. The effect was more Jerry Lewis than Bela Lugosi, but at least it was something. I wore my white Sunday shirt, and tied a big square of black satin around my neck for a cape. I practiced the stare and hand movements of Lugosi as depicted in the advertisement for the Aurora monster kits. Arching the back of my hand really hurt, but I kept at it. No pain, no gain.

The missile crisis waned, but my interest in Dracula and monsters remained. Although Cleveland television was blessed with one of the country's best horror movie hosts—Ghoulardi, portrayed by the late Ernie Anderson—I was deprived of the Universal horror classics for most of the 1960s. The Cleveland stations dropped the "Shock!" series of Universal monster pictures long before my interest in horror was piqued (although I still remember seeing, and being fascinated by, *Frankenstein Meets the Wolf Man* on TV around the age of seven). Ghoulardi specialized in AIP and Allied Artists pictures from the late 1950s, and so my only access to the Universal films was frustratingly second-hand, through illustrated features in magazines like *Famous Monsters of Filmland* and *Castle of Frankenstein*.

My first monster magazine (meaning the first one I actually owned, took home, read to pieces) was the April 1963 issue of *Famous Monsters*. This, of course, was the *Dracula* "filmbook" issue with PHOTOS FROM BELA LUGOSI'S OWN SCRAPBOOK. I had been haunting the magazine rack at Jay's Drug Store for several months, and had surreptitiously read, over a period of several store visits, the previous issue on *Bride of Frankenstein*. My parents had already laid down the law on *Mad* magazine— it was a "sick," subversive rag, never to be brought into the house again—and I can't really remember how I convinced my father to buy *Famous Monsters* for me, but I did. I took the magazine to my room and read it from cover to cover, and then I read it again.

Dracula didn't just come out of some graveyard—he had a whole *castle*, with big winding staircases where he could strike poses and strangle victims.

There were no castles in Garfield Heights, but I lived in a house opposite a big Catholic hospital and its adjacent convent. The hospital was modern; the convent was one of the only really old buildings anywhere nearby; old, dark, and, to my imagination, castle-like, with mullioned windows and skulking nuns. A popular suburban legend had it that the nuns were charged with the grim nocturnal task of secretly burying amputated limbs on the convent grounds (since it was a Catholic hospital, any leftovers from operations couldn't be cremated). It didn't take much for me to start imagining the black-robed sisters as a secret coven of vampires—I even wrote some stories in which they came flapping down from their fortress into our blue-collar neighborhood of tract houses to slake their unnatural thirsts at the throats of working-class sleepers— just the way Dracula decimated the peasant population in Transylvania. In my catechism classes, the nuns always spoke ecstatically of drinking the blood and eating the body of Christ. Since Christ couldn't be expected back anytime soon, it seemed only logical that the sisters might well have to find other sources of nourishment. I always half-expected to see a red trickle escaping the corner of one of the nun's mouths—hard, dry mouths, with lines at the corners like little fishhooks. But the trickles never came.

Unable to see *Dracula*, I imagined *Dracula* everywhere. The convent was the castle, my neighbors were the unsuspecting villagers, and the knotty-pine window seat in my room became my "coffin"—I made "handles" out of metallic gift-wrap tape. (Later, I had a transportable, backup "coffin" in the form of a big corrugated box I would fill up with my monster magazines and other treasured possessions and drag down to the basement during the inevitable spring and summer tornado alerts. Let the house get blown to smithereens—my monsters weren't going anywhere!)

Odd as it may strike younger readers, there were no VCRs or Blockbuster Video outlets in the early 1960s, no cable networks showing film classics 24 hours a day, no real way to see classic movies unless a television station decided to show them to you. On Saturdays during the school year, I began to haunt the newspaper morgue at the Cleveland Public Library downtown, filling out call slip after call slip to have wheeled carts of bound, 1931 copies of the *Cleveland Press* and *Plain Dealer* delivered to me from the bowels of the earth. I wanted to know what it was like to be alive in 1931, and see *Dracula* approaching, inexorably, in the movie advertisements. From *Famous Monsters*, I knew that the movie had been released in February 1931, so I started there, not knowing that back in the 1930s, movies didn't open at the same time all across the country, and that cities like Cleveland sometimes had to wait a month or more for the latest releases. The newsprint was brittle, and turning the pages, one fragile leaf at a time, was very slow going. Finally, in March 1931, the first ads appeared: HIS KISS WAS LIKE THE ICY BREATH OF DEATH, YET NO WOMAN COULD RESIST! My hands started trembling. The ads were small at first, but each day they got bigger, like a vampire's hard-on. WHAT DOES HE DO AT NIGHT? WHERE DOES HE GO DURING THE DAY? WHO IS THIS STRANGE, AWFUL MAN, DEAD 500 YEARS AND YET ALIVE?

I looked at the other advertisements to see what the 1931 people waiting for *Dracula* to arrive in Cleveland looked like. The slouchy, art deco women in the department store ads were the perfect victims, dazed and somnolent, Depression-age "nifties" who couldn't wait for the icy breath of death. I imagined them lining up at the Hippodrome theater on Euclid Avenue, a sea of cloche hats and clutch purses, a hushed murmur of obedient anticipation. Since I knew deep down that *Dracula* had to be the greatest movie ever made, it surprised and disturbed me that a lot of the original reviews were pretty lukewarm. But from these capsule descriptions, I could at least piece together an idea of the kinds of things that went on in the film. *Famous Monsters* had published a lot of pictures from *Dracula*, but for some reason it didn't tell the story, and this was almost as frustrating as not being able to see the movie. I had my school librarian order a copy of the Stoker novel on inter-library loan. It was the old Modern Library edition, with a picture of Dracula on the cover that didn't look anything like Bela Lugosi—he had a big droopy mustache—and this confused me. I inhaled the whole book in the course of an afternoon, and could tell right away that it was very different from the movie. But it gave me some clues.

You must understand that my quest to see Tod Browning's *Dracula* started at the age of 10 and was not successful until I was 16—in other words, the whole ordeal was the equivalent of more than half of my life at the time I began the hunt. As the years rolled on, my despair at ever seeing the film increased. Oh, there was that 10-minute eight-millimeter Castle Films abridgment, but it only used the boring parts of the movie— there wasn't a single shot of Transylvania, the castle, and the staircase! I scoured the weekly issues of *TV Guide*, praying that Cleveland's long embargo on the Universal horror films would be lifted, but no such luck... week after week, Ghoulardi kept showing things like *Attack of the Crab Monsters* and *The Hypnotic Eye*. One week, however, my heart almost stopped when I came across the listing: *Dracula (Melodrama, 1931) Bela Lugosi, David Manners*. Could this really be real? Then I looked at the channel—it wasn't Cleveland, it was *Erie, Pennsylvania.*

I knew we didn't get the Erie stations, but maybe, just maybe, something could be worked out. Every now and then some far away stations crackled through—once, through considerable static, our set had connected with a station in Detroit. So it *was* possible. I had a whole week before the Saturday, 11 P.M. broadcast to make it work. I did everything I could to maximize our chances. I got a long length of television antenna cable and fashioned a kind of supplementary dish out of coat hangers and window screens. I hung it out of my upstairs bedroom window, pointed skyward, vaguely in the direction of faraway Erie. Like the kites in *Bride of Frankenstein*, I tried to pull the lifeforce of a great monster from out of the skies. But my contraption failed to capture *Dracula.* Crushed and defeated, I observed the time of the broadcast by re-reading the old copy of *Famous Monsters*, and sorting the considerable collection of *Dracula* stills I had amassed by mail order from Movie Star News in New York City. It was my only consolation. Why did I have to be born in Ohio? What had I done to deserve such punishment?

One day, in 1968, my mother looked up from her newspaper and announced, "Well, David, I guess you're finally going to see *Dracula*."

Was I dreaming?

She showed me the entertainment section of the *Plain Dealer.* There was a long strip ad with sprocket holes like a strip of film, running from the top to the bottom of the page. The Old Mayfield Theater on the East Side of Cleveland was inaugurating a new program of screening revivals—first, the ad announced, there would be sparkling new 35-millimeter prints of W. C. Fields and Mae West comedies, and then, *right there in*

Millions the world over have felt the effect of Dracula's peculiar charm (Bela Lugosi and Helen Chandler in 1931's *Dracula*).

the middle of the ad—ONE WEEK ONLY—BELA LUGOSI IN "DRACULA"—BORIS KARLOFF IN "FRANKENSTEIN."

The originals!

I spent the next several weeks in a state of indescribably tense nervous excitement... which dissipated considerably when the film began. I don't know what I expected from *Dracula*, but I certainly didn't expect it to be a slow, stagy movie that got slower and stagier as it went on. *Could this be all there was?* It was extremely disorienting. Lugosi didn't have much dialogue; mostly he just stared... there was this stupid bit with an armadillo... you never found out exactly what Renfield did with the maid... there wasn't any music. And so on.

But the opening two reels of the film riveted me, for reasons I was not ready to fully admit or explore. I went back to the Old Mayfield on Saturday and sat through *Dracula* and *Frankenstein* twice. A few months later the films showed up downtown at the

Hippodrome (where *Dracula* had its Cleveland premiere in 1931). I went again, and stayed all day. I wanted to see that opening part of *Dracula* again and again, even if I had to sit through the slow parts, along with *Frankenstein* (a film I found far less interesting). What grabbed me was the strange, stylized encounter that opened the movie: a highly affected, middle-aged man with pancake make-up and painted lips invites a young man to his castle, stares at him intently, plies him with a combination of alcohol and drugs, tells the women to go away, and gets the guy unconscious on the floor and crawls on top of him for the fadeout.

Monster movies have always provided people, especially kids, a way to think about sex without having thinking about it too directly. For a large part of my adolescence, *Dracula* and other horror movies gave me a way to simultaneously engage and avoid scary sexual issues—homosexuality in particular. When I was downtown at the library, digging into *Dracula*, I always noticed that there was someone in the last men's room stalls who never left or moved or made any kind of sound that would indicate he was actually using the facilities, at least not in the ordinary fashion. You could go back three hours later and he would still be there, waiting with the patience of the dead. Now, of course, I realize that the guy trolling the toilet was, in a sense, Dracula, the Big Sucking Sound of my adolescent nightmares.

Monsters took a back seat to college and career in the 1970s, but in the late 1980s, the Count began scratching at my window once again. I was living and working in Greenwich Village, and it took me quite a long time to realize that the energy fueling the vampire's reappearance in my life wasn't the H-bomb, but the explosion of the AIDS epidemic which was creating devastation all around me. The fearful interplay of Dracula, blood borne plagues, and gay issues had reawakened with a psychic vengeance. I had my parents send me the box of monster magazines and *Dracula* photos which had rested undisturbed in my bedroom closet for years. It didn't occur to me that, in writing a proposal for what would eventually be *Hollywood Gothic*, I was actually "bargaining" with the Count and all the body-fluid horror he represented, trying to control and contain and explain him between the sturdy covers of a book.

In 1989, W. W. Norton and Company offered me a contract for *Dracula: The Book of the Film*, which would have been a lavishly illustrated edition of the 1931 screenplay, as well as a complete documentation of the little-known but technically superior Spanish-language version which had been filmed on the same sets with a different cast and crew. The incomplete negative was on deposit at the Library of Congress, I had studied the work print, and was convinced that my book might spur a full restoration of the film (the only source for the missing material was said to be in Cuba). Unfortunately, even with the backing of the American Film Institute, I was unable to obtain rights to the screenplay from Universal, and had to completely revamp the book proposal as a project that did not require studio licensing. I quickly became immersed in documenting the stories of all the people in *Dracula*'s long history who had become obsessed in one way or another with the character and the story: Bram Stoker, his wife Florence, and her amazing campaign to destroy the plagiarized film adaptation, *Nosferatu*; producers Hamilton Deane and Horace Liveright, and of course, Bela Lugosi. Needless to say, my own obsession rivaled almost any chronicled in the book.

In 1989, in a moment of supreme irony, I found myself in Havana, the focal point of all the Cold War jitters that got me interested in Dracula in the first place. I had been exchanging telexes for several months with Hector Garcia Mesa, the director of the

The 1931 Spanish *Dracula* is available today thanks largely to the efforts of historian Skal.

Cinemateca de Cuba. (I don't know to what extent American communications with Cuba are screened or snooped on, but I've always wondered whether my correspondence was surveilled by intelligence busybodies wondering what all the references to "Dracula" were *really* about.) Garcia Mesa confirmed that the Cinemateca indeed owned a "very nice" complete print of the Spanish *Dracula* and I was welcome to come study it.

I obtained a journalist's visa from the U.S. Treasury Department and booked a three-day trip to Havana. I was surprised I didn't have to fly through an intermediary foreign country; Continental Airlines conveniently had regularly scheduled flights out of Miami, but didn't advertise the fact. The flights left in the middle of the night, packed mostly with Cuban Americans with relatives on the island, who have special travel privileges most of us don't know about.

Cuba, of course, had been linked in my mind to the terror of personal annihilation at a very early age, so somehow it wasn't all that surprising when we were herded off the plane into shuttle buses by soldiers with machine guns. The REVOLUTION OR DEATH billboards along the road to the airport were a little startling, too. But I soon found that the Cubans were extremely friendly and accommodating. Was this really the country whose bad behavior in 1962 had sent me running to the arms of Dracula?

When I arrived at the Cinemateca the next day, Garcia Mesa wasn't there and nobody knew who I was or what I was doing. I had a moment of complete panic. Fortunately, there was one staff member fluent in English who was able to save the trip. The print of *Dracula* was still at the repertory theater where it had just had a public screening, and it would take a day to get the Count in his canister back to his archival resting place. Could I come back tomorrow?

I killed time wandering around Old Havana, much of which seemed like an overheated vision out of J. G. Ballard: once-beautiful mansions and art deco houses in the style of Miami Beach, their grounds overgrown with foliage and their outer walls sunblistered with peeling paint. I had my date with Dracula the following morning, via an ancient movieola that projected the missing third reel of the Spanish *Dracula* film on a battered index card clipped above the machine. I cringed when the technician repeatedly let yards of film unspool all over the floor—this was, after all, the only copy of this particular footage anywhere in the universe; the original negative had crumbled into dust, and, unlike Dracula himself, couldn't be reconstituted for an onscreen encore. Later, they projected the reel over and over for me in a screening room, where I stood in the middle of the seats with a camera and tripod, snapping the images I would use in my book.

I expected to be rewarded handsomely for my efforts on behalf of Dracula, but in the end, unlike Renfield, I wasn't even offered bugs. Despite a lot of publicity and some lavish reviews, I didn't profit a nickel on the American edition of *Hollywood Gothic*. All the advance money, and more, got poured back into research and out-of-pocket expenses. Universal finally got hold of the Cuban reel and restored the Spanish film, which ended up on *Billboard*'s Top 40 video list for eight weeks in 1992. It would have been nice if the studio had acknowledged in some way my efforts to spur the restoration, but it didn't (instead, the press kit from MCA Home Video simply used verbatim, unattributed chunks of text from *Hollywood Gothic*, and shot their publicity photos from the printed book).

I've been a largely unpaid flack for Dracula ever since. I've lost any real desire to be a vampire (I've appeared on far too many talk shows with real-life blood drinkers to be susceptible any longer to *that* fantasy). Perhaps the real moment of truth came on a trip to London when I was given the chance to try on one of Christopher Lee's original Dracula capes. Now, Christopher Lee is about seven feet tall (or something); I'm five-six. Nonetheless, I pulled the thing on and dragged it over to a full length mirror to get a good look at my transformed, Dracula self.

It was pretty pathetic. It looked like one thing on Christopher Lee, but on me it resembled... well, a collapsed circus tent. I learned an important lesson: short guys can't wear capes, but we can write books about people who do.

The book you've just finished reading should be more than enough evidence of Dracula's staying power in the modern imagination. For me he's always had specific associations with very personal themes of sex and death which some of you will relate to, and others won't. But it's the essence of Dracula's genius for survival to be all things to all people, a cultural as well as fictional shape-shifter. I hope you've enjoyed *Dracula: The First 100 Years* as much as I have. Dracula himself may be a novelist's fantasy, but his legacy in popular culture, as outlined in this volume, is tangible and real. To his presence, influence and meaning, attention must be paid.

I'll be loyal to you, master. I'll be loyal.

A Dracula Discography

As Stoker's vampire casts no reflection, it stands to reason that Dracula's voice would not record either.

Despite that limitation—which would seemingly put an end to this entry—Dracula's voice has often haunted vinyl, tape, and disc technology.

While it can be argued that Dracula is a major influence on the "Gothic" music scene (yet another crime on his record!), Dracula's main interests seem to lie in rock-n-roll's musical coffin.

Television's horror-film host

Zacherley had a hit single and album with *Dinner With Drac* (1958), which became a perennial Halloween favorite on Dick Clark's *American Bandstand*. The most memorable lyric, "For dessert, there was bat-wing confetti, and the veins of a mummy named Betty. I first frowned upon it, but with ketchup on it, it tasted very much like spaghetti!" was popular in schoolyards around the country.

Zacherley had a run for his money with Bobby (Boris) Pickett's *The Monster Mash* (1962). Though Pickett sings in a sly send-up of actor Boris Karloff's voice, he also interjects a few lines as Bela Lugosi's Dracula. His *Monster Mash* album also includes such "Dracula" numbers as *Blood Bank Blues* and *Transylvania Twist*. Like Dracula, the album rose unexpectedly from the dead to become a hit all over again in the early 1970s.

Actor Gabriel Dell terrified young listeners with a Dracula monologue (closely imitating Lugosi's voice) in the album *Famous Monsters Speak!* Movie-Dracula Christopher Lee also cut a record adaptation of Stoker's *Dracula* in 1966 (now a hard-to-find collectible), and told a Dracula anecdote on 1974's *Hammer Presents Dracula*, featuring the music of James Bernard.

Former Beatle Ringo hitched his Starr to the Count for his album, *Son of Dracula*, and the Marvel Comics Group released one of their Dracula comics complete with 45 RPM recorded adventure in 1975. The uncredited actor playing Dracula sounds like a villain from a James Bond movie.

The scores of various Dracula films have also been recorded, notably John Williams' lush score for John Badham's 1979 *Dracula*, and Wojciech Kilar's work for Francis Ford Coppola's 1992 *Bram Stoker's Dracula*.

One of the most tasteless Dracula-inspired songs came from the rock group Bauhaus: *Bela Lugosi's Dead*. The editor of this volume had the pleasure of interviewing prominent attorney Bela Lugosi, Jr. at a vintage radio convention in 1995, where a member of the audience asked how Lugosi, Jr. felt about the song.

"How do you think I felt?" he replied.

Dracula, though undead, is still very much alive. Bauhaus, however, is dead, with no signs of resurrection.

—Bob Madison

A DRACULA FILMOGRAPHY
An Opinionated Listing
by Bob Madison

Even a brief overview of all the significant Dracula and vampire films ever made would take up this entire volume. So, instead, I offer here a listing of the films that have had an impact on the genre, along with a brief analysis. (Film titles are followed by country of origin and director.)

1921
Drakula (Hungary; Karoly Lajthay)
Though lost, many scholars believe this Vilma Banky vehicle to be the first Dracula film.

1922
Nosferatu: A Symphony of Terror (Germany, F. W. Murnau)
Max Schreck lurched into nightmarish infamy as Graf Orlock (Count Dracula) in this early version of Stoker's novel. To prevent copyright infringement, all the characters' names were changed and Stoker's sprawling narrative streamlined; the effort was in vain, as Stoker's widow sued anyway. Mrs. Stoker attempted to have all prints of Murnau's classic destroyed, which is ironic in that *Nosferatu* is of one of the few vampire films to enjoy the status of a world classic. A fascinating creation from beginning to end, *Nosferatu* has rarely been equaled in the decades of vampire films to follow.

1927
London After Midnight (USA, Tod Browning)
A lost film, with only some tantalizing photographs of Lon Chaney's make-up surviving to whet the appetites of film fans everywhere. Its legend grows with each decade, and when, if ever, this film is found, it would have to be *magnificent* to merely satisfy film buffs.

1931
Dracula (USA, Tod Browning)
This film immortalized Stoker's character while changing it completely. Though creaky with age, *Dracula* is still compelling thanks to Dwight Frye's dynamic Renfield and Bela Lugosi's magnetic Count. Though dozens of actors were to play Dracula in the ensuing decades, none have claimed title to the role as completely as Lugosi: the Hungarian actor turned the vampire into a pop culture icon recognizable the world over.

Dracula (USA, George Melford)
This Spanish-language version of the Browning film, made on the same sets at night with different actors, is better than its American cousin in every particular with the

exception of Lugosi. Without his charisma to drive the film, even this better version falls flat. Considered a great rarity for many years, the Spanish *Dracula* is now available thanks largely to the champion efforts of film and pop culture historian David J. Skal, the dean of Dracula scholars.

Vampyr (France/Germany, Carl Dreyer)
Not as much fun as the Universal thrillers of the same era, but a fascinating alternate portrait of vampirism nonetheless. While its mannered, dream-like approach can make for some slow going, Dreyer's film is a must see for the serious vampire buff.

1933
The Vampire Bat (USA, Frank Strayer)
Not a real vampire at all, but just Mad Scientist #1 Lionel Atwill victimizing villagers and draining them of their blood. The root of all this madness? To better feed his ghastly science experiment... looking for all the world like a sponge in the bottom of a fish tank. (Which it probably was.) Look for Dwight Frye further refining his role as creepy madman, Fay Wray as the ingenue, and a young Melvyn Douglas, dreaming of better days ahead.

1935
Mark of the Vampire (USA, Tod Browning)
Director Tod Browning takes another shot at *Dracula* (in a way), with mixed results. Actually a remake of his earlier *London After Midnight*, here Browning uses the same strategy of finding a killer by employing actors to pose as vampires and scare him into confession. Bela Lugosi looks impressive as "Count Mora," as does Carroll Borland as his daughter "Luna," but Lionel Barrymore hams outrageously and the film is too puffy to be taken seriously.

1936
Dracula's Daughter (USA, Lambert Hillyer)
A truly terrific film, the last to be produced during the first cycle of classic Hollywood horror films. As Dracula's daughter, Gloria Holden is very effective, an obsessively evil, larger-than-life lesbian. The screenplay neatly inverts the original, beginning in London and ending in Dracula's Transylvania castle. Though earlier scripts were wonderful and outrageous (including one that promised orgies, whips, and bondage, and a sorcerer turning Dracula's followers into swine), the finished film remains an impressive piece of work. Its influence is nearly as great as that of its predecessor, with novelist Anne Rice frankly admitting that *Dracula's Daughter* was an inspiration to her. The gay subtext so important to vampire films today can be traced to this polished production.

1939
The Return of Doctor X (USA, Vincent Sherman)
Humphrey Bogart as a scientific vampire in this sequel that owes nothing to its original, the far superior *Doctor X*. Bogie, according to legend, had little affection for this film, calling it "a stinking picture" that he "should've left to Karloff or Lugosi."

1940

The Devil Bat (USA, Jean Yarbrough)

Bela Lugosi breeds gigantic vampire bats to avenge himself on the men he believes swindled him. Lugosi's talents are many and varied: not only can he create giant bats, but he can mix a pretty mean aftershave as well. (The bats are attracted to a lotion of his invention.) Though not great cinema, *Bat* is completely priceless for Lugosi's charm and uncanny way with dialogue. Watch this and then repeat to yourself: "Try it here, on the tender part of your throat."

1941

Spooks Run Wild (USA, Phil Rosen)

More Lugosi fun as the actor, now relegated to low-budget programmers, prowls the film's shabby sets in his Dracula costume. He deserved better, but the film is still watchable.

1943

Dead Men Walk (USA, Sam Newfield)

B-movie veteran George Zucco as two brothers, one good, the other, a vampire. A great premise that is never fully realized by a pedestrian script and low-budget production values. Universal's B-movie unit could have turned this into a minor masterpiece.

Son of Dracula (USA, Robert Siodmak)

Lon Chaney, Jr. is the only actor to make the vampire look like a wrestler disguised as a headwaiter. Barring that crippling defect, the film is an interesting riff on the Dracula theme, placing the vampire in the American South. Part Southern Gothic, part *Our Town*, *Son of Dracula* needed only a stronger, more charismatic actor to have achieved classic status.

1944

House of Frankenstein (USA, Erle C. Kenton)

Dracula appears in little more than a cameo in this Monster Rally, produced by Universal Pictures. The studio was interested in producing kiddie fare at this point, and dusted off Dracula, the Wolf Man, and Frankenstein's Monster for horror fans, and even considered, but later dropped, the Mummy. Though John Carradine's interpretation has many partisans, he seems strangely uninvolved, delivering a distant performance that lacks energy, fire, or wit.

The Return of the Vampire (USA, Lew Landers)

Bela Lugosi returns as Dracula (in all but name) in this interesting nod to the vampire legend. Lugosi is given a werewolf sidekick (Matt Willis) to help in the fun, as the vampire eyes young Nina Foch, the niece of his nemesis. Not as good as it should be, but the visuals maintain a true Gothic look and Lugosi is as memorable as ever.

1945

House of Dracula (USA, Erle C. Kenton)

Carradine returns as the Count, here seeking a cure for his vampirism. He is destroyed by Dr. Onslow Stevens (whom he has infected with the curse), but Lon Chaney, Jr.'s Wolf Man enjoys a cure and a moonrise, in this final serious entry in the series.

Isle of the Dead (USA, Mark Robson)
This spooky Val Lewton production is only a quasi-vampire film, with loony Boris Karloff searching for the vampire-like entity prowling an isolated Greek island. No fireball, but a creepy classic nonetheless.

The Vampire's Ghost (USA, Lesley Selander)
Interesting variation of the vampire theme with character actor John Abbott prowling the African veldt. A compelling film despite its B origins, and it sits well with the viewer long after screening. For offbeat atmospherics and novel premise, this is the vampire film of the 1940s to catch.

1946
Devil Bat's Daughter (USA, Frank Wisbar)
Rosemary LaPlanche proves her father's innocence in this sequel to Bela Lugosi's *Devil Bat*. Funny, I could've sworn the old guy was guilty...

Valley of the Zombies (USA, Philip Ford)
Interesting mainly for the performance of actor Ian Keith, who was considered for the part of Dracula in both 1931 and for 1948's *Abbott and Costello Meet Frankenstein*. *Zombies* is an okay programmer, and Keith is suitably creepy, but it could've been more. Keith's vampire drains the blood of his victims and replaces it with embalming fluid, which makes him, in a way, the most considerate of all bloodsuckers.

1948
Abbott and Costello Meet Frankenstein (USA, Charles Barton)
The perfect monster comedy... a genre often attempted, but rarely done successfully. Bela Lugosi repeats his Dracula performance on film for only the second time and, though burdened by age and illness, still holds the central position in the action and among the monsters. Though many serious horror film aficionados believe this to be a low point for the great Gothic characters, *Abbott and Costello Meet Frankenstein* is actually a well-tailored and affectionate comedic valentine. Dracula and company are treated with greater respect in this film than they would in later (and lesser) "serious" horror films, including most of the output from Hammer Films. *Abbott and Costello Meet Frankenstein* proves that a clever horror comedy can be pulled off, but the feat was only duplicated once, with Mel Brooks' *Young Frankenstein*. Both films are a must for any video collection.

1951
Mother Riley Meets the Vampire (UK, John Gilling)
Bela Lugosi again trades on his Dracula persona in this entry in England's *Mother Riley* series. The Hungarian actor is quite funny in his scenes, and makes a credible foil for drag star Arthur Lucan (Mother Riley). Recommended.

The Thing from Another World (USA, Christian Nyby and [uncredited] Howard Hawks)
As terror films moved away from the cobwebby crypts of Transylvania and into the
stars, vampires went with them. Though ostensibly a science-fiction film, *The Thing* is
more horror picture than anything else, with James Arness as the killer carrot from
space draining the blood of soldiers and scientists in a remote Arctic outpost. Watch it
with the lights off... but not alone. Ineffectively remade by John Carpenter.

1953
Drakula Istanbulda (Turkey, Mehmet Muhtar)
Adaptation of *Dracula* from Istanbul. No print seems to exist in the U.S., and I'd love
to see it.

1957
Blood of Dracula (USA, Herbert L. Strock)
First part of Herman Cohen's trio of teenage monster films (the other two being *I Was a
Teenage Frankenstein* and *I Was a Teenage Werewolf*), this drive-in favorite has Sandra
Harrison becoming a vampire-killer at her exclusive girls' school. Pretty awful, but
Harrison's vampire make-up is becoming something of a 1950s pop icon in its own
right.

The Vampire (USA, Paul Landres [also known as *Mark of the Vampire*])
Actor John Beal turns vampire due to a chemical dependency-caused imbalance. Fascinating... as this all happened just one year after Bela Lugosi's death and celebrated
drug addiction cure. Equal parts science-fiction and horror, *The Vampire* continued to
move the undead out of a mythical Middle Europe and into everyday America.

1958
Blood of the Vampire (UK, Henry Cass)
Sir Donald Wolfit slums deliciously as an evil scientist performing experiments with
blood, hiding within the safe confines of a Victorian prison. Wolfit was the inspiration
for the play and film *The Dresser*, and the unhappily alcoholic actor is here made-up to
look like Bela Lugosi. He manages to deliver a sterling performance, giving this inexpensive programmer better than it deserves.

Dracula (USA/TV)
John Carradine reprised his Dracula role in this television version which, at this writing, seems to be lost.

Horror of Dracula (UK, Terence Fisher [known as *Dracula* in the UK])
Peter Cushing's incisive performance as Van Helsing galvanizes this, England's streamlined, *Classics Illustrated* version of Stoker's novel. Though not the definitive interpretation, Jimmy Sangster's script has pace and forward momentum. Christopher Lee,
on screen for a total of seven minutes, is adequate as an athletic Dracula, but his performance has been wildly overpraised. In later films his dialogue and screen time are
pared down even further, but his weaknesses as an actor remain apparent. The final
confrontation between Van Helsing and Dracula is still gripping, but Cushing and Fisher
topped it with the next film in the series, *The Brides of Dracula*.

It! The Terror From Beyond Space (USA, Edward L. Cahn)
One of the many inspirations for Ridley Scott's *Alien*, *It!* is a snappy, 1950s creature feature. Its taut screenplay and realistic playing elevate the film above more standard science-fiction fare, and the design of the blood-drinking monster-on-the-prowl is a delight. The original title substituted *Vampire* for *Terror*.

The Return of Dracula (USA, Paul Landres)
Veteran actor Francis Lederer plays Dracula like a James Bond villain in this entertaining update of the character. This clever amalgam of Cold War jitters, Hitchock's *Shadow of a Doubt,* and drive-in horror chills would've made an effective first film in a series. Unfortunately, the picture was overshadowed by Hammer's Dracula film, and a series never materialized. That's a shame, for Lederer's Dracula is a wonderful piece of work, combining subtlety, wit, and style.

1959
Curse of the Undead (USA, Edward Dein)
This film taps into the era's twin boyhood obsessions: vampires and cowboys. Michael Pate is a vampire gunslinger in this entertaining flick, but the Old West setting is done so cheaply that it looks more like a Ghost Town than a thriving Western outpost.

Plan 9 from Outer Space (USA, Edward D. Wood, Jr.)
Many critics call this Bela Lugosi's final film, but really, it's not. Lugosi appeared in some footage that director Edward D. Wood would later incorporate into this, his *magnum opus*. Aliens plan a world takeover by reactivating the dead... and that's about all that can be said about the plot. A perennial favorite with the witless "Bad Film" crowd, *Plan 9* is simply sad and embarrassing.

Uncle Was a Vampire (Italy, Stefano Vanzina)
Forgettable vampire farce with a deadpan Christopher Lee performance. Bela Lugosi did it first and better with *Abbott and Costello Meet Frankenstein*. (*Uncle Was a Vampire* is better, however, than Hammer's horror comedy, *Horror of Frankenstein*. But that's not saying much!)

1960
Black Sunday (Italy, Mario Bava)
Some striking imagery has made this import from Italian maestro Mario Bava a classic. Supposedly based on a Gogol story (but don't believe it), *Black Sunday* made an impression on a whole generation of Baby Boomers, one that simply will not fade.

The Brides of Dracula (UK, Terence Fisher)
Hammer Films' one true Gothic masterpiece is a stylized re-telling of Tennessee Williams' *Suddenly, Last Summer*. Evil Baroness Martita Hunt trolls young women for her vampire son, fey, pretty boy David Peel. Peter Cushing is magnificent as Dr. Van Helsing, and one wishes that Hammer continued the series with the adventures of Van Helsing and jettisoned Lee's one-note vampire. Here, Peel does quite well as the effete aristocrat, adding a welcome note of decadence to his performance. The ending remains a stunner.

The Little Shop of Horrors (USA, Roger Corman)
Talking plant drinks blood and eats human flesh. This mix of farce and home-movie filmmaking would achieve cult-movie status, later remade as a big-budget musical with Rick Moranis and Steve Martin, directed by Frank Oz.

The Vampire and the Ballerina (Italy, Renato Polselli)
More Italian vampires. Like *Black Sunday*, a film of sometimes haunting imagery.

1961
Atom Age Vampire (Italy/France, Anton Giulio Majano)
Mad doctor tries to restore his wife with the glands of other women. Help yourself.

Blood and Roses (France, Roger Vadim)
A very loose update of *Carmilla*, more explicitly lesbian in Europe than the United States. Oft times lovely to look at, but a little much.

1963
Black Sabbath (Italy, Mario Bava)
Boris Karloff stars as a vampire in the final tale of this anthology film. His old magic had not diminished, and his creepy, spooky line-readings are a joy. An intelligent horror film with a fine cast, not to be missed.

The Kiss of the Vampire (UK, Don Sharp)
Hammer returns to the vampire genre with a vengeance, as a honeymooning couple become entangled with a cult of vampires. The ending, with the vampire cult attacked by some of the phoniest killer-bats ever seen in movies, was originally conceived for *The Brides of Dracula*.

1964
Batman vs. Dracula (USA, Andy Warhol)
Any bets?

Dr. Terror's House of Horrors (UK, Freddie Francis)
Anthology horror film hosted by the great Peter Cushing, playing a character named "Schreck" (in homage to Max Schreck). The final sequence, staring Donald Sutherland, featured vampires. Nifty programmer.

The Last Man on Earth (Italy/USA, Sidney Salkow and Ubaldo Ragona)
Vincent Price is the last human being alive after a plague leaves the rest of humanity in a vampire-like state. This adaptation of Richard Matheson's *I Am Legend* benefits strongly from Vincent Price's presence, as the actor plays against type as the film's hero. Overlooked (or passed over) by most horror film aficionados, *The Last Man on Earth* is ripe for a major rediscovery. Highly recommended.

1965
Planet of the Vampires (Italy/Spain, Mario Bava)
Capt. Barry Sullivan is stranded on a planet where the inhabitants take over the bodies

of his dead crew members. As man spent most of the decade racing to reach the moon, movie-makers were secure in their knowledge that vampires would be there, waiting for us.

1966
Billy the Kid versus Dracula (USA, William Beaudine)
Oh boy. John Carradine tackles Dracula once more in this, one of the classics of inept cinema. Pretty much what you would expect from the title.

Dracula—Prince of Darkness (UK, Terence Fisher)
Christopher Lee's Dracula victimizes two English couples on holiday. The actor plays the role mute, which adds to his performance immeasurably. Francis Matthews is fine as the hero, and he bears a remarkable vocal similarity to Cary Grant! Hammer's last decent Dracula film.

Munster, Go Home! (USA, Earl Bellamy)
Al Lewis reprises his television role of Grandpa Munster in this feature-length adaptation. If you like the series, you'll like this, too.

Queen of Blood (USA, Curtis Harrington)
More vampires in space, as unnerving Florence Marly dines heavily on a rocket's crew, including Dennis Hopper and John Saxon! Basil Rathbone plays the earth-bound scientist, and director Harrington does well with this futuristic melodrama.

1967
Blood of Dracula's Castle (USA, Al Adamson)
John Carradine is demoted to butler as Alex D'Arcy (who?) plays Dracula in this cheap, exploitation quickie. Director Adamson will use Dracula again in *Dracula vs. Frankenstein*, with the same undistinguished results.

Dr. Terror's Gallery of Horrors (USA, David L. Hewitt [also known as *Return from the Past*])
Dracula and a werewolf duke it out in the final scene. This anthology film, hosted by John Carradine, was a favorite when I was in grade school. I rather liked it then, but it has been years. The first widescreen Dracula film.

The Fearless Vampire Killers or: Pardon Me, But Your Teeth Are In My Neck (UK, Roman Polanski)
Roman Polanski's vampire comedy is not everybody's cup to tea (or blood), but it continues to have many devoted supporters. It's impossible to watch Sharon Tate in this film and not think of her eventual murder at the hands of Charles Manson and his cult followers.

Mad Monster Party? (USA/UK, Jules Bass)
A masterful children's film. Stop-motion fantasy in which Dr. Frankenstein (the voice of Boris Karloff) invites the world's greatest monsters to a convention at his isolated island stronghold. Dracula, of course, plans a takeover. With clever songs, wicked

dialogue, and smart character designs, *Mad Monster Party?* is one of the most delightful artifacts of the "Monster Boom" of the 1960s. Find it, buy it, own it.

1968
Dracula Has Risen from the Grave (UK, Freddie Francis)
This most financially successful Hammer Dracula proves that there's no accounting for taste. Christopher Lee pulls the stake out of his own heart as the film's atheist hero tries to kill him... the actor is later impaled on a giant cross. And those are the high points.

Night of the Living Dead (USA, George A. Romero)
Only rarely does a horror film come along that radically changes the genre; George Romero's *Night of the Living Dead* is one of them. A space-borne plague reactivates the unburied dead, who feed upon the living. The film takes place mostly in an abandoned farmhouse as the heroes fight for life. A dark, unhappy, and bitter film that tapped into the sentiment of the times, when optimism was at a low and the belief that God was dead was at a high. Mercilessly panned when it opened, the film has since become a cult classic. Highly recommended, but watch it with friends and all the house lights on.

1969
Taste the Blood of Dracula (UK, Peter Sasdy)
You'll love this: a peddler (Roy Kinnear), kicked out of his coach, happens upon Dracula just as he disintegrates atop his silver cross (see *Dracula Has Risen from the Grave*). The many characters present at the end of the earlier film must've instantly went out for a smoke, for Kinnear scoops up some of the vampire's scarlet ashes, only to sell them later to randy Victorians hungry for thrills. Lee actually speaks about three lines of dialogue here, none of them memorable. At the end, the Count has what appears to be a religious experience and drops dead. We should all be so lucky. The score by James Bernard is beautiful, and deserves a much better film to accompany it.

1970
Count Dracula (Spain/West Germany/Italy, Jess Franco)
Christopher Lee proves that the role of Dracula as conceived by Bram Stoker is utterly beyond him in this cheap, muddled re-telling of Stoker's novel. The actor, usually stiff and windy, is near comatose here. Herbert Lom tries to lend a note of class and professionalism to the proceedings, but he is thwarted by a dreadful script and insipid direction.

House of Dark Shadows (USA, Dan Curtis)
Barnabas Collins and the rest of the gang from television's first Gothic soap opera make it to the movie screen. Considerably better than the often inept television show, with Jonathan Frid almost proving that he is an actor after all. Perfect Saturday night fare. Followed by a non-vampire sequel, *Night of Dark Shadows*.

Count Yorga, Vampire (USA, Bob Kelljan)
Robert Quarry plays a caped bloodsucker in modern-day California. A huge drive-in

hit when first released, and something of a cult classic today. Quarry camps it up delightfully as the title character.

Countess Dracula (UK, Peter Sasdy)
Hammer's take on the story of real-life blood Countess Elizabeth Bathory. Ingrid Pitt does what she can with the script; sadly, this is Nigel Green's last film.

The House That Dripped Blood (UK, Peter Duffell)
Anthology horror film features final story (by Robert Bloch) about a vampire's cape that possesses a horror film star (Jon Pertwee). Deliciously funny, and the film's other stories are equally strong.

Jonathan (West Germany, Hans W. Geissendorfer)
Polemic posing as a Dracula film. It has something to do with fascism and identity, I think. Lauded by the intellectual press, *Jonathan* remains murky and incomprehensible to most (including this author).

The Vampire Lovers (UK, Roy Ward Baker)
Hammer's first version of *Carmilla*, an excuse for cheap lesbianism and tawdry innuendo.

Lust for a Vampire (UK, Jimmy Sangster)
Hammer's second version of *Carmilla*, another excuse for cheap lesbianism and tawdry innuendo.

Scars of Dracula (UK, Roy Ward Baker)
Phony looking vampire bats, a red-eyed Christopher Lee, and the Victorian version of the swinging 1960s. Lee is struck by a bolt of lightning... proving it's not nice to fool Mother Nature.

Scream and Scream Again (UK, Gordon Hessler)
Vincent Price, Peter Cushing, and Christopher Lee appear in this science-fiction-horror film. The three never share screen time (indeed, Cushing's role is little less than a cameo), and the muddled script is plagued by stops and starts. Evil Vincent Price creates human replicas that drink blood, but Christopher Lee proves to be even more evil.

1971
Daughters of Darkness (Belgium/France/West Germany, Harry Kumel)
Vampires, lesbians, and some sumptuous cinematography.

Dracula vs. Frankenstein (USA, Al Adamson)
Zandor Vorkov (who?) plays Count Dracula as a living echo chamber complete with ray gun ring. Dr. Frankenstein (J. Carrol Naish) and Dracula revive the Frankenstein Monster in the back of a rundown carnival. Both Dracula and the Monster look as if their costumes were provided by the local Woolworth's, and it's a pretty safe bet that they were. The last film for both J. Carrol Naish and Lon Chaney, Jr., both of whom deserved a better sendoff.

The Night Stalker (USA/TV, John Llewellyn Moxey)
One of the finest made-for-television movies ever. Vampires enter the modern world as reporter Darren McGavin tracks a vampire-killer in contemporary Las Vegas. Comes complete with a "wow" finish, and McGavin was never better. For those who like their supernatural thrills grounded in some semblance of reality, *The Night Stalker* cannot be beat. This film was recently released on video tape, and there are few better ways to spend $10. Followed by a sequel (*The Night Strangler*) and a television series, both inferior.

The Omega Man (USA, Boris Sagal)
The second go-round for Matheson's *I Am Legend*, and not nearly as good as the Vincent Price film.

The Return of Count Yorga (USA, Bob Kelljan)
Essentially a remake of the first film, though Robert Quarry is fun.

Twins of Evil (UK, John Hough)
Twice as bad as it should be. Peter Cushing abandons his Christian soldier interpretation of Van Helsing to play Gustav Weil, a religious fanatic. He's terrific, and one wishes this performance would find its way into a better film.

Vampire Circus (UK, Robert Young)
Vampires come to town as part of a traveling circus, and the village starts going to hell in a handbasket. Though acrobats turn into panthers during performances and seem to be able to levitate, villagers never connect the circus and the growing circle of tragedy in their town. This muddled, murky movie makes no sense at all... and has a greasy, sweaty, makeshift feel to it. Almost impossible to view in a single sitting, *Vampire Circus* is for Hammer completists only.

1972
Blacula (USA, William Crain)
William Marshall actually appoints himself well as an African prince cursed by Dracula. Pretty neat for anyone eager for a peek at early 1970s urban America, and of particular interest to sociologists and nostalgia buffs. One of the decade's few "blaxploitation" films to merit survival.

The Deathmaster (USA, Ray Danton)
Robert Quarry drops his patent leather pumps for hippie drag to star as an undead guru. Typical.

Dracula A.D. 1972 (UK, Alan Gibson)
Peter Cushing returns to the series too late to save it. Dracula is resurrected by some bored "young people" in mod London. They leave before Drac himself appears, allowing Christopher Lee to bore viewers. Hammer doesn't have the courage to back-up its own concept: the behavior of the film's "kids" was anachronistic by 1972, and Dracula never leaves his moldering, Gothic church to mix in the contemporary world. Somehow, Cushing manages to emerge unscathed.

Grave of the Vampire (USA, John Hayes)
Truly frightening exploitation quickie, and a perfect example of the vitality of the early 1970s B-vampire movie. Vampire rapes woman in an open grave. Years later, his son comes looking for revenge. Brutal, mean, and utterly compelling, *Grave of the Vampire* is the type of movie Hammer *should've* been making.

The Mystery in Dracula's Castle (USA/TV, Robert Totten)
Johnny Whitaker and company track jewel thieves while filming their amateur Dracula flick at a seaside resort. Monster-crazed kids of the early 1970s responded strongly to this mix of the Hardy Boys and Dracula, and it can still conjure a nostalgic smile today.

1973
Andy Warhol's Dracula (Italy/France, Paul Morrissey and Antonio Margheriti)
Dracula goes to Rome in search of virgins, only to vomit blood (lots of it) in the toilet. Hunky Joe Dallasandro got to them first, you see, providing sex and Marxist philosophy to a trio of very needy sisters. Some found this post-modern take smart and sophisticated. Most did not.

The Ghastly Orgies of Count Dracula (Italy, Ralph Brown [Renato Polselli])
I must confess that I haven't seen this film. But the title is quite terrific, isn't it? Say it once or twice to yourself and see if you can repress a smile.

Satanic Rites of Dracula (UK, Alan Gibson)
Peter Cushing returns as Van Helsing's grandson in this interesting failure. Van Helsing and granddaughter Jessica (Joanna Lumley) track down occult terrorists who seek to destroy the world with a new strain of bubonic plague. Christopher Lee's Count Dracula is behind it all. In an unusual change for the series, the film actually provides Lee with dialogue, which he makes the least of. Cushing's older Van Helsing could've easily been the focal point of a series of Sax Rohmer–type thrillers, but it never happened.

Scream, Blacula, Scream (USA, Bob Kelljan)
Mixes Blacula and voodoo. Not to everyone's taste, but effective. *Scream, Blacula, Scream* was a box office disappointment, so goodnight, sweet African prince, and flights of angels sing thee to thy rest.

1974
The Bat People (USA, Jerry Jameson)
Scientist bitten by a vampire bat on his honeymoon becomes horrible bat man. No, he doesn't fight criminals in Gotham City, which is the only cliché missed in this poor programmer.

Captain Kronos: Vampire Hunter (UK, Brian Clemens)
Hammer attempted to infuse new blood into the vampire myth with this tale of a swashbuckling vampire hunter. It didn't.

Dracula (USA/TV, Dan Curtis)
Jack Palance takes a stab at the bloodthirsty Count in Richard Matheson's adaptation of

Stoker's novel. Interestingly, while the performances and direction are sound, it is Matheson's screenplay that falls short. Palance never returned to the part, but his brooding, Byronic intensity helped re-envision the role—a reinterpretation of Dracula as a tragic figure that continues to this day. The original broadcast was postponed by Watergate coverage, proving that Nixon was a *real* monster.

The Legend of the Seven Golden Vampires (Hong Kong/UK, Roy Ward Baker [also known as *The Seven Brothers and Their One Sister Meet Dracula*])
A major Hammer embarrassment, where they degrade and debase the character as no other studio had ever done before. This mix of Dracula and martial arts adventure is sure to please no one, and deserves more "Bad Film" plaudits than the entire Edward D. Wood oeuvre. Peter Cushing, a fine actor, looks pained and embarrassed.

Old Dracula (UK, Clive Donner [also known as *Vampira*])
After spoofing James Bond in *Casino Royale*, actor David Niven returned as Dracula in this low-energy farce. Niven is, as always, a delight; the film is not.

Tendre Dracula (France, Pierre Grunstein)
Peter Cushing plays an actor famous for his horror film roles, and is seen briefly in full Bela Lugosi–Dracula regalia. Cushing looks so good in costume that it's a shame he never essayed the role; his sensitivity and warmth might've done something special to Dracula, and anticipated what Frank Langella did a few years later.

1975
Deafula (USA, Peter Wechsberg)
The first vampire movie in sign language!

Spermula (France, Charles Matton)
Porno for people *really* into capes.

1976
Dracula and Son (France, Edouard Molinaro)
Christopher Lee proves that it's not only his performances in the Hammer Draculas that are funny in this French farce.

Martin (USA, George Romero)
Is Martin a confused, dangerously psychotic teenager, or is he actually an 87-year-old vampire? George Romero's creepy film has an unnerving *cinema verite* feel, and John Amplas as Martin provides one of the finest performances in contemporary vampire films. *Martin* contains considerable graphic violence and dark and dangerous sensuality... and is even a penetrating examination of obsession and psychosis to boot. A must for any serious vampire fan, Romero's film transcends genre boundaries. A minor masterpiece, and simply the best post-war non-Dracula vampire film.

Rabid (Canada, David Cronenberg)
Porn-star Marilyn Chambers teams with director David Cronenberg for this film about

a young woman who drinks blood through a nifty little attachment in her armpit. First dates beware!

1977

Count Dracula (UK/TV, Philip Saville)
Louis Jourdan plays Dracula in this three-part BBC version of Stoker's classic. Literate, moody, atmospheric, and genuinely frightening, this is the best Dracula ever produced for television. Though Jourdan is not Stoker's idea of the monster, he is icily creepy. This adaptation continued to move Dracula out of B-horror movie country and re-establish him as a class act. One of only a handful truly magnificent adaptations, but beware: most television prints cut the more gruesome sequences.

McCloud Meets Dracula (USA/TV, Bruce Kessler)
John Carradine stars as an aged horror film star who may, or may not, be a crazed vampire/killer. Nice to see the old pro again, and Dennis Weaver's McCloud makes an amiable foil. Made for television, and a diverting time waster.

1978

Dawn of the Dead (USA, George A. Romero)
The second part of Romero's zombie trilogy, and one of the most graphically violent films ever made. There is some smart commentary on America's consumer society as ghouls take over a shopping mall, but the film leaves a dank taste in this viewer's mouth. Not to be seen after a large, spaghetti dinner.

Dracula's Dog (USA, Albert Band, [also known as *Zoltan... Hound of Dracula*])
Title says it all: a dog.

1979

Dracula (UK/USA, John Badham)
Stoker's novel and the Deane-Balderston play receive an opulent, romantic treatment in this lush thriller. Langella delivers a complex, brooding, witty and romantic performance in the title role, rescuing the Vampire King from the clutches of indifferent actors. Thanks to director John Badham and stars Langella and Laurence Olivier, Dracula was once more big-budget, A-movie material. If you can only see one version of *Dracula*, make it this one.

Love at First Bite (USA, Stan Dragoti)
George Hamilton trades his tan for graveyard pallor in this funny—though sometimes crude—comedy. The script has Dracula coming to present day New York after being exiled from Transylvania by the communists, who hope to turn his castle into efficiency apartments. Though the film dates visibly as an artifact of the 1970s, its appeal remains.

Nightwing (USA, Arthur Hiller)
A horde of ravenous vampire bats attack in this non-supernatural thriller.

Nocturna, Granddaughter of Dracula (USA, Harry Hurwitz)
John Carradine and Yvonne De Carlo (Lily, from *The Munsters*) are the aging vampires in this undead disco comedy. Like having Novocain injected into your face.

Nosferatu the Vampyre (West Germany/France, Werner Herzog)
Klaus Kinski plays the rodent-like vampire in Werner Herzog's remake of F. W. Muranu's classic. With magnificent cinematography, Herzog made a film that *looks* a lot better than it is.

Salem's Lot (USA/TV, Tobe Hooper)
Filmmaker Tobe Hooper rejected Stephen King's darkly handsome vampire Barlow, opting instead for a *Nosferatu*-like monster, played by veteran heavy Reggie Nadler. James Mason and David Soul are quite good, but this over-long television movie is only middling. Stay with the book instead.

1980
The Monster Club (UK, Roy Ward Baker)
Vampire Vincent Price puts the bite on former Dracula John Carradine in this pallid anthology film. You can safely give it a miss.

1981
The Munster's Revenge (USA, Don Weis)
The Munsters of 1313 Mockingbird Lane return... Al Lewis and Yvonne De Carlo, as Grandpa (Dracula) and his daughter, Lily, look fine, but the series is way past its prime.

Saturday the 14th (USA, Howard R. Cohen)
Horror comedy whose cleverness is all in its title. Richard Benjamin, who was so amusing in *Love at First Bite*, is wasted.

1983
The Hunger (UK/USA, Tony Scott)
Euro-trash vampires suck their way through the United States. David Bowie looks great while disintegrating, and Susan Sarandon and Catherine Deneuve shine. Glitzy and stylized, *The Hunger* is like most of the 1980s: glossy, but empty.

1985
Day of the Dead (USA, George A. Romero)
Final chapter in George Romero's zombie trilogy... here the series, like some of the corpses, shows its age.

Fright Night (USA, Tom Holland)
One of the most enjoyable and entertaining vampire movies ever made, Tom Holland's *Fright Night* is a hoot from start to finish. Chris Sarandon is impeccable as a vampire who seemed to step out of the pages of *GQ*, and Roddy McDowall hams heroically as aging horror star, Peter Vincent (read Peter Cushing and Vincent Price). Made-up to look like the elder Cushing, McDowall's excesses only underscore the film's flamboy-

ant plot and infectious high spirits. When high schooler William Ragsdale can't get the police to believe him that his neighbor, Sarandon, is really a vampire, he enlists the aid of McDowall, a broken-down actor forced to act as host of the local Fright Night program of horror films. And the fun begins. With nods to everything from Lugosi's *Dracula* to Jess Franco's *Count Dracula*, Holland has created the ultimate cinematic valentine to vampire movies and the kids who love them.

Lifeforce (UK/USA, Tobe Hooper)
Space vampires—they suck the life energy from you—attack London. Look for a pre-*Star Trek* Patrick Stewart in a small role.

Once Bitten (USA, Howard Storm)
Jim Carrey stars in this teen sex comedy masquerading as a vampire film. He's as obnoxious as ever.

Transylvania 6-5000 (USA/Yugoslavia, Rudy De Luca)
Jeff Goldblum a long way off from *Independence Day* and *Jurassic Park*. This comedy never lives up to its potential, and also stars Ed Begley, Jr.

Vampire Hunter D (Japan, Tayoo Ashida, animated feature)
Animated Japanese vampire film: technically brilliant, but nasty. *Vampire Hunter D* helped usher in a new generation of Japanese animated fantasies.

1986
Little Shop of Horrors (UK/USA, Frank Oz)
Musical version of Corman's low-budget romp, with Steve Martin especially funny as a sadistic dentist. A musical about a giant, man-eating plant shouldn't work, but somehow it comes off magnificently.

The Midnight Hour (USA/TV, Jack Bender)
Television movie with a cast of familiar faces (LeVar Burton, Shari Belafonte, etc.) where a curse turns school kids into vampire-ghouls. Three demerits!

Vamp (USA, Richard Wenk)
Singer Grace Jones bares big teeth in yet another teen-vampire-sex comedy. Jones is one of the more interesting artifacts of the Reagan era.

1987
The Lost Boys (USA, Joel Schumacher)
I Was a Teenage Vampire, 1980s style. With plenty of style, verve and fun, director Joel Schumacher takes on teens, bikers, rock-n-roll, vampires, and a rotting California boardwalk in this surprise hit. Originally intended as a vampire-recast of Barrie's *Peter Pan*, the film instead mutated into this crowd-pleasing blood fest. I like this one a lot, although I'm sometimes ashamed to admit it. An early showcase for Kiefer Sutherland.

The Monster Squad (USA, Fred Dekker)
Duncan Regehr's Dracula recruits Frankenstein's Monster, the Mummy, the Creature

from the Black Lagoon, and the Wolf Man to attack a small town containing an amulet and the gateway into chaos. Naturally, it's up to a bunch of kids to stop them. If you've grown up on the Universal classics, it's impossible not to have a warm spot for this nifty kid's movie... I even know horror film buffs who *cry* at the ending. For viewers who have managed to retain a child-like sense of wonder, catch this movie and share it with your favorite kid.

My Best Friend Is a Vampire (USA, Jimmy Huston)
Vampirism as a metaphor for homosexuality, as Robert Sean Leonard learns the ropes of his "alternate lifestyle" from older man-vampire Rene Auberjonois. Watched in that frame of mind, an interesting riff on young people coping with emerging, different sexuality, masked as yet another teen-vampire-sex comedy. No classic, but it will keep sociologists busy for decades to come. What is David Warner *doing* in this movie?

Near Dark (USA, Kathryn Bigelow)
Vampirism as a white trash dream of empowerment, as a "family" of vampire "good old boys" suck their way through the American heartland. The cast is superb, especially Adrian Pasdar as the cowpoke who gets bitten by love. The only loose cannon is Bill Paxton, who mugs inappropriately. A terrific ride the first time around, but does not hold up after repeated viewings.

A Return to Salem's Lot (USA, Larry Cohen)
Larry Cohen, the contemporary Edward D. Wood, was the mastermind behind this tepid, bloodless vampire flick that would've been booed out of drive-ins 20 years earlier. Yes, that's June Havoc.

Vampire at Midnight (USA, Gregory McClathcy)
Vampire psychologist charges for the hour, but is only available for 50 minutes. This psychological take on vampirism is sometimes too smart for its own good, but definitely worth a look.

1988
Dance of the Damned (USA, Katt Shea Ruben)
Vampire shows stripper that life is worth living. Remade as *To Sleep With a Vampire* in 1992.

Fright Night Part II (USA, Tommy Lee Wallace)
Director Tommy Lee Wallace destroys any chance for a series of *Fright Night* films with this indigestible sequel. Ragsdale and McDowall return, but the concept and script are not up to their performances. A waste and a shame.

Lair of the White Worm (UK, Ken Russell)
Ken Russell's delirious version of Bram Stoker's novel seems like a bad acid trip. For all of that, it has a certain camp appeal. The kind of horror film that appeals to those who make a point of not liking horror films, this film is guaranteed to offend aficionados of the genre.

Waxwork (USA, Anthony Hickox)
David Warner is the curator of a wax museum where the figures exist in an alternate reality, which Zach Galligan and his pals learn to their peril. The Dracula sequence is an over-the-top treat, and Patrick Macnee is on hand to help save the day. A hoot!

1989
Nick Knight (USA/TV, Daniel Taplizt)
Vampire cop. So what else is new?

Transylvania Twist (USA, Jim Wynorski)
Supposed comedy. Transylvania is rapidly becoming a tourist trap.

Vampire's Kiss (USA, Robert Bierman)
The defining vampire film of the decade, *Vampire's Kiss* explores vampirism as a metaphor for me-first Reaganism. Nicolas Cage, in his breakthrough role, is a powerhouse. Not to be missed, *Vampire's Kiss* is the most fascinating non-Dracula vampire film of the 1980s.

1990
The Reflecting Skin (USA/Canada, Philip Ridley)
Small boy is convinced that his widowed neighbor is a vampire. When his older brother returns from military duty and starts to grow ill, the boy's conviction grows. Terrific... *Fright Night* for people who don't like vampire films.

1991
My Grandpa Is a Vampire (New Zealand, David Blyth)
Al Lewis returns as a vampire (but not Grandpa Munster) is this melodrama.

My Lovely Monster (Germany, Michel Bergmann)
Monster steps from the screen of a silent movie and charms a little girl in German revival house. An engaging comedy that completely deflates once the two characters come to the United States and befriend a bunch of sleazy Hollywood types. Watch the first half, rewind, and devise your own ending.

1992
Bram Stoker's Dracula (USA, Francis Ford Coppola)
Simply one of the grandest, most opulent tellings of Stoker's classic novel. Gary Oldman's Dracula is a magnificent creation, working best in the early scenes in Castle Dracula. Sadie Frost nearly steals the show as Lucy, and actors Bill Campbell, Richard Grant, and Cary Elwes do fine jobs as her trio of suitors. Screenwriter James V. Hart follows the continuity of Stoker's tale closely, and the rousing chase to Castle Dracula will set pulses pounding. A significant moment in Dracula cinema.

Buffy the Vampire Slayer (USA, Fran Rubel Kuzui)
Could have been much funnier, but it's amusing to watch Donald Sutherland earn his retirement money. The resulting television series is far superior.

Dracula Rising (USA, Fred Gallo)
Blonde Christopher Atkins stars in this erotic take on the Dracula myth, produced by Roger Corman to capitalize on the success of the Coppola *Dracula*.

Innocent Blood (USA, John Landis)
Vampire vixen attacks the mob in this vampire comedy from John Landis. Robert Loggia steals the show as the Mafia don who gives a whole new meaning to the phrase "underworld figure."

John Landis Recalls *Innocent Blood*

I certainly have always enjoyed horror and vampire movies. *Horror of Dracula* is a good movie, not the brilliant movie that the fans think it is, but it's very good. Lee's entrance, and the presence, magnetism and power he brought to it, made Dracula sexy in an attractive and feral way. But I also think Lugosi is terrific and has gotten something of a bum rap lately. His performance has been imitated and parodied so often that we forget the *power* of his performance. I think he's the definitive Dracula.

The vampire film I remember the most fondly from my boyhood is a Japanese Samurai vampire movie: *Kuroneko*. When I was a kid growing up in Los Angeles there was a movie theater called the Toho La Brea, which used to play Asian films. I used to go there once a month or so to see Samurai movies. *Kuroneko* is a wonderfully disturbing movie, and full of some of the most outlandish imagery ever seen in a vampire film. I remember the hero being lured into the home of seductive mother and daughter vampires, and the whole audience screaming at him to get the hell out of there! *Kuroneko* was a terrifically outlandish, physical kind of vampire movie.

I tried to capture that same quality with *Innocent Blood*. I'm very proud of *Innocent Blood*. I made a conscious decision that the vampires would not have fangs. In the original *Dracula*, Bela Lugosi didn't have fangs—neither did Langella in the 1979 remake. I've always thought it was odd that vampires would have these stiletto fangs that darted in and out only when they were hungry. I sincerely believe that one of the reasons *Innocent Blood* didn't do as well in U.S. as it should've is that the audience didn't know it was a vampire movie!

Innocent Blood came about because I had gotten a script that I liked called *Red Sleep*, written by Richard Christian Matheson and Mick Garris. It had a great show business premise and was set in Las Vegas. The idea was that the King of Vegas Entertainers was also King of the Vampires. It played with the idea and imagery of the other Kings of Vegas for their respective decades: Sinatra, Elvis, Wayne Newton, and, now, Siegfried and Roy. He's all of them combined into one super entertainer, who is, in fact, King of the Vampires. Vegas is so grotesque already, I thought it was perfect! I took it to Warner Brothers after I had it rewritten by Harry Sheer, who did a very funny draft that was really a sly poke at show business.

Warner Brothers was horrified—they thought it was something like a horror film with musical numbers—which, of course, is exactly what I wanted to make! So they gave me the *Innocent Blood* script, written by Michael Wolk, which I thought was really clever and enjoyed very much. I thought vampires and the Mafia was as clever as vampires in Vegas, and that you could do a lot with it. When Robert Loggia is given this power, this gift you might say, of vampirism, at first he is bewildered by it. It's only after he fully understands it that he can exploit it. I thought it potentially amusing and powerful... and outrageous. I was impressed by Robert Loggia and the courage of his performance, he caught the outrageous tone of the script and really matched it.

I remember when researching *An American Werewolf in London*, I learned that almost all the werewolf lore we have came from Curt Siodmak (who wrote the screenplays for many of the Universal horror classics of the 1940s, including *The Wolf Man*). In his screenplays, werewolves have always been victims through a curse or disease. But my research found that in the old days, witches could turn into wolves at will. Interestingly, I had much the same experience with *Innocent Blood*. In researching vampires I discovered that so much of what we believe to be ancient lore about them actually all comes from Bram Stoker and *Dracula*.

—John Landis

Sherlock Holmes: The Last Vampyre (UK/TV, Tim Sullivan)
Jeremy Brett's Sherlock Holmes faces the possibility of vampirism in this, a very loose retelling of Conan Doyle's *The Sussex Vampire*. Roy Marsden is suitably mysterious, but the show belongs to Brett's Holmes.

1994
Interview With the Vampire (USA, Neil Jordan)
Neil Jordan's bloated version of Anne Rice's bloated novel lacks pacing, romance, or scares. Tom Cruise, despite the author's final approval, is simply out of his depth in a role that demands a more flamboyant, classical actor, and Brad Pitt is dull enough to give dead people a bad name. The homoeroticism of the novel lacks any sexual heat on film, and there is no chemistry between the two leads. Antonio Bandaras is wasted in a role that makes him look like Morticia Addams in need of a shave, and Christian Slater's screen time is unfortunately limited. In the final reel, Pitt's Louis goes to the movies, seeing such films as *Gone With the Wind* and *Superman*. It is a tragic miscalculation on Jordan's part to show clips from other, better films so near the end of his own *Heaven's Gate*.

Nadja (USA, Michael Almereyda)
Essentially an updated remake of *Dracula's Daughter*, with some terrific business added. Nadja (Elina Lowensohn) likens Dracula to Elvis ("He was like Elvis in the end... already dead, surrounded by zombies"), and Peter Fonda delivers a career-destroying performance as a wigged-out Van Helsing type. Very popular with New York audiences, *Nadja* is guaranteed a cult following; well deserved.

1995
Dracula: Dead and Loving It (USA, Mel Brooks)
Mel Brooks' sometimes funny Dracula spoof is nowhere near as clever as his earlier *Young Frankenstein*. The film, however, does have its moments, and Leslie Nielsen obviously studied Bela Lugosi's vocal inflections carefully. Peter MacNichol's Dwight Frye impression is terrific, and the actor comes close to stealing the film. Some beautiful photography and Mel Brooks' performance as Van Helsing are added benefits.

Vampire in Brooklyn (USA, Wes Craven)
Wes Craven and Eddie Murphy do disservice to the vampire genre in this eminently forgettable film, while putting additional nails in the coffins of their own careers.

1996
From Dusk Till Dawn (USA, Robert Rodriguez)
The film's first half—tracing the careers of psychopathic brothers George Clooney and Quentin Tarantino (who also scripted)—is a magnificent evocation of *film noir*. If only it continued in that vein, *From Dusk Till Dawn* may have been a minor masterpiece, along the lines of *The Grifters*. Instead, the film takes an abrupt left-turn, transforming into a grotesque, over-the-top vampire action-comedy. While the second half is amusing, it nowhere has the bite and verve of its first, more serious half, leaving the viewer with the feeling that two very disparate films were mindlessly stitched together.

Just a moment, Ladies and Gentlemen!
Just a word before you go.
We hope the memories of Dracula and Renfield won't give you bad dreams,
so just a word of reassurance.
When you get home tonight and the lights have been turned out
and you are afraid to look behind the curtains and you dread to see
a face appear at the window... why, just pull yourself together and
remember that after all *there are such things!*
—Dr. Abraham Van Helsing, *Dracula: The Vampire Play*,
by Hamilton Deane and John L. Balderston

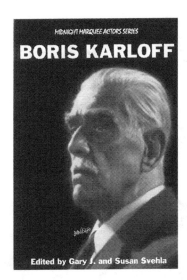

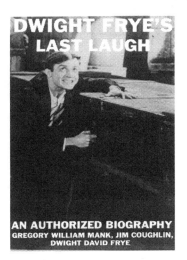

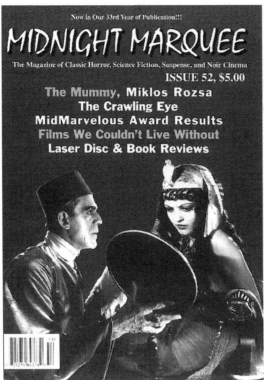